Wine and Society

Wine and Society

The Social and Cultural Context of a Drink

Dr Steve Charters M.A., M.W.
Lecturer in Wine Studies and Wine Marketing
Edith Cowan University
Perth, Western Australia

AMSTERDAM • BOSTON • HEIDELBERG • LONDON • NEW YORK • OXFORD
PARIS • SAN DIEGO • SAN FRANCISCO • SINGAPORE • SYDNEY • TOKYO
Butterworth-Heinemann is an imprint of Elsevier

Elsevier Butterworth-Heinemann
Linacre House, Jordan Hill, Oxford OX2 8DP
30 Corporate Drive, Burlington, MA 01803

First published 2006

British Library Cataloguing in Publication Data
A catalogue record for this book is available from the British Library

Library of Congress Cataloguing in Publication Data
A catalogue record for this book is available from the Library of Congress

ISBN-10: 0 7506 6635 8
ISBN-13: 978 0 7506 6635 0

For information on all Butterworth-Heinemann publications visit our website at http://books.elsevier.com

Typeset by Charon Tec Ltd, Chennai, India
www.charontec.com
Printed and bound in Great Britain by MPG Books Ltd., Bodmin, Cornwall

Contents

List of Figures

List of Tables

Preface

This book is the result of a long-term interest in the way in which we create and use wine throughout the world. My interest has been developed first as a keen consumer, then as a member of the wine industry, and now as an academic involved in teaching others about wine and its marketing. Wine is a product which by its very complexity can keep people enthralled, but I also think that the way we view it and imbue it with meaning adds to the enjoyment it can offer. Additionally, wine is a drink with a great history and part of its fascination is the fact that the way it was viewed and consumed many thousand years ago – from the time it was first produced – still informs our attitudes to it now. Yet at the same time many of those attitudes go unremarked not only by consumers but even by those involved in making, marketing, selling and writing about wine; what I am attempting to do here is to expose the origins of our views about wine as well as consider how, in the modern world, the way that we treat the drink may be evolving.

This book is designed primarily as a text for higher-level undergraduate and postgraduate students, including those involved in wine marketing, tourism, hospitality, leisure and oenology. I have also, however, tried to make it accessible for the general wine lover, who may have no academic impetus to think about the place of wine in society and how cultures shape its use, but is nevertheless interested in these things.

This book analyses the motivation and perspectives of both those who make and those who drink wine. It uses insights from anthropology, sociology and psychology to deconstruct the meaning wine offers, especially its symbolic function, and in doing that it may appear to be cold and objective about the product itself. But wine offers great pleasure, excitement and fun; it stimulates, consoles and thrills, and in the academic dissection of its place in society this should never be forgotten. It is enjoyment rather than cold analysis, after all, which brings us to wine in the first place and continues to provide its fascination. Nevertheless, I think that with all its complexity this fascination can be piqued and enhanced by a deeper understanding of how we use it. I believe that knowledge enhances rather than impedes enjoyment.

Acknowledgements

My interest in the subject of the relationship of wine to the societies which produce and consume it was originally given shape in a series of seminars run by Prof. Tim Unwin at Edith Cowan University. Whilst my ideas have developed since then, much of what I explore in this book owes its genesis to Tim's enthusiasm for and insight into the subject, and I am grateful to him for sparking some of the themes which have been expanded on here. What I have written also builds on both my research and teaching over the last 7 years, particularly one course which tries to help students consider the social and cultural context of wine. I am grateful to the thought-provoking input of my students over the years, which has helped to shape this more than they would realize.

The wine industry is one of the most co-operative and open industries in the world; its members love to share their passion and ideas, and that makes it one of the most enjoyable products to be involved with. Crucially, I must acknowledge the contribution of Dr Patrick Farrell M.W., who wrote much of Chapter 12 and gave the key medical and scientific background to it, something which I could never have done, and who responded with great patience and courtesy to my persistent requests for details. A number of people provided information whilst I was researching this book. I am grateful to Mike and Mireille Oakes for giving me a lot of time in Fitou, with great hospitality and stimulating discussion. Jean-Pierre, Sylvain and Bernadette Faixo offered forthright views and a great tasting in the same place, as did Katie Jones. Sue Birch from Wines of South Africa and Lynne Sherriff M.W. facilitated my collection of much of the information about South Africa and the development of its industry. Mike Beverland has helped my understanding of authenticity, and Tuomas Meriluoto has given insight into wine distribution in Finland. Even before I began to write this others have assisted my research, especially Nicholas Maillet, Drew Noon M.W., Sharon Wild, Jim Smith, Peter Leske, Kate Loughton, and Craig and Carolyn Drummond. Particular thanks are due to Simone Pettigrew for hours of support and assistance on consumer behaviour-related topics and for incisive discussions about a number of the issues raised in this book. Many others in the wine industry have given time and information over the years which has informed what I write, and more importantly they have shared great bottles of wine with me which I have enjoyed. Additionally, Mike Beverland, Tim Unwin, Mike Oakes, Craig Drummond and Cathy van Zyl M.W. have read parts of the book and I appreciate the comments they have made on it. The greatest thanks, however, must go to my family who put up with the fermentation of this project then had to endure a lengthy *élevage*, and particularly my partner Anita who now knows far more about wine and society than she ever wanted to and has added intelligently throughout the whole process.

Some of the chapters here make use of qualitative research that I have conducted with consumers and the wine industry. Qualitative research depends substantially on the time and input of its informants and, though they are pseudonymous when quoted, I am indebted to them for the time they gave up to help me.

Part of Chapter 3 and occasional allusions elsewhere are drawn substantially from a paper given at the Bacchus to the Future conference at Brock University in 2002. The section on involvement in Chapter 7 is based on a co-authored paper published by the *Journal of Research for Consumers*, Issue 5, in 2003. Additionally, some of the consumer quotations used in the section on aesthetic consumption in Chapter 9 are taken from a paper previously published in the *Journal of Wine Research*, Issue 2 of Volume 16, in 2005. I appreciate the respective editors' permission to incorporate extracts from those papers here.

Part One: Context

1 Introduction

Consider the following documents. The first is the back label of a Robert Mondavi Wines' cabernet sauvignon:

> **Napa Valley**
>
> CABERNET SAUVIGNON
>
> Wine has been with us since the beginning of civilization. It is the temperate, civilized, sacred, romantic, mealtime beverage recommended in the Bible. Wine has been praised for centuries by statesmen, philosophers, poets and scholars. Wine in moderation is an integral part of our culture, heritage and the gracious way of life.
>
> Taken from Fuller (1996).

The following comes from an online press notice from 2005 sent out by the wine magazine, *Decanter*:

http://www.decanter.com/news/62288.html

Latest News

Bomb blast damages La Baume

March 11, 2005
Adam Lechmere

A bomb was detonated at La Baume winery in the Languedoc on Monday night, in an apparent protest against the power of large companies.

There were no injuries and no stock was affected but the blast damaged the barrel cellar and roof.

It is alleged a group called Comite Regional d'Action Viticole (CRAV) took responsibility for the attack, in the form of a scrawled message on the wall of the chai.

The bomb – a stick of dynamite – was detonated by means of a crude timing device. Tim North, UK director of Les Grands Chais de France, which owns La Baume, blamed 'a small minority of extremists' who had 'not moved with the times' and had 'strong feelings against global companies.'

'Many people in that part of France understand the world is changing and people are no longer content to drink cheap *vin de* pays. But there are others who have not moved with the times and they have strong feelings against global companies.'

Les Grands Chais de France is the country's biggest wine exporter and its second biggest wine company. Its biggest brand is JP Chenet. In the past 12 months the company has massively expanded its portfolio.

North also said 'one or two' other sites had been targeted by CRAV that night.

Meanwhile, two thousand years ago the Roman author, Pliny wrote:

> Even in the most favourable circumstances, the intoxicated never see the sunrise and so shorten their lives. This is the reason for pale faces, hanging jowls, sore eyes and trembling hands that spill the contents of full vessels; this the reason for the swift retribution consisting of horrendous nightmares

> and for restless lust and pleasure in excess. The morning after, the breath reeks of the wine-jar and everything is forgotten – the memory is dead. This is what people call 'enjoying life'; but while other men daily lose their yesterdays, these people also lose their tomorrows (Pliny the Elder, n.d./1991).

All of these refer to the same product – wine, yet they reveal such different views about it. The first extract lauds the civilized nature of wine and its contribution to a 'gracious way of life'. In the second case its significance to a group of grape-growers in the south of France is such that they will attack and bomb those they think are threatening its role in their life. Meanwhile the third comment warns against its dangers and the retribution it can bring on the drinker. Meanwhile the value of wine in international trade has now reached $111 000 000 000 per annum – so that consumers spend more on it each year than cosmetics, and three times as much as recorded music (Anon., 2005d). It is thus not merely a product which stirs strong passions, but one which is economically of great importance.

Wine has been giving pleasure to people for over 8000 years. Indeed, it may have been significant in human life even before bread was being made (McGovern, 2003). But wine does not just give pleasure. It is, perhaps more than any other drink (with the possible exception of tea), a product which has a substantial and far-ranging symbolic significance. Some of the associations with which we imbue wine date back the full 8000 years to the dawn of its production. Others may be of more recent origin yet are still fundamental to how and why we consume, and to the selection of wines which we make. For those who wish to understand wine – because they have to market and sell it, or because they are wine producers, or merely because they enjoy drinking it – knowing about these issues is a necessary precursor to a more effective engagement with the product. Pleasure and meaning are the starting point of the process of exploration.

The relationship of wine to society – to the culture of those who make it, to the consumer, and in the wider context of wine's place in the community – is a vast topic and this study can do no more than introduce some of its key aspects. This chapter will introduce the topic. Critically it explains the aim of this book: how it is structured, its key themes, and some definitional issues.

The aim of this book

This is not a marketing text nor is it a study of the consumer behaviour of wine consumption – although both the marketing and consumer practices in relation to wine figure large throughout. There are other texts which may be more focused on the marketing of wine *per se*. Neither is this a book about the structure of nor international trade in wine – although much of what is discussed here has an impact on wine commerce and the ebb and flow of different wine styles. It is, perhaps, best seen as a precursor to a text on wine marketing, focusing as it does on how the production of wine itself shapes perceptions about the product, how the consumer may gain from it a range of meanings, and how society tries to control it. It has the aim of helping the reader to understand some of the cultural forces which have shaped both how wine is made and the way in which it is consumed. This is relevant to those who wish to understand the nature of wine consumption, who may market wine, or who may be involved in ancillary activities such as wine tourism or the hospitality industry – and it is to these people that this book is primarily addressed.

A number of key themes permeate the book. Most of these will be expanded substantially in the following chapters, but a few core ideas are best established at the outset, so that the reader is clear about the author's own perspectives – perhaps biases – on the subject. These themes include the following:

- The core of wine production and consumption is shaped by historical, geographical and cultural factors. The way producers approach their wine is moulded by where they have learnt how to make it and, crucially, the understanding their culture has of what wine is and how it should be made. Consumers, likewise, drink wine with varying attitudes which are shaped by those myriad features which shape consumer behaviour around the world, from climate through religion to food – as well as a range of symbolic factors.
- That wine takes different forms in its production, and is made by individuals and organizations which have very varied ideas about the nature of what they are producing. The type of organization the winemaker works for, therefore, has an impact on how the product is understood and thus how it is made.
- That the motivation to consume wine is multifaceted; it is more than just the pursuit of 'a drink that tastes good'. This is explored in more detail in Chapter 7.
- That there is a substantial 'mythology' surrounding the production and consumption of wine. We attach a range of meanings to wine, and tell various 'stories' about it which legitimize consumption, and explain its importance to us and – in the case of winemaking – justify much of what is done to the wine.
- That there is a great deal of ambivalence surrounding wine and its use. Broadly – as the extracts at the start of this chapter exemplify – wine

is significant and enjoyable but it contains a negative side which cannot be ignored and the connotations it conveys are finely nuanced.

- That all of these factors give wine a substantial social and political relevance, although the outworking of this is culturally variable.

The structure of this book

The book is divided into five parts. The first – this chapter and the following one – sets the context for the study, outlining the core themes that are considered, and summarizing briefly the history of wine, viticulture and the trade in wine. Although this is not a historical work many of the factors which frame our consumption of wine stem from how it was made and consumed in the past – often the distant past. Each chapter will feature, to a greater or lesser extent, a historical dimension and consequently it is necessary for the reader to have a broad understanding of the historical spread of the vine and wine at the outset.

The second part (Chapters 3–6) deals with the social and cultural aspects of the production of wine. This includes an analysis of how the production of wine itself, as a cultural object, can vary from place to place. It also considers how different organizational structures shape varying attitudes to winemaking. A distinctive feature of wine production is also how it is categorized, both by attempts to classify its quality, or to fix it in the place where the grapes were grown; those factors, with the linked idea of terroir, are covered. This part finishes with a review of how attitudes to wine production are changing in the modern world, and how those changes have an impact on how wine – as a cultural object – is made.

Part Three (Chapters 7–10) focuses on the consumer. It starts by considering what motivates the consumer to drink wine – the experiential, symbolic and utilitarian benefits which wine offers. The symbolic benefits are particularly complex, and the two subsequent chapters in this part examine some of the specific meanings that may be attached to wine; the related issues of religion, fertility and sex along with the idea that wine can be used to establish status, and then the concept that wine can be the marker of a civilized life – a complex notion, which includes a number of issues often seen today to relate to lifestyle. The final chapter in this part again looks at changing wine in the modern world – but in this case from the perspective of the consumer, rather than the producer.

The fourth part of this book (Chapters 11–14) moves from the consumer as an individual to the wider perspective of society as a whole. It considers the nature of wine fraud, how it is perpetrated and how it is controlled – including, at times, how what is misleading may be legalized. The important issues of health and the abuse of wine are also dealt with (in a chapter co-authored with Dr Patrick Farrell M. W.). Stemming directly from this is an examination into the motivations and methods of those who are opposed to wine, and would like to see its consumption strictly limited, or even abolished. These issues are then brought together in a chapter on the politics of wine; how states use, control and protect it. The whole book is then pulled together in Chapter 15 with a conclusion.

Each chapter features a number of detailed examples of specific points, as well as case studies and illustrative extracts from relevant research. These items are clearly boxed and are included to develop specific ideas and add flesh to some of the theoretical discussion. The reader who merely wishes to follow the argument or who has some detailed knowledge of the specific topics can skip those boxed materials and still maintain the sense of the argument. In some cases the illustrative material is based on the author's own research output (which has generally been qualitative) and therefore features the particular perspective of individual wine drinkers. In those instances it comes with the usual academic caveat about qualitative research that it should be trustworthy but may not necessarily be generalizable across a full range of consumers (Wallendorf & Belk, 1989). Additionally, each chapter ends with a bibliographical note which will recommend further reading for those who wish to explore the issues raised in more depth.

Some qualifications and definitions

One caveat is important at this stage. This is a book about the wine industry. The wine industry, however, differs from country to country. In wine-producing countries (France or Australia, for instance) it is very much considered to be those involved in growing grapes and making wine. In non-producing countries, such as the United Kingdom or Sweden, the industry comprises those involved in distribution. In the United States and Germany it is more confused, as both producers (particularly in California and South-Western Germany) and distributors are significant. In all of these countries wine writers, critics and retailers are important.

A second qualification is that the study assumes a basic knowledge about how wine is made and about the geography of wine. If readers wish to further their knowledge in this field then the bibliographical note at the end of this part contains recommendations on further reading in wine generally.

One definitional issue is also relevant. In common speech the term 'table wine' normally refers to a wine which is not fortified or sparkling. However, in European legal parlance table wine has a different interpretation, used to distinguish it from what is considered to be a quality wine (explained in more detail in Chapter 2). To avoid confusion the term table wine is used throughout in this very strict definition. The term 'light wine' is used to define a wine which is neither fortified nor sparkling.

A number of abbreviations are used throughout. Generally these are defined in the text. Table 1.1 gives details of common abbreviations related to area or volume in the wine industry and used in this book.

Table 1.1 Abbreviations

a.b.v.	Alcohol by volume
hL	Hectolitre (100 L)
ha	Hectare (an area of 100 m by 100 m)
hL/ha	Hectolitre per hectare (used to measure the amount of wine from a specified area of vineyard)
g/L	Grammes per litre
mL	Millilitres

Bibliographical note

There are a series of excellent books which can offer an introduction to the world of wine. *Hugh Johnson's Wine Companion* (Johnson, 1997) and *Jancis Robinson's Wine Course* (Robinson, 2003) are elegantly written primers. More substantial encyclopaedias on the geography of wine include *The Global Encyclopedia of Wine* (Forrestal, 2000) and *The New Sotheby's Wine Encyclopedia* (Stevenson, 2005). In Australia one of the best introductions – both simple and clear – to how wine is made and why it tastes the way it does is *Australian Wine: Styles and Tastes* (Iland & Gago, 2002). There are many detailed outlines of the specific wine-producing countries and regions of the world – the most comprehensive set is the Mitchell Beazley Classic Wine Library. For those who want to understand more about winemaking then *The Art and Science of Wine* (published as *The Vintner's Art* in the United States) by James Halliday and Hugh Johnson (1992) is the most accessible starting point. If the reader only ever has one book, however, it must be *The Oxford Companion to Wine* (Robinson, 1999). The next edition is due out in 2006 and this book is the closest to a single work which details everything about wine it is possible to know.

2

The history of wine

As noted previously, this is not a text on the history of wine. However, much of the context in what follows is historical, so it is therefore useful to preface the main part of the book with a brief overview of the spread of wine and the development of the wine industry. This chapter will give an outline of the history of wine since it was first made – perhaps about 6000 BC – to the present. The aim of this is not so much to convey a mass of information (all of which is available elsewhere) as to raise issues that will be relevant in later chapters. This chapter will also focus on key social and technological changes which had an impact on the societies which produced wine and the ways in which it was viewed and consumed.

In order to aid in the understanding of the time scales involved in the history of wine and to help readers place the timing of various developments outlined through the course of this chapter, there follows a time chart of the last 9000 years (see Figure 2.1). This shows both general developments in world history alongside changes in the production of and trade in wine. Later Figures (2.3 and 2.4)

Figure 2.1 Nine millennia of the history of wine.

Date	*World history*	*Viticulture and Winemaking*
7000 BC	Neolithic period	
6000	Pottery vessels first made	?Vines first cultivated
		Wine in the Zagros mountains
		Resinated wine produced
5000		
4000		
		Wine drunk in Mesopotamia
	Bronze Age in the near east	Wine recorded in Egypt

(continued)

Figure 2.1 *(continued)*

Date	*World history*	*Viticulture and Winemaking*
3000	Sumerian and Egyptian empires	Grape pips in northern Greece
		Vineyards recorded in Egypt
		Trade in wine between Crete and Egypt
2000		
	Iron Age in the near east	Resinated wine in Greece
	?Trojan war	
1000	King David in Israel	Phoenicians export wine
	Rise of Greek city states	Hesiod writes on Greek wine production
	Alexander the Great	
	Roman Empire	Large agricultural estates

AD 1	Life and death of Christ	Development of barrels for storage
	Emperor Constantine becomes a Christian	
	Fall of Rome	
	Dark Ages in Europe	
1000	Norman Conquest of England	Growth of ecclesiastical vineyards
	Medieval period in Europe	
	Spanish Empire in the Americas	Vines planted in S. Africa and S. America
	Large European empires	Technological revolution in winemaking
2000	Expansion of new wine markets	

do the same in more detail for the past 2000 and 350 years, respectively (based on the key works of wine history detailed in the bibliographical note at the end of this chapter) but it must be noted that some historical changes are long term and cannot be absolutely precisely fixed, and certain dates shown are, by the nature of the figures, only broadly accurate.

The prehistory of wine

Wine appears to have been made at least 7400 years ago (McGovern, 2003); archaeologists using molecular biology have discovered traces of wine in pottery vessels from the Zagros mountains, in what is now Iran, from 5400 BC. In fact, argues McGovern (one of the foremost archaeologists in this field), wine was almost certainly developed first further to the north at the foot of the Caucasus mountains, and dating of grape pips suggest this occurred at least back to 6000 BC. It seems probable that this part of the world (around modern-day Georgia or Armenia or towards Kurdistan) was the original home of wine (Unwin, 1996), and from there it spread south towards the civilizations of Mesopotamia and Egypt; early stories about the origins of wine, such as Noah in the Bible and Gilgamesh (Anon., n.d./1972), suggest the authors of these narratives saw wine originating from that direction. In any event, the natural limits of wild grapevines were from present-day Lebanon and northern Syria and Iran, along the coast of Mediterranean Turkey and the Black Sea through the Caucasus region; somewhere there wine originated.

A note on grapes and varieties

Most modern wine is made from the grapevine species known as *Vitis vinifera* (literally the 'winemaking grape'). This was the only species of grape growing naturally in the Middle-East at the time when plants were first domesticated. Over the millennia a number of varieties of *Vitis vinifera* have been spawned – with names we know today, such as riesling or grenache. New grape varieties can be produced by crossing two existing varieties: pinotage, widely planted in South Africa, has cinsault and pinot noir as its parents. Archaeologists can trace the spread of viticulture by recovering and analysing *Vitis vinifera* grape pips.

As well as *Vitis vinifera* there are many other species of vine; some of these are in Asia but a number come from the Americas – such as *Vitis labrusca* or *Vitis riparia*. The quality of wine made from these is generally considered to be substantially inferior to that from *Vitis vinifera* grapes (Robinson, 1999), although some wine is still made from these species for local markets in the United States and Canada. Hybrid vines are those created by crossing *Vitis vinifera* vines with American ones. This produces vines which may have qualities drawn from both parents, although traditionally the quality of their wine is not seen to be as good as pure *Vitis vinifera* and their use is banned in many European countries.

Wine is made from the juice of fruit and grapes are an especially likely source of wine. Grapes are juicy, so that a lot of liquid can come from them. The grape skins attract yeast cells – essential to the process of fermentation. Additionally, for significant fermentation to occur a minimum sugar level of about 10 per cent is required – which grapes have (McGovern, 2003). Thus, whilst with some technical experience other fruit (such as dates) were later used to make wine it is likely that grapes were the only fruit which could initially produce a fermented drink in the neolithic period. It is probable that people selected the sweetest grapes which were, because of their sugar content, most likely to produce a successful fermentation.

The production of wine required one technological advance and helped to spawn others. The key requirement for wine production was pottery. Although animal skins or shallow wooden containers could have been used, before pots were made there was probably no secure way of containing large volumes of juice for long enough for fermentation to take place. The first wine may well have owed its existence to a woman (as they tended to be the gatherers of wild fruit). Probably some split grapes were left for a few days in a pot and went through a form of partial carbonic maceration (where fermentation using enzymes rather than yeast takes place within unbroken grapes, as well as ordinary yeast-based fermentation which occurs in juice). When the pot was recovered after a little while the juice was drunk and found to have changed; it had less sweetness, but also acted as a drug on the person who drank it. From there it was a simple step to crush grapes deliberately and leave them for the (misunderstood) fermentation to happen. In this interpretation wine is the result of a chance event – although others suggest that, if wine was preceded by the discovery of mead, an alcoholic drink made from honey, it may have been deliberately created (Phillips, 2000). In any event the resulting wines would have had an erratic production, with varying flavours and dangers of all kinds of spoilage. But, crucially, they had alcohol in, and the best would have tasted acceptable. As will be examined further (Chapter 8), the mystery surrounding the creation of wine made it seem to be a magical liquid and that only added to its appeal.

The discovery of wine occurred during the neolithic period, that part of the Stone Age when people began to hunt less and cultivate crops and keep herds of domesticated animals. As part of the growth of agriculture early farmers developed sufficient knowledge about their crops to reproduce those which were highest yielding, or most resistant to disease, or more flavourful than others. This inevitably happened with the wild grapevines and so, from one species, different varieties of grape developed, and within each variety a form of clonal selection took place to ensure the reproduction of the most useful vines.

The spread of the vine

The mystique of, and pleasure afforded by, wine made it desirable. Thus both the drink and the cultivated vine were taken to new regions, often away from the original home of the wild grapevine. Broadly vines flourish best between the lines of latitude of 30 and 50 degrees (depending on altitude and other climatic variables). Thus, from the Caucasus cultivation of the vine and knowledge of winemaking was pushed north, west into modern Turkey and south towards the civilization of Sumer (traded down the Tigris and Euphrates rivers to city states such as Ur and Uruk) at some point soon after 4000 BC; from there the drink reached Egypt by about 2600 BC (McGovern, 2003). As will be seen, wine became significant in these two civilizations but, whilst both made some wine, the vine was towards its southernmost limits here, and for these people the large-scale production of wine was never feasible. This meant that its use tended to be reserved for the social elites.

Wine was, however, one of the first products that were widely traded. It was transported from modern Kurdistan down to Ur and Babylon; from Crete and Lebanon to Egypt (McGovern, 2003) and later from Phoenicia (modern Lebanon) to the western Mediterranean (Phillips, 2000). Trade of a key commodity was one driver of this expansion, but imperial conquest was also significant. Hittites (from central Anatolia), Greeks and later Romans took the vine with them to produce local wine as they established colonies.

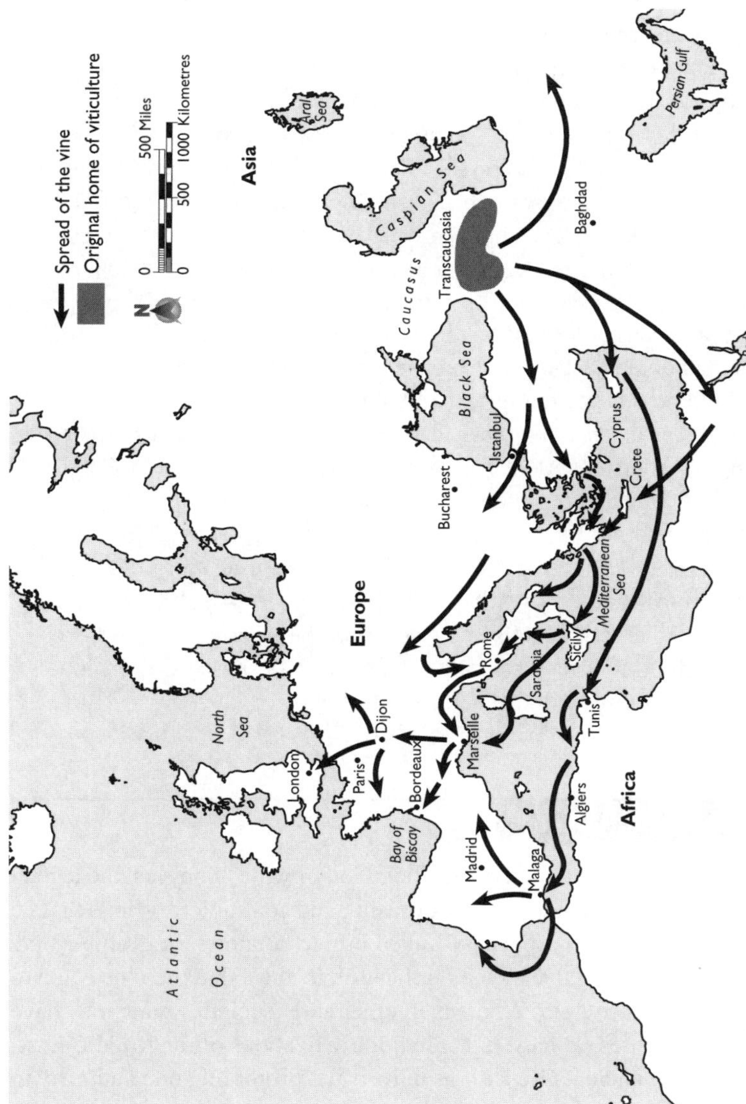

Figure 2.2 The spread of viticulture and wine from its origins until the end of the Roman Empire.

What was prehistoric wine like?

It is hard to be clear about what early wine would have been like. It seems likely that most wine was red (Phillips, 2000), and it is probable that it was not the crystal clear liquid we drink today but was fairly hazy. It was almost certainly of a comparatively low alcohol (perhaps 8–10 per cent alcohol by volume, a.b.v.), at least until methods such as late harvesting to develop sweeter wines became common. In the heat of Mediterranean countries it could rapidly spoil, so that vinegary or dull, oxidized wines were doubtless common. However, the ancients had one way which could be used to protect wine against spoilage, which was the addition of tree resins containing anti-bacterial compounds capable of killing acetobacter (McGovern, 2003). Resin from the terebinth tree or the Aleppo pine, or the Arabian incense myrrh all acted in this way. Essentially such an addition created an ancient form of retsina; the aroma, – whilst an acquired taste, would also cover the absence of flavour in any wines made from over-cropped or under-ripe grapes. It is clear that for a number of millennia many – perhaps most – wines were resinated in this way (McGovern, 2003). Wine would often have been blended before use (possibly with herbs, spices or other flavourings), and may well have been watered down (Johnson, 1989; McGovern, 2003). The Romans were certainly flavouring wine with wormwood, roses and violets (Edwards, 1984), although in the case of roses the petals had to be steeped in the wine for 21 days, suggesting substantial oxygen contact. Possibly the flavouring was essential to hide the otherwise oxidative nature of the wine.

The Greeks and Romans

Greek wine culture was bound up with their God of wine Dionysos; the legend of the God, whilst (like most myths) confusing and contradictory, tells that he came from the east – and especially linked him to Anatolia, or even beyond, to Iran and Iraq (Dalby, 2003). One implication is, thus, that the vine came to mainland Greece from Asia. Whereas in other early societies wine may have been reserved to elites (at least in the major civilizations of the Middle-East) the use of wine in ancient Greece was universal – prompting one authority to talk about 'democratic drinking' (Phillips, 2000).

It was, perhaps, at this time that the traditional Mediterranean nutritional triad of wheat (for bread), olives (oil and food) and grape (fruit and drink) crystallized. These three foodstuffs have formed the core of the diet for the region over the last 4000 years or so. Wine was certainly widely used in the Mycenaean period, before the supposed fall of Troy, and continued as Greek civilization began to flourish around Athens, Sparta and other city states in the first millennium BC. The Greek author, Hesiod, wrote a poem entitled Works and Days in about 800 BC in which he discussed agricultural matters (Hesiod, n.d./1999). Part of the poem talks about viticulture, such as when to prune. He also discusses harvesting, and talks about how, once picked, the bunches of grapes should be dried in sun for 10 days, and then in the shade for a further five, before the juice should be pressed off for fermentation to start. A similar process is still used in the *passito* wines of Valpolicella and Soave today to make rich, often sweet, wines.

Although this was a peasant-based society even the richer, urban Greeks integrated wine into their social structures. The symposium (literally a 'drinking together') was a formal social event at which people ate a meal, then drank wine while discussion took place (Unwin, 1996). The drinking and discussion was led by an appointed leader for the event and each was governed by a series of rituals. The wine would be mixed in specially designed bowls with water, in proportions determined by the leader (only 'barbarians' drank undiluted wine). A series of drinking games could be played. The discussion may be on serious philosophical or political topics (so that Plato named one of his philosophical dialogues *The Symposium*); alternatively it could be on more mundane matters. The Greeks were also the first society to systematize the medical use of wine, especially after the time of Hippocrates (Lucia, 1963).

The Greeks were great seafarers. As well as planting in their own country they took wines and vines to the western Mediterranean. They were responsible for the first vineyards in southern Italy, where vines even now may be low trained in the Greek style as a result of the advent of the Greeks over 2500 years ago – and some southern Italian grape names, such as greco and aglianico, are testament to the variety's origin. They also took wine, and later grapes, to their outpost at Massilia – modern-day Marseilles (Johnson, 1989) – and so bear responsibility for the origins of wine in France, a factor which is still traded on by those marketing the wines of that region today (see Figure 2.3) (Gade, 2004).

In the early part of the Roman Republic, wine was not so widely consumed; only after about 200 BC did its use become more usual (Phillips, 2000). When it did spread, however, it became very common. The Romans, being great organizers, were also amongst the first to produce a number of systematic treatises on agriculture, including viticulture. From Cato (around 200 BC) via Varro and onto Columella (about 65 AD) these guides provide a mass of detail

Figure 2.3 The history of wine over the last 2000 years.

Date	*World history*	*Viticulture and wine*
200 BC	***Expanding Roman Rule***	Cato's treatise on agricultural management
100	Julius Caesar	Columella's *On Agriculture*
	Augustus establishes Roman Empire	
0	Birth and life of Christ	Pliny's *Natural History*
	Emperor Nero	Edict of Domitian
100 AD		
		Development of Barrels in Gaul
200		
	Roman Empire split into East and West	Vines in Burgundy and the Mosel Valley
300	Emperor Constantine becomes a Christian	

400	Romans leave Britain	
	Fall of the Roman Empire	Vines in the Loire Valley
500	Saxon invasion of England	
600	Foundation of Islam	
	Viking raids on Britain	
700	Moslems conquer most of Spain	
800	Charlemagne crowned as 'Emperor'	
900		
1000	***Middle ages***	
	Norman Conquest of England	42 vineyards recorded in England

(*continued*)

Figure 2.3 *(continued)*

Date	*World history*	*Viticulture and wine*
1100		Abbey of Citeaux gains vineyards in Burgundy
	Bordeaux is part of the English empire	
1200		
1300		
	Renaissance begins	
1400	Fall of Constantinople to Turks	Portuguese settlement of Madeira
	Moslems finally expelled from Spain	First distilled alcoholic drinks
1500	Spanish settlement of the Americas	Vines in Chile
	Reformation across northern Europe	First fortified wines
1600	Thirty years war devastates Europe	
	Age of the scientific revolution	The 'New Clarets'

1700	Developing consumer society in Britain	Dom Pérignon
	Industrial revolution in Britain	Constantia flourishes in South Africa
1800	Development of rail transport	M. Chaptal, agriculture minister in France
	Age of European imperialism	A 'golden age' – then phylloxera
1900	War and depression	Start of appellation systems
	Cold war	Expansion of 'new producing countries'
2000		Growth of new markets

about grapes and how they were grown. It was not necessarily the love of literature which prompted this however. With increased economic power investment in productive land became important. Guides to the use of land were designed to maximize its value to the owner. Cato, for instance, is very hard nosed about the use of slaves on properties. Financial profit, rather than mere subsistence, became a major inducement to grow and expand vineyards. The focus that the Romans gave to agriculture also meant that wine became subject to legislation. At various stages the worship of Bacchus (the Roman equivalent of Dionysos) was outlawed, women were forbidden to drink wine on pain of death, and around 92 AD the Emperor Domitian ordered half the vineyards outside central Italy to be cut down to encourage greater production of wheat (an edict which was widely ignored, but not repealed for almost another 200 years (Johnson, 1989)). Wine also featured in much of the literature of the period, especially the poetry of Horace. Additionally, it became an object for connoisseurs; vintages were graded, places of origin were compared and even grape varieties were assessed for the qualities they could offer (Pliny the Elder, n.d./1991). The best wines were expected to age for some time, improve, and become collectable items (Unwin, 1996).

To facilitate the trade in wine there was mass production, on a vast scale, of long, two-handled pots called amphora. These amphorae were used throughout the ancient world to store all kinds of goods; archaeologists, by tracing their movement around the Roman Empire from remains at archaeological sites, can follow the transport of wine and even gain some clues about the origins of wine traded. By the end of the first century AD the remains of amphorae suggest that wine was widely distributed through what is now Spain and France, and even into parts of Germany and England (Unwin, 1996). Wine had become a key-traded commodity.

The development of barrels

Amphorae were the main means of storing wine around the Mediterranean for over 2000 years (McGovern, 2003). They were heavy, and – with a pointed end – hard to store upright, but easy to carry and pour from. However, at the end of the first century AD a revolution in the storage of goods began. Under the influence of craftsmen from Gaul, barrels became a major storage container – the Celts were skilled woodworkers. Oak especially is malleable and watertight, making it an ideal container. Coopers could shape it in many ways, and the barrel became the main means of storing wines (Unwin, 1996). Whilst the precise reasons for the change from amphorae to barrels are ill-understood, crucially wood was lighter and less breakable than pottery – consequently it was cheaper in the long run, and by 300 AD barrels had replaced amphorae (Johnson, 1989).

There was, however, one unexpected consequence of the shift from amphorae to barrels. With a good seal, wine could be stored anaerobically and age for some time in amphorae, just as it can in a bottle today. Barrels are good storage containers – but they are not anaerobic. Wine styles will have changed rapidly. The long-term ageing of wine would have declined substantially and with it some of the cachet of connoisseurship. The famous Roman doctor, Galen, discusses the ageing of wine in 169 AD, but after him, as Hugh Johnson (1989, p. 74) says 'we have no commentator on the progress of the Roman taste in wine'. Instead, for the next 1600 years, wine would have been subject to more obvious spoilage and rapid oxidative development; most wines would have had to be drunk within a year of vintage at the most or they would have ceased to be pleasant.

The 'Dark Ages' and the medieval period

The decline of the Roman Empire was long and slow but with the barbarian invasions of the fourth and fifth centuries AD also bloody and violent. With historical hindsight we may see it as the end of civilization; it certainly was the collapse of empire, of economic power and of trade. But for most people, life went on; it was more uncertain, but farms were still run, and peasants eked out a living whilst trying to stave off disease and famine. Included in this was the need to tend vines and produce wine, if only for personal consumption.

In insular, peasant-based societies, however, technological development may be slow and tradition rather than knowledge is the determinant of viticultural practice (Loubere, 1978). In this situation, and with political organizations often in a state of flux, the repository of knowledge was the church. Whilst, as Unwin (1996) has noted, the church's influence on preserving viticulture may have been exaggerated, nevertheless the fact that wine was central to the religious rites and that clerics kept alive libraries, reading and enquiry meant that they were able to maintain some viticultural knowledge. At times, as religious institutions became richer, they also developed some economic power, allowing them both to generate production and consumption of wine.

From 630 AD onwards, however, a new threat arose – not to civilization, but to the use of wine. The expansion of Islam accelerated towards the end of the life of the prophet Mohammed and, as will be seen in Chapter 13, the new religion forbade the drinking of wine. Arabia, Mohammed's native land, was too warm to make wine although it imported it, but the Islamic empire quickly spread through the countries of the eastern and southern Mediterranean. As they converted the local population so the use of grapes for wine production declined. By the beginning of the eighth century AD the Arabs had crossed the Straits of Gibraltar, conquering Spain and Portugal within 11 years. From there they were into France and only defeat at the Battle of Poitiers in 732 turned them back into Iberia. They would remain there, though defending a shrinking nation, for another 760 years. Nevertheless, although the Koran proscribed wine drinking, in practice a more tolerant approach was often taken – with even rulers drinking. Under Islam in Spain many people were prepared to accept wine consumption. The other point to be made is that those subject races who did not convert were generally allowed to practice their own beliefs in peace; Islam was usually very tolerant, at least to 'people of the book' – Jews and Christians.

As cohesive political rule slowly became more established during the Middle Ages, trade in wine began to grow again. The states of northern Europe were always keen to purchase wine. The fact that for 300 years from 1154 AD Bordeaux was an English possession helped develop the English fondness for Claret. The Rhine became a major artery for the transport of the wine made on its banks. As the Middle Ages progressed increased urbanization and annual fairs and market towns helped provide new forms of distribution. Nevertheless, despite a few developing trade routes, it should not be forgotten that most wine was consumed at the place where it was made.

Ultimately the wine trade began to organize itself. Brokers became the King's formal agents in France, with an agreed code of behaviour (Brennan, 1997). The Vintners' Company, a guild which operated a closed shop for the trade in wine in England, was incorporated in 1437 (Unwin, 1996) formalizing the importance of wine in a country which produced very little.

Throughout all this the role of the church remained critical. In many ways its varying arms were both the large viticultural conglomerates and the wine tourism operators of their day. In order to shorten their time in purgatory richer people would make gifts to the church; in wine-producing regions that could include land – so that bishoprics and monasteries gradually amassed collections of prime vineyard sites. The fact that the monks personally owned nothing ensured the concentration of this economic power in these organizations. Monasteries especially preserved the knowledge of how to make wine but also had the economic resources to spend on good equipment and to expand their knowledge base. Monasteries would provide hospitality to travellers; in viticultural areas that allowed them to showcase their wines to nobles, royalty and emissaries passing through.

The 'Age of Discovery'

From the beginning of the fifteenth century onwards maritime Europe began to explore well beyond its own boundaries. The Portuguese explored down to southern Africa; the Canary Islands and the Azores were claimed by Spain. In 1420 Madeira was settled by the Portuguese – later the island would gain key markets for its wine as a stopping post for ships going south through the Atlantic. Then, in 1492, Columbus sailed across the Atlantic and the Spanish crown claimed Central and South America, starting in what is now Mexico; vines were taken there by the 1520s (Unwin, 1996). This expansive approach was given impetus by the fact that the Ottoman Turks, who were Muslims, captured the last vestige of the Roman Empire – Constantinople – in 1453 (renaming it Istanbul), and for the next century pressed on through the Balkans conquering Christian territories. Old sources of wine were disappearing and new ones had to be found.

A complicated series of factors affected both consumption and the newly planted viticultural regions of the Americas. First, the impact of religion – the desire to convert the world for Catholicism (by force if necessary) and to outflank Islam – was a driving force. Conversion necessitated the sacrament, and proselytizing Jesuit missionaries in the middle of Patagonia or Franciscan friars in Baja California needed wine. (It is no coincidence that a synonym for one of the most widespread grape varieties in areas of former Spanish rule is 'mission'.)

However, the demands of the mass for wine were quantitatively limited. Perhaps of greater importance was a desire by settlers to create a 'new Spain' (Unwin, 1996). Recreating Spain, rather than adapting to the new, was fundamental to the approach of the first settlers. In Spain their beverage of choice was wine, and so – they considered – it should be in the colonies. The Spanish colonists also, for all their religious fervour, required some consolation for having left their homeland. Alcohol was one of the major comforts in a strange and hostile land. Shipping wine to the Americas from Europe was expensive and detrimental to the wine. Ultimately the settlers saw local vineyards as the answer to their need for drink (Unwin, 1996).

However, the perspective from Europe was different. The key factor there was the requirement to protect European vineyards, which meant the need to 'control' the development of viticulture across the Atlantic. In 1595 a ban was placed on new plantings in the Americas by Philip II of Spain in order to try to protect markets for Spanish wines. This seems, like previous attempts by rulers to control markets, to have been unsuccessful (Unwin, 1996).

The final phase of the period of discovery (at least for viticulture) came much later, with the settlement of Cape Town by the Dutch in the middle seventeenth century, and the English colonization of Australia and then New Zealand 140 years later. However, by that time much had changed in the area of wine production (see Figure 2.4).

Revolutions: Science, technology, consumption and politics

From the seventeenth century onwards two substantial changes in intellectual outlook began to have a major impact on the world of wine: one was the revolution in scientific understanding and the other was a major change in how goods were viewed and products consumed. Both of these changes had their origins in the revolution in critical thought prompted by the renaissance. Essentially, until the renaissance a fact was taken as given because long-established authorities (for instance, Aristotle and the Bible) determined it was so. One effect of the renaissance was to legitimize the questioning of traditional knowledge. This had obvious results in (say) astronomy following the work of Copernicus and Galileo but it also spread to many other fields of scientific investigation. At the same time the growing wealth flowing into Europe from trade, as well as the need to improve the infrastructure which enabled that trade to take place, provided an economic stimulus to greater exploration of the physical world and how it could be harnessed to benefit economic growth.

As science developed a broader understanding of how the physical world functions, and as European resources increased in the wake of overseas empires, so technology began to develop. This was to have a substantial impact on how wine was made in general, and on specific styles of wine in particular. The first area of impact was in the distillation of grape spirit and fortified wines. Distillation in fact predated the renaissance and was, paradoxically, probably a product of Arabic civilization. The Arabs invented distillation as a general means of concentrating liquid (and in the process also gave us the word alcohol – from al-kohl, signifying the essence of a substance). The first fortified wine was probably made by the mid-sixteenth century (Younger, 1966). At some point soon after, in the reign of Elizabeth I, Spanish wine producers realized that Sherry could be fortified (Jeffs, 1992). At this stage fortification may well have been merely an easy way for producers to create a wine with the 15.3 per cent a.b.v. at which flor most easily grows on the surface of the wine in an open butt. A little more than a century later the first experiments with fortifying Port took place, making a paradoxical wine, deeply red and tannic yet sweet.

Figure 2.4 An outline of recent wine history.

Date	*World history*	*Outline of Viticulture and wine*
1650	Dutch establish the Cape Colony	Botrytis recorded in Sauternes
		Pepys tastes Chateau Haut-Brion
	'Glorious Revolution' in England	First South African wines produced
	Age of consumer revolution	First sparkling champagnes appear
1700	Union of England, Wales and Scotland	Methuen treaty benefits Portuguese wines
		First Médoc wines appear in Britain
	Age of Agricultural revolution in Britain	
		'Three bottle a day' men

(continued)

Figure 2.4 (*continued*)

Date	*World history*	*Outline of Viticulture and wine*
1750		Christies start wine auctions
	Age of Industrial revolution in Britain	
	American war of independence	Thomas Jefferson plants vines in Virginia
	Settlement of Australia by Europeans	Tokay and Constantia are the 'great' wines
	French revolutionary period	Confiscation of French monastic vineyards
1800	Napoleonic wars	M. Chaptal, agriculture minister in France
	Fall of Napoleon	Development of riddling in Champagne
	Victoria becomes queen of Britain	First wines in the Hunter Valley
		Growth of temperance movements
	Californian gold rush	Expansion of Californian viticulture
1850	Great exhibition of Paris	Médoc classification
	Australian gold rush	Pasteur discovers the activity of bacteria
		Time of phylloxera
	Agricultural depression in Europe	Rapid expansion of Algerian vineyards
		Rise of prohibition movements

1900	Death of Queen Victoria	Riots in Languedoc
	First World War	Riots over the demarcation of Champagne
		First comprehensive local AC system
	Great Depression	Establishment of French AC system
	Second World War	
1950	Cold war	Rapid technological change in production
	Formation of the EEC	
	UK joins the EEC	Market expansion in Anglophone nations
	Spain, Portugal, Greece join the EU	Increased sales of non-European wines
	End of the communist bloc	Phylloxera and Pierce's disease in California
2000		Decline in markets for traditional wines

Technology also made possible the sparkling wines which come from Champagne. Although effervescence in wine had been recorded throughout history (and may even be alluded to in the Bible), the process was ill-understood so that producing it was erratic, and a sparkle may well have been associated with faults in wine. When it did occur it was because, in cold northern regions such as Champagne, the drop in temperature in autumn could suspend fermentation by sending the yeast into hibernation. When the temperature rose again in spring the fermentation would restart and if the wine was by that stage in an enclosed container the carbon dioxide produced would remain dissolved in the wine; however, given that almost all wine was stored in barrel, and the gas could escape from such an environment, this occurrence was rare. In the middle of the seventeenth century a combination of events changed this. First, processes for producing harder glass were developed; this meant bottles became safer receptacles for wine (Unwin, 1996). At the same time the use of corks as bottle stoppers became widespread (in place of cloth, or poor-fitting wooden bungs which had been utilized previously). Corks could provide a complete seal and an environment had been produced in which gas could be trapped in the bottle. At the same time the more widespread use of bottle-and-cork allowed wine to age again over the long term in a near anaerobic environment, returning to the days of amphorae.

Contemporaneously there was another change in the way wine was produced – thought at the time to be more significant still both by stabilizing wine and allowing it to age. This was the introduction of racking wine between barrels and then topping it up to pre-empt oxygen contact (Briggs, 1994). The Dutch also introduced to Bordeaux the practice of burning sulphur sticks in empty barrels to help preserve the wines with which they would be filled (Phillips, 2000). For fuller-bodied red wines, such as those of Bordeaux, this marked a change in the styles of wine made.

Changes did not just occur in production, but also in the vineyards. Before 1708 wine designated as Médoc was unknown in England (Peppercorn, 1991) and Claret came primarily from the Graves region south of Bordeaux. From 1680 Dutch expertise in land reclamation had allowed the land north of the city to be drained so that it could be planted with vines – thus one of the great wine regions of the world was created (Faith, 1999; Phillips, 2000).

Following on from changes in production came a revolution in consumption. From about 1680 onwards attitudes to consumption began to change radically and with those changes the volume and type of goods consumed increased (McKendrick et al., 1982). This began in Britain (McKendrick et al., 1982), then possibly the Netherlands (Ger & Belk, 2005) followed by other countries.

The desire for consumer goods had existed for some time (for instance, in the renaissance (Jardine, 1997)) but a series of factors changed the process of concerted consumption from being the privilege of a few to the right of many. First, overseas trade and the development of empires provided new wealth that could be spent on more than mere subsistence – a factor given new impetus as the industrial revolution created yet more wealth. At the risk of oversimplification whereas previously spending and luxury were considered the preserve of the rich – and sinful if committed by those of lower social status – by the late eighteenth-century consumption was seen as a logical, necessary and commendable result of production. At the same time the rapid expansion of printing and the widespread development of newspapers, pamphlets and handbills meant that advertizing became widespread, as did the recording of new fashions. Meanwhile the idea that information was to be eagerly sought out became more common. All of this created a climate of fashionability where to consume, to be different and to know about the latest products was important (McKendrick et al., 1982). These factors combined later with a growing 'romantic' sensibility which itself saw goods (especially if they had aesthetic value) as being morally strengthening (Campbell, 1987). Novelty itself involved two contradictory forces: the desire to imitate one's betters (thus to drink what they were drinking) and the aim of being ahead of the crowd, of drinking what no one else had yet discovered or could afford.

Fashionability, novelty and the desire to consume had an impact on wine. It was in this period that the 'new French Clarets' (Unwin, 1996), appeared – led by Haut-Brion which Pepys recorded drinking in his diary and followed by the new wines of the Médoc. This was also the age in which Champagne, Port and Madeira became popular; new wines offered novelty value. During the eighteenth century the growing wealth of the middle class allowed them to drink more wine so that in due course the accoutrements of aesthetic consumption – books about wine, auctions and later the careful matching of food and wine – became more common. This change particularly emphasized the appreciation of wine, and the consumer's understanding of it. Meanwhile, as the consumption of wine grew in non-producing countries so the need for new places to make wine or new means of getting it to markets speedily became necessary.

One impact of these developments was to highlight a difference between varying wine markets. The period since the eighteenth century has also seen the development of a consumer market for premium wine. However, in much of southern Europe wine remained a drink consumed where it was made, by rich and poor alike. This period also saw the growth of less obvious but quite specific markets for bulk wine. Phillips (2000) notes that wine became the 'staple alcohol' of Paris (uniquely in northern France, where beer was otherwise the principal drink), and that this accelerated after the development of the French railway system.

Meanwhile the eighteenth century became the great age of political revolution – crucially in France but also, in the wake of Napoleon, through much of central Europe as well. The ownership of vineyards was changed dramatically; the church lost most of its wealth and its land was taken from it. However, using a Marxist analysis this was not a proletarian revolution so it was not really the peasantry who benefited. Rather it was the bourgeoisie who gained and the new masters of the vineyards were the middle and lower-middle classes. Négociants, landlords and the moderately well-off small local farmers who could raise some money to buy a little of the expropriated land were the ones who gained. The revolution had one other key influence on the shape of vineyard ownership. The Napoleonic code, a comprehensive legal system which was introduced not just in France but also other parts of Europe, provided that inheritance should be split equally between sons on the death of a parent. In many parts of the continent, such as Burgundy and Alsace, the Rhine and Austria, this meant that land ownership fractured, often into economically unviable units. Production of grapes and the economic resources to make, and even more to market, wine became more separated than they had been.

The 'golden age' of wine

The period from around 1810 until 1875 has been termed by Hugh Johnson (1989) the golden age of wine. This is in many ways an apt term, even if there have been other golden ages and despite the fact that the roots of this era lie in changes that were taking place in the previous century. In northern Europe the industrial revolution and the influx of wealth from expanding overseas empires was providing a growing middle class with resources for luxuries, some of which included wine. Legal structures were changing to facilitate credit and investment was becoming more widespread – so that it was easier to expand production. Producers could buy more, with a 25 per cent increase in land under vines from 1835 to 1869 and yields rising from under 15 hL/ha in the 1840s to 23 hL/ha in the 1860s and 1870s (Loubere, 1978). Another key change was heralded by the free-trade agreement between France and Britain in 1861 (Unwin, 1996), which led to a period when tariffs on wines were almost entirely ended – thus ensuring that export growth stimulated production not merely for the French but also for the Germans and Spanish and to a lesser extent Italians.

Crucially, also, the pace of technological change was accelerating yet further and improving both the production of wine and speedier and more effective distribution. The first production changes began in the regions where wines had the widest market and produced the greatest income. Champagne is the classic example. Early in the eighteenth century came the realization that alcohol was created by the conversion of sugar. When this was understood it was easy to increase the alcohol level of wine by adding sugar (a process named after M. Chaptal, Napoleon's minister for agriculture). It was also possible to control the second fermentation of sparkling wine by adding a precise amount of sugar before sealing the bottle. At the same time, the invention of riddling meant that clarifying Champagne became easier, a method which reached its apotheosis after the means to freeze the plug of dead yeast cells in the neck of the bottle was introduced in 1889 (Stevenson, 1986).

Technology also had a major impact on distribution. First railways, then steam ships, meant wine could travel within countries and even around the world more rapidly, remaining fresher and unspoiled for longer. Preservation was aided by better methods of chilling which also protected wine. Markets in places like New York and Chicago could be more easily serviced, as well as outposts of the burgeoning European empires. This in turn increased profit to producers which could be reinvested in applying science to improve viticulture and production (Loubere, 1978).

The changes in science and technology were epitomized by Louis Pasteur. The greatest French biochemist of the age (and a lover of wine), he was commissioned to examine why wine spoilage occurred. He concluded that it was bacterial in origin and showed ways in which it could be treated – resulting in wines with much lower volatile acidity and fewer other faults (Robinson, 1999). He also explained how fermentation occurred – another key requirement if wine production was to become a carefully controlled process – although he himself did not in fact discover yeasts.

The technological developments in production were mirrored in changes in the vineyard. With academics such as Jules Guyot and Jules-Emile Planchon a new scientific rigour was brought to vine physiology and soil science (Loubere, 1978). Vineyards which had regularly been polycultural, with competing crops, were turned into monocultures so that growers could give vines their undivided attention. In areas where planting had been *en foule* (haphazard, at often extremely high density of up to 40 000 vines/ha) trellising and ordered training were introduced, and systematic pruning methods adopted. This was not merely a French phenomenon; in Italy reforming politicians, such as Count Cavour (in Piedmont) and Baron Ricasoli (in Tuscany) transformed their vineyards (Loubere, 1978). Treatments such as Bordeaux mix to combat mildew were also invented and saw widespread use.

Improving quality, growing wealth and speedier distribution made wine more valued. The golden age then increased the desire to classify the wine – to highlight those which were especially good, so that they could be even more sought after. Thus in 1855 the merchants of Bordeaux classified the wine of two areas around their city – the Médoc (59 wines) and Sauternes (26 wines) – grading them according to their price on the market. This only represented a small proportion of wine made in the region but it enhanced the fame of all Claret; even those who could not afford to buy the classed growths sought to drink Bordeaux because of the cachet by association (Ulin, 1996).

As the major European wine regions were gaining in reputation and economic strength, so new wine regions were also developing. Until the middle of the nineteenth century the Cape Colony in Southern Africa had had some success in supplying the British market. That success soon vanished, but it was replaced by growth in supplies to the United Kingdom from both Victoria and California. In each case the stimulus to the growth was the same – gold. Gold rushes caused a massive population influx which needed to be supplied with alcohol. As this happened the improvements in the storage and transportation of wines meant that export as well as local markets could be accessed. For California that export market was the east coast of the United States, for Australia it was Britain.

In the context of this book these sources of wine along with South America and New Zealand are termed the 'new producing countries'. The idea of the 'New World' is imprecise, as South Africa, for instance, does not fit neatly there even though its wine industry has developed in the last 300 years. In any event it is hard to describe Australia, for instance, with an aboriginal heritage which dates back at least 40 000 years, as part of a new world.

Depression and decline

After the golden age came a reaction. From about 1875 a decline set in across the wine regions of Europe, later affecting the whole world. In part this was more than just a problem for the wine industry and presaged a substantial period of economic and social restructuring in both rural and urban areas. There was a general agricultural depression throughout Europe from 1873 to 1896. To a certain extent this depression resulted from better agricultural production methods, which increased yields along with the improved distribution methods which have already been noted.

Another general cause for malaise was war, which disrupted production and depressed economies over the longer term. In 1870 France and Prussia fought a war, as a result of which France ceded Alsace to what became Germany. More substantial was the Great War, fought from 1914 to 1918, which drained the economies of Germany, Italy and France, depressed many of their major overseas markets and continued to reduce economic growth for long after the armistice.

Other problems were more specific to viticulture itself. Better transport improves distribution but it also spreads pests and diseases. Oïdium, a form of mildew which affects quality and yield, arrived in Europe at the end of the 1840s. It harmed vineyards substantially, although it was soon discovered that dusting with sulphur controlled it. Much more devastating was the arrival of phylloxera, a barely visible North American insect which arrived in Europe having been brought in by ship on the roots of a vine from the United States (Campbell, 2004).

Phylloxera and its impact

Phylloxera vastatrix first attacked vineyards in the Rhone valley in southern France from 1863 onwards with a subsequent, separate outbreak around Bordeaux (Campbell, 2004). Over the next 40 years the insect spread through the country and beyond and had devastated most of Europe's wine regions by 1914. Phylloxera has a complex lifecycle but, critically, the larvae of the insect burrow into the soil and gnaw at the roots of the vine, extracting sap. Its natural habitat was the roots of American vine species but these plants had developed resistance to the insect and their roots merely calloused over when damaged, so that the plant remained healthy. The roots of *Vitis vinifera* vines have no such resistance and after a period the vine dies. The insect then moves on to a new vine and the destruction spreads to neighbouring vineyards. As the vineyards of the southern Rhone were destroyed it was quickly discovered that the common factor was the American louse which had arrived on the roots of American vines on a ship to Marseilles. In searching for food it had discovered local vinifera vines and started feeding from their roots. Those vines were not tolerant of it, their roots decayed, and they began to die.

The insect was named phylloxera vastatrix – the 'female devastator', because of its lifecycle. It is hermaphroditic and a single female can lay up to 20 million eggs in a season – enough to ensure a rapid progress. Vineyards and whole viticultural regions became entirely unproductive. As a result the French resorted to other means to satisfy their thirst for wine. This was the period of great vineyard expansion in the French colony of Algeria. Domestically other types of 'wine' became common.

Imported raisins, added to water and tartaric acid and crushed, could be fermented. Even less authentic were the fermented concoctions produced from sugar syrup, colouring and flavouring (Campbell, 2004).

The French puzzled for years about how to deal with the scourge of phylloxera (Campbell, 2004). It would not tolerate sandy soil – however that was of little use, for few vineyards were planted in sand. It could be dealt with by flooding a vineyard for 100 days – but that was rarely possible or practical. Some specific chemicals injected into the soil would kill it – most effectively carbon disulphide – yet they were dangerous, expensive and temporary in effect. One solution was to import resistant American grapevines. These tended to produce inferior wine (Robinson, 1999) but they, or hybrids created by cross-pollinating an American vine with *Vitis vinifera*, were widely planted in the immediate aftermath of phylloxera (Campbell, 2004). Ultimately the best solution was to graft scions of *Vitis vinifera* varieties onto rootstocks from native American vines. That way you could keep your cabernet or sémillon, but protect it from devastation. There was, however, a protracted debate in French viticultural circles about the efficacy of the various methods of dealing with it and it was many years before grafting became widely adopted as the means of control. In the interim hundreds of thousands of hectares of vine had been lost, some of them never to be replanted, and the viticultural map of Europe changed. The insect is now endemic through much of the world, although it has not reached Chile, the sandy central plain of Hungary is spared it, and in Australia it is confined to Victoria and a small part of New South Wales.

In the mid-term the cost of phylloxera was high for grapegrowers. The long-term effects, moreover, were radical. First, the structure of the French wine industry changed profoundly, as many small peasant growers lost their livelihood (Campbell, 2004), and others replanted with alternative crops (Ulin, 1996). The industry began to consolidate as only those with some capital could afford to replant with grafted stock. There was a social impact to this for in many places the countryside began to empty as men left to find more stable work in towns (Loubere, 1978). Consolidation, however, resulted in owners who were determined to make vineyards economically viable; these producers started to pay more attention to viticultural research and were more ready to experiment in order to maintain their livelihood (Loubere, 1978).

Second, the viticultural landscape changed dramatically. Until phylloxera Paris had had a small wine region; after it was devastated no one replanted. Further south large wine-producing areas were lost or reduced substantially in size (Campbell, 2004). Replanting accelerated the ordering of vineyards, increasing the number that were trellised and carefully laid out. Rigorous vineyard management became the order of the day (Loubere, 1978).

Third, the ampelographic make-up of the country changed dramatically. Low-quality hybrid or American vines were planted – a mistake that would take a century to remedy. More to the point, when replanting took place, growers took the chance to rationalize their vineyards. In many ways this made sense; the old habit of mixing varieties in one plot, including both red and white grapes, began to be phased out. On the other hand old, often high-quality varieties disappeared, like carmenère in Bordeaux, because they could be replanted with more productive vines.

Resulting from a combination of the general decline in the vinous economy due to phylloxera and from the establishment of the high reputations of some select regions from the earlier golden age was the spread of fraud. The demand for wine meant that some unscrupulous producers were prepared not just to adulterate or concoct wine but also to pass it off as something else. Foreign wine (especially Algerian) was repackaged as French, and French wine from lesser regions was sold as being from somewhere more reputable (Campbell, 2004). Bottling wine at the premises of the producer was not common at the time; much was matured and then packaged by merchants, so that such fraud was relatively easy to commit.

Whilst viticultural fortunes rose at various times and in various places during this period, there was nevertheless a general sense of decline, even of total failure, which led inevitably to dissatisfaction amongst *vignerons*. Rioting became common in much of France. The rejuvenation of the southern French industry in the wake of widespread replanting meant that dearth was replaced by a surplus which was hard to sell in competition with cheap imported wine and this only increased the discontent. By the first decade of the twentieth century severe unrest spread through French wine regions. It was directed at different targets. In Languedoc opposition focused on imported, chaptalised or fraudulently produced wine – in 1907 five people were killed by army fire at a demonstration. In Champagne violence was directed at limiting who was within the designated Champagne viticultural region – and would thus benefit from the higher price grapes used for such a famous wine would obtain.

One final factor began to threaten the health of the wine industry. This was the period of the growth of temperance movements and particularly the campaign for total abstinence. This development is considered in more detail in Chapter 13, but particularly in North America and Scandinavia, to a lesser extent in Britain and Germany yet even, in a small way, in Mediterranean Europe, large-scale campaigns developed to prevent people drinking and – as an ultimate goal – to ban any alcoholic drinks. Whilst this may not have had such a great effect on European wine production, it did dramatically affect viticulture in the United States and New Zealand. It also had an emotional impact; suddenly, after 7 millennia of winemaking, the drink was being castigated for causing poverty, disease and misery.

It is worth commenting, however, that whilst there may have been a general depression for wine producers over this period, it was not universal, nor always contemporaneous. Phylloxera reached different countries at different times. Only France had the problem of substantial competition on its domestic market from an alternative supplier in Algeria. The South African wine industry fell into decline in the 1850s, well before that of Europe, whilst wine production in Australia rose continuously from 1850 until the end of the 1890s, stabilized for about 20 years and then rose again substantially from 1918 to 1930.

The twentieth century

One might have expected viticultural fortunes to rise in the euphoria of the years after 1918 but, whilst things only became noticeably worse in the United States because of the introduction of prohibition, they did not really improve anywhere else. There was a sense of post-war economic drift which ended in the depression, rather than improvement.

The response of business and of governments was to try to find ways to protect the wine industry. The first was to stem the spread of fraud by offering internal legal protection to the more reputable regions. The first comprehensive appellation system, demarcating wine regions, was not in France but in Portugal before the First World War. However, the French system, begun voluntarily in Chateauneuf-du-Pape in the 1920s and then enshrined in French law as a national structure in 1935, is the most well known. Meanwhile in 1930 Germany instituted a national wine law designed to improve the quality of wine. It banned the blending of German and foreign wine, controlled chaptalisation and prohibited the use of hybrid grape varieties (Brook, 2003).

More general types of economic protection were applied. Tariffs were restored to protect wine from external competition and government subsidies began to appear (Phillips, 2000). Co-operatives were also developed in many countries. Portugal, for instance, made wide use of them – as did Australia and South Africa – in order to give hard-pressed growers access to a regular market for their grapes, and to enable capital for production processes which small producers could never afford. At the same time a new form of wine trade with multiple outlets and seeking to sell much cheaper wine developed, especially in the United Kingdom. This was allied to an expansion of advertizing intended to stimulate a wider market (Unwin, 1996).

Most of these processes were just developing when the Second World War struck, effectively delaying any recuperative effect. In the aftermath of the war the key focus of most wine-producing nations was the reconstruction of Europe. For wine this had a number of effects. First, the need to gain valuable foreign currency meant that some of the defeated nations – notably Germany and Italy – put a lot of effort into producing cheap, affordable wines. In places like the Rhine valley and Valpolicella this resulted in planting vines away from traditional high-quality vineyards and into more fertile valleys. Yields were high but quality declined. Some of these wines – especially liebfraumilch in the English market – became widely popular, but in the longer term they reduced the reputation of the country or region in which they were produced because of the focus on making them as cheap as possible.

Also significant was the European drive towards unity, driven partly by the desire for collective economic growth and partly to ensure that co-operation would end further wars in the continent. This led to the formation of the European Economic Community (EEC) in 1957 – later to become the European Union (EU) – with the aim of harmonizing markets and production processes across the member nations (Unwin, 1996). As France was considered to be the leading wine nation in the world the EEC broadly adopted a form of the French appellation system across all of its wine-producing member states (although, as will be seen in Chapter 5, with local variations, especially in Germany). Additionally it established a comprehensive and substantial support mechanism for agriculture – including viticulture. This resulted in policies designed to encourage and bolster production throughout what is now the EU, particularly in less economically thriving rural areas in the south of the continent.

Quality wine and table wine

The harmonization of wine laws across Europe based on the French model led to the formal institution of a two-tier system for wines. The upper part of the hierarchy was designated as 'quality wine produced from a specified region' (QWPSR). In France this was substantially appellation controlée wine (though also included the minute volume of *Vin Délimité de Qualité Supérieure,* (wine designated as superior quality). In Italy this included *Denominazione di Origine Controllata* (DOC) and – later – *Denominazione di Origine Controllata e Garantita* (DOCG); equivalents exist now in all wine-producing European Union (EU) countries. QWPSR has to be produced within a demarcated area and usually has to comply with other production controls, most noticeably controls on which grape varieties may be planted in the region and the imposition of maximum yields in the vineyard in order to avoid excessive cropping. Other controls often include minimum sugar or alcohol levels and ageing periods.

The lower category of wine is called table wine. Within France table wine cannot, in principle, declare a vintage nor state a grape variety or place of origin. It is nameless and may be blended from a number of countries. This was modified slightly in the 1970s with the introduction of the category known as *vin de pays* (country wines) in France, quickly copied in other EU countries. *Vin de pays* were introduced as a spur to the improvement of table wines. They are technically table wines, but by exemption can state a vintage year, grape variety and place of origin. They are also, however, subject to controls on yields, although these are not as strict as those for QWPSR.

The other issue that was crucial in the post-war period was the rapid acceleration of technological advance (Charters, 2003). This could be seen in viticulture – with the growth of vine crossings, sprays and fertilizers, and later the development of scientific canopy management systems – and also in wine production. The development of hygienic winery practice, temperature control, cultured yeast to control fermentation and very effective methods of stabilizing wine, including filtration, became widespread. At the start of the post-war period the core research for the industry was centred on France and Germany, but from the 1970s onwards both Californian and Australian institutions were producing equally good if not better results.

The reason for the geographical shift in research output was because wine production was no longer an essentially European concern. Californian wines began to penetrate international markets in the 1970s, followed by those from Australia, New Zealand and Chile; later South Africa, also a large producer, began to export more actively. As production spread, so did consumption. People in northern European markets, such as the United Kingdom, Scandinavian countries and Holland, began to drink more. Meanwhile in some of the new producing countries which had traditionally drunk beer rather than wine (the United States, Australia and New Zealand), habits began to change and consumption soared. Most recently countries in East Asia have become increasingly keen to enjoy wine.

As markets changed, so did wine styles (Charters, 2003). Sugar became a major food flavourant in the twentieth century; thus the taste for slightly sweet wines grew. Later, the impact of technology (particularly anaerobic handling in wineries) started to produce fewer faulty and many more obviously fruity wines – often given some oak character. Ripe, sweet-fruited, oaky wines came into vogue. At the same time a move away from very sweet and certainly from very alcoholic drinks led to a decline in the popularity of fortified wines which had been the mainstay of consumption in many Anglophone markets. This change in wine styles has not been universally popular, with some seeing in it the debasing of traditional wine quality.

Recreating old wines

History is important not merely because it sets context but because it continues to be used and reinterpreted in the contemporary marketing of wine. One way in which this may occur is in the modern reference to old wines, or the tradition of producing wine. Thus Champagne Veuve Clicquot makes much of the fact that early in the nineteenth century Madame Clicquot 'invented' the means of riddling wine. Even more useful is when an old wine can be recreated, to give it instant historical cachet.

Towards the end of the eighteenth century there were two wines which vied with each other for being the most famous in the world. One was Tokaji, from Hungary, and the other was Constantia, from the eponymous region south of Cape Town, in what is now South Africa. The Constantia farm was established in 1685 by Simon van der Stel. On his death it was split, but two of the successor companies agreed to sell a wine labelled as 'Constantia'. In the middle of the following century one of van der Stel's successors, Hendrik Cloete, built a fine cellar at Groote Constantia for making wine and replanted the vineyards with aromatic grape varieties, especially muscat. Cloete established a method of late harvesting so that the grapes became almost raisined on the vine, concentrating their sugar levels and resulting in a sweet, perfumed wine. This wine, known as *Vin de Constance*, rapidly became highly sought after; Jane Austen referred to it in her novels and Napoleon loved it enough to have it shipped to St Helena when he was exiled there.

With changing trade relationships between Britain and her colonies in the middle of the nineteenth century the market for *Vin de Constance* collapsed, phylloxera devastated the vineyards and ultimately the wine was made no more. The Constantia estate from which it came was divided into three and sold on.

Then, in 1980, a new owner, Duggie Jooste, purchased one of the successor estates, Klein Constantia. He determined to restore the reputation of the wine farm to its former glory, investing heavily in production at the property. In 1986 a trial version of the famed old wine was made, though not sold; subsequent vintages were put onto the market (Lloyd, 2002).

It is not just the name which harks back to the days of the wine's fame 200 years ago. The winery claims to have replanted with vines descended from those originally used to make *Vin de Constance*. The method – late harvesting – is said to be identical. The wine is sold in a bottle based on a centuries old design which was used for the wine 150 years ago or more, with a distinctive asymmetrical shape and bulbous flask-like base – the design has been trademarked to protect its use (du Plessis, 2005).

At this point history shades into myth. In a book published in 1997 the wine was described as one of the 44 best wines of the world; in 2002 the magazine *Wine and Spirits* in the United States put Klein Constantia on a list of the world's 25 great vineyards (Jooste, 2005). In 2000 soil from its vineyards was bound into cubes of crystal and included in a collection of the 'nine most mythical vineyards of the world', alongside the greatest of French sites. When the wine finally appeared on the British market, in 2002, one leading wine writer ended an article about it with the phrase 'welcome back'. *Vin de Constance* is also building up a series of recommendations from international wine critics, including Robert Parker, the *Wine Spectator* and Stephen Tanzer (Lloyd, 2002).

On the basis of less than 20 modern vintages the wine is attaining the status of a classic and, whilst there is no doubting the intrinsic quality of the wine, each time it is discussed its history is referred to; it is a wine which cannot escape its past because the past has been used to provide its market position. However, is it the same wine? Production similarities with the wine of 200 years ago have been noted. On the other hand, whilst winemaker's notes on its production (Lloyd, 2002) describe how the producers try to 'mirror the old Constantia wines', processes include mechanical pressing, transferring the juice to stainless steel tanks, adding specially cultured yeast to start fermentation, filtering the wine and cold stabilizing it. None of these methods would have been known to the makers of old Constantia wines two centuries ago; to that extent the wine remains a modern reinterpretation of what was made in the past.

Bibliographical note

The development of this chapter is based on some major academic interpretations of the historical development of wine. Tim Unwin's *Wine and the Vine* (1996) is a substantial work of interpretation, complex at times but extremely enlightening and probing. No less rigorous, but more discursive and perhaps accessible is Rod Phillip's *A Short History of Wine* (2000). One other helpful book, which concentrates on all forms of drink but is entertainingly written and has some interesting insights into wine, is Andrew Barr's *Drink: An Informal Social History* (1995). Equally stylish, well researched and easy to read is *The Story of Wine*, by the eminent wine writer Hugh Johnson (1989). The early development of wine is covered by McGovern (2003), although the molecular science becomes detailed at times. For a cohesive examination of the modern French industry in one region the books by Brennan (1997) and Guy (2003) are very interesting. For the wine industry's own perspective on the last 100 years *A Century of Wine*, edited by Stephen Brook (2000d) is very accessible.

Part Two: The Production of Wine

3

The nature of wine

This chapter investigates how wine's nature has an impact on the methods used to produce it, and in turn how those production issues inform the way in which it is perceived. It will focus on four key issues. The first considers how wine's attributes are bound up in its biochemistry. This specifically means that it has been considered a 'healthful' product for much of its history and it has also been an important means of obtaining sweetness and sugar. Second, it is suggested that wine operates as two different products; both as a bulk drink without aesthetic connotations, and as a premium product, with a core aesthetic focus. There is then an examination of whether or not wine is 'produce' or 'product' and how perspectives on this shape the varying perspectives with which countries view their product and how it is marketed. Finally it is argued that wine production can be a key element in the expression of national identity, which again shapes how its production is carried out.

The physical benefits of wine

A healthy drink

For much of its history wine has been perceived to be a healthy drink – with good reason. Its combination of alcohol and acid level means that only two bacteria can survive in it (acetic and lactic) and, whilst both of these can affect its taste – even, in the case of acetobacter, turning it to vinegar – neither are harmful to humans. Water, on the other hand, was a medium which could sustain microbes such as typhus and cholera and, until the development of effective sanitation and water purification from the 1850s onwards, was much more dangerous to consume unless boiled. For this reason alcoholic drinks were widely available, and in northern Europe, away from wine regions, beer became the drink of choice. Until the mid-nineteenth century low-alcohol beer was the standard drink issued for breakfast in English public schools (Barr, 1995, p. 58). Wine is sanitizing.

This notion that wine is a healthy drink has pervaded the general perception of the product. Wine was often prescribed for various maladies by Hippocrates, the founder of modern medicine, and by many influential later doctors (see Chapter 12). Even in the modern era many southern European countries have seen wine to be healthy for the nation, so that it is often considered to be in a different product category from other forms of alcohol. An American anthropologist in the 1960s reported seeing a French mother give a young child watered wine to drink yet was told by the same mother that she would not let her children touch alcohol (Anderson, 1968). The French philosopher, Roland Barthes, noted the mythic health giving properties of wine – especially that it could make the weak strong – whereas milk, which was 'calming' was nevertheless much less symbolically significant for his nation (Barthes, 1957/2000, p. 58).

The importance of sweetness

In an age when sugar is cheap and readily available it is easy to forget that before the eighteenth century, and the development of sugar plantations (later supplemented by sugar beet), sweet substances were at a premium. Honey and dried fruit, such as dates and figs with a concentration of sugars at the expense of water, were the main sources; the limited supply of these (especially of dried fruit in northern Europe) made them luxury goods. Wine could be made sweet by leaving the grapes to desiccate (either on the vine or on mats after picking) as recorded by Hesiod in the eighth century BC (Hesiod, n.d./1999). Dry grapes, with an excess of sugar, precluded the fermentation of grape juice to dryness, making the resulting wine another attractive source of sugar. From the sixteenth century AD onwards this method of making sweet wine was supplemented in two ways: first by fortification, which achieved the same effect by arresting fermentation; second by the use of botrytized grapes. Until the nineteenth century sweet wines tended to be the most prestigious and popular in the world. Only in more modern times has this taste changed (albeit slowly), a trend which has its origins about 150 years ago. Even currently it is possible to recall the popularity of sherry (almost invariably of the medium-dry to sweet variety) in many anglophone countries until about 30 years ago.

The two wines

The idea of the two wines

Almost invariably those who discuss, sell or write about wine refer to it as if it were a single, homogeneous product, albeit in various styles. Where differences between wines are considered they relate to colour, variety, country of origin or winemaking (for instance, sparkling, oaked or botrytized wines). It is suggested, however, that these variations, while relevant to specific groups of distributor or consumer, are not the fundamental way of distinguishing wine. Rather, there are two types of wine in the world and these are distinguished on the basis of both the culture of their production and the culture of their consumption. Effectively these function – in marketing terms – as two distinct products. One is a bulk product. It may or may not be mass produced, but is nevertheless generally purchased in large volumes (either direct from a vat, or in containers larger than the traditional 750 mL bottle) and is referred to as bulk wine. Consumption of this product takes place substantially in countries which produce wine – but not exclusively in Europe. Bulk wine consumption is widespread, for instance, in Australia and New Zealand. This kind of wine – consumed merely as a beverage – receives little focus from the wine industry which naturally tends to promote its premium product, and almost no attention from wine critics and writers. Nonetheless, it is economically important. In France basic *vin de table* was 49 per cent of all wine produced in 1999 (although 31 per cent of this was the subcategory of *vin de pays*) (Ribereau-Gayon, 2001). In Australia at the end of the 1990s over 56 per cent of all wine sold was in casks of 2 litres or more (Travers, 1999). In New Zealand there is a marginally lower proportion of bulk wine sold – but it still accounts for about 23 per cent of sales by volume (Beverland & Carswell, 2001). It has been suggested that worldwide there was '23 per cent of the value and 60 per cent of the volume of world wine production in the non-premium category in 1999' (Anderson & Wittwer, 2001, p.74). In non-producing countries consumption of bulk wine is much less important but it is clear that historically this was not always the case. Duguid (2003) makes the point that in the 'grog shops' of Victorian England brand name was unimportant where intoxication was the prime aim of wine consumption.

On the other hand one also finds premium wine. This is designated explicitly as such in Australia (Geene et al., 1999), when it is based on price, or as 'quality wine produced from a specified region' (QWPSR). Premium wine is not sold in bulk form. Its distinguishing feature in Europe is likely to be its region of origin and in most of the new producing countries that it carries a vintage date. It is almost invariably sold in 750 mL bottles.

It is necessary to stress that this distinction is not one of market segmentation, but more fundamentally about the type of product consumed. Indeed, the markets for the two types of wine can themselves be segmented, particularly the premium wine market. So, for instance, Perrin and Lockshin (2001) have one segment for the bulk wine market but three segments of the premium wine market. Indeed some approaches to segmentation ignore the bulk market altogether (Spawton, 1991). Rather than segmentation, therefore, this distinction is about both the origin of the wine and the consumption purposes to which it is put.

Distinguishing the two wines

The distinction between these two types of wine can be made clear by examining two aspects of the purpose of consumption – aesthetic appreciation and social reward – and then also by considering the origin of the different wines.

Aesthetics

Premium wine is drunk with a primarily aesthetic goal, rather than being consumed fundamentally for lubrication. One of the benchmarks for premium wine quality is said to be aesthetic evaluation (Amerine & Roessler, 1976). Part of that aesthetic process is the careful complementing of wine with a specific food – so that many wine books now have sections on pairing food with an appropriate wine, and in some cases entire works are dedicated to the principles of food/wine matching (Simon, 1996). It has been suggested that this is a comparatively new approach to consumption – at least in a country like France which drinks both bulk and premium wine. What was once drunk for nutritional benefit is now consumed because the drinker enjoys its taste (Demossier, 2005).

In contradistinction bulk wine is used primarily as a lubricant with food, or for its alcoholic impact, rather than primarily for any aesthetic qualities. In support of the former instance one can cite the general use of a local wine by consumers throughout much of the Mediterranean region, irrespective of its colour or style. Historically that drink may have been piquette (Loubere et al., 1985), with little aesthetic value. Even today there are those who will drink whatever happens to be locally accessible. In this kind of society wine is primarily selected not for its aesthetic value, nor to match specific food, but because of the dictates of custom or availability. Consumption of wine in this fashion has its roots in the well-established fact, noted above, that it is a much safer drink than water. The way wine is utilized in this manner is clearly as an accompaniment to food as a lubricating agent – rather than as a drink to be savoured.

Social purpose

Traditionally the role of wine in establishing the consumer's status within consumer cultures is well recorded (see Chapter 9). This may merely be the function of the cost or reputation of the wine, but in more complex situations it may result from the application of 'connoisseurship' (Phillips, 2000; Tomlinson, 1990). Such a use only applies to premium wine, however. On the other hand one can observe the bulk product where social distinction has little relevance, except possibly in the negative – as a form of anti-elitism – for it offers no opportunity for personal differentiation. With a label which may give no vintage, grape variety or region of origin, and very often no label at all, the opportunities for establishing 'distinction' are minimal. It is fair to suggest that in the traditional wine producing nations of Europe, consumption of this product took place generally amongst rural peasants in the region of production itself as part of a local polyculture (Unwin, 1996), and even today production for personal use continues (Calabresi, 1987). One also still observes carafes of unnamed wines automatically placed on the table for general use in cheap French bistros or Italian trattorias.

The geography of production

The key requirement for bulk wine is that it is cheap. The production implication is therefore that it is produced in a warm to hot region, for two reasons. First, so that a large volume of wine can be produced, for the temperature allows ripening of greater volumes. Second so that there is greater security that the crop will ripen from year to year, guaranteeing the consistent volume which a product with small margins requires. Thus bulk wine is made in the San Joaquin valley of California, whilst rarely up the road in cooler Sonoma; in Puglia and not Piemonte. As well as heat, access to large volumes of water for irrigation also helps to ensure high yields. (Traditionally Europe has eschewed irrigation, although the decision of Spain to permit irrigation even for quality wine means that now only France and Germany truly remain bastions against the idea of watering vines.) It can be noted, however, that even in regions which have hitherto produced bulk wine, there may be a new pressure to shift to 'quality'. In the Griffith area of New South Wales, for instance, trebbiano and muscat gordo blanco grapes were mainly planted by Italian migrants to provide them with the kind of wines which they were used to drinking in their homeland; as the Australian wine industry expanded these same grapes were adopted to produce bulk wine for wider consumption (Pritchard, 1999). Recently, however, the expansion of export markets and an increasing taste for premium wine has produced a shift to classic varieties. Interestingly this move has been mirrored by a change of marketing of the region's wines, so that its Italian heritage (linked to everyday drinking wine) has now been dropped from marketing materials in favour of themes which promote a quality focus (Pritchard, 1999).

On the other hand whilst premium wine may come from hot regions it is more likely to come from cooler climates. A bulk wine producer could not easily risk the threat of frost which comes with plantings in (say) Touraine, where in 1991 the average yield was only 10 per cent of normal. At the same time there is an assumption amongst some wine producers that the most intense wines – and therefore those of highest quality – tend to come from cooler areas (e.g. Jackson & Schuster, 1994).

However, the difference between the two wines is about more than their geographic origin – it is also about different attitudes to the land on which the grapes are grown, the idea of terroir (see Chapter 5). Premium wine is designated by its origin from a specific region – even a specific vineyard. Bulk wine has no such designation or interpretative function – and the category of table wine in Europe is explicitly designed to exclude it, by banning any stated region of origin on the label.

The geography of origin is therefore about both the *type* of environment in which the grapes are grown, and the viticulturists' *relationship* to that environment. One wine is considered to reflect the land on which the grapes are grown; the other is merely an agricultural crop. (It is worth noting, however, that this begins to change with the introduction of the category of *vin de pays* in France and similar classes of 'superior' table wine in other European Union (EU) countries.)

Consequently wine which results from warm to hot climatic regions with high yields and with less vintage variation tends to be perceived by wine experts as less intense and possibly less complex than wine made in cooler areas and from lower yields. It can be argued that bulk wine therefore offers less in the way of aesthetic stimulation – which means that appreciation and connoisseurship have less scope to operate. In turn this means that status-seeking behaviour is less available to offer social reward to the consumer. There is thus a direct relationship between the distinct production methods and consumption goals of both premium and bulk wine. At the same time, for premium wine the geography of origin allows yet further forms of distinction. The connoisseur's knowledge of specific sites in Burgundy (for example) with an ability to place wines tasted blind in their terroir – thus proving their connoisseurship – reinforces this link between place of origin and consumption purpose.

Note that the argument outlined here is also not a distinction between large-volume brands and 'quality wine'. All quality wines are essentially branded (i.e. they have a distinctive label or name and offer added value to the consumer (Lockshin et al., 2000)). If anything, it is the bulk wines which are less likely to be branded – at least for those sold from the cask at the cellar door. This practice, now most visible in southern Europe, has also been common in the new producing countries. Wines are available in this way, for instance, in the Swan Valley in Western Australia, and even in the early 1990s Villa Maria – a New Zealand producer determined to promote an image of high quality – sold cheap, non-branded, fortified wines offered straight from the barrel to cellar-door visitors.

Democratic and elite wines in the past

This proposition – that there are in fact two distinct 'wines' throughout the world, both culturally and economically – does not reflect something that has happened recently. Rather it has deep historical roots. Compare two assertions from Unwin's (1996) history of viticulture and the wine trade. The first quotation comments on consumption in Egypt:

> From the end of the fourth millennium and the beginning of the third millennium BC wine appears to have been used by kings and priests (p. 68).
>
> It is also evident that wine was the preferred drink at all levels in Greek society. Unlike the situation in Mesopotamia or Egypt, where beer was the drink of the poor, the arrival of the vine in Greece brought with it the consumption of wine throughout the social order (p. 99).

Egypt produced little wine – partly for climatic reasons, and perhaps because it had relatively little available arable land for a comparatively large population. Wine there was a product for the elite. On the other hand Greece had neither of those constraints. In the Mycenaean era wine consumption may have been limited to the elites but later, and probably by the eighth century BC, most small farmers had at least a few rows of vines for their own wine production (Wright, 1995). This integration of wine into Greek society was repeated amongst the Romans (Phillips, 2000). In those places wine became a democratic drink, even if a few premium wines were reserved for the richest. This distinction has continued through history, and it can be noted in passing that the split denoted by premium and bulk wine has been implicated in social unrest at times (Holt, 1999).

The impact of the two wines

It could be argued that a similar distinction, between the basic (or bulk) and the premium exists for most products. However closer examination suggests that this is not the case, and most goods do not operate so dichotomously. One talks of the luxury as opposed to family cars, for instance, but their cost means that such goods are invariably luxuries for consumers (and thus 'premium' products), whatever the type purchased. Few consumer non-durables offer the consumer both an aesthetic and status purpose for consumption – so that one can argue that most goods are on a single price continuum from cheap to expensive, rather than the either/or of bulk and premium wine. There are two possible exceptions which mirror the dichotomous nature of wine. The first is cheese, where there is a clear distinction between the bulk and the premium product (Kupiec & Revell, 2001). The second is clothing, where status, taste and even origin could be considered to have created two distinct kinds of product, where haute-couture is intrinsically different in purpose and production (design) from a tee-shirt bought at a discount store.

It has been common for wine marketers to attempt a segmentation of various national wine markets (for instance in Australia: Bruwer et al., 2001; Hall & Winchester, 2000; Johnson et al., 1991; Perrin & Lockshin, 2001; Spawton, 1991). Almost all of this work, however, fails to distinguish bulk from premium wine. Indeed, in one recent article (Bruwer et al., 2001) 'basic wine drinkers' (a segment which includes all bulk wine consumers as well as those who drink bottled wine at around $10 per bottle) are said to comprise merely a quarter of all wine drinkers, each consuming just 0.6 of a bottle per week on average. This is despite the fact that bulk wine comprises 50 per cent of all wine consumed in Australia. Thus the extent of the proposed market segment completely underestimates its volume share of the market.

The different social purpose of bulk and premium drinkers is very relevant to marketing professionals. Brand management becomes more complex if one realizes that one deals not merely with different market segments but with what are, for marketing purposes, essentially different products. The purported 'shift to quality' amongst contemporary wine consumers (Brook, 2000b; Phillips, 2000) is inevitably having an impact on the position of bulk wine and the evidence suggests that its consumption is dropping dramatically, especially in southern Europe. How the marketers of the product respond to this development is critical – but they are unlikely to be effective as long as bulk and premium wine are viewed as fundamentally the same.

It is also important that those who comment on wine are aware of the relevance of the distinction made between the two wines. Wine can have a symbolic or semiotic significance (discussed later – see Chapters 8 and 9). It could be suggested that many of those symbolic functions (for instance those related to religion or fertility) can be applied to both bulk and premium wines. However, other symbolic processes (especially relating to status, seduction and celebration) may only have a relevance to premium wine. Thus Bourdieu (1986), for instance, uses wine as a means by which distinctions of taste can be made. That may well be accurate for Parisian society (at all socio-economic levels) but could have much less relevance for rural southern French society. This is not to negate the semiotic relevance of wine, but to suggest the need for some subtlety in how it is interpreted, depending on the type of wine being used.

Produce or product?

There is another fundamental difference in the way that wine producers view their product. This again depends in part on where the wine is made, but it also stems historically from the time when wine was first produced on a large scale. In summary it is suggested that in some countries wine is treated as a form of agricultural produce; in others it is primarily viewed as a product, produced by an industry (albeit using agricultural raw materials).

For much of its past wine has been produced in pre-industrial societies, and many of the traditions about, processes for, and attitudes to the product in European wine regions stem from that age. Wine is thus the result of what farmers do, as bread, oil, meat and cheese also stem from farming activity. For most of the past millennia farming has broadly been a subsistence activity; the farmer made enough to live on and probably only sold a small surplus of production for cash. As suggested above, this applied to wine as much as to other forms of produce. This can be seen in the development of protection of origin (appellation) in Europe. Court cases in the nineteenth century granted trademark guarantees for wines based on the specific region in which the grapes were grown, rather than on the flavour characteristics of the wine. This was in contradistinction to the concurrent development of industrial patents, where the focus was on a specification – and thus standardization (Stanziani, 2004). Wine was thus seen as the non-standard product of a place, not the result of an industrial technique.

On the other hand Australia and New Zealand were settled as the industrial revolution was underway in Britain, and the Californian wine industry began as industrialization was taking hold in the USA. One of the impacts of the industrial revolution was to focus on consumer goods, rather than staple produce (a perspective that was reinforced as the mass of workers left the countryside, with its dependence on seasonal agricultural production, and moved to towns and cities where products were made all year round). The individuals who developed the wine industry in the new producing countries, whilst still seeing the raw materials stem from the work of agriculture, were themselves the result of a place and an age which considered their goods to be products. The specification (comprehensively detailing factors such as residual sugar, levels of additives, pH and acid levels) has now become a major tool in shaping wines made as products, in distinction to the non-standardized approach adopted by European courts in the past.

This can perhaps be seen more clearly using clothing as an example. For most of history clothing has been the result of agriculture; wool, leather, cotton and flax all come from the land, either grown in it or from animals fed by it, and generally created in cottage industries. Today we do not see our clothing as agricultural produce but as a thing, an item made in a factory. The industrial revolution took wool or cotton away from the land. Instead raw materials were grown or raised in British colonies, then exported to Britain so that cloth or garments could be made, before the end result was re-exported to the rest of the world. Today's cotton tee-shirt comes from a factory, not from a field, a perspective that has been reinforced by the development of synthetic fabrics over the last half century.

This distinction between produce and product can be seen in some of the ritual which surrounds wine. European winemakers are often still inclined to celebrate St Vincent's day on 22nd January each year. St Vincent is the patron saint of wine, and his festival takes place in the depth of winter, when the vine is dormant, in part as a supplication for a good harvest in the coming year. In Burgundy, for instance, a major festival is organized to celebrate the saint's day which now attracts up to 100 000 visitors (Demossier, 2005). Likewise it is common in Europe to have a vintage celebration (Calabresi, 1987). Such celebrations are much less widespread in California or the

Antipodes, and where they do occur they are more likely to have their origins as a marketing exercise than a ritual marking the passing of the seasons.

The new producing countries have a different approach. Consider the following comments, made on an Australian radio programme (Mitchell, 2001):

> Many people would see grape growing as a farming exercise but as a matter of fact we are now seeing in the grape growing industry aerial surveys of vineyards, aerial spectroscopic analysis of vineyard performance and highly sophisticated computer programs to then go and say to the grape grower you've got to rectify your practices in these areas. That to me is not low tech, that's high tech. (Peter Høj, Director, Australian Wine Research Institute).
>
> I think being at the pointy end is where we want to be and . . . you just have to do that otherwise you're just going to be a farmer and bugger being a farmer. You know we want to make a difference and put our mark on the place. (John Edwards, Grapegrower).

Peter Høj's perspective is significant not because the techniques he outlines would be ignored in Europe, but because of his opening comment – which suggests that grape growing is no longer a 'farming exercise'. John Edward's comment about the 'pointy end' is a reference to being in the vanguard of technological application in the vineyard. Without that you are no more than a farmer, who, by implication, does not change the way things are done but merely responds unquestioningly to what each year brings.

In part this product-focused approach may be based on the fact that, unusually for something produced from an agricultural base, wine comes at various levels of quality, and a premium (which is often substantial) can often be charged for that which is perceived to be the best (Thode & Maskulka, 1998). Wheat, sugar beet or canola fall within a fairly limited range of grades and with minimal variations in value, whereas wine is processed, and those production processes can be seen to contribute towards the added value which accrues to the product. One can also suggest, however, that wine quality had a minimal relationship to technology before Louis Pasteur began his investigations into the microbiological spoilage of wine in the middle of the nineteenth century. Only since then has process become so important as a guarantor of quality and process sits clearly within the domain of industrial production rather than agricultural place.

The split focus on growing or process is also seen in who is considered to be responsible for the production of large-volume wines, especially bulk wine. In Europe and South Africa many of these wines come from cooperatives which, as will be seen in Chapter 4, are controlled by growers. In the new producing countries it is the large companies which make the wines. They source grapes from growers but the growers have no influence over how the wines are made nor on their resulting style, and economic control of production resides not with the growers but with the producers. Likewise, the nomenclature used to describe what a producer does is also significant. In Europe the term 'winegrower' may be used to explain their role (Ulin, 1996), implying that what is drunk springs naturally from the soil. In the new producing countries the term winemaker – which focuses on process – is much more common, although in some places (especially California) those producers who are trying to associate their approach to wine with a more European perspective will explicitly use the former term.

It could be argued that the one exception to this neat division of old and new producing countries centres on Champagne. Champagne, as the wine style is now drunk, was founded less on agriculture than on a series of technological processes (corks and hardened glass to trap the second fermentation, the careful measurement of sugar and addition of cultured yeast to start the second fermentation, riddling and freezing to aid disgorgement). Thus one journalist has suggested that it is no longer the result of agriculture, even though it may be made from grapes (Voss, 2005). This in turn, Voss (2005) has claimed, has taken it out of the traditional 'cyclical' nature of wine and made it a category of its own.

The significance of the agricultural versus industrial approaches

It needs to be stressed that neither the industrial nor the agricultural approach is, in essence, innately superior. Both may produce good (or bad wines), they may even produce similar wines. However, the significance is in how the producer of each views their product, and in turn this has implications for how it is marketed and how it is understood by consumers.

One sees the differences, for instance, in the debate about whether or not vines should be irrigated. Historically irrigation has been prohibited throughout much of Europe for the production of quality wine. The argument has been that to irrigate a vineyard tampers with what nature offers; it may result in excessively high crop levels, reducing the quality of the wine and it also helps to hide the distinctive nature of the vintage. Wine, as an agricultural product, is subject to fluctuations of weather, and there is a strong feeling amongst some producers that vintage variation is a positive aspect of the product, adding personality to what is consumed (for instance, the Bordeaux producer Peter Sichel in Halliday & Johnson, 1992, p. 20) and offering greater diversity to the consumer. To many winemakers in the new producing countries, however, such an approach flies in the face of what science has to offer; if irrigation can enable you to make wine at a cheaper price (by increasing yields) or if it can preserve the consistency of the product, by remedying water shortage in dry years, then why should that be a problem? Neither perspective is necessarily wrong, but it is important to note that each is rooted in a fundamentally different approach to what the wine producer is doing, and that a failure to agree is less about being able to prove or disprove that one way of making wine is better and more about divergent philosophical and cultural frameworks.

This, of course, is a simplification. There are many producers in the new producing countries who decide not to irrigate (though generally because they believe that will improve quality, rather than for any cultural reasons). There are many others who think it helpful to irrigate in the first 4 or 5 years of the vine's life, to help it grow rapidly and securely, but not thereafter. It is also worth pointing out that the vineyard manipulation has taken place in much of traditional Europe. The Médoc – one of the bastions of a traditional approach – is viable vineyard land because much of the area was drained in the eighteenth century, and but for this it would not be able to produce grapes (Faith, 1999). This fact is conveniently forgotten today by many of those Bordelaise who most ardently oppose irrigation. It is also necessary to add that the contrast of agricultural and industrial is not about differences in how wine is made. Producers with an agricultural focus often use the most advanced technology in the winery; once the grapes are grown the means of turning them into wine can be as sophisticated as possible. Rather, the dichotomy focuses on how the wine is primarily seen; as produce, which may then be processed as cheese would be from milk, or as product, with the processes pre-eminent and the raw materials subsidiary.

There is also a marketing dimension to this. If wine is agricultural produce, then it can be sold as such. Barr (1995) has noted that Beaujolais nouveau, a wine generally considered by critics to be dilute and unexciting, is still drunk, even by expert consumers who would normally dismiss such a mediocre drink. The reason, he suggests, for such a suspension of critical judgment is that its very early release (on the third Thursday in November following the northern harvest) is as a celebration, perhaps a thanksgiving, for that year's vintage. On the other hand many wines from the new producing countries are not sold on the strength of their agricultural roots, but on the basis of consistency and product quality; the fact that they deliver the same flavour profile with the same intensity from year to year (Demossier, 2004). This is an issue which will be considered further in Chapter 6.

An interesting problem with this argument of the industrial versus the agricultural is where South Africa sits. It is often considered to be a new producing country, and certainly the aromatic profile of its wines tends more to the ripe fruit forwardness of California or Australia. However, its first grapes were planted before the Médoc was drained, and its wines were successfully exported to Europe by the mid-eighteenth century which was broadly the start of the industrial revolution. Significant here is the fact that South Africans do not refer to wineries, as an American or Australian would, but to wine farms. One of the first Cape Colony farmers' pressure groups, the Boeren Beschermings Vereeniging was established in 1878 with the aim of opposing the excise placed on wine and spirits. It was a farmers' group campaigning on wine issues reflecting an agricultural outlook (Welsh, 1998). It is also worth noting that a visitor to South African wine farms today will find many references to terroir, and the importance of finding the correct soil for the grapes. Whilst a concentration on terroir is not essential to an agricultural focus (it also appears to a greater or lesser extent in other new producing countries), nevertheless the persistence with which South African winemakers refer to the idea – certainly more than those in Australia and New Zealand – may be symptomatic of a perspective which emphasizes the agricultural rather than the industrial.

Even where, in the countries where wine is perceived to be a product rather than produce, there is a focus on terroir it tends to be secondary to production processes. Brian Croser, in Australia, is an outspoken advocate of the idea of 'distinguished sites' – the importance of matching grape variety to vineyard, and of searching out the best vineyards which will create the best wine. Even he, however, says that precise and technologically sound winemaking practices must be adopted before the winemaker can afford to experiment with more traditional methods of production (Hooke, 2004); it can be suggested that for Croser production must precede the reflection of terroir.

Wine and the expression of national identity

The idea that wine can represent a nation's identity is probably of recent origin. It is likely that wine was seen to be one of the achievements of a specific and local region for many years before that. It is certainly true that wine has had a long link with religious affiliation. One of the defining characteristics of the Greeks during the period of Ottoman overlordship was that they, as Christians, drank wine (indeed it was part of the eucharist, one of the outward symbols of their faith.) As Moslems, the Turks were forbidden wine.

However, the specific link between national self-image and wine has taken longer to evolve. The relationship is most clearly expressed in France. The idea that French cuisine is more refined and exquisite than that of other countries has a long history (Mennell, 1985). Until the sixteenth century the idea of 'French' wines meant wine made around Paris (Ulin, 1996). The concept of 'the wines of France' came into being towards the end of the seventeenth century – but the idea was that wines were a 'jewel in the French crown' rather than a symbol of French popular solidarity (Briggs, 1994). It was, perhaps, natural that the reputation of their wine would follow that of their food, although that may have had more to do with distribution than quality. French wines were more easily transported to rich export markets such as London, Hamburg and St Petersburg than those of other Mediterranean countries and to a certain extent reputation followed trade. With the overthrow of the French monarchy the significance of the country's wines was transferred to the nation itself. In 1872 Professor Planchon, a French academic who was a leader in the battle against phylloxera, said '[Burgundy] wines are one of our nation's glories. If Burgundy should be wiped out – along with Bordeaux – one could say that France itself had been overthrown' (quoted in Campbell, 2004, p. 102). Nevertheless, the myth that French wines are superior is now widely believed. This is true in France, where in 1965 it could be said that 'without wine, France would probably not be France' (Sedoun, Lolli and Silveman, quoted in Demossier, 2005, p. 145). The idea is also accepted in much of the rest of the world.

However, the mere assumption that a country's wine is best does not in itself incorporate wine into that nation's identity. That is a much more complex process, and – in the case of France at least – resulted from a shift in the regional importance of wine to its national importance, so that wine came to be seen as a 'national treasure' (Ulin, 1995, p. 524). Kolleen Guy has charted this change for Champagne from about 1850–1914 (Guy, 2003). Champagne, along with Bordeaux, was the first French wine to achieve wide international recognition and market penetration. At the same time there was an increasing local awareness of the importance of the Champagne region – an awareness that manifested itself in the desire to protect the name of the product to the benefit of those who grew Champagne grapes or made the wine (the two were not identical and often had different interests). The focus for this protection was against French outsiders who sought to defraud the honest *vigneron* (or a Champagne house) from his birthright. Whilst vinous fraud was undoubtedly being perpetrated on a wide scale this battle took on mythological importance for the region. Meanwhile, because the Champagne region had gained such international significance, and because the sense of place and of regional product had become highly symbolic for the French nation, so the battle to protect the *Champenois* from fraudulent outsiders became a battle for the country as a whole. By 1914 defrauders were seen to be an external enemy, undermining the soul of France and then the Great War only increased the strength of these views; the soil was watered with the blood of Frenchmen who had fallen in the trenches across the Champagne region (Guy, 2003). Thus, as Guy (1997) has argued, 'In contending for its interests, the community actively participated not only in the construction of modern France but also in the ongoing process of negotiating a "French" identity' (1997, p. 303). This integration of wine generally and Champagne specifically into the French self-image can only have been strengthened by the country's 40-year struggle against phylloxera (Campbell, 2004). This idea that wine is essentially France's gift to the world remains until today. Barthes, for instance, claimed that:

> Wine is felt by the French nation to be a possession which is its very own, just like its three hundred and sixty types of cheese and its culture. It is a totem drink (Barthes, 1957; 2000, p. 58).

Thus, the poet Apollinaire wrote, during the First World War:

> I am like you soldier, comforting myself
> With a quart of plonk,
> Which makes all the difference between the Boches and us
> (quoted in Gautier, 2002, p. 22: Author's translation).

This approach can still inform French advertising. In late 2004 an advertising campaign was launched in the United Kingdom by Burgundian producers attacking competition from the new producing countries. One advertisement, which explicitly focused on Australian wines, showed a winemaker digging dried up red soil, with a caption 'Andrew, the tenacious New World grower, pursued his fruitless quest for the ruby in Burgundy wines'. Beneath that another caption notes that over the centuries 'wine growers from Burgundy have brought out the best and most beautiful in the Pinot Noir through a combination of factors Andy won't find down under'. The message is clear; Burgundy produces the world's best pinot noir, and it cannot be replicated elsewhere.

It would be wrong to suggest that the correlation of wine with national identity is only a French issue. It may be most obvious there but the relationship undoubtedly exists elsewhere. Hungary refers to its most famous wine – Tokaji – in its national anthem (Friedrich, 2000). Such an approach to the national significance of wine is reflected in the view that physical place shapes human character as much as history or upbringing. This idea has a long history within the discipline of geography, and was given forcible expression in France a century ago by the geographer Paul Vidal de la Blache

(Guy, 2003). The notion still has currency, as the following quotation from the novelist and travel writer Lawrence Durrell suggests:

> Just as one particular vineyard will always give you a special wine with discernible characteristics so a Spain, an Italy, a Greece will always give you the same type of culture – will express itself through the human being just as it does through its wild flowers. We tend to see 'culture' as a sort of historic pattern dictated by the human will, but for me this is no longer absolutely true. . . . I believe you could exterminate the French at a blow and resettle the country with Tartars, and within two generations discover, to your astonishment, that the national characteristics were back at norm – the restless metaphysical curiosity, the tenderness for good living and the passionate individualism (Durrell, 1969, p. 156f).

The relevance of national identity may have other, rather wider impacts on wine consumption. The Finns, for instance, speak a non-European language. Their nearest linguistic neighbours are the Estonians and the Hungarians. It is a long-established albeit distant sense of commonality with the latter which means that Tokaji is, even to this day, the most widely sold sweet wine in Finland, even though where light wine is concerned the Finns are more likely to drink western European or non-European wines.

Conclusion

The point of this chapter is to set some contextual ideas about the nature of wine itself. Specifically, it is important to realize that 'wine' the drink, as fashioned by the producer, is not a single product, but comes in multiple forms; it may be a premium product, with key symbolic and aesthetic functions, or it may be much more utilitarian in purpose. To that extent, it is probably unlike almost any other goods in having two distinct and unrelated product types. Further, it may not even be seen as a product by some, but as produce – part of nature's bounty rather than a created thing which science and technology empower a person to shape. Finally, the physical properties of wine also imbue it with meaning. It is sweet, so it has been sought by those on a diet devoid of sugar, and it is healthful – a perspective which remains until this day, although no longer automatically accepted, as will be seen in Chapter 12.

This all sets the scene for how the physical product provides some meaning to those who drink it. Next it is necessary to examine the organizational structure of those who make wine, and to consider how those structures may shape different ways of interpreting the drink.

Bibliographical note

For an expansion of the idea of the two wines see Charters (2002). Tracing the historical perspective on this topic and other issues raised in this chapter can be done in the historical works, such as Guy (2003) – particularly for notions of national identity – and especially Loubere et al. (1985) on European approaches to wine production. For a demonstration of the alternative, product-focused approach to winemaking, Halliday's (1994) *A History of the Australian Wine Industry 1949–1994* shows the attitude to wine production in a new producing country.

4

The structures of wine production

The nature of wine shapes how it is viewed – but so does the organization which makes it. This chapter considers the different kinds of wine producer around the world, their organizational structure and how the varying background of each moulds their perspective on what they make. It first examines the smallholder and farmer, then co-operatives and négociants. These are predominantly based in Europe (although it also considers some migrant groups who settled in the new producing countries), and tend to have quite a long history as organizational structures. Consideration then moves to family companies. Following that large producers (including those in public ownership) throughout the world and, in the new producing countries, the role of the boutique producer, will be examined; both of these tend to be the most modern business types used in the wine industry.

There are two key questions which the chapter seeks to address. The first is to ask why people are in the wine industry. This is important given that the family operation making bulk wine primarily for their own consumption is dying out.

The second and dependent question is to examine how each of these categories views their wine. The relevance of this is that, whilst the main aim of producing wine is to sell it to make a living, beyond that what a boutique producer may be trying to do with their wine could be substantially different from what a co-operative is doing – and this will have an impact on the messages they convey about it, and how they market it.

Contextually, however, it is useful to remember the difference between management and ownership. Staff who work in the organization may have a different perspective from those to whom it belongs. The Champagne house, Krug is a good example of this. The company is part of the luxury goods conglomerate Moët Hennessy–Louis Vuitton (LVMH). LVMH is a public company, owned by a number of shareholders, whose overriding goal is to seek a good return on their investment and its managers are charged with ensuring that. The house of Krug is still run by the family who founded it – reporting to LVMH management. They may, however, have family traditions and a sense of family reputation to uphold, which could conflict with the company's goals. The family member who is the senior winemaker may have aims which are different still – distinct from both the shareholder's aim for profit and the family's stewardship of their heritage. (It must be stressed that this is only an example, and there is no suggestion of conflict between the Krug family and their parent company.)

Smallholders

Historically smallholders would have been considered peasants and some may still use the term for (in France at least) it has no negative connotation (Echikson, 2004). As already noted, Mediterranean agriculture is considered to be based on a trinity of wheat, olives and grapes, and for much of the last 4000 years it is these three which would have formed the core of any producer's crops (Unwin, 1996). On top of this a small farmer may have had other resources to supplement his (rarely her) income; perhaps a few sheep, goats or cows, some hens or a few fruit trees. In more northerly wine regions a similar structure of production could apply albeit with different crops. Even in 1999, in Austria the average vineyard holding was only one and a half hectares (Österreichische Weinmarketing Service GesmbH, 2005), which is insufficient to guarantee a living. The peasant economy based on the subsistence agriculture of the medieval period was further influenced by the Napoleonic code, which split land ownership yet further.

Yet, despite the continuing existence of smallholders, they are substantially less common than they were. The key event in much of Europe which began their demise was the onset of phylloxera. Substantial capital was required to achieve replanting on American rootstocks and even if a smallholder could afford the grafted stock there would be a hiatus of at least 3 years before the vines produced another crop, and 7 years before yields were optimized. Few could sustain such an interruption to their livelihood; some gave up agriculture altogether, others gave up viticulture and focused on other crops. Many sold their vineyards, and when the land was replanted became wage labourers on the same sites (Campbell, 2004). This was not something limited to the poorer parts of southern Europe. Even in Champagne, it has been noted, the production of basic wine, still rather than sparkling and sold for everyday consumption locally and in cafes, ended with the destruction of the vineyards (Guy, 2003). Replanting only became profitable if it was for the production of luxury sparkling wine.

A variant on the smallholder developed in the new producing countries. Australia and New Zealand, especially, have been settled by numbers of non-Anglophone migrants who brought viticultural and even wine production skills with them. The Barossa Valley in South Australia was settled in the 1840s by Silesian Germans, who famously shaped the valley's culture and acted as a catalyst for wine production there (Faith, 2002). Later settlers from the former Yugoslavia, especially the Dalmatian coast, went to New Zealand, where they were involved in founding a number of companies including Babich, Villa Maria and Kumeu River (George, 1996). In both these areas the original smallholding culture has been transformed into newer production structures. However, in the Swan Valley of Western Australia a more traditional approach, introduced again by Yugoslavs and also Italians, still persists, with a number of the traditional producers such as Talijancich and John Kosovich Wines remaining small.

To the extent that smallholders remain, why do they grow grapes and (perhaps) make wine? The essential answer to that is that it is part of their inheritance, and a way of making their (often precarious) living, probably as part of a mixed farm. The result of this is that they do not necessarily aim for quality, nor for any aesthetic recognition for what they do. Rather, their produce will provide them with their own drink for a year. It may provide friends, relatives and neighbours with a cheap, everyday wine. Some of the producers may also be able to sell a little in local towns, to cafes, or to a passing tourist trade prepared to buy something cheap *en vrac* rather than seek out the more prestigious names in the region. However, it varies from country to country. In central Europe the proprietor of a small vineyard is today less likely to be a farmer than an urban dweller who has a full-time job and maintains the vineyard at the weekends. However, in all places they are declining. In Germany there has been a conscious move towards *flurbereinigung* – the rationalization of small vineyard holdings, in order to make them more viable (Brook, 2003). In other parts of Europe fewer of the current generation wish to remain in small-scale farming, with the intensive work and limited returns it entails. In the new producing countries wineries which were established by migrants are turning themselves into boutique producers – or sometimes growing into something more substantial (Ramsay, 2002). Critically, the cost of producing wine in a technological age is making it difficult for mixed farmers or small vineyard owners.

Historically small producers may have been able to make wine by using a communal village press, or hiring such a facility from a more affluent producer who was able to outlay the capital for such equipment. In many cases, however, that was not possible. As a result other organizations had to make the wine from the smallholder's grapes. The main organizations which were able to do this were négociants and co-operatives, and they require some consideration.

Négociants

Two key problems hampered the small grapegrower. Already mentioned is the difficulty in obtaining capital for production equipment. Additionally, distribution beyond the immediate locality, and especially to the rich markets of northern Europe, was prohibitive with a small volume of wine. One response to this problem was found in the growth of merchants and distributors, usually termed négociants in France. The precondition for being a négociant was access to capital. This allowed the merchant to buy wine from a wide range of sources, then blend and mature it (which meant being able to hold stock for a period) and ship it (often in cask, later in bottle) to other markets. Initially the négociant might generally buy recently fermented wine, but in time they expanded to take in other ways of sourcing the product. In Burgundy today a négociant may buy wine but equally could buy grapes and control the wine production process, or even buy pressed juice ready to ferment. Additionally they will probably hold some parcels of vineyard land in their own right – often extremely good sites. Hence the négociant is not merely a wholesaler but also a company which matures and bottles wine, may make it, and could even have vineyard holdings. Using négociants had substantial advantages in a region where there were so many small, often scattered vineyard holdings. A négociant can buy wine from a number of producers in the village of Gevrey Chambertin. Those wines which come from *premier cru* sites could, if desired, be blended into a single wine labelled AC Gevrey Chambertin

Premier Cru. Wines from the lower-quality village sites could be blended into a mere AC Gevrey Chambertin. Lesser wines still could be blended with wines of other villages to make generic Burgundy. Négociants became particularly important during the eighteenth century, when there was a move to standardize wines (Loubere, 1978), and they increased their holdings substantially in the viticultural depression which followed phylloxera.

Historically négociants have been very powerful. This especially applies to the most reputable wine regions, such as Bordeaux, Burgundy and Champagne in France and, although they are not called négociants, with the Port Houses. The highest return was to be made from the most famous wine; it therefore made sense to invest capital in these wines, rather than the product of the Roussillon or Ribatejo. The Bordeaux négociants came to be the most powerful arm of their wine industry; many, in fact, had German, English or Irish origin (reflecting the markets to which they were exporting), and when the famous Médoc classification of 1855 was established it was the négociants rather than the chateaux who determined it (see Chapter 5). This power lasted until the 1970s. From then, however, in both Burgundy and Bordeaux their power waned owing to a complex series of factors, two of which were paramount. The first relates to the varying strata of wine produced by the négociants. If you produce a range of wine from *premier cru* to generic Burgundy, but with the former selling for five times the price of the latter, there is considerable incentive to 'increase' the production of the former at the expense of the latter. This could be done by blending in lower-quality wine, or even by shipping in wine from other regions to bolster the blends (Hanson, 1982). In some cases this was exposed – most notably with the highly influential house of Cruse in Bordeaux during the 1970s (Faith, 1999). In other cases such fraud was suspected, or known but unproven. The result of this was that the reputation of négociants generally sank until the 1980s (Robinson, 1999) and continuing deception, such as that perpetrated in Burgundy by Bouchard Ainé in 1987, when wines were given a misleading (and superior) designation of origin accentuated this decline (Mansson, 1996). The other reason for the waning influence of négociants was the increasing power of producers. As the price paid for the best Bordeaux and Burgundy rose rapidly, especially after the great 1982 vintage in the former region, the most sought-after producers had more economic weight, and began to exert more control over their markets, appointing – even buying – their own distributors.

How do négociants view their wine? They are primarily merchants, and therefore the starting point is that it is something to be traded. From that it can be viewed as a commodity, a good which is used to make money. Many négociants would reject that definition, especially smaller, family companies with prestigious viticultural properties of their own. Nevertheless, there is no doubt that wine buyers and critics view négociants today with a certain amount of caution, even if they willingly support the better ones, because of a perceived willingness to promote volume rather than quality.

In Burgundy, if not in Bordeaux, the influence of négociants has begun to rise again. This is in part due to a new wave of merchant, committed to making high-quality wine. Typical of these is Olivier Leflaive, scion of one of the most respectable domaines in Puligny Montrachet, who has branched out into producing wine from other people's grapes. Unlike more traditional négociants he prefers not to buy finished wine, seeking to control the whole of the production process himself in order to guarantee quality (Loftus, 1992). This influence is paralleled by the development of high profile and reputable négociants in other regions, such as Chapoutier, Jaboulet and Guigal in the northern Rhone.

Co-operatives

The background to co-operatives is complex. Of primary note is that they generally predominate in areas where négociants are not influential which, by extension, tends to be those areas which produce cheaper wine with less potential profit; thus there are co-operatives in the southern rather than the northern Rhone Valley, in Dão rather than the Douro Valley. Even within regions this division takes effect. There are strong co-operatives in southern Burgundy (the Maconnais and the Cote Chalonnaise) but not so much in the prestigious Cote d'Or.

Co-operatives are owned by their members. Thus grapegrowers in a village or group of villages can apply to become members of – shareholders in – the co-operative. All the members share in the direction of the co-operative but it is normal to elect a president and management committee to run the organization just as a company has a board of directors. The committee appoints oenologists or winemakers to handle production and these days they would probably also employ a marketing manager.

Co-operatives have their origins in a combination of political factors. The first is in radical politics; co-operatives reflect a left-wing perspective on industrial structure (Ulin, 1996), albeit one that has more of a basis of anarchism and libertarianism than traditional socialism. (It is often forgotten that rural southern Europe, in places like Andalucia, produced major centres of anarcho-syndicalism (Woodcock, 1975).) The second factor to influence the development of co-operatives was much more statist. At a time when rural economies were in retreat with agricultural prices all falling and small producers threatened by cheap imports central government felt threatened by rural unrest (see Chapter 14). Early in the twentieth century encouraging smallholders to pool their resources and sell wine produced cheaply from their entire joint crop was one way of avoiding disturbances and shoring up a regional support base. It also seemed to be a way to preserve the status quo and avoid even more radical political solutions which may have undermined the social order further (Loubere, 1978). The politicization of the co-operative movement meant that in Italy, for instance, there were Communist co-operatives and Christian Democratic co-operatives. Your party allegiance would determine which one you joined. It was one of the ironies of the cold war that, as Lambrusco became fashionable in the United States, it was the communist-run Riunite co-operative outside 'red' Bologna which capitalized on the wine's popularity with its own brand. No doubt much of the profit from sales in the 'land of the free' found its way back into the Italian Communist Party's funds.

A secondary feature – more appropriate to the later development of co-operatives towards the middle of the twentieth century – was the increasingly rapid development of oenological technology. New equipment and new scientific techniques required substantial expenditure. As previously noted this was beyond the means of most smallholders and, by the end of the nineteenth century, was beginning to increase the power of the négociants (Loubere, 1978). However, a co-operative which was large could more easily access the technology for the benefit of all – especially if government financial support was available to assist them. Given the opposition of many small growers to the perceived aggression of the merchants the co-operative was seen to be a very attractive way forward, especially to growers who were already used to working mutually in syndicates to protect their common interests (Loubere, 1978).

Crucially, the political support offered extended easy access to cheap capital and to fiscal incentives, including – for instance – an exemption on taxes paid on dividends in France. They were also exempt from paying for a licence to carry on their business, which was expensive in France (Loubere, 1978). However, easy access to capital was limited to those who would undertake to modernize production (Ulin, 1996).

Whilst many co-operatives were formed in Europe, they were not limited geographically. South Africa saw substantial numbers formed, including the overarching South African Co-operative Winegrowers Association (KWV). In the warm Riverland region of South Australia the Berri-Renmano co-operative operated from 1918 onwards (Faith, 2002); later demutualised it formed one half of BRL Hardy, the major Australian company now incorporated into Constellation Wines. In California by the 1950s of the five biggest wineries two were co-operatives (Geraci, 2004). In these instances, however, the co-operatives were formed not due to any progressive political ideology but in order to optimize market power at times of declining markets. Despite this, they still suffered from the same weaknesses as co-operatives in Europe.

Mutuality was a strength of co-operatives but also their failing. It was comparatively effortless to be a member – and many grapegrowers remain co-operators merely because it gives them an easy life; this (combined with a natural rural conservatism) made the co-operatives reluctant to pursue change. This inertia has meant that whereas in the mid-twentieth century with the support of government funding co-operatives were often well equipped and fairly dynamic, since then this dynamism has been allowed to slip. Concrete fermentation vats were not replaced with stainless steel, continuous presses did not give way to pneumatic ones. Oenological conservatism was paralleled with a reluctance to engage in modern marketing techniques. The fiscal benefits which co-operators have received, which could be construed as being anti-competitive, may also have reinforced this inertia.

As well as inertia another problem stemmed from the fact that all the members were grapegrowers. They viewed their business as one of growing grapes, rather than producing wine – and even less were they interested in marketing it. As grapegrowers they tended to specify that they were paid for the volume of grapes they produced, rather than their quality. Sometimes a premium was paid for higher sugar levels, but sugar is only one, imprecise indicator of quality; high sugar does not preclude damaged or diseased grapes. Differential payments for grapes from better sites would be resisted – members with lower-grade land would not want to get less than their neighbours. The result was that rural viticulture was preserved, but potentially at the expense of wine quality. Whilst substantial domestic markets for cheap wines remained that was not necessarily a problem but, as domestic consumption in southern Europe began to drop drastically from 1970 on and new markets required wines with reasonable technical quality, so co-operatives have begun to be threatened. This lack of concern for production often remains today. The wine writer Stephen Brook, when reviewing the wines of the Roussillon region of southern France, commented that 'at the Lesquerde cooperative I watched grapes arriving during the harvest and was surprised at the seeming lack of quality control at the reception area. When I asked the director if he had the right to refuse grapes, he frankly replied: "Non". Not an encouraging sign' (Brook, 2005, p. 49). The agricultural perspective breeds a short-term outlook; the co-operators see the end result as payment for the grapes, not sale of the wine, so it is hard to develop a dynamic market-focused ethic in the organization. Having said this, in some places, particularly the premium wine regions of Italy, there were co-operatives which in the early days pursued a high-quality, high-price policy (Loubere, 1978).

How then, do co-operators view their wines? Primarily as an extension of grape growing; thus as a means to allow smallholders to make money and preserve their livelihood in a precarious rural economy. It takes extreme discontent to persuade a co-operator to secede – as Nicolas Maillet in the Maconnais village of Verzé did in the late 1990s because he felt that his village co-operative had no commitment to wine quality. His annoyance showed foresight. By June 2001, when he was beginning to find new markets for his wine made under his own label, the co-operative still had half of the previous year's vintage left unsold in storage – a critical problem when the next vintage was less than 3 months off.

This dismal picture is not universal. There is a long list of dynamic co-operatives making good wine and actively marketing it, including many in France such as Veuve Devaux in Champagne and La Chablisienne in Chablis, as well as Araldica in north-west Italy and the Cooperative Virgen de Fatima Pedrosa in Ribera del Duero, Spain. These companies have become major players in the modern world of wine. But for each of these progressive organizations there are a number which change too slowly to compete in contemporary wine markets, and it has been shown in Spain that co-operatives are much less likely to add value than other forms of wine-producing organization (Sanjuan & Albisu, 2004).

How successful are co-operatives? Two perspectives

One of the more dynamic co-operatives in Europe is Mont Tauch, based at Tuchan, about 30 km north-west of Perpignan. It was founded quite early – in 1913 before the main wave of co-operative development – and has recently taken over three other regional co-operatives. Mont Tauch produces 60 per cent of the entire production of AC Fitou, plus smaller amounts of a few other AC wines as well. They draw their grapes from 7000 plots managed by 250 growers. Each grower has, on average, 4 ha of land under vine.

For over 18 years the administration and marketing of the co-operative has been managed by outsiders – that is, by staff who are not co-operators.

Whilst the members of the co-operative still have the final say this outside blood has provided a dynamism and global perspective often lacking at other similar organizations. They have a sales team whereas most other co-operatives just sell to négociants. The organization has developed a 'selection scheme' – a system whereby they offer their members extra for good quality grapes – in some cases doubling the payment. They now require their members to give 24 hours notice of the arrival of grapes so they can plan for them, and the winemaker can even defer receiving them if it does not fit with winery plans. The co-operative's approach is mirrored in the investment in the winery which is very modern. The winemakers can vinify each co-operator's grapes separately, which permits monitoring of quality and greater control over the final blend of each wine.

The co-operative has been selling to the UK for 20 years – and almost half its sales are now into that country, so they have used that to try to focus their brands on specific market segments. Crucially the organization has developed a number of premium brands, such as *Les Douze*, which takes the wine from just 12 of the best growers in each year and transforms it into a high-quality product which has been praised by critics such as Jancis Robinson MW and Tom Cannavan. The co-operative's dynamic marketing director, the English-born Katie Jones, suggests that whilst some members are cautious about the changes they see other co-operatives failing elsewhere and the growers not being paid, and consequently would never reverse this dynamic approach – a perspective which is confirmed by some of the co-operators.

However, not everyone is happy with the co-operative. One local smallholder who is not a member suggests that there are too many restrictions on members – and at the same time, the co-operative is still required to take any grapes that come. He dismissively points to an AC vineyard run by one of their members which used to crop at 120 hL/ha (against a maximum for the appellation of 45 hL/ha). The co-op have worked with that grower to reduce yields, so it is now at 90 hL/ha – merely double the maximum allowed. Wine made from these grapes is too dilute to make good wine and needs modification. They may have to blend good grapes, from better sites, with bad, making a mediocre but drinkable wine yet at least ensuring their members can all get paid. Other members comment on how the management of the co-operative has changed. They used to have open members' meetings to discuss everything – and these would regularly dissolve into major arguments and even, on occasion, fist fights. In order to push through their fairly radical programme general members' meetings are now limited by the co-operative's officials to a single annual general meeting. The organization is now run by a *conseil d'administration* (management committee), which, though elected at the AGM, is carefully vetted to ensure it comprises sound members who will agree with the management's vision. Other decisions are considered by various co-operative 'commissions' – with members carefully selected to ensure they will contribute effectively, but will not rock the boat. Recommendations from the commissions are not binding, but are sent up to the *conseil d'administration* for a final decision. This means that effective decisions are made, and such focus has contributed to the organization's success – but at the same time it means it has moved away from its original democratic ideals and is much more carefully managed.

Meanwhile the co-operative's focus on marketability does not receive universal approval. One co-operator noted that their drive to plant syrah – a very trendy, saleable variety at present – means that they are encouraging members to rip out old vine carignan and grenache; less fashionable varieties but capable, when the vines have some age, of making distinctive, interesting and long-lasting wines.

Family companies

Whereas négociants and smallholders are almost entirely a European phenomenon, and co-operatives predominantly so, family companies are common in the wine industry across the world. Certainly the European family companies have a long tradition – the Antinoris in Tuscany trace their involvement with wine back to 1385 and the Frescobaldis, from the same region, to before that. Nevertheless families in the new producing countries like the Mondavis, Gallos, Fistonichs and McWilliams have been extremely influential in the modern world.

In one sense it is duplication to include family companies in this analysis. Many of them are smallholders or boutique wineries. Others, like the Gallos, are amongst the largest wine companies in the world. Nevertheless, there is a dimension to family companies that overlays these other structural paradigms and deserves to be dealt with separately. Additionally, whilst one can argue that family businesses operate in all industries and therefore they bring nothing distinctive to the production of wine, this is belied by the identification of person with place and the particularly long history associated with many of the families involved in wine businesses.

Family companies may only last for a couple of generations, or they may continue for centuries. However, the pressures they face in a business environment where both globalization and consolidation are accelerating make their continued existence increasingly precarious – at least when they are any more than a very small producer. However, other factors may also work in favour of small family businesses. In France, for instance, a whole family may be the taxable, rather than individuals, making it attractive for children to work for their parents and having, effectively, a tax-free income whilst they stay in the business.

Smyrnios et al. (1998) offer four definitions of a family business. Two are particularly useful:

1 where 50 per cent or more of the ownership is held by a single family, or
2 a single family group is effectively controlling the business.

Additionally, a family business could be controlled by two or more families. On this basis many – perhaps most – of the world's wine businesses are family owned. In Australia at the end of the 1990s 84 per cent made that claim (Charters & Loughton, 2000). However, such ownership may be disparate. The McWilliams company, based in New South Wales and founded in 1877, has many family members as shareholders after six generations of involvement in wine production.

Two key issues for family businesses are control and succession planning. Control requires family members to agree on the policies pursued by those who manage the company; they also have to decide who will manage – whether it is a member of the family, or if it is better to appoint an outsider as manager, as the McWilliams family have done with Kevin McLintock, the CEO of their company. When a family member is manager there are major dangers that the policies they pursue will be unpopular with other family members. Chateau d'Yquem, the most famous producer of Sauternes, was owned by the Lur Saluces family until 1999. Compte Alexandre Lur Saluces had been the long-time manager of the chateau and was regarded by many outsiders as being Yquem – but he only owned 13 per cent of the company's shares (Echikson, 2004). He was unpopular with other members of the family who accused him of being autocratic and giving them little return from the family business (Stimpfig, 2005b). In the end they sold to LVMH, even though the property had been part of the family's inheritance for almost 220 years. Family relationships may not become that bitter but it is still the case that business decisions can merge with and hinder familial relationships, as the father and sons in Robert Mondavi Wines have acknowledged (Nossiter, 2004).

Another key issue for family wine businesses is how ownership and management will be passed to the next generation – if at all (Charters, 2001). This becomes especially complex where there is substantial inheritance tax legislation, or where the company is publicly owned but managed by a family (as was the case with the Mondavis in California). If a family business is to retain its distinctive character, however, this issue needs to be addressed. It may be complicated where some family members in a succeeding generation wish to retain ownership of a winery and others do not.

How does a family business view its wine, and its wine business? There are two related answers to this. The first is to suggest that it is an inheritance, something that is held in trust for future generations. This may be especially applicable to family businesses which have been in operation for some time, and was made explicit by Alexandre de Lur Saluces, of Chateau d'Yquem, who, when asked for his marketing plan, said 'I don't have one . . . I just want to preserve the fabulous inheritance I have received' (quoted in Echikson, 2004, p. 131). Inheritance can also be used as a marketing device, so that the neck label of wine bottles sold by the Hugel company of Alsace state that it has been in the wine industry since 1639, offering a sense of reliability and authenticity for the product. This sense of a close relationship between a family and a place has resonance with consumers. There is now a book, *Bloodlines and Grapevines: Great Winemaking Families of the World* (Ray, 2004) devoted to the concept. The second aspect of the attitude of family business owners to wine is that it is a lifestyle choice. This probably applies more to newer entrants to the industry than long-term businesses, but certainly is the major incentive for involvement with the wine industry in the new producing countries, where lifestyle is also viewed as a greater indicator of a successful family business than financial return (Charters, 2001).

It can also be tentatively suggested that family companies like to work with other family companies. A number of joint operations have been established linking family businesses. Before the company was purchased by Constellation Wines, Robert Mondavi Wines had combined projects with the Rothschilds (of Mouton-Rothschild) in California, the Frescobaldis in Italy, the Chadwicks of Errazuriz in Chile and the Oatleys of Rosemount in Australia and California. The Gallo family have linked with the McWilliams in Australia.

The first families of wine

There is even an international organization which aims to link some of the most well known family companies around the world – Primum Familiae Vinum. This includes Champagne Pol Roger, the Torres family from Spain, the Antinoris and seven others. The organization's stated aims, detailed on its website, are interesting.

'The families which comprise PFV are conscious they each share a common ambition of excellence and efficiency, they are custodians of a part of their respective national heritages, and they face the same problems of fiscal pressure and the transmission of the family business to the next generation.

These points give rise to fruitful exchanges of views during regular general meetings of all members, and have led the association to elaborate a 'PFV charter' which can be summarised as follows:

- To promote and defend the moral values that are the backbone of family businesses.
- To exchange viticultural/oenological information and promote traditional methods that underline the quality of the wine and respect for 'terroir'.
- To promote the moderate consumption of wine, which is considered to be a cultural tradition of conviviality and of 'savoir-vivre'.
- To exchange useful information on all aspects of their businesses.

PFV members aim to defend and promote the traditions and values of family-owned wine companies, and ensure that such ideals survive and prosper for future generations' (Anon., 2005c).

It has been noted that family companies come in all sizes. However, whilst few of them are very large, a number feature as medium-sized companies within their respective markets. This gives them particular problems, for they have neither the economies of scale of the very largest, nor the intimate control and production flexibility of the smallest. Some family companies have determined to grow in size, to gain the economies of scale. The Antinori company based in Tuscany followed this approach with a massive expansion programme throughout Italy after 1985, as well as developments in Hungary and the United States; their production is led by the three million bottles produced each year of the sangiovese based Santa Cristina – a very substantial production level (Belfrage, 2001).

Public companies and large enterprises

The large wine company is entirely a creature of the modern world. It is also much more in evidence in places where wine is viewed as a product rather than as produce; thus particularly in the United States, Australia and New Zealand; to a lesser extent in South Africa and Chile. (The key European exception where public companies are widespread is Champagne, where it can be argued that the production method distances the drink from the idea of produce more than anywhere else.) It can be surmised that wine as product fits more neatly with organizations where emphasis is placed on market orientation rather than creating the goods (see Beverland (2004) for a consideration of market orientation).

Not all large wine companies are publicly owned. The world's second and fourth largest (at the time of writing), Constellation Wines and Gallo, are owned by American families. Nevertheless, increasingly individuals and families do not have the capital required to control an organization of that size. Companies like Constellation achieved their position in an era of small companies, and it is unlikely that new entrants to the industry would now be able to replicate that.

The key to ownership of large companies is that they are, therefore, public. Historically that meant that individual investors shared ownership, but increasingly it is institutional investors such as banks, insurance companies and pension funds who dominate shareholders' registers. It also means that control of a company can move and be passed around. One of the features of the last decade has been the increasing interest of drinks conglomerates – often spirits producers, sometimes brewers – in purchasing successful wine producers. Thus the Australian brewer, Fosters, purchased Mildara Blass in Australia and used the leverage of that powerbase to buy up the Beringer winery in the United States and then Southcorp back in Australia. Diageo, the huge drinks company which owns Johnnie Walker whisky, Smirnoff Vodka and Gordon's Gin – as well as Guinness – purchased Chalone in the Napa late in 2004 – having already bought Sterling Vineyards, Beaulieu Vineyard and Blossom Hill in the same area, allowing for substantial concentration and developing economies of scale. However, although these are the giants of the wine world, a sense of proportion needs to be retained. Most are not, on an international scale, huge companies. Nor, with the possible exception of the major Champagne houses, are any wine companies truly multinational in the sense that they have major markets across a wide and diverse range of countries. Rather they would be defined as transnational; their markets cross a number of countries. Furthermore none of them, with the exception of LVMH, are sourcing wine from more than about four countries. Crucially the three largest wine-producing companies have only 7 per cent world market share for their brands as opposed to 25 per cent for the three major spirits companies and 27 per cent for the equivalent number of beer companies (Heijbroek, 2003).

A number of wine producers have used the opportunity of turning their privately owned business into a public company in order to use the share issue to raise capital so that they can fund expansion. The problem with this is that once a company is public the original entrepreneur who set it up no longer has complete control of it. A series of major Australian wine industry figures have found this to be the case, some of whom have been excluded from the new organization; Len Evans with Rothbury (now part of the Fosters group), Brian Croser with Petaluma (now owned by the brewer Lion Nathan), Andrew Pirie with Piper's Brook and Peter Lehmann with Peter Lehmann Wines. Only the latter successfully fended off a hostile take-over bid by Allied Domecq and then it necessitated the involvement of a Swiss company who paid substantially in excess of the Peter Lehmann Wines' market value in order to gain control (Hibberd, 2005). It is, paradoxically, the success of these high-profile wine entrepreneurs in their single-minded pursuit of quality which has made their companies so attractive to third parties.

Large companies may have been started by an individual or family who have varying reasons for entering the business. However, the momentum established by their size means that they tend to take on a life of their own and, most noticeably when they are public, the focus is on making a return; wine is therefore a commodity, which is used to make profit. Wine may be the sole focus of the company, or may be part of a portfolio which includes other drinks (Lion Nathan, Diageo, Allied Domecq) or other goods such as fashion with LVMH. As a secondary driving force one can note the tendency towards monopolization within capitalism. This was noted by Marx (Marx, 1867/1976), who, whilst he did not foresee all aspects of the development of capitalism accurately, noted that companies in a sector have a tendency to combine because higher profits are to be made by reducing competition and increasing market share, to the point where a monopolistic supplier of a product type has substantial economic power. Whilst this has happened much less with wine than with beer and spirits it is nevertheless the direction in which the international industry is currently moving. In California, for instance, there were

1300 small producers in 1936 but barely 270 in 1960 (Geraci, 2004). In some countries this tendency towards monopoly production is now very advanced; Montana in New Zealand, merged with Cooks Corbans at the end of the twentieth century. It was purchased by Allied Domecq in 2001 and now produces well over half of the country's wine. It has also happened in some specific wine sectors, so that in Champagne LVMH, who own Moët et Chandon, Mercier, Ruinart, Veuve Clicquot and Krug, are responsible for over 35 per cent of the region's wine (Leahy, 2003).

Large companies have a reputation for producing bland, even poor quality wine, and in certain countries, such as Spain, there may be a limited truth in that (Sanjuan & Albisu, 2004). However, they can also produce good, even very good wine. Southcorp, in Australia, are responsible for Penfold's Grange, the country's most famous wine, and LVMH in France make Dom Pérignon and Krug *Grande Cuvée* – again both reputable and very expensive.

Boutique producers

The idea of the boutique producer is perhaps the most recent of all the organizational structures dealt with in this chapter; the term is only about 10 years old, and is essentially applied in the Anglophone new producing countries. A boutique winery or producer is very small scale, perhaps no more than one individual or a couple, may be including an employee or two. It may well also be a family business, although many are in their first generation of ownership, so it is hard to be categoric about that. Boutique producers have gone into business for two reasons. The first is that it is a lifestyle choice. Research in Australia has shown that for small wineries (with a turnover of under £200 000 p.a.) lifestyle is the main motivating factor for being in the business. Gradually, however, the importance of lifestyle diminishes slightly and other factors become more important, so that by the time that turnover exceeds £2 000 000 p.a. ambition-related issues are the most relevant. Thereafter, by the time a business attains £8 000 000 p.a., money is equally as important as lifestyle as a reason to run the winery (Charters & Loughton, 2000). Whether those who focus on lifestyle choose to keep their business small, or if with those companies which grow dramatically the original lifestyle goals are superseded, is uncertain.

It can be suggested that another factor affects how boutique winery owners view their wine. The lifestyle they seek is a wine-related lifestyle, and they come to that with specific ideas of what they want to do about wine. Consider the following comments, both from Australian winemakers working in boutique wineries, each of whom had been asked about what they try to achieve with the wines they make:

> Hal: The unobtainable . . . . You're constantly aiming for something that is possibly unachievable, that's why you keep doing it – because you never really get there. And it changes from year to year, your definition of what you're aiming for, I guess, so it's an evolution in the way you go about it.
>
> Nick: We're . . . trying to achieve some individuality. . . . It's very easy to fall into a trap of making a stock standard wine.

What both these winemakers are expressing is the idea that wine must have some value beyond merely functioning as a beverage; that it has interest, identity, perhaps even an aesthetic dimension. Hal later said that 'you put your heart and soul into making a wine'. Most of those who operate a boutique winery would understand these ideas. They are not just in the business in order to live in an attractive rural area (a tourism operation would offer this as effectively). The lure is the desire to shape a distinctive wine, an individual product which can be identified with them. It is this goal, and not merely the lifestyle, that distinguishes the boutique winery operator from traditional smallholders or co-operators. Indeed, when small winery owners in Australia were asked why they decided to establish their business the most popular response was 'for a personal challenge' – ahead of personal development or lifestyle opportunity (Charters & Loughton, 2000). That challenge encompasses the desire to produce wine which marks their identity.

Making choices

Mike and Mireille Oakes moved from London to the south of France in the late 1980s – although without the intention of growing grapes. However, when he needed to earn an income Mike took employment as a casual vineyard labourer with a local winemaker. He took to the work, and subsequently bought some vineyard land. He now works 10 ha with Mireille and his eldest son who works full-time with him. The family own 6 ha of vines themselves and manage about four *en métayage* (where they run the vineyard, and pay a share of the grapes to the landowner after each harvest), with the vines in forty different plots around the village. Mike is a member of the local co-operative, which takes his grapes each year. He is a hard worker, and committed to producing high-quality grapes; as a result of this commitment the co-operative has used some of his grapes in a 'super-cuvée' each year, along with a few of his fellow co-operators. Nevertheless, whilst he can see the benefits which the co-operative offers, he is not uncritical of it, and is particularly concerned that little distinction is ultimately made between him – who produces healthy, flavourful grapes at low yields – and some of his neighbours who care less and overcrop their vines, substituting quantity for quality. The trouble is, he claims, he is now too old to start making wine on his own account; it takes all available time just to tend the vines, without having to sell wine as well. Even if he could persuade a local winemaker to vinify for him, under French law the wine would have to be on his premises by 15th November each year for him to claim that he has made it as part of a family operation. Nor is the idea of a partnership with another local appealing. As soon as he joins with someone else he and Mireille cease to be running a family business, with all the concomitant tax and administrative benefits that affords, and would become a limited company, required to keep much more detailed records and facing a less amenable tax regime. He has a commitment to improving the quality and reputation of the appellation in which he is situated but he is very limited in how he can pursue that goal, within the structures and legal framework available to him in the south of France.

Conclusion

The answer to the question 'why are people in the wine industry?' may seem obvious; it is to make wine. But, as this chapter has suggested, it is not as simple as that. Members of the wine industry aim to make a living but how they do this, and the other factors which colour the combined goals of making wine and money can be complex. They may manage their vineyard because it is what their family have always done – perhaps as part of a farm or smallholding; wine (more probably grapes) is just another crop, and maximizing income is more important than any idealistic idea of making a premium drink. They can be in the business to trade, because they are merchants; a commitment to the individuality and quality of their product may or may not exist alongside that. They may have made a lifestyle choice – they enjoy the romance of wine and perhaps its connection with the land or aesthetic value. Alternatively they may be shareholders, potentially having no interest in the commodity beyond the money it will make them. How people view the product informs what aims they have with the wine they make – what kind of wine they are after. Because they may view it in different ways, this also affects the image they have of it, and therefore the type of concept they will seek to promote to consumers.

Bibliographical note

For a now outdated but nevertheless insightful description of life with an Italian smallholder and his family see Calabresi (1987). An excellent introduction to the growth of négociants, and how they replaced brokers, is contained in Brennan's (1997) study of the development of the wine trade in north-eastern France, and Nicholas Faith's *The Winemasters of Bordeaux* (1999) details their decline in one region with great clarity. For an excellent example of the problems facing a modern co-operative Echikson (2004, pp. 195–217) profiles Sauveterre. Ulin (1996) gives a detailed explanation of the origins of co-operatives, although his work is marked by a very specific theoretical perspective and a number of errors in vinous matters. There has been no specific study of large wine companies nor of boutique wineries but Charters (2001) contains useful background on family businesses in Australia, including information about smaller producers.

5 Classifications, appellations and terroir

As soon as wine became an elite product there was an impetus to grade it and to protect and enhance the value of the 'better' wine. Essentially this became a form of adding value to the product for both the consumer and – crucially – the producer. Grading in this way was based historically on where the grapes were grown, and defining wine by the place of its origin is fundamental to the European wine industry and is becoming increasingly important in much of the New World. This chapter examines why classification, demarcation and a sense of place became important, how they are used to achieve marketing differentiation and how there are subtle differences of approach between the single vineyard, communal origin and larger demarcated areas. It also looks at the 'benefits' (or otherwise) that classification and origin provide to the consumer.

The origins of wine differentiation

Once the supply of wine expanded and could not be controlled by elites there was a need to establish relative quality. This was necessary so that elites could maintain their status by consuming the best – at the same time as giving themselves an enhanced enjoyment from wines which were sweeter, or more pleasantly flavoured. They felt that they were, as 'superior' members of their community, entitled to appreciate the superior wine. Where wine was a democratic drink this was less of an issue, although even in those cultures the elites would still prefer to mark out their status in the same way. It is worth noting that such differentiation is not solely important for grapewine nor in the western world. The Lele of the Kasai – in Democratic Congo – drink palm wine which they categorize into thirteen different quality levels, depending on the type of tree used, the maturity of the tree, the age of the wine and its taste ('sweet' or 'fierce'). For them different categories of wine are considered appropriate for different social groups (Ngokwey, 1987).

As early as the time of Tutankhamen wine was marked as 'good quality' for the Pharaoh (Johnson, 1989), with some wines even being termed 'very, very good' (McGovern, 2003, p. 123) . Such an approach, of guaranteeing the quality of the wine, was just as much in the interests of the producer as the elite consumer; to prove that your wine was better was to increase your return on it. It consequently engendered the view that some sites were better than others for producing wine. Thus, in classical Greece Pramnian was mentioned in the Iliad as making one of the most famous wines (Unwin, 1996). By the late Roman republic a series of sites in Italy were designated as being the best, which effectively created an early system of *grands crus*. At the same time the fact that wines could be stored for long periods in *amphorae* – and thus could age slowly – allowed vintage to be used as a means of establishing quality. Wines from the year of the consulship of Opimius (121 BC) were notoriously of high quality even into the first century of the Empire (Unwin, 1996).

As barrels supplanted *amphorae* as the main container for wine, the drink underwent much more substantial contact with air and as a result aged more rapidly – usually needing to be drunk within a year of the harvest. Vintage could no longer be used in the same way for differentiation, so the focus increasingly returned to where the grapes had been grown. Tastes varied from century to century, but sweetness was often a defining feature of quality. In a French poem entitled 'The battle of the wines' and dated to 1224, 70 samples were judged by an English priest (Phillips, 2000). A prize was awarded ultimately to the wines of Cyprus – where, with Commandaria, they still make rich, sweet red wine. Later, according to Shakespeare in Richard III, the Duke of Clarence opted to be killed by drowning in a butt of Malmsey; not, at that time, from Madeira in the Atlantic, but another sweet wine made on the coast of the Peloponnese.

With the impact of the consumer revolution the desire to discriminate between wines became much more widespread, and again allowed vertical distinction (between vintages) alongside horizontal distinction (between place). It also saw the fine tuning of differentiation based on place. It was no longer a case of the Bordeaux producing better wine than Cahors, but variations based on the specific area within Bordeaux.

Classifications

Classifying vineyards and the wines they produce has been perceived to be a useful guide to their quality for over 500 years. Vineyards in parts of France and Germany were graded before the end of the seventeenth century and Hungary had all of its vineyards ranked in five grades early in the eighteenth century (Robinson, 1999). However, the fashion for ranking wines is very much one of the modern era, with a focus on consolidating consumer recognition for the wines of a region.

Classification in practice: The Médoc

Probably the most famous classification in the world is that of the Médoc, established in 1855 as part of the Great Exhibition in Paris during that year, when the wines of Bordeaux were used to exemplify French vinous culture. Fifty-nine chateaux were awarded the accolade of *Grand Cru Classé* (which translates literally as a 'great classed growth'; perhaps classified site would be a more accessible term). The producers were further categorized at five levels, from first to fifth. There were four top wines, which included one from outside the Médoc and to the south of Bordeaux, albeit a chateau whose quality would not brook an exception (Briggs, 1994). This classification has lasted to the present day. The fortunate chateaux still note the fact that they are a classed growth on their labels, and consumers give credit to which of the five levels a wine is accorded when they select them. Such is the venerable tradition of the last 150 years which surrounds these wines that it is impossible to conceive of it changing.

The classification was the work not of the producers in the Médoc, but of its brokers (Markham, 1998). Indeed, much of the history of its establishment is a history of how the merchants, far more powerful at the time than those who made the wine, used the classification to enhance their power and undermine attempts by the chateaux to increase their influence. The way in which the brokers decided on the five levels of the classification was to use what they knew best: price. Rather than taste or historic reputation it was market mechanisms which decided on the top four wines, and then the cascade of others below them. It could be argued that the merchants were hardly unbiased observers in the whole process. Setting the classes was one way of helping to stabilize wine prices, a factor which would work to their advantage in any bargaining process. Furthermore, it was – with the one noted exception – only wines of the Médoc which were included. Other top chateaux of the Graves had no place in it; even less wines of the right bank such as St-Emilion or Pomerol. One reason for this is that the Médoc was the favourite source of wine for the British, and the industrial might of Britain made them the key export market for the wine; the region they favoured consequently sold for the highest price. The Dutch preferred wine from various origins on the right bank, but they were less prosperous than the British, and so paid less. Indeed, even one Médoc producer, Chateau Cantemerle, was originally excluded from the classification because it had only been sold to the Dutch until a couple of years before Universal Exhibition. It was only included as a late entrant, after the original list had been finalized (Markham, 1998). It is thus important to realize that whilst many people now believe that the classification is based on place – where the chateau is situated – it is primarily based on price.

Nevertheless, whilst apparently fixed as firmly as the 10 commandments (and perhaps having the same significance for wine lovers), Dewey Markham, in his comprehensive analysis of the classification (1998), makes the point that when it was established it was only expected to have a limited impact; it was designed solely for the Paris Exhibition. More than that, it was only the latest in a succession of such classifications which had been developed by individuals and organizations over the previous century. As such it was a fairly contingent assessment; others had included different chateaux in the list, and varied their level in the process.

Furthermore, in the time since the classification, the Médoc has changed. Some chateaux included in the original classification have disappeared. Others have bought and sold land – so the first growth, Chateau Lafite, for instance, has added a further 23 ha to its area under vine since then. Nevertheless, the classification is not attached to the land, but to the chateau, even if the core of the vineyard has altered. In this respect this classification differs from earlier ones in other countries. They focused on the vineyard; this focused on the wine. Additionally one can note that the varietal makeup of Médoc wines has altered since 1855. Cabernet sauvignon is more important; carmenère has vanished; malbec, which was significant, has almost disappeared. There has also been other overt human intervention. In 1973 Chateau Mouton-Rothschild was promoted from being a second growth to a first growth (see Chapter 14). Finally it is fair to note that the revolution in winemaking over the last 30 years, and the increasing overseas demand for good Bordeaux (first from the United States, later from east Asia) has prompted many producers to make a dramatic improvement in the quality of their wine. This has led to the concept of the 'super seconds'; wines classified as second growth (or even lower) in 1855 which are beginning to push close to the first growths in the way that the quality of their product is perceived – chateaux such as Leoville Las Cases and Cos d'Estournel are regularly mentioned in this context, along with a number of others. Further, for the super seconds, as reputation increases, so does the price they can charge for their wine. In this way what happened in 1855 is reversed. Critics revise the reputation of a producer, and that in turn results in a higher price.

Above all, the 1855 classification was a product of the golden age of wine (Johnson, 1989), the age of economic growth and of emergent markets, and a time when wine was a good way to earn a living. It resulted from the era of the expansion of trade and of imperial certainty in what Europe could achieve. As such it was a symbol of the triumph of wine generally, and French wine in particular, before the onset of depression, war and phylloxera.

As a result two questions are relevant. How much credibility should have been accorded to the classification in the first place, and how relevant is it today? The answer given by wine critics is that it remains a useful rule of thumb – but is not exact and there are some who consider it unjust (Echikson, 2004). There seems to be some general agreement that if it were reworked today some which were excluded in 1855 would be included (such as Chateaux d'Angludet and Potensac) and some would be promoted – the fifth growth Lynch-Bages being a prime example of this. Fewer are prepared to be explicit about demotions – or even exclusions from the list. The American critic, Robert Parker, however, has offered his own revision of the classification. He includes wines from across the region, not merely the Médoc, resulting in the inclusion of more wines in total. He suggests 15 first growths (including the original five from the 1855 classification) down to more than 50 fifth-growths (Parker, 1986).

Classifications in the modern world

Other classifications, based on the one developed in the Médoc, have been adopted in Bordeaux. A less well-known classification of Sauternes was established in 1855. Another was adopted in the Graves region in 1959 for both red and white wines (with some chateaux classified for both, some for red only and some for white only). St-Emilion also created one in 1955. In this case, however, the classification provided for regular revision every 10 years, with the possibility of promotion and demotion. Whilst revisions have not kept precisely to the timetable, they have taken place (the last in 1996) and both promotions and demotions have occurred, making it a far more useful spur to improving quality than the more inflexible versions. Pomerol, a region which has been one of the most exciting performers on international wine markets over the last 30 years, has no classification; that has not stopped wines such as Chateau Pétrus being amongst the most expensive in the world.

Burgundy, as one would expect from the key domestic rival to Bordeaux, also has a classification system, with its roots nearly as old, dating back to 1861 (Robinson, 1999), although critics recognized an informal classification – using sites that are still noted for their quality, such as La Romanée Conti and Richbourg – at least as far back as 1827 (Loubere, 1978). However, whereas the Médoc classification is price related, the Burgundy one is based firmly on site. This is, in part, inevitable in a region where the vineyards themselves may be split up amongst many grapegrowers. It is a simpler system than Bordeaux. Wines may be regional (such as generic *Bourgogne*), they may have a village designation, such as Gevrey Chambertin, they may come from a vineyard designated as a *premier cru*, or, at the very pinnacle, from a *grand cru*.

Generally few classifications have succeeded outside the most prestigious regions of France. However, a variation on the theme operates in Australia. Langton's, one of the country's major auction houses, launched its Classification of Distinguished Australian Wines in 1991. This began with 34 wines, including one designated as outstanding (Penfold's Grange), and in its 2005 incarnation comprises 101 wines, 11 of which are now classed as outstanding. Whilst the qualifications for inclusion are quite complex the primary basis for the classification is the price the wine has attained on the domestic secondary market. The classification has been criticized, specifically because it is based on price and not the quality of the wine, and because it uses apparently arbitrary criteria for its judgments, particularly by requiring the wines to have been made for a number of years. As a result an excellent new wine may suddenly appear, and may even command high prices but would not be included in the classification for some time until it had shown consistency over a number of years (Oliver, 2000). The critics of the price-based classification do not explain how the quality of a wine is to be judged. However, despite the criticisms, classifications do offer the consumer a short-cut to the potential quality of a wine – a factor which has prompted some to argue that California should create a classificatory system to improve public awareness of how good the state's wines are (Thode & Maskulka, 1996).

One other classification system has been commenced recently, in Germany, where the Association of German Prädikat Wine Estates (VDP) agreed a system based on three levels, with detailed production specifications for those who seek inclusion. The classification is not uncontroversial (Brook, 2003). At the top level are the 1120 ha of 'first growths' but a criterion for inclusion at this level is that the wines have to be dry. To many critics and consumers who love the great *spätlese*, *auslese* and *trockenbeerenauslese* of the Mosel and the Rheingau this will appear to be a strange requirement, excluding what are generally perceived to be some of the country's greatest wines.

The success of classifications

Based on his research on the Bordeaux system Markham (1998) suggests that there are three criteria for a classification to be successful. The first is that a region must have an outstanding reputation for quality over the long term; only Bordeaux, Burgundy and Champagne have that in France (though probably one could argue about the Rhone, maybe even Alsace). Perhaps, though, on the basis of the Australian example, that should be modified; there must be a market which believes in the exceptional quality of the area classified. Second, Markham argues that the wines must be linked to the named producer at every step of the production process. Again, this could be questioned. Even in 1855 many Bordeaux wines would be shipped to Britain to finish their *élevage*, before being bottled there. Today grapes for a wine like Penfold's Grange may be grown by independent contractors who then sell on to the company. Nevertheless, it is undoubtedly true that the producer must have an element of control throughout the process if the wine's quality level is to be preserved. The third criterion is that the producer must have a long term 'identity'; thus there must be a distinctive name which the consumer can relate to for an extended period. Again, whilst this may be a precondition of success for the individual producer within the classification, it is less certain how this relates to the classification as a whole. In Bordeaux producers have come and gone. Even so, the fact that Burgundy, where producers change but the quality of the vineyard remains, does not have a classificatory system that is as historically significant as its rival's suggests that there does need to be a group of highly regarded producers who exist for a long term. Perhaps the Napa Valley, and maybe the Barossa Valley, are two regions which are close to fulfilling this criterion.

The economists' perspective on the idea of classification is interesting. A study carried out by Landon and Smith (1998) investigating the relationship of reputation to price concluded that the consumer pays attention to both long-term reputation (the 1855 classification) and shorter term perceived quality (as determined by influential wine critics). However, the former – the long-term reputation – has greater weight, with the implication that a price premium only comes when that reputation has had some time to be confirmed. This does appear to fly in the face of the recent financial success of the so-called *garagiste* wines of the Bordeaux right bank (like Chateau de Valandraud) as well as some newly rejuvenated producers such as Chateau Pavie. Perhaps, however, their price fluctuations whilst high, are short term when compared with chateaux such as Ausone or Latour with histories spanning centuries, and there is evidence that the prices paid for 'new wave' producers may be on the wane (Kakaviatos, 2005).

Landon and Smith also make the comment that one strange effect of the classification is that even though it has never been amended it remains an effective guide to quality. In economic terms a situation like that – with a stable, unchallenged, long-established quality endorsement – would have encouraged producers to coast, for there is no effective process to enforce continuing quality control. Surprisingly this has not happened. They comment that the producers clearly have a means to implement the maintenance of quality amongst themselves (Landon & Smith, 1998). In practice the only 'enforcement mechanism' seems to be the continuing commitment of the producers to maintain what they see as their inheritance, or a tradition which has to be preserved for the greater good of their country, or the world of wine. Even when a producer's quality standards have dropped – most notoriously with the first growth Chateau Margaux in the 1970s (Robinson, 1999) – a determination to restore the chateau to its former position (often combined with new ownership) seems enough to resurrect the previous adherence to high-quality standards.

Crucially one can note the benefit of collective action to promote quality for a region like the Médoc. It acts to the lasting benefit of a number of producers in the area, as opposed to individual action which just gives long-term benefits to a single producer (Thode & Maskulka, 1996). For a new producer, promoting the quality of the region may have fewer immediate benefits, but in the longer term to be recognized as a leading producer in a high quality region may give more substantial recognition, and offer higher rewards. It could be argued, for instance, that this has begun to work for wineries such as Heitz, Stag's Leap and Diamond Creek in the Napa Valley. Additionally it can be suggested that classifications (the promotion of the best individual producers) tend to occur when a wine region is comparatively successful: Sauternes and the Médoc in the 1850s, Graves and St-Emilion in the 1950s, and Australia from the 1990s onwards. As we shall see, appellation systems (the defence of all producers within a specific region), tend to be a response to decline and economic depression.

Paradoxically it is also true that whilst classification consolidated the prestige (and therefore economic power) of the elite wines, it also made fraud more attractive (Ulin, 1995). The more that successful wines provided a high return, and the more that an 'objective' benchmark fixed their superiority, the more attractive it was to outsiders to either claim to be one of those wines, or to assert falsely that they had the endorsement provided by the classification. The great age of fraud followed shortly after the Médoc classification.

Classification by vintage

One other way in which wine can be classified is by vintage. In those classic wine regions of the world where the climate is cool or just warm the variation in weather from year to year has a direct impact on the way a wine tastes, and thus on its quality rating. Certainly by the time of the Romans there was an awareness that wines of some years were preferable to others (Unwin, 1996). In most French, German and Italian regions vintage is seen to have a substantial impact on wine quality, and Port and Champagne have 'vintage' wines which are only declared in the very best years; in all other years the wine produced is blended into a non-vintage style. In southern Europe and in many of the new producing countries where it is warmer the variation in weather from year to year may be less marked. Even there, however, vintage is not irrelevant. Australian wines from the 1998 vintage (a year of drought conditions which reduced yields and enhanced concentration) were considered to be very good quality, and eagerly sought after on release.

The importance of vintage as a means of classification is primarily significant for premium wine. This does not mean that vintage is not relevant to the consumer of bulk wine – and it will affect the taste and style of the wine particularly when it has been made on a small scale. (Modern industrial techniques and large scale production make it easier to smooth over flavour differences from year to year.) There is no doubt that a local consumer of *vin de table* may well register a better or worse year for their preferred drop, but that discrimination is much more personal, and of little use in making social distinctions.

Vintage as a means of classification is very important in two categories. First, it allows for differentiation by investors. Wines from good years are noticeably more secure as an investment than those of poor years; appreciation is greater and the decline in value after the period of peak drinking is much lower (see Chapter 10). The second point to be made is that the use of vintage as a means of making statements is important. There is a world of difference between offering a guest a 1990 and a 1991 Bordeaux. The former was a hot, dry vintage, with excellent ripening conditions. The wines are perceived to be intense, well balanced and flavourful. The following year had a very cold spring and a dismal, wet summer. The grapes ripened imperfectly, and the resulting wines can be green and unexciting. The knowledgeable consumer, offered either of these, may use the wines to make judgments about their relationship with whoever is providing them with the wine.

Appellations

Whilst reworking existing classifications has become a pleasant activity for some critics and interested consumers, the emphasis has moved away from grading wine and towards a focus on where the wine comes from. This trend began in France towards the end of the nineteenth century (Loubere, 1978; Vaudour, 2002) and the appellation system became enshrined in law in France in the early part of the twentieth century. It then spread, especially with the formation of the EEC, throughout western Europe. As such it is the dominating mode of differentiating wine throughout the world, against which all other modes are judged.

The origin and spread of appellations

The first attempt to define and restrict the origin of specific wines was not French. Prior to the twentieth century demarcation occurred in Tokaji (1700), Chianti (1716) and the Douro Valley (1756). In each case this was undertaken to protect producers of an already established wine from others who wished to pass off their own wine, from outside the region, as more reputable. In the latter case such protection was accompanied by rules determining how the wine was to be made, and outlawing (for instance) the addition of elderberry juice to deepen colour (Robertson, 1992). It is also worth noting that the first comprehensive national appellation system in Europe was instituted in Portugal from 1908 onwards (although this did not have the impact that the later French system had), and that Spain also had some delineated areas as the French system was being legislated for (Sanjuan & Albisu, 2004).

The classic explanation for the origins of the French *appellation controlée* (AC) system is economic. From the mid-1870s much of western Europe was in the grip of an agricultural depression. The price of grain dropped by almost 30 per cent from 1865 to 1900, and the cost of wine by over 25 per cent in the same period, albeit with a brief increase in the 1890s (Loubere, 1978). At the same time, the impact of phylloxera was devastating overall production. Exports dropped from 3.98 million hL in 1873 to 2.05 million in 1891 (Loubere, 1978). Meanwhile growing temperance movements were threatening markets overseas, and even having an impact on sales in France (Loubere, 1978). At the same time other sources of wine, such as phylloxera-free Algeria were developing. Imported wine increased from about 800 000 hL in 1870 to over five million after 1900. Although there was then a slight improvement the Great War, followed fairly soon by prohibition in the USA and then depression, merely compounded the decline. Concurrently passing-off began to be practised on a wide scale. The increasingly fluid market in wine, a result of the golden age, combined with the premium always accorded to the more reputable producers and regions, was an incentive to the producers of cheaper wine (including some from overseas) to rebadge their product as having a more prestigious origin than was the case. This had already been seen on the UK market, particularly from 1860 onwards (Duguid, 2003) and was increasingly common in France. Consequently, the argument runs, the need to protect established producers and regions in the face of falling returns, insect predation, overseas challenges and fraud (which cheated both the producer and the consumer) resulted in a process which guaranteed the origin of the wine. At the same time once an appellation is established, there is then a further inducement for the producer to maintain quality, because if they have to invest to get the benefit of what is effectively a regional trademark they will not then compromise that benefit by reducing the superiority of the wine (Stanziani, 2004).

However, it can be argued that this explanation on its own is not enough. Controlling imports would probably have been a more effective means of supporting a depressed domestic market than an AC system. It may well be that social and cultural factors were as important. The agricultural depression occurred during (and helped to accelerate) a substantial shift in population from country to towns and cities (Loubere, 1978). One commentator writing 50 years later said of this time 'whole villages were just abandoned . . . presenting a scene of desolation and ruin that we would not see again until the end of the Great War when we could go back into the villages of our liberated regions' (Henri Hitier, quoted in Campbell, 2004, p. 225). It can be suggested that those who remained would have had a sense of loss, perhaps even despair, as the rural way of life which had existed for so long appeared to be disintegrating. This was set against the political backdrop of the rapid and complete French defeat in the Franco-Prussian War of 1870. For a country which believed in '*la gloire*' (the glorious heritage of France) such a defeat undermined its self-image dramatically. This was followed by the bloody struggle of the First World War which, though won, drained the country further of self-esteem as it relied on British and American support to gain victory. On top of this the wine industry had further demoralizing problems; the curse of phylloxera increasing consumption of non-French wine, and the incomprehensible rise of temperance with its idea that wine, so long considered overwhelmingly health-giving, was in fact a debilitating drink. Even amongst committed wine drinkers there was a growing resistance to a product which was, by the first decade of the twentieth century, widely perceived to be contaminated – and thus not truly representative of natural rural produce (Loubere, 1978). A combination of factors – the blow to national pride, rural demoralization, and challenges to the wine industry's belief in its own importance – thus engendered a major loss of confidence. In the light of this the AC system, with its emphasis on marking boundaries to protect against the untrustworthy outsider (Guy, 2003), plus its other requirements which enshrined traditional grape varieties, and tried to guarantee product quality, can be seen as a means of protecting a discrete rural way of life. Appellations were about self-image, self-respect and enhancing both of these in an increasingly alienating world as much as about economic protectionism.

A form of demarcation was established in a few regions early in the twentieth century, including Champagne in 1908. Champagne was a region which, because of its prestige and very effective international marketing, was a prime target for unscrupulous competitors (Duguid, 2003). However, a major dispute took place within the region over who would be within the demarcated area, and who outside. The authorities found that drawing lines on a map to include and exclude was not as easy as they hoped (see Chapter 14). At the same time, although without the equivalent unrest, demarcation took place in areas as diverse as Bordeaux and Banyuls; yet no overarching national system was established. The major push for a national system began after the First World War. Chateauneuf-du-Pape had suffered particularly from passing-off with its wine regularly being blended with lesser local wine but sold as genuine Chateauneuf, and at the same time the president of the local syndicate, Baron Le Roy, was concerned to ensure the quality of wines which were produced locally so that poorer quality versions would not undermine the position of those who were committed to producing to a high standard

(Loubere, 1990). As well as delimiting the geographic area within which the grapes could be grown, a series of other requirements were voluntarily adopted by producers in an attempt to guarantee the final quality of the wine. Some of these requirements were ultimately integrated into the national AC system, although others, such as the requirement for a compulsory *trie* of 10 per cent of the crop (the exclusion of grapes, in order to force the removal of those which were most diseased or unripe), remained a local provision. The success of what was achieved in Chateauneuf formed the basis for the national system adopted in 1935.

Gradually appelation controlée (AC) regions were demarcated throughout France; the designation meant that an AC wine was considered a 'quality wine'. There is also no doubt that the quality of wines produced within AC demarcations improved as yields were controlled, hybrid vines rooted out and consistent production practices implemented. It is often forgotten that establishing an appellation was expensive. In Cassis, in the south of France, over 30 per cent of all growers went out of business from 1950 to 1960 because they did not have the resources required to comply with the AC regulations (Gade, 2004). However it is critical to note that not all wines have an AC designation. Although the system has become widely established over the last 70 years, still only about 50 per cent of all French wines are technically quality wine. The rest are classed as table wine, which cannot state a region of origin, grape variety or vintage year – although the introduction of *vin de pays* in 1974 modified this somewhat. Crucial to understanding the system, however, is the fact that quality relates directly to demarcation – to lines drawn on a map. If a producer is inside the line they are deemed to make quality wine associated with a specific place; beyond the border and they cannot make quality wine, and cannot adopt the name of the origin.

The formation of the EEC in 1957 prompted the spread of AC systems. As noted earlier, because France was considered the world's leading vinous power it was used as a template for a common demarcation system, initially in Italy and Germany, later in Spain, Portugal and Greece. Thus the system with two classes, quality wine and table wine, was adopted throughout the EEC. The French model was modified however, to take account of local circumstances. In Germany, where the northerly latitudes mean that attaining fruit ripeness is a key concern, there is a two-tier system, with a geographic designation overlaid with a categorization of the wines based on ripeness. A *Qualitätswein bestimmter Anbaugebiete* (QbA) Mosel spätlese thus gives indication both about where the grapes were grown and their sugar content at harvest as part of the quality wine designation.

Appellations as intellectual property

Internationally, appellation systems are seen as a form of intellectual property. The World Trade Organization is currently considering how they can be enforced internationally and how they should operate to protect producers, yet in a manner which does not inhibit trade (World Trade Organisation, n.d.).

Stanziani (2004) has considered the development of appellations as the development of a trademark. The French law of July 1824 protected trademarks, whilst specifically excluding trademarks based on place – except for those related to wine production; wine, thus, was recognized at this time to have a legally valid connection with its origin. (Interestingly, brand marks were only protected from 1857 onwards, which may be one reason why the French focus more on origin than brand even today). By the 1840s producers were taking legal action to protect their regional name, and by 1887 a court 'asserted that the Champagne appellation would henceforth be exclusively reserved to wines grown and made in the Champagne region' (Stanziani, 2004, p. 157). In 1905 a general law on fraud and falsification was applied specifically to wine and used by grapegrowers as the basis for early demarcation – but it is worth noting that this law was mainly designed to protect consumers. However, by 1911 it was clear that legislators considered the needs of the producer to be identical to those of the consumer.

Stanziani notes, however, that there was an early debate about whether regional designation should protect just the grower or if it could apply to merchants also. For instance, could a négociant based in Bordeaux have regional trademark protection for wine which he marketed made from grapes grown in the Languedoc? Merchants argued strongly for the latter, particularly in Bordeaux and Champagne, but in the end it was the land which was protected.

The legislators of the time also debated whether or not appellations should cover organoleptic quality, or merely where the grapes were grown. There were strong arguments in favour of the former, but in 1911 the French parliamentarians explicitly excluded any such approach, saying their legislation did not 'seek to guarantee the uniform quality of the products it protects. It simply wishes, by establishing their origin, to prevent the appellation used to designate them from being fraudulently usurped' (quoted in Stanziani, 2004, p. 162). In fact, as will be seen later, the nationwide appellation system did attempt to influence quality, but not to define it, and this approach has evolved into a perspective which sees quality as primarily residing in the reflection of place and not in the taste of the wine.

Legal frameworks

As will be quite clear by now appellation systems are essentially geographic. However, that geographic nature varies from region to region. In Burgundy it is based very much on specific site, with a number of individual vineyards having their own AC. In Bordeaux, as in the northern Rhone, it is much more focused on the commune, or a small group of communes. In Alsace, as in Champagne, it is regional, covering a very substantial area.

As well as delineated area, however, AC regulations were also designed to preserve viticultural tradition and – as best could be done 70 years ago – to enhance quality. Thus only permitted varieties could be grown in a region; syrah, which had a residual presence in Bordeaux (Briggs, 1994), was prohibited there. Specific viticultural techniques were prescribed, so that sémillon in Bordeaux has to be pruned to seven buds on a cane, and only four methods of vine training are available in Champagne. Vinification methods may also be established, such as the minimum ageing of Muscadet on its yeast lees in order for the wine to qualify as being *sur lies*.

Three key controls aim to guarantee quality. The first is the implementation of maximum yields. Typically a yield in hectolitres per hectare (hL/ha) is set as a maximum, often on a cascading scale for quality so that red AC Bordeaux can be cropped at up to 55 hL/ha, AC Haut-Médoc at 48 hL/ha and Pauillac at 45 hL/ha. The core idea is that if the vines crop at too high a level the resulting wine will be thin and lacking in extract, so that the intention is that in the more prestigious regions yields should be kept lower to maintain the area's reputation. It is fine in theory but the system also provides for a variation of up to 20 per cent over the set yield (the *plafond limite de classement*). This is supposed to vary to take account of different vintage conditions but in practice becomes regularly applied, meaning that there is generally a dilution of controlling yield as a dimension of quality compared with the intention of the founders of the system.

The second quality control is to set a minimum alcohol level for the wine in each region. This is based on the idea that higher alcohol means riper grapes. It is an indicator of quality, but only a rough one. The final control is the *agrément* – a process of compulsory tasting which takes place in many of the AC areas. Theoretically wines have to pass a tasting test to qualify for AC status. However, the tests are applied by local winemakers, who are hardly without a potential conflict of interest (Norman, 1996), and what the wines have to show is not so much organoleptic quality than that they conform to the expected type of wines from the region – quite a different criterion. In the mid-1990s almost 98 per cent of wines passed the *agrément* – hardly suggesting that the lowest quality wines are invariably weeded out (Johnson, 1996).

The third way in which quality has been controlled is by limiting the grape varieties which can be planted in an AC area. This currently produces criticism both in Europe and overseas as being far too restrictive on producers. Why should a grower be forced to plant one variety if a far better wine could be made from another (Lombard, 2002)? However, in the early part of the twentieth century the problem was the widespread use of hybrid vines which only made very mediocre wine. The point of limiting the varieties which could be planted was less to preserve some notional and archaic vinous heritage than to end the spread of poor-quality grapes and thus reduce the volume of poor-tasting wine.

Some new producing countries are demarcating their wine regions – on occasions under pressure from Europe, which seeks to maintain a focus on the origin of wine, and to give legal protection to the 'intellectual property' of regional names. In the USA demarcation has happened with American Viticultural Areas (AVAs). These are based on topographic and climatic influences, and the boundaries are supposed to mark a geographically cohesive area. However, an AVA can be declared without reference to other demarcated areas, so they may overlap or lack contiguity in a haphazard fashion. A similar, though more structured, process is taking place in Australia following a trade agreement with the European Union, with the establishment of Geographic Indicators (GIs). However, in both countries demarcation is limited to creating boundaries. Restrictions on the use of grape varieties, controls on yields and prescriptive production techniques form no part of the process, and would be vigorously resisted by winemakers.

The impact and effectiveness of appellation systems

There is no doubt that appellation systems have had an impact. As noted, quality undoubtedly improved as a result of the national system in France in 1935, although the results may have been more ambivalent in other countries such as Italy (see below). They have also had other effects. In the Cassis region of France the AC regulations specified 13 possible grape varieties, but the effect of the quality designation has been to rationalize those, with a focus on varieties perceived to be good. Bourboulenc, authorized but seen locally to be rustic is barely used; marsanne, recognized as an improving variety has jumped from 4 per cent of the blend in white wines in 1980 to 40 per cent today (Gade, 2004). It is thus important to understand that demarcation systems are not necessarily static and conservative; they encourage wine regions to develop and modify with time.

How effective are systems which protect and market wine based on their region of origin? In Spain, Gil and Sanchez (1997) have suggested, the *Denominación de Origen* (DO – the Spanish equivalent of the AC) is more important than brand or vintage when consumers select wines, although for some segments (such as low income consumers, and older females living in urban areas) price is equally or sometimes more significant. In Greece it has been suggested that some consumers will pay a premium for wine with a designated origin (Botonaki & Tsakiridou, 2004). Tustin and Lockshin (2001) undertook a research project to evaluate the importance of region of origin as a factor in wine selection in Australia. When product involvement was analysed they suggested that for high involvement consumers region of origin had the most significant impact on choice (brand name was of less importance). For low product involvement consumers price was more vital – though after that region was also relevant. Certainly, the use of an appellation adds value for the producer; it has been noted in the Aragon region of Spain that the 51 per cent of DO wines produced account for 80 per cent of the worth of sales (Sanjuan & Albisu, 2004).

However, there has been substantial criticism of AC systems in recent years – and most noticeably about the restrictions it places on producers (for a good summary see Jefford, 2002a). Thus, for instance, in Beaujolais the only available red grape variety is the unfashionable gamay; the ability to plant cabernet sauvignon or shiraz could enable local producers to expand markets, rather than send unsold wine for compulsory distillation (Lombard, 2002). Additionally there are claims that the system impedes, rather than enhances, actual product quality (Lombard, 2002). Some have suggested that by replacing the 'real' quality of the wine with a superimposed 'geographic' condition quality actually deteriorated:

> 'We used to buy on quality. The appellation controlée legislation caused the quality of Burgundy to fall' remarked the father of Yves Thomas (of négociant Moillard-Grivot). It is an interesting point, and perhaps true in the short term (Hanson, 2000, p. 94).

The expansion of the quality wine produced from a specified region (QWPSR) system to other countries also proved ambivalent in its results. The Italian equivalent of the AC system, the *Denominazione di Origine Controllata* (DOC) has been subject to much criticism on the grounds of unreliability, political interference (see Chapter 14) and because it had no organoleptic assessment as part of its process. This produced the paradoxical result that many producers seeking to make the very best wines worked outside the national quality system, so that they have deliberately relegated their wine to the designation of *Vino da Tavola*, in the process creating the idea of the 'super Tuscan'; an organoleptically higher quality wine with a lower QWPSR designation (Belfrage, 1999). This ambivalence is also reflected in variations in the volume of QWPSR wine produced in different countries. Germany classifies around 95 per cent of its production as quality wine each year while in France the figure is closer to 40–50 per cent (Robinson, 1999). Such variability cannot be explained by the assertion that more German wine than French wine each year is 'good'.

A further criticism relates to the problem of drawing lines on maps; who is in and who is out? The argument over the boundaries of the Coonawarra region of South Australia is evidence of the importance of this (Fish, 2001; Steiman, 2001). Coonawarra has traditionally been considered to make its best wine on a long strip of *terra rossa* soil; red soil overlaying limestone. However, grapegrowers with vineyards on the surrounding black, clay-dominated soils naturally argue that their wines are just as good. The situation is complicated by the fact that pockets of red soil exist outside the main central strip. When Australia began to draw up its GIs the initial determination restricted the Coonawarra designation to the red strip. This was opposed by a number of well-known producers, led by Brian Croser who had the very reputable Sharefarmers vineyard to the north of the strip, and ultimately the decision was overturned. There were problems for both sides in this argument; if red soil does produce better wine, then the inclusion of other areas will dilute the quality of Coonawarra wines and reduce the reputation of the best. On the other hand producers on black soil who have sold their wines at a premium for decades – using the Coonawarra name – suddenly faced the loss of that premium, and thus a substantial reduction in income.

A final issue is whether or not appellation systems actually guarantee quality. They certainly include regulations which tend to enhance quality, but in the end what they guarantee is origin. This, in itself, is sufficient for a number of European wine experts; the quality resides in the wine's *typicité*. However, for many wine consumers outside the traditional European wine-producing countries the typicality of a wine in itself does not prove the quality of what one is drinking (Basset, 2000). In this case quality is based ultimately on what is tasted in the glass (Charters & Pettigrew, 2003b). Consequently, the different perspectives on wine quality are not those of degree, but relate to the essence of what it actually is. Neither approach is necessarily right or wrong, but there is a total failure to connect between the organoleptic approach and that based on *typicité*. A variant of this dispute suggests that quality – as *typicité* – is primarily a device to protect producers (especially when they make less enjoyable albeit 'typical' wines), whereas the consumer has moved on from basing choice on the wine's origin to its grape variety (see Chapter 6).

Terroir

Defining terroir

Classifications and appellations operate within a legal framework. Terroir is more of a philosophical and viticultural idea, so that placing it in this chapter may seem strange. However, terroir underpins the process of demarcation so that the concept fits neatly here. It is also important to note that terroir is at the centre of a substantial current debate about what wine is, and how it should be understood. Indeed, whole books have been devoted to terroir, and 'understanding' its impact on what is drunk (e.g. Wilson, 1998).

Defining terroir is hard; much ambiguity surrounds the notion. The word is French, and has a relationship to *terre*, the soil, land or territory, but terroir itself is not identical with the idea of soil although many wine experts may make that assumption. It has been said that vines 'don't eat rock *per se*, but sip on mineral concoctions dissolved from them' (Wilson, 1998, p. 28). Traditionally there have been claims that Chablis has the aroma of the flint found in the vineyard soil, or that Mosel riesling is slatey (Desseauve, n.d. pp. 7, 199) although there is no scientific evidence that wines can assimilate flavour from the rock type on which the vines are planted (Gladstones, 1992). Literally, terroir can be seen as the area within which grapes are grown, but even that is imprecise, and deals only with the physical manifestation of the term. One commentator on the subject has offered four interrelated interpretations: the growing vine (nutriment); territory (space); advertising (slogan); and identity (conscience) (Vaudour, 2002, p. 118). That may seem rather abstruse, but terroir certainly does have overlapping meanings.

Terroir can first be interpreted as a strictly physical concept; in this context it means the entire natural environment of a vineyard. Vines respond to three environmental components (Halliday & Johnson, 1992). The first is the climate within which the vineyard is situated – a combination of temperature, day–night temperature variation, sunlight, rainfall, wind and frost. The second is topography. This includes aspect (a southerly facing slope in the northern hemisphere can dramatically improve the likelihood of ripening) as well as other natural features like rivers and mountain ranges, and those added by people, such as rows of trees acting as windbreaks. Finally, physical terroir includes the soil, which provides drainage and water access, a medium for necessary nutrients as well as reflected and reradiated heat. There are few people involved in wine production around the world who would disagree with this concept of terroir as the threefold physical context of the vine. More controversially, Moran (2001) adds a human element to this, claiming that human activity has adapted sites and had an impact on their relationship with the vine, so that it is incorrect to place more emphasis on geography rather than the cultural environment. Even in this case, however, the discussion is about the tangible existence of the vine and the vineyard.

The idea of the impact of terroir on a wine's character is taken further, however. It is possible regularly to taste wines made by the same producer, in the same way, but from adjoining vineyards, and notice differences between them. These variations, consistent from year to year, are put down to the distinctive terroir of the vines. Historically this was seen to be a result primarily of the soil in which the vines were rooted; more recently increasing emphasis has been placed on the topography of the vineyard, especially its aspect, as having a fundamental role in shaping differences between wines. Whilst this perspective is seen to be very European (and has its origins going back over five centuries or more), it is not exclusively so. Leeuwin Estate in Western Australia, renowned for making one of the country's best chardonnays, regularly base their premium wine substantially on block 20 – a specific vineyard which they have come to recognize consistently gives them more concentrated and balanced fruit than any of the surrounding plots of the vine.

Some wine producers take this notion of terroir providing differentiation further. It is not merely that the wine tastes different, but that it is – almost philosophically – a different object, because it represents a specific plot of land. In this way the physical substance of the wine is subordinate to its role as a marker for where it came from. (Some might see in this a similarity to the Christian concept of transubstantiation – where the eucharistic wine becomes the very blood of Christ). Wine is therefore considered to be an interpretation of that place so that one could argue that Cote Rotie is above all a wine from the 'roasted slope'. The fact that the wine is made using the grape variety syrah is incidental, and that variety is utilized simply because syrah has been established as the best medium for the interpretation of Cote Rotie as a place. This interpretation of terroir may well have its roots in the growing attachment to the land during the 75 years of depression and decline from 1870; if you fear that rural life is being threatened then to imbue your plot of land with a mystical sense of importance becomes important in establishing your own worth. In this way the land almost develops its own sense of personality (Vaudour, 2002), something which harks back to ancient spirits of rivers, hills and woods. Indeed, for some this view of terroir sees it as less a geographical concept than a historical one; it is a notion which is a continuing reinterpretation of the past – of the history of a sense of place – by wine producers (Demossier, 2004). It has been suggested that terroir is becoming increasingly important in an age of globalization as a counter movement, 'patrimonialization' develops. Patrimonialization expresses the idea that local heritage – including foodstuffs – is important and worth defending, and may bring together a wide range of individuals such as food advocates, high-involvement consumers and regional and agricultural lobby groups (Gade, 2004).

At this level there is clearly a relationship between terroir and demarcation. For those who consider terroir important a wine is good to the extent that it portrays that terroir. Quality is consequently related to origin and *typicité*. Thus, it has been suggested 'typicality characterizes a collective taste memory, which has matured over a long time, through several generations of people, and refers to geographically referenced products. It is the shared perception of how generations of people from a given place expect the wine should taste'(Vaudour, 2002, p. 120). Although terroir at this level is widely adopted as a concept in Europe, and often in the new producing countries also, its origin is shrouded in mystery. There is some suggestion that it has origins in the medieval period (Guy, 2003), although it has also been noted that in the early nineteenth century to describe a wine as having a *gout de terroir* was considered derogatory (Spurrier, 1998).

There is a fourth aspect to terroir which occurs when terroir is used as a marketing device. The importance of differentiation in a fragmented market as a means of promoting wine has already been commented on. For many producers the ability to mark their wine out as different from all others because of its origin can be invaluable. This is perhaps most apparent in Burgundy, where, for the very best wines (the *grands crus* and *premiers crus*), the AC is coterminous with the vineyard boundary; the vineyard, in turn may be owned by just a few owners, or even a single person. The need to distinguish site from site has spawned a number of books (e.g. Hanson, 1995; Norman, 1996) and regularly inspires tastings to compare the wines of different vineyards. This point has already been considered in the discussion about appellations. Environment alone may be insufficient to explain the reputation of a wine, so trade, scarcity and demand converge to enhance its fame (Vaudour, 2002). This use of terroir as an aid to marketing may not be relevant for most wines (see Chapter 6) but, it has been suggested, wine marketers are aware that the extra value they offer some consumers is in conveying this sense of place (Fridjhon, 2004).

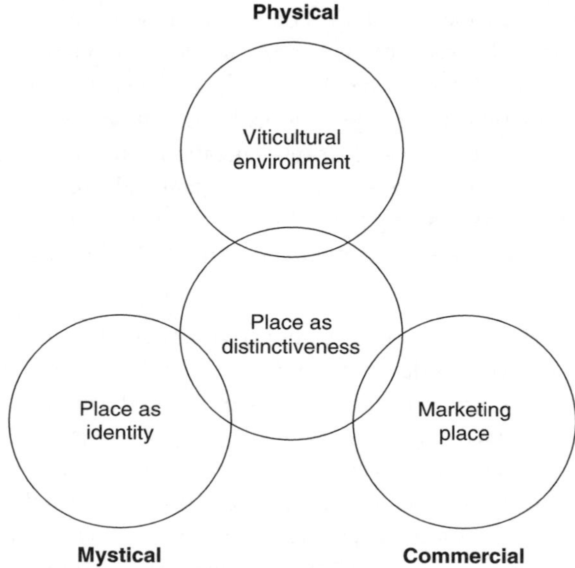

Figure 5.1 The interlocking concepts of terroir.

This fourfold interpretation can be envisaged graphically, as shown in Figure 5.1. In this example terroir is conceived as a tension between the physical (or viticultural), the mystical sense of place, and its role in marketing – with the use of terroir to make distinctions the unifying factor. Distinctions reflect diverse viticultural environments, they fix identity, and they are used as a means of promoting the wine as one which stands out from all others.

Debating terroir

It might be thought that within Europe terroir is a particularly French obsession – but consider these two quotations. István Szepsy, of Tokaji in Hungary, says that 'the terroir is the most important thing in the life of Tokaji' and the producer La Rioja Alta in Spain claims that soil and climate are very important in wines with terroir characters. Both of these represent a perception of what shapes their wine – historically and culturally, as well as environmentally – which is widespread across the continent.

Even outside Europe winemakers in the new producing countries are increasingly seeing the location of origin as a key aspect in shaping the style of their wine. There are many examples one could offer; for instance, Josh Jensen's specific selection of his limestone-based Mt Harlan vineyards for wines based on the Burgundian varieties of pinot noir and chardonnay in California, or Brian Croser's commitment to the idea of 'distinguished sites' in Australia, including the Petaluma 'Tiers' Chardonnay. There is also some evidence, in Australia at least, that consumers are responding and making the region of origin of a wine a major factor in their decision-making processes (Tustin & Lockshin, 2001). At the same time, bulk wine in Australia is invariably sold without a designation of origin – even for the more 'upmarket' small-volume boxed wines, such as those produced by Yalumba.

Nevertheless, the new producing countries have always been more cautious about terroir. With the ability to irrigate, the overall climate and the water-bearing capacity of the soil have been less important, so that the focus has been primarily on temperature (Hancock, 1999). There has also been a sense that Europeans use the idea of terroir to show how their wines are 'better' than wines from other places. This perspective sees terroir as elitist (Jackson, 2002), and designed to exclude others, rather than merely to promote good wine. This view has been reinforced recently by some aspects of European marketing, most obviously a campaign by Burgundian wine producers designed to suggest that non-European winemakers will never make wine of the same quality as Burgundy because they cannot replicate its terroir (see Chapter 3). Conversely there are also those who remain sceptical that terroir has any impact whatsoever on the taste of wine. The Canadian oenologist and wine writer Ron Jackson has commented that 'terms such as terroir (to describe flavours supposedly derived from particular vineyard sites) are figments of the imagination' (Jackson, 2002, p. 194). Yet despite this apparent 'European/non-European' dichotomy, even within the new producing countries there are differences of approach. It has been suggested that Californian wine producers are particularly inclined to follow the European lead (Matthews, 2002), and certainly any visitor to South Africa is struck by the regularity with which winemakers there refer to terroir in discussing their wines.

Further, it is significant that whilst the term terroir is widely used, how it is understood in practice – even at the physical, viticultural level – may vary. The Champenois, for instance, regularly promote the terroir of their region, so that a promotional brochure has a section headed 'A very special terroir' (Anon., 1998). However, Champagne is a blended wine (with up to 140 different components for, say, Moët et Chandon non-vintage brut), the region stretches over 70 km with a number of topographies, and it is an area where it could be argued that – except for climate in the very broadest sense – the production methods used are far more instrumental in shaping the wine than the individual sites from which the grapes come. Selling the terroir of Champagne is romantic but the concept bears little relationship to the distinctions made by Burgundians between the 27 ha of le Montrachet, Batard Montrachet and Chevalier Montrachet, each vineyard producing nuances which mark its wine out from the other two. Terroir, consequently, informs the AC system (a legal framework) yet there is no legal definition of the concept (Hancock, 1999), and conflicting understandings of what it means in practice. It has, indeed, been observed that in the nascent AC systems courts and legislators were prepared to define the physical components of a demarcated region (boundaries, grape varieties and viticultural practices) but refused to determine the organoleptic characters imparted by terroir (Stanziani, 2004). Indeed, such is the indeterminacy of the Champagne terroir that one popular writer has suggested that Champagne producers could move from producing a homogeneous product to one where the reflection of local terroirs would offer more individuality and interest (Jefford, 2002a).

What this also results in is the fact that different wine professionals may use the same language, promoting the notion of terroir, but defining different things. The author Lawrence Osborne (2004) comments on two producers in the Languedoc region of France, Aimé Guibert and Jean-Pierre Jullien, both of whom promote *vins de terroir*. Guibert, however, a former businessman and incomer to the region, has imported non-indigenous varieties to his winery, Mas de Daumas Gassac, such as cabernet sauvignon from Bordeaux and viognier from the Rhone valley. These, however, he argues make a wine which reflects the place where the vines are planted. Jullien, whose family have made wine for many years and who is steeped in the often confrontational viticultural history of his region, uses the traditional local varieties such as picpoul and cinsault – because these are the varieties of the terroir, of the local place. For Guibert the terroir is the environmental impact of the vineyard on the wine; for Jullien it is the complete sense of place, including its history (Osborne, 2004).

Terroir: A small producer's perspective

Much has been written by the academics and the opinion leaders of the wine world about the relevance of terroir. What do the less well-known think it is? Jean Pierre Faixo runs a family business with his wife and son at Paziols, a small town in the far south of France. The family have about 25 ha under vine, and make a range of wines under local appellations. Terroir, for him, is a complex and multi-layered concept.

First, it is the exposure of the true nature of the soil; the grape variety is the conduit for the vineyard. Thus the vine roots need to probe deep down; the wine should show the composition of the soil. This is 'in order to get the taste of the minerality – the best mineral qualities of the terroir'. You can only do this if you keep the yields low. Additionally the vinification of the grapes translates the terroir into wine. This means you have to experiment with your different sites, and you have to keep samples of wines for many years, in order to trace how the wine develops, and how the terroir continues to be revealed in the wine.

Jean-Pierre and his family make four wines under their local appellation. Two of them, carrying the name of their brand, the Domaine de Roudene, have labels which are identical in appearance, except that one is red, and one is blue. When asked about the difference they explain that each comes from a different terroir; 'taste them, and they are different', so they are selling the customer the ability to drink two distinct places. However, there is no indication of this on the bottle, and thus nothing to help the consumer understand how or why the wines are individual. Jean-Pierre counters by explaining that they explain to their customers the difference, and their agents can do the same. However, only 15 per cent of their customers have direct contact with them at the cellar door, which places a lot of responsibility on the agents to understand and transmit such a complex idea.

Terroir is used across the world as a justification for and endorsement of the quality of wine. Another interpretation, however, may be that when a wine, or an entire region, becomes successful the profits of that success are put back into maintaining and improving quality. In practice that may mean improving the processes used for production (better clones, more new barrels, the most up-to-date equipment). That in turn enhances quality – but the enhanced quality is credited to the quality of the vineyard and/or the region rather than better technology (Beverland, 2005).

Conclusion

Notions of terroir and demarcation spring from specific historical circumstances around the decline of viticulture (in France especially) from 1870 onwards. Other specific historical circumstances have given the concept a transnational significance (across Europe) and – in negotiation about wine worldwide – an international dimension. This has led to a focus on wine expressing place which may be in conflict with a more modern consumer-focused perspective that makes the primary goal of wine to be that it tastes good. Both approaches are now bound up in marketing conflict as countries seek ever more focused ways to sell their wine in a world where there is now substantial over-production.

Classification offers another means to assist in marketing wine – but it too is limited in approach, generally relating potential quality imprecisely to price, or possibly an expert evaluation of a vintage. All of these processes reflect an attempt to fix the quality of wine, an aesthetic product in which the concept of and criteria for quality are notoriously misunderstood (Charters & Pettigrew, 2002; 2003a).

Bibliographical note

Markham (1998) offers an excellent introduction to the origins and impact of the Bordeaux classification. Loubere (1990) does the same for the origins of the AC system. Wilson (1998) gives a detailed account of the geology of French wine regions but without considering inconsistencies and variations, and without truly fixing the physical role of terroir; Hancock (1999) gives a clear alternative perspective. Moran (2001) and Vaudour (2002) give more up-to-date and measured analyses of how terroir operates.

6 Modern wines

Past attempts by producers to add value to wine focused on where the wine came from, and how it could be classified. However, in the contemporary world as much emphasis is placed on other forms of enhancing its worth, particularly via the active branding of mass-produced products and the creation of aesthetically appealing high-premium wine. This chapter contrasts the large-volume brand, and icon and cult wines. It also considers how changing production – including the impact of new technology – and changing tastes have an impact on what is produced, specifically considering both the decline of fortified wines and the rise of varietal wines. The focus remains that of the wine producer; this chapter therefore needs to be considered in tandem with Chapter 10 to see how these developing approaches to wine have an impact on the consumer.

Large-volume brands

Dynamic branding, often accompanied by the simplification (reduction) of choice has been a major feature of much product management over the last half-century. It is generally accepted, however, that wine marketing has lagged behind other products in this respect – mainly as a result of the fragmented market wine offers. Yet in the last 20 years there has been a proliferation of large-volume branded wines on the market, especially in Anglophone countries and particularly – though not exclusively – produced by large companies based in the new producing countries. However, it is not the case as many wine critics suggest that aggressive branding of wine is a recent phenomenon; there is evidence that it was being developed by British distributors with Claret, Port and Champagne in the Victorian era (Duguid, 2003). Indeed it is ironic, given the current focus on the strength of brands from the new producing countries, that the first example of light wine which had substantial branding (in this case benefiting from downwards brand extension) was Mouton Cadet, developed by the owner of Chateau Mouton-Rothschild, Baron Philippe de Rothschild, in 1932 (Littlewood, 1985). This wine evolved from the large volume of consistently made cheap wine which sprang out of the new Bordeaux co-operatives in the 1930s and now sells 1 million cases per annum (Echikson, 2004).

Despite Mouton Cadet, generally volume brands were not significant in the light wine market until about 1990. The contrast with the development of spirit brands, which have moved towards international branding more obviously than wine, is telling. What has been central to consolidation in the marketing of spirits is that whilst different countries have different preferred product types (vodka in Poland, Russia and Scandinavia, bourbon in the USA, rum in much of Central and South America), within each product category a few brands have been established as worldwide leaders. With wine, at least until recently, national tastes have varied substantially, and the symbolic significance of wine (especially its association with status – the need to drink what is 'appropriate' – and national identity) have tended to focus consumption on a limited range in each country, and a range which may not be widely consumed outside that country. The comparison with gin is interesting. Five major gin brands globally account for 63 per cent of the market, and the five largest producers of gin have 75 per cent of the market share. Similarly, with rum the top five international brands jointly command a 41 per cent share of the market (Euromonitor, 2004). Such global reach has become very attractive for some in the wine industry where the top five producers account for less than 5 per cent of all sales; the ability to develop a genuinely transnational brand, recognized in many or most of the world's wine markets, has become a key aim. Stephen Millar, the head of the wine division for Constellation wines (the world's largest producer) has said that 'There is no Coca-Cola . . . of the winemaking world. We certainly intend to be just that' (Hughes, 2003). The advantage for consumers, of course, is that in making such wines widely available the security which is offered by branding is more easily accessible (Aaker, 1996). The desire to establish transnational brands has reflected the growing consolidation in the wine producing sector – a point noted by Demossier (2004):

> The growth of multinational and transnational corporate enterprises is a powerful force for global convergence of values and behaviour, especially in relation to taste. Secondly, these economic transformations have permitted a substantial increase in the quantity and quality of wines produced, and one of the effects of growing competition has been the transformation of wine into a high-quality product that is increasingly sold through chains or supermarkets (2004, p. 95).

Such a perspective, stressing consistency, convergence and commonality of style is not universally popular, and it has been suggested that a designation of appellation gains more consumer recognition than brand in parts of Europe, such as Spain (Sanjuan & Albisu, 2004). Nevertheless, again there appears to be a shift in the wine world. Whilst some European producers still complain about the danger presented by 'branded' wines from other continents, others realize that dynamic branding is popular with consumers and that it is necessary even in traditional wine-producing regions; the influential Bordeaux négociant Yvon Mau is one of these (Williams, 2004a).

Lockshin et al. (2000) have given one of the most helpful analyses of how a wine brand operates. They note that an effective brand helps to define a company's worth, but with fast-moving consumer goods generally, gaining large market share may be its most important impact. However, with wine it may be slightly different. Drinkers may search out less well-known products for variety, even though they use traditional cues in order to rationalize their choices. They also stress that the fact that wine is an agricultural product, subject to the vagaries of weather and disease, means that it cannot be treated in the same way as merely manufactured products; controlling the brand is a tougher challenge. Based on the work of Spawton (1991) they go on to suggest that brand 'hierarchies' exist; country, region, domain, producer, distributor and retailer are in descending order of importance. Each stage of the hierarchy can provide an element of the total brand equity, because each stage can help to foster positive responses leading to brand attachment.

What is a wine brand?

Given that there is no general agreement on the nature of a wine brand this seems to be an impossible question to answer. In their review of wine branding Lockshin et al. (2000), following previous marketing academics or practitioners, give five current definitions of what a brand might be:

- The consumer's overall concept of what the product is.
- The complete marketing mix (product, place, price and promotion).
- A series of associations.
- A way in which a product can be differentiated.
- A process enabling consumers to short-circuit difficult consumption choices.

It can be suggested that the last two of these are not what a brand is, but what it does. It is also interesting to observe that some of these focus on the consumer, but others are of benefit to the producer and it is worth recalling that the word brand stems from the mark burnt onto a bale or box of produce to identify the merchant or producer of the goods, thus symbolizing ownership. This is crucial, because brands exist not just because they offer the consumer something, but because they also give a benefit to their maker. Maybe, therefore, it is best to think of a brand as having a two-part definition:

1 It is a symbol or name which marks a product as clearly belonging to a specific producer or distributor (Kotler et al., 1994).
2 It is something which adds value for the consumer over the merely functional benefit of the product (Bradley, 1995). In the case of wine this extra value may be a reduction in the potential risk arising from purchase (Mitchell & Greatorex, 1989).

Professor Larry Lockshin, head of the Wine Marketing Research Group at the University of South Australia, goes further than this. He claims that with wine it is necessary to look at the 'Brand Constellation'. This comprises:

> all the potential label cues, which consumers could use in making a wine choice. The Brand Constellation would include the company name, but also some or all of the following: colour of the wine; country, region, sub-region and vineyard; price including discounts; varietal names or combinations; winemaker(s); and style (sweet, light, heavy, tannic, etc. – often on the back label) (Lockshin & Hall, 2003, p. 13f).

Some would argue that this goes further than merely the brand, and actually refers to the totality of the product; attributes, quality and value – which in themselves are more than just the brand. Other researchers have placed more emphasis on the end result for the consumer, suggesting wine branding is about creating an attractive lifestyle (Thode & Maskulka, 1996). In any event, it is worth noting that the longest continuously recognized brand in the world is probably a wine: Chateau Haut-Brion, from the Graves region of Bordeaux, which has been marketed under its brand name at least since the time of Samuel Pepys in the mid-seventeenth century.

Brands offer wine consumers a great advantage. The wine market is one of the most fragmented in the world. Enter a wine store, and you may face anything from 400 to 4000 different products on display. No other product type (with the possible exception of women's clothing) offers such a range. Wine also has an aesthetic dimension, where knowledge may be important (with concomitant opportunities for the superior display of conspicuous consumption (Fattorini, 1994) and for status-based distinction (Demossier, 2004)). This means that the uncertain consumer (which includes most drinkers) may find choice a threatening proposition. This uncertainty has been accentuated over the last 50 years by the wide range of new products appearing on the market, especially from the new producing countries. For consumers who are unable or unwilling to engage in information-seeking activity the use of brands can give security, which can be obtained without undertaking wine education courses or reading about the product (Lockshin, 2002). Thus, in commercial research carried out in the United Kingdom, it was suggested that 48 per cent of customers use brand as a primary influence on product selection, and 25 per cent use price. Fewer use country of origin and variety. Consumers therefore see taste and familiarity as providing them with most security rather than price and even more than where the wine originates (Evans, 2004).

However, the large-volume wine brand is not universally popular in the wine world. Many recent commentators have complained that it reduces the diversity and excitement of the product (e.g. Atkinson, 1999; Goode, 2005; Jefford, 2004). The argument focuses on three different issues. The first is that very technically 'correct' wines tend to taste the same; thus the wines lose their individuality – which is related to the fact that winemakers increasingly travel the world to work, and production techniques are becoming more standardized. Related to this is the fact that the wines are typically simple and fruity, lacking the complex flavours that many more highly involved consumers seek; rather, it is suggested, large-volume branded wines are made to appeal to a kind of 'lowest-common-denominator drinker'. Finally there is the complaint that because of their standardization they are obliterating the sense of place – the typicité – that quality wine should have (Demossier, 2004). To a certain extent – though not entirely – this criticism parallels a desire to protect traditional wine styles, especially those from Europe, combined with a criticism of the product of the new producing countries. This parallel is not absolute, however. There are French wines, particularly those made in the south, which critics would object to, and there are certainly wines from California, New Zealand and Australia that the critics admire (Jefford, 2004). Others are more subtle in their objections. An American critic, Larry Walker, comments that whilst he would not choose to drink the large-volume brands they are at least fresh and palatable, unlike many of the fault-ridden wines of the past. He adds that they deliver pleasure at a reasonable price and are increasingly ensuring that former non-wine drinkers are coming to enjoy the product (Walker, 2005). Walker and other commentators like the South African Michael Fridjhon (2004) claim that large-volume branded wines and artisanal, terroir-focused wines are now two distinct products, the one catering for the mass of the drinking public the other for a small group of connoisseurs. As suggested in Chapter 3, however, it could be argued against this view that, whether as a luxury product or a mass-produced commodity, premium wine serves both to satisfy an aesthetic demand from drinkers – the delivery of good taste – and allows for forms of social differentiation, so that both large-volume brands and more expensive wines are two aspects of the same product.

Cult and icon wines

Icon wines are those which are perceived to be the greatest expression of wine production a country or region (even perhaps the world) can attain. In Australia they are given a monetary value of Au$50 or greater (Geene et al., 1999), although such a crude analysis may well be eschewed by many wine critics. In any event, icon wines are expensive and are therefore very desirable for a wine producer. A cult wine is an icon wine of sorts, but whereas an icon wine may be decades or (as in the case of *cru classé* Bordeaux) centuries old, a cult wine tends to be of very recent origin, and indeed much of its appeal lies in the fact that few other people have heard of it. To this extent icon and cult wines may reflect the marketing idea of fashions (mid-term) and fads (short-term) (Kotler et al., 1994), although there is no reason why a faddish wine cannot become a fashionable wine, and ultimately a long-established classic.

Cult wines

A cult wine in the making

The following is an extract from the wine list of an Australian distributor, 'The Spanish Acquisition', based in Melbourne.

Domino de Pingus (Pingus, 2001)

With only six vintages released, Pingus has already joined that elite club of producers whose wines combine a true sense of their origins with fiercely singular personalities. While other wines from Rioja and Ribera del Duero had achieved international recognition, Pingus was the first wine to transcend traditional Spanish winemaking. Peter had created a great, mammoth, supple testament of a wine – in short, a new archetype. With only a few vintages released, Pingus has already joined that elite club of producers – Raveneau, Chave, Giacosa – whose wines combine a true sense of their origins with fiercely singular personalities.

Pingus was established in 1995 by Peter Sisseck, who had already made a name for himself as winemaker at Hacienda Monasterio. He located three separate plots, each containing very old vines of Tinto Fino, and established the winery. His aim was to produce 'an unmistakably Spanish, terroir-driven wine . . . a garage wine'.

Peter's tiny production of fewer than 500 cases comes from three parcels of ancient, head-pruned Tempranillo vines. His true genius is demonstrated in the vineyard. The gnarled old vines have been carefully husbanded back to health – the trunks straightened, lowered and pruned back to 1–2 buds per stump. Yields tend to an incredibly low 9 hL/ha.

'Tinto Fino is important,' he explains. 'A lot of cuttings of Tempranillo have come in from Rioja, so not all vineyards in Ribera del Duero are Tinto Fino. There is a difference. All the vines in my plots are very old. They have never been fertilized nor treated with pesticides and all grow following the traditional *en vaso* system. They are perfect.' Like a top chef, Peter carefully seasons the young wines, controlling their exposure to oxygen and utilizing lees contact to give the final wines their exotic textures. After fermentation in large wooden vat, the wines are raised in 100 per cent new French oak.

The first Pingus, 96, got 96 points on debut from Parker, and the rest as they say . . . Worth $700 plus on the open market, it is actually a profitable speculative purchase here in Australia – but we would urge that it be kept and enjoyed, for it really is a remarkable, individual wine . . . and a far cry from the 'made for Parker recipe wines we see so much of – all extract, oak and sugar but devoid of finesse or individuality'!

What this wine list describes is a cult wine, it has only been produced since 1996 – and it contains some idea of how a cult wine can be established. The wine needs to be impressive, an attribute which can be obtained by very low grape yields on old vines, resulting in concentrated flavours, enhanced by a substantial amount of new oak. It helps if the area in which the wine is produced is recognized as improving, as Ribera del Duero is, for then the wine's incipient reputation can feed off other wines in the region. So that it is popular the world over it is important that the wine is in an international style (thus it can 'transcend traditional . . . winemaking'). Production should be small, so it begins to attain a reputation that it is hard to obtain – and when it is bought its rarity value accords real status to the consumer. Finally – and this is where the element of chance has an impact – it needs endorsement by a key gatekeeper (such as, in this case, the American critic Robert Parker) whose recommendation of the wine adds an element of market certainty to the other factors which help to shape the wine. This combination of events usually results in a very rapid increase in the market price of the wine (at least on the secondary market, if not from the producer). Such a process is now international, as witnessed by the success of – amongst many others – Screaming Eagle in the United States, Torbreck in Australia and Valandraud in France, as well as Pingus in Spain.

The fact that a wine attains cult status should not be seen as a condemnation. It is a precondition of such wines that they are good quality and very intense, although that is not necessarily the same as greatness. They should be enjoyable. But to a certain extent (given substantial resources and access to appropriate land) cult wines can be shaped; only the celebrity endorsement has some uncertainty. It is, however, much harder to create an icon wine, which has much longer-term market recognition.

Icon wines

Beverland, (2003; 2004) has examined the critical success factors for icon wines, and suggests that there are six of these. A major criterion seems to be product integrity (which includes quality and attention to detail). Effective marketing is also a key issue, although paradoxically many of Beverland's informants claimed not to do any marketing. It may be (although this is not a point made by Beverland) that this kind of company relies heavily on the development of effective customer relationship management, but fails to see that as part of a marketing process. Beverland also highlights the importance of gatekeeper endorsements and notes the significance of a sense of history in the company but the kind of culture which seeks to build links with both the past and the present. Finally it is suggested that these companies have a 'value-driven emergence'; there is no grand design for their success, but it arises out of their strong commitment to the other brand components. It is worth noting that some of these are important to cult wines (particularly product integrity, endorsement and relationship marketing).

Interestingly Beverland's (2003; 2004) analysis is mirrored by a historical perspective – in this case on the development of the Champagne industry during the nineteenth century. Guy (2003) comments on the adoption of advanced marketing techniques, and explicitly highlights the use by the Champenois of relationships with clients to promote their wine. Endorsements (in this case primarily from royalty or nobility) were also used as a promotional tool. She further observes that the Champenois explicitly used their history to enhance the cachet of their product (especially in the development of the myth of Dom Pérignon), yet at the same time allowed Champagne to be seen as the wine of the modern world so that it became the appropriate drink with which to salute modern inventions such as planes in the first decades of the twentieth century. Crucially, Champagne was promoted as a quality wine, with great attention to process (and the application of modern technology), and that commitment to quality as a value, attached to respectability, drove much of the development of the product.

Creating an modern icon wine

There are also those who would like to 'create' an icon wine today (presumably skipping the role of cult wine). In a recent press release the Australian company Evans and Tate announced 'the keenly anticipated domestic release of their Redbook Chardonnay 2001' produced in the Margaret River region of Western Australia. This is a wine which claims to be the 'ultimate expression' of their white wines, 'the very apex of our art'. This wine has been the result of a project with the University of Western Australia using modern 'scientific' viticultural techniques to locate the best sites for the wine, which in turn allows them to shape the 'flavour precursors' to make the highest-quality wine. The company's executive chairman, Franklin Tate, noted that 'whilst Margaret River currently produces superb chardonnay, I believe that our children will live in a society where icon Chardonnay is synonymous with Margaret River around the world'. It may not therefore be this wine which becomes an icon wine, but the region at least can attain that. The recommended retail price for the Redbook Chardonnay is Au$62.95 – putting it above the Australian industry's threshold for icon status.

The critical distinctions between cult and icon wines are that the former have little track record. Those who buy them are gambling that they will develop one. Other differences emerge from Beverland's (2003; 2004) analysis. The sense of history (inevitably), the 'bridging' culture and perhaps value-driven emergence are less obvious with cult wines, although with time they may attain them. It is interesting that Beverland (2004, p. 458) suggests that a sense of history can be created. New Zealand wineries of comparatively recent origin will develop the story that they have been 'pioneers', the first to exploit a region or a variety, in order to attain a form of differentiation. It can also be suggested that cult wine producers eschew advertizing; perhaps this results from the low volumes often produced, which mean advertizing is not cost effective, or it may be that in trying to create a sense of exclusivity for the wine they want to offer the cognoscenti the chance to discover something that the regular premium wine drinker knows nothing about. Icon wine producers may advertize, though not to stimulate sales so much as to reinforce brand awareness and an appropriate image.

Changing styles

The impact of new technology

Technological development has had an impact on wine styles throughout history; the development of barrels as storage by the end of the first century AD, the use of distillation to create fortified wines about 1400 years later, and the use of cork and bottle to stimulate sparkling wine production in the seventeenth century. However, the pace of oenological change has quickened substantially in the last 60 years, and this has allowed the development of more variation in wine styles than previously.

There are five related technological factors which have recently had an impact on the characteristics of wines. The first stems from a clear understanding of the importance of hygiene in the cellar in order to minimize wine spoilage. Connected to this are two other developments: the greater use of anaerobic handling, to preserve freshness in the wine, and the ability to keep wine cool – especially during fermentation – which preserves its more fruity aromatics. These together result in styles of wine which are cleaner and fruitier than wine tended to be in the past. Whilst good hygiene is adopted as best practice the world over, there has been a greater tendency to focus on overt fruit characters more in the new producing countries (with the result that European countries are often said to make wines with more developed, secondary or savoury aromas).

The fourth technological development has been the ability to improve the stability of wine – even, ultimately, to be able to filter it so finely that yeast cells are extracted from it. The impact of such filtration is that wines are less likely to spoil, and especially that sweet wines can be made without the danger of refermentation in the bottle or other damage occurring. This resulted in the post-war popularity of off-dry and medium-dry wines which appealed to consumers in an age of increasing sugar consumption. Steen in South Africa, liebfraumilch in the UK and white zinfandel in the United States are all manifestations of this phenomenon. Even today, as sweet wines are increasingly seen to be more unfashionable, producers regularly make a 'dry' chardonnay, but leave 6–8 g/L residual sugar in it; barely detectable sweetness, but enough to add softness and smoothness to the wine.

The final development is less a new technology than a reworking of an old one. Oak barrels have been the main storage vessel for wine for over 2000 years. For much of that time the barrels would be reused many times, so that whilst the wine's flavour developed due to oxygen contact during storage; it was also an effective way to encourage natural stability and clarity in wine. The danger of reusing old barrels was the increased risk of microbial spoilage which could ruin the wine. The richer producers, however, could change their barrels more frequently, and with new barrels came a greater flavour of new oak – the spicy, creamy, perhaps vanillin or coconutty characters which are perceived to marry so well with many white and red grape varieties such as chardonnay and cabernet sauvignon. As it became clear that such wines were popular with consumers so the use of new barrels became much more widespread – but now oaked with the primary aim of providing flavour enhancement and complexity, rather than merely for storage or stability. However, the cost of barrels made them prohibitive for use with the cheapest wines. As a result other techniques were used to impart oak flavour without the cost. Hanging bags of oak chips in fermentation tanks, or macerating the wines with oak staves are key ways of achieving this. Thus wines could be created which offered the consumer modified, perhaps enhanced, oak-derived flavour for minimal cost. The excessive use of oak is regularly condemned by critics and it may be that its use has declined somewhat in Australia and the United States over the last decade or so, but – as the note about Pingus above suggests – it seems that such wines retain continuing popularity with the consumer.

Varietal wines

One of the major changes in the promotion of wine over the last 50 years has been the switch from focusing on a wine's origin to the grape variety or varieties used to make it. Varietal labelling first appeared in the United States under the influence of Frank Schoonmaker (Robinson, 1999); trying to pinpoint the style of a wine by knowing the grape variety used seemed easier to consumers than coming to grips with generic 'Burgundy' or 'Hermitage'. Additionally, in an effort to improve quality in the less established winemaking countries there was a focus on using 'classic' varieties rather than grapes with less well-defined characteristics (Robinson, 1999). It is worth noting, however, that varietal versus origin labelling is not necessarily an old world/new world split. Parts of Italy and Germany (as well as Alsace in France) have always emphasized the grape variety in describing their wines. Nevertheless some European producers, with a perspective that sees the quality as being rooted in place, and perhaps fearful of competition from the new producing countries, have been actively attempting to reduce its use. In the late 1990s there was even a proposal in France to forbid producers from including the name of a grape variety on the label, an idea which was unsuccessful and which is increasingly ignored as producers of appellation controlée (AC) wines seek to maximize the marketability of their product by specifying the variety's name. Varietal labelling is now becoming dominant, particularly because it is easy for consumers to understand. However, it has been argued that for an effective wine brand to exist focusing on the origin – which presupposes that some sites are better than others – is more beneficial than variety, which produces lowest-common-denominator wines and ignores the aspirational side of wine consumption (Atkinson, 1999).

It is instructive to understand the deeper differences between varietal and origin-based labelling. The latter is established on the agriculture, produce and the terroir concept; place, one's identity and a sense of tradition all feature. Varietal labelling, on the other hand, presents a product with 'ease of understanding' the aim, to make it consumer-friendly. Therefore, to the extent that there is a dichotomy between origin and variety it relates to much deeper-rooted approaches to wine than merely the rejection or embracing of change.

A case study in change: The decline of fortified wines

Changing tastes are reflected in changes in the consumption patterns of wine styles. Fortified wines were first developed about 300 years ago when it was realized that the addition of distilled grape spirit would halt fermentation. The resulting wine was protected against bacterial damage which made it ideal for use on board ships during the age of European imperial expansion. The wine was also, at least if fortification occurred before the end of fermentation, sweet – a greatly prized characteristic. In the eighteenth century, Port became the English gentleman's drink, Madeira was popular on both sides of the Atlantic and a century later Sherry had become one of the favourite beverages of British society (Johnson, 1989).

In a number of non-wine-producing countries (especially in the Anglophone world) consumption 40 years ago was still dominated by fortified wines, particularly Sherry and Port. By the twenty-first century consumption of these wines had slumped, replaced in their traditional markets by light wines. The change in production of one of the lesser-known fortified wines is a good example of this. The volume of Marsala, produced in Sicily (a drink effectively created by the English), peaked in 1960 at 450 000 hL. By the middle of the 1970s production had halved, and by the end of the 1990s it was less than 125 000 hL. In 1997 less than 16 000 L of the higher-quality wine (i.e. that which is drunk rather than used for cooking) was made (Belfrage, 2001). Marsala is effectively an 'extinct' wine, with Madeira possible following close behind (Liddell, 1998). Meanwhile Sherry, whilst not yet extinct, has seen international sales drop by 53 per cent from the 1970s to the year 2000 (Cobb, 2001).

The reasons for this change are complex. Perhaps most important is the fact that fortified wines have high-alcohol levels: at least 15 per cent, and more regularly between 17 and 20. Both health and legal constraints (with random breath testing becoming more common around the world and stiffer penalties for drunk driving) mean that fewer people are prepared to drink fortified wines, especially away from home.

Taste is also a key issue. Increasingly consumers are preferring to buy dry wines – or at least wines that are not perceived to be sweet (Wright et al., 2000). With the exception of fino Sherry fortified wines are sweet. Combined with this is the fact that consumers are tending to look for fruitier styles of wine. Many fortified wines are oxidative in character and thus display less pure fruit aromas, so that for wine drinkers who learnt to enjoy Languedoc chardonnay or New Zealand sauvignon blanc these styles are unfamiliar. Fino Sherry especially, with its flor-induced characters of saltiness and yeast, can seem very strange when compared with most modern wine styles.

The combination of sweetness and high alcohol also means that fortified wines are generally not perceived to be food-friendly. Certainly there are supposed 'classic' matches between fortified wines and foods, such as Port with stilton cheese and soup with dry Sherry (Simon, 1996), but even these reveal some of the problems these wines face; the kind of formal meals which include a soup and a cheese course are much less common than they used to be. Thus, as is commonly the case, where just one or two wines have to last an entire meal drinkers are much more likely to consider a chardonnay and/or a dry red wine most appropriate.

Perhaps crucial, however, is the issue of image. When a new generation of drinkers began to develop in the 1980s, focusing on light wine, fortified wine was perceived to be the wine of the previous generation. Sherry was for 'maiden aunts' (Pettipher, 2005) and Madeira for 'old people' (Ray, 2001). The combination of unfashionable sweetness, lack of varietal labelling, perhaps even the brown colour they often display (rather than bright lemon yellow or deep plum) which signalled the fact that they were old-fashioned, together has made them unpopular.

Some producers of fortified wines are trying to reverse this trend. Port has not suffered the same decline in sales that similar wines have endured by careful positioning and opening up new markets, so that worldwide sales actually increased by 18 per cent from 1990–2000 (Cobb, 2001). Thus, they have promoted late bottled vintage wines very successfully in the United Kingdom whilst they have persuaded increasing numbers of American consumers to buy vintage ports. Sherry producers are also campaigning hard to win greater acceptance, especially for fino and manzanilla Sherries. The minimum alcohol level for these wines has been reduced to 15 per cent and the Spanish have actively promoted these styles with Mediterranean and tapas-like food (Pettipher, 2005). There has been, since the year 2000, just the first sign that this activity may be reversing the downward trend but it is too early to be certain about this (Pettipher, 2005).

Conclusion

Wine is not a static product; whilst some classic names can last for centuries generally fads come and go fast and fashions change – albeit more slowly. The spread of consumption in parts of the world, together with the application of modern marketing techniques, have resulted in a range of mass-produced products. These are designed to simplify choice and increase security for drinkers but are also perceived to standardize the product. The cachet and rewards of producing highly reputable wines means more producers are using techniques designed to 'create' cult, even icon wines. At the same time some other long-established styles are fading in popularity and may ultimately disappear.

Bibliographical note

This book is not a text book on branding. However, developing an effective brand is an essential part of modern wine marketing. A good general starting point on the nature and management of brands is Aaker's work, *Building Strong Brands* (1996). For a consideration of how brands operate specifically in wine Lockshin et al. (2000) offer an insightful perspective. An interesting historical investigation which exemplifies many of the ideas set out in this chapter and applies them to the Champagne region is Guy's (2003) *When Champagne Became French: Wine and the Making of a National Identity*. Beverland's (2003, 2004) work is the only major academic analysis of the idea of icon wines.

Part Three: The Wine Consumer

7

The motivation to drink wine

This chapter aims to analyse the reasons why people may drink wine. It suggests a threefold model, looking at the utilitarian (physical) benefit, symbolic reasons and experiential motivation, noting however that the latter two are most important. Much of the emphasis in this chapter is on using the paradigms of consumer research as a means of exploring motivation; however, consumer research draws widely on anthropology, sociology, psychology and history, and insights from these disciplines will also be applied, where relevant. The second section of this chapter considers the cultural context of consumers, their values, how segmentation can be applied to provide some understanding of the impulse to drink and the role of involvement as a motivational factor.

The exploration of consumer motivation then uses a consumer-focused research project to explore wine drinkers' own views on why they drink and a range of symbolic and experiential factors will be explored, including historical tradition, situation (including the importance of food), cultural factors, self-image, enjoyment and relaxation. It is necessary to add, however, that the focus of this chapter is on what prompts people to drink – not what prompts their choice. Thus activity related to the selection of wine, a major focus of consumer research, is not primarily relevant.

Introduction

In looking at the context for drinking behaviour given by the social sciences it is necessary to start with a caution. Usually the viewpoint of social scientists is that wine consumption *per se* is not the primary focus, but rather it is used as an exemplar of a more significant subject which the researcher wishes to address. This has been neatly summarized by Heath (2000, p. 167):

> A fundamental curiosity about most of what is written about beverage alcohol especially by scientists, health professionals and other researchers, is that so little acknowledgment is made that the great majority of people who drink do so because they find it enjoyable and pleasurable.

Thus, the main focus of existing research is inclined to be on issues of alcohol abuse, establishing status, or social relationships. However, it seems relevant in this chapter to consider wine consumption as an end in itself and not just as an aspect of aberrant behaviour or a tool of social interaction.

Consumer researchers utilize insights from the social sciences, but see wine drinking primarily as an act of product consumption and consider the consumer's engagement with the product as the keystone of the process. Drinking behaviour, therefore, must be seen in the light of the consumer's social and cultural context. Wine is often drunk as part of a group process, and it is a product imbued with substantial social meaning (Thornton, 1987; Unwin, 1996), which may vary from culture to culture (Barr, 1995; Charters & Pettigrew, 2002). This inevitably makes it more complex to analyse and increases the difficulty of interpreting its cultural function.

Analysing consumption

When you ask people why they drink wine they tend to come up with a series of answers. If you repeat the exercise a number of times you may see the same responses recurring, as suggested in Figure 7.1.

In this example, each of the responses has been grouped with a number of others. Broadly the first column relates to physical or utilitarian reasons for drinking wine (in fact these are the least likely to be mentioned, and the least important for most consumers). The second column details reasons which are generally experiential in character (sometimes called hedonic) – they link to what people feel when they drink. The third column can broadly be classed as symbolic; these factors are connected to messages we convey when we drink – either to other people, about how we want them to see us, or to ourselves, relating to the self-image we try to create. Note that this is not a neat division. Thus, for example, the impact of alcohol may be utilitarian for an alcoholic who craves the drug, or a factor in self-image for another drinker.

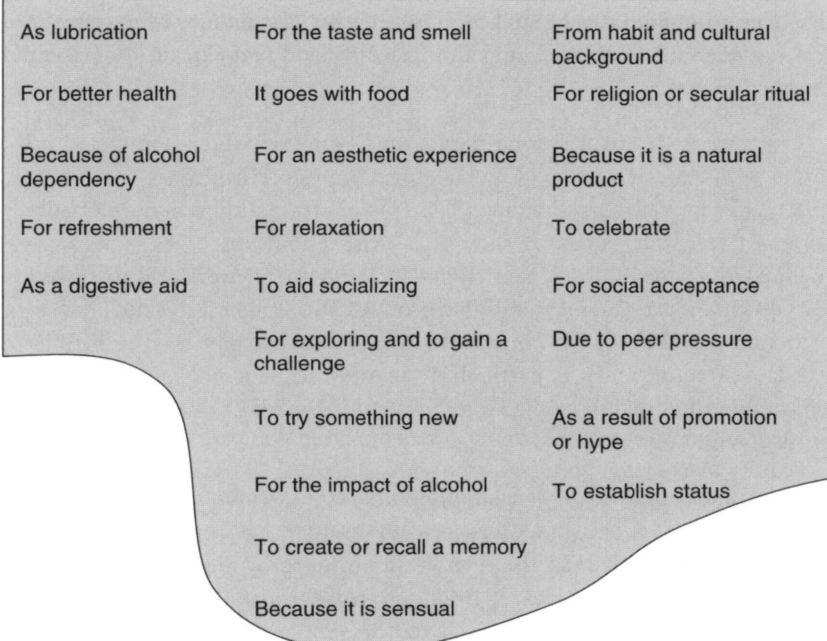

Figure 7.1 Why do people drink wine?

A framework for wine consumption

The discipline of consumer behaviour developed with a focus on the utilitarian dimension of consumption – that is, the distinct physical and functional benefits provided by a product. Its methods tended to concentrate on consumers' cognitive processes, particularly information gathering and processing as determinants of consumption behaviour. This includes, for instance, the stream of work based on Fishbein and Ajzen's theory of reasoned action (Ajzen & Fishbein, 1980; Fishbein & Ajzen, 1975), subsequently applied to wine by Thompson and his colleagues (Thompson & Vourvachis, 1995; Thompson et al., 1994). In this interpretation the consumer is seen to be very much a cognitive analyst of precise functional benefit, weighing up the pros and cons of various product alternatives before buying the most cost-effective in the circumstances.

Two challenges to this unidimensional approach developed. The first, stemming from a psychological perspective, came from the work of Dichter (1964), later developed by Levy (1981; 1986) and then others. This approach focused on the symbolic meaning of consumer goods and thus how we use products to convey messages about ourselves. 'Symbolic consumption' as a paradigm has produced substantial bodies of research into, and explication of, consumption behaviour. It has been suggested by Richins (1994) that the symbolic use of consumption can be split by separating representations of interpersonal ties (an outward directed focus) from identity and self-expression (an inner directed focus).

In the early 1980s a second paradigm developed which contrasted utilitarian with experiential and hedonic consumption (Hirschman & Holbrook, 1982; Holbrook & Hirschman, 1982). This interpretation was developed in a series of research papers to show that experiential processes (fun, amusement, sensory stimulation, excitement and enjoyment) were closely linked to the consumer's engagement with the product. It was also suggested that sensory cues are likely to be non-verbal and affective rather than reducible to words – a factor which is particularly relevant to wine consumption, where sensation rather than language may frame the drinker's engagement with the product (Solomon, 1990).

This triadic approach to consumption (utilitarian, symbolic and experiential) is regularly used in consumer research at present. It has been noted that there are cultural differences in the relative importance of the three purposes of consumption (Wong & Ahuvia, 1998), so that, for instance, in Chinese societies the display of close family ties may be a more important symbolic goal than in European cultures. Nevertheless, as a broad approach to consumption it has both some validity and some acceptance, so that we can use these three approaches – the utilitarian, symbolic and experiential – as a means of analysing consumption purpose. It is necessary to stress that no single act of consumption falls into just one category, nor is a repeated act of consumption invariably given the same motivational weighting at each repetition. Drinking a wine in solitude may focus much more on the pure pleasure in the taste, whereas drinking in public may be primarily concerned with conveying messages to other people (Groves et al., 2000).

One can conceptualize how this tripartite analysis works as applied to wine in Figure 7.2. Wine consumption tends to be weighted away from the utilitarian, but otherwise potentially equally concentrated on the experiential and symbolic categories, or possibly tending towards one or other of them depending on the precise situation of consumption.

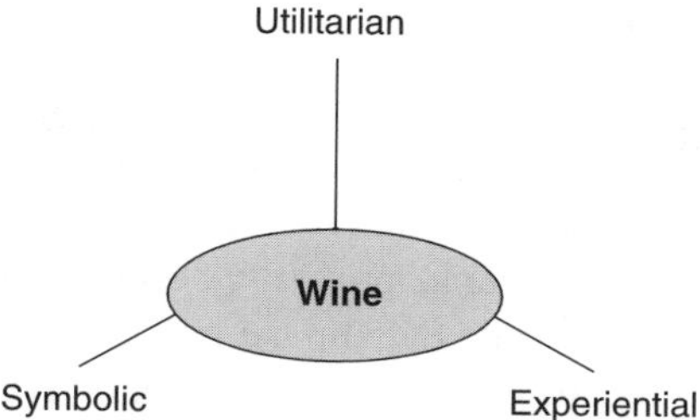

Figure 7.2 A purposive analysis of wine consumption.

It should be noted that consumption must be defined in the broadest terms: drinking, acquiring and collecting are all elements of the process. Buying is not the primary element of consumption, merely one – possibly minor – part of it; imbibing is generally the focal point of wine consumption.

The role of cognition, affect and sensory perception

It will be clear from this analysis that some of a wine consumer's motivation is very cognitive; that means consumption is thought out, and rationally stimulated (Thompson & Vourvachis, 1995). Other aspects, however, are more affective; broadly, they are more emotional, and may be less conscious than the cognitive responses. Thus, for instance, it has been suggested in Australia that wine is subconsciously perceived to be more sophisticated than beer, and therefore more appropriate as a female drink (Pettigrew, 2003). Further, some people's response to wine may focus on the sensory. There is, for example, evidence that the bitterness of alcohol makes wine inherently unpleasant for some consumers (Bartoshuk, 2000). This threefold series of responses – the cognitive, affective and sensory – underpins the competing motivational factors which influence consumers' overall desire to drink wine and their desire to drink a specific type of wine in a given situation.

What shapes the wine consumer?

This is not a text on consumer behaviour, and does not aim to explore the general basis for consumption motivation in detail. However, a summary of the factors which influence the wine drinker's motivation may be useful. This includes a brief consideration of their cultural context, the role of personal values in shaping consumption motivation, how segmentation can help us uncover the reasons for wine drinking and – crucially – the role of the consumer's involvement with the product.

The consumer's cultural context

It is well established in consumer research that the social and cultural background of consumers may have an impact on why they consume. Physical environment, for example, is relevant. A consumer is more likely to expect to drink wine in Italy than in Iceland, primarily because wine has been made in Italy for over 2500 years, while the climate in Iceland precludes its production. Cultural environment is also important; many religions proscribe the consumption of wine, the most well-known being Islam. Some political and economic contexts may dissuade people from drinking wine; for instance the traditional approach in Sweden was to impose high taxation on alcoholic drinks and limit their distribution to monopoly outlets to encourage people not to consume (Nycander, 1998). An individual's personal characteristics may also be relevant. Some people of Chinese and Japanese origins flush easily if they use alcohol, a factor which may make them less inclined to drink. Additionally the consumer's age may also have an impact. It has been claimed that in the United States whilst members of Generation X (broadly those born between 1965 and 1979) are reluctant to drink wine, seeing it as a Baby-boomer indulgence, members of Generation Y (born from 1979 onwards) are increasingly willing to drink wine – as long as it is red.

The consumer's values

One core element of consumer behaviour theory which relates to motivation is the impact of an individual's values. The idea is that motivation, and thus decision making in consumption, is guided by values held by the consumer and consequently the appreciation of wine is carried out in the light of satisfaction of those values.

The analysis of values in the process of consumer decision making began in the late 1970s (Gutman, 1982) with the application of the work of Rokeach (1968; 1973). Rokeach, a psychologist, investigated the theory of values and suggested the concept of terminal and instrumental values, the former being a desirable end state and the latter a preferable form of conduct which may ultimately lead to a terminal value (Rokeach, 1968, p. 160). Amongst the terminal values listed by Rokeach were 'a sense of accomplishment', 'a world of beauty', 'pleasure', 'self-respect' and 'social recognition', all of which have a plausible link with the motivation to drink wine. It is especially relevant to note the potential importance of wine in marking one's status and validating self-worth (Bourdieu, 1986; Richins, 1999) and establishing identity (Belk, 1988).

In consumer research, values are linked to the consumer's motivation by use of the 'means-end chain'. The idea of the means-end chain is that motivation, and thus decision making in consumption, is guided by values held by the consumer and consequently post-consumption evaluation is carried out in the light of satisfaction of those values. In order to make this link the consumer is asked a series of questions about why a product is important to them, and they are then probed further about why the issues they raise in each answer remain important. The point at which they can give no further answer is the point at which their core value, applicable to consuming that product, is reached. Thus 'the means-end chain is focused on the linkages between where a person wants to be and the means chosen to get there' (Gutman, 1982, p. 68).

Some wine-related marketing research has used the means-end chain as a framework for assessing consumer motivation. Judica and Perkins (1992) applied it to the consumption of sparkling wine (Figure 7.3). Their analysis concluded that accomplishment, self-esteem and family life were fundamental values sought after by wine consumers which were relevant to drinking behaviour. Additionally they suggested that for high-involvement drinkers 'belonging' was a core value to aim for. Nevertheless, their research should be viewed cautiously as they did not include happiness or pleasure as terminal values and other research into wine consumption suggests these would be

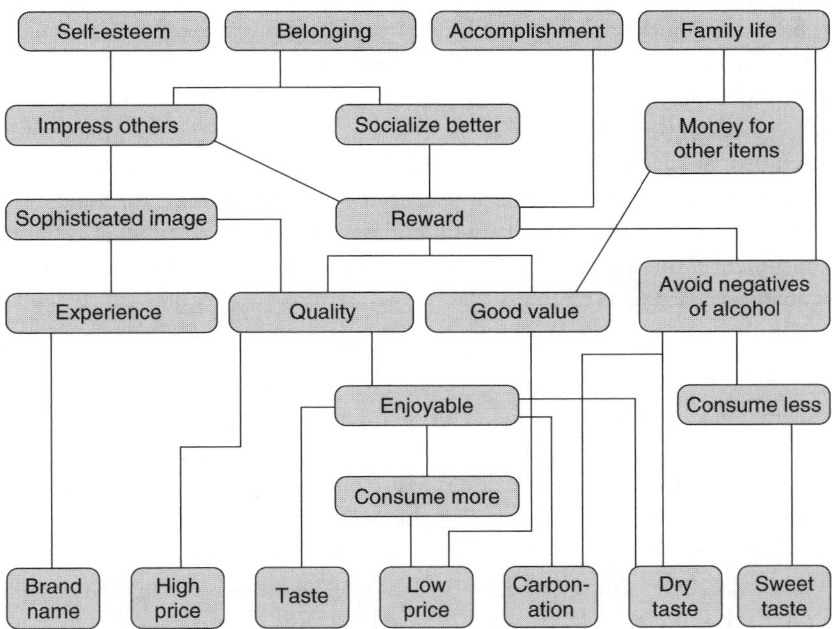

Figure 7.3 Laddering goals and values for sparkling wine consumption (adapted from Judica & Perkins, 1992).

of fundamental importance. They also use the idea of 'reward' as an interim consequence between the consumption object and the final values, and it could be suggested that reward is so broad as to be meaningless.

The means-end chain has also been used for segmenting consumers (Hall & Lockshin, 1999; 2000), again offering insights into why people may choose to drink wine. Thus, for instance, a segment categorized as 'beverage wine drinkers' tends to link their wine consumption to a key value of 'inner harmony'. Another segment, the 'connoisseurs', connects wine consumption to five values, including (*inter alia*): a sense of accomplishment, a comfortable life and social recognition. This idea of the means-end chain has also been used to correlate values, consumption motivation and the situation in which drinking occurs (Hall & Lockshin, 1999).

The consumer's involvement with wine

The concept of involvement is a useful tool for understanding wine consumers. A definition of involvement characterizes it as 'a person's perceived relevance of the [consumption] object based in inherent needs, values and interests' (Zaichkowsky, 1985, p. 342). The important part of this is relevance – emotional and motivational – but the focal point of the idea is on the consumer; it is not the product which itself generates involvement. Consumers' involvement may be situational, so that they are only involved with a specific purchase or brand, but our concern is with what is termed enduring involvement; the long-term relationship the consumer has with wine. Involvement is often described as either high or low (Zaichkowsky, 1988), but in practice (at least for wine) it is probable that it operates on a continuum, from the consumer who drinks occasionally, with no interest whatsoever in what is being consumed, to the connoisseur who reads about wine, visits wineries and goes on wine courses (d'Hauteville, 2003).

Some work into the impact of involvement in wine consumption has been carried out and involvement has been seen to affect the importance consumers place on price as an indicator of a wine's quality. It has been claimed that low-involvement consumers are more likely to rely on price as a cue and, whilst high-involvement consumers pay some attention to price, they are more likely to use grape variety (Zaichkowsky, 1988), although this conclusion has been disputed (Quester & Smart, 1996). As one would expect, heavy wine consumption has generally correlated with high involvement (Dodd et al., 1996; Goldsmith & d'Hauteville, 1998), at least in the English-speaking world. In these instances involvement has also correlated with education about and passion for wine, a desire to know more about it, and a pre-disposition to buy more and pay more for it (Dodd et al., 1996). High involvement with wine is additionally linked to a consumer's likely innovativeness – the willingness to search out and try new products – as well as the probability that they will become an opinion-former, and influence the less involved consumers around them (Goldsmith & d'Hauteville, 1998). Consequently, involvement has been shown to be a key determinant in the formation of consumers' perspectives on wine and their motivation to drink it. Critically, low-involvement consumers order the attributes of wine differently from the way that high-involvement consumers do, placing less emphasis on region of origin and style (Quester & Smart, 1998). Low-involvement wine purchasers, it has been suggested, are less cognitively involved with the correlates of wine (i.e. less inclined to seek information) than high-involvement consumers (Lockshin & Spawton, 2001). It may be that high-involvement consumers are more likely to pay attention to wine writers than any other consumers (Lockshin, 2002). There is a category of wine consumer, at the very highest level of involvement (perhaps less than 1 per cent of all drinkers), who ultimately seem to attempt to take on some of the characteristics of the wine professional (Charters & Ali-Knight, 2002). Consequently the professional practice of formal wine tasting can be embraced by a consumer as a way of indicating how highly involved they are with the drink (Fattorini, 1994).

It is hard to quantify the number of high-involvement consumers in any one market, although within the context of wine tourism it has been suggested that these drinkers comprise about 33 per cent of the total market (Lockshin & Spawton, 2001). However, no formal research has been done to establish a precise figure for varying involvement levels in consumption generally across various countries.

An outline of how involvement level may relate to consumption behaviour in an Anglophone country is set out at Figure 7.4. It is important to note that

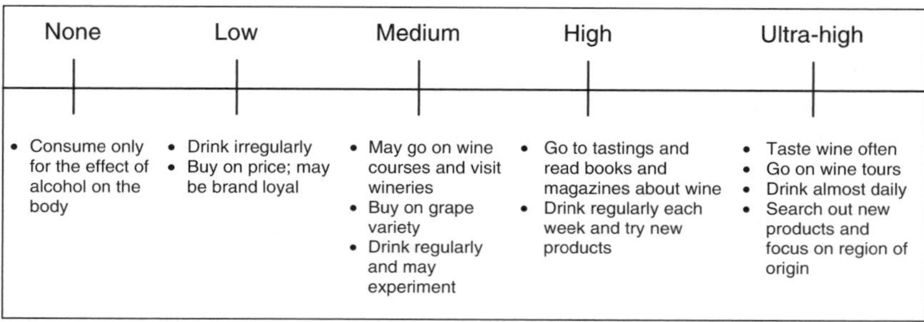

Figure 7.4 Involvement and wine consumption behaviour.

this is a simplified analysis and no individual fits precisely into such stereotypes. However, it does give an indication of the relationship.

Nevertheless, it is worth remarking that cultural factors have an influence on a consumer's involvement with wine. Whereas, in Anglophone countries, the amount of wine consumed tends to correlate with the level of involvement, in France there is a category of traditional wine drinker who consumes a great deal of wine, yet has a very low level of involvement in the product (d'Hauteville, 2003). Similar, high-volume traditional consumers in Greece have been shown to have very little knowledge about wine (Botonaki & Tsakiridou, 2004). This form of consumption is particularly related to the use of bulk wine, as outlined in Chapter 3.

Why do people drink wine?

The marketing perspective: Segmentation

We can start this section by observing that segmentation is a marketing tool which is not primarily about motivation. Rather it is a form of splitting consumers up into linked categories, in theory enabling marketing managers to target the ultimate purchasers of their products more precisely. However, in the process of segmenting wine consumers it is possible to learn something about what may inspire them to drink wine. Segmentation primarily applies demographics, psychographics (the emotional, value-based and attitudinal characteristics of the consumer) and purchase behaviour (such as price paid) to break up the potential market on the basis of generic differences between customers.

In the Anglophone world the most comprehensive attempts by academics (as opposed to private companies) to segment the wine market has been undertaken in Australia. The initial attempt at segmentation of this market was carried out by Spawton (1991), who proposed four segments of wine drinker:

- *Connoisseurs* are knowledgeable, regular drinkers with a broad spectrum of tastes.
- *Aspirational drinkers*, who focus on the social aspects of drinking. They are risk averse and like to learn.
- *Beverage wine consumers* are very keen consumers, with little desire to 'appreciate' the product and loyal to one style.
- *New wine drinkers*, who are yet to establish preferences. They drink socially, like coolers, and are unsophisticated.

Subsequent research developed Spawton's approach to segmentation, and suggested a group of consumers focused on 'enjoyment orientation' rather than the 'new wine drinkers' (Hall & Winchester, 2000). However, the exact nature of enjoyment was not examined in any more detail. More recently Spawton's segments have been modified further, with the suggestion of two more (Bruwer et al., 2001; 2002), which are 'ritual-oriented conspicuous wine enthusiasts' and 'fashion/image-oriented drinkers' (Table 7.1). This body of work therefore suggests that social drinking, enjoyment, conspicuous drinking (with elements of ritualistic benefit) and a focus on projecting a trendy image may be key motivators for different consumers.

Table 7.1 Comparison of Australian wine market segmentation research studies

Spawton (1991)	*Hall & Winchester (2000)*	*Bruwer et al. (2001)*
Connoisseurs	Connoisseurs	Ritual-orientated conspicuous wine enthusiasts
		Purposeful inconspicuous premium wine drinkers
Aspirational	Image concerned	Fashion/Image oriented
Beverage	Risk averse	Basic
New wine drinkers	Enjoyment-oriented	Enjoyment-oriented social drinkers
Main premises		
Risk reduction strategies and expectations can form a segmentation basis. The product meets psychological and social needs	Personal values and situation combine to create segments. Each segment desires different product attributes	Lifestyle is the key factor which links wine product to the attainment of values

Adapted from Bruwer et al. (2001, p. 107).

An alternative form of segmentation concentrates not on the attitudes and background of the consumer, but on the occasion at which the product is consumed. This perspective was pioneered in the United States by Dubow (1992). Dubow carried out cluster analysis to analyse why wine consumers drink in varying contexts, and concluded that the only motivational factor which applied across a number of situations was the taste of wine. Additionally he produced one specific segment focused on social drinking – with an emphasis on celebration and fun – and another primarily concerned with food enhancement.

Developing this theme the theory of reasoned action (which assumes rational consumers making fully informed choices about consumption) has been applied to wine drinking situations in the United Kingdom (Thompson & Vourvachis, 1995). Thompson and Vourvachis noted the significance of taste as a factor in drinking wine, although again there was no exploration of exactly what taste gives to the consumer. They further commented on the social dimension of wine drinking (Thompson & Vourvachis, 1995). Gluckman (1990) has also investigated wine consumption, and concludes that 'esteem' and 'self-actualization' are the most important needs of the consumers of premium-branded wines (Gluckman, 1990, p. 32). His focus on the inner-directed symbolic use of wine fills out the understanding of motivation by pointing out the importance of issues related to esteem and self-fulfilment, but he does not explain his research method or data collection process, and much of what he claims appears to be assertion with little evidence to support it.

Within Australia the approach developed by Dubow (1992) has been integrated with the idea of the means-end chain, thus linking situation with the consumer's values. Hall and Lockshin (1999; 2000) combine both perspectives by evaluating the drinking situation against its resulting consequences. They concluded that complementing meals, using wine to impress and enhancing the drinker's mood were situations in which drinking wine was considered positively.

The segmentation-focused research all stresses the importance of taste to most consumers, the relevance of social factors, the relationship of wine to food, the occasional need to impress and the benefit of wine in enhancing the drinker's self-image. Crucially, however, the weight attached to these may vary depending on the situation in which the wine is drunk, and other than categorize the main forms of motivation the precise detail remains to be filled in.

The anthropological perspective

Anthropological inquiry into drinks consumption has only really developed over the past three decades, and it generally considers all alcoholic drinks, rather than singling out wine specifically. Douglas (1987a) suggests that drink is significant primarily as a social act, and that it operates in three ways. First, for its celebratory role, where drinking is often used to strengthen social ties. Second, drink also allows us to provide a discernable structure to the abstract organization of our social world. Thus, for instance, a drink can be utilized as a marker for the division of work time and private time, and for group boundaries – who is in and who is out (Gusfield, 1987). A prime example of this is connoisseurship, which is used both to identify the drinker and to mark the quality of the wine (Douglas, 1987a). Thirdly, drink may be a tool used to help us escape the bounds of our current social world and instead to construct an alternative, better world:

> There is also a sense in which drinks perform the other task of ritual. They make an intelligible, bearable world which is much more how an ideal world should be than the painful chaos threatening all the time (Douglas, 1987a, p. 11).

Recently research has focused more on the experiential reasons for drinking (Heath, 1995; 1999; 2000), with an awareness that enjoyment is key to the consumer's experience of the drink and its taste (Peele, 1999), whilst also stressing its role in socializing. This research has also noted the transformative, inspirational aspect of consumption, which may at times be almost spiritual (Heath, 1999; Marlatt, 1999).

An interesting anthropological investigation into consumption in France has proposed the historic existence of four types of drinking behaviour (Nahoum-Grappe, 1995). These include the situational consumption of wine with food; social drinking (often away from the home); celebration and consumption for aesthetic ends. However, cultural difference has an impact here. Nahoum-Grappe (1995) focuses primarily on wine. An equivalent anthropological exploration of drinking in Australia notes that its basis in an Anglo-Saxon, masculine, frontier-type, rural society provided a tendency to drink beer rather than wine which only began to change with increased affluence and the influence of southern European migrants in the twentieth century.

The sociological perspective

Sociological research into why people drink wine generally falls into one of two categories (other than the view that it is merely dysfunctional behaviour). The first of these considers consumption behaviour, including wine drinking, as part of a greater analysis of society's structure. Important as part of this approach, and crucial as a contribution to the overall sociological understanding of consumption motivation, is Bourdieu's (1986) study of social differentiation. His thesis is subtle and complex but essentially is that consumers are classified by their taste and that taste results from the interplay of social origin, educational background and 'trajectory' (the direction of one's social mobility). All of this results in differentiation – 'distinction' as Bourdieu terms it – which marks out the social class and subclass to which we belong. These distinctions are made within fields of preference – specific examples of which could include products such as drinks, plays, clothes or cars. Bourdieu's study has a direct bearing on how the motivation for drinking is understood. He argues that if what we do socially is to attempt to classify ourselves, and be classified by those around us, then how we display our 'good taste' is critical. Consequently, Bourdieu claims, the enjoyment of wine generally and specific wines in particular help to establish where we fit into society; it defines the groups of which we form a part, and those from which we are excluded, or exclude ourselves. In this context wine, it has been claimed, is 'a food for hierarchies' (Demossier, 2004). Thus the consumption of wine is crucially about defining who we are, by differentiating ourselves.

Bourdieu's argument is solidly backed by empirical research, but it deals with the macro rather than the micro. Consequently it fails to account adequately for the selection of specific 'fields of preferences' made by individuals. Thus, whilst those with high cultural and low economic capital (for instance university lecturers) show a marked tendency to prefer 'legitimate art' (they become what may be termed connoisseurs), he does not account for why an individual may invest time in wine rather than classical music, or in poetry rather than the novel. Nor, within the fields of preference, is he entirely convincing about the selection of one product style rather than another; why, for instance, should the university lecturer prefer the wines of Burgundy to those of Bordeaux?

An alternative perspective is given by sociologists who, unlike Bourdieu, accept the existence of an independent aesthetic. In certain cases this standpoint situates wine as part of that aesthetic tradition (Grunow, 1997). Wine consumption is therefore considered to produce an aesthetic response, and a sense of pleasure. Grunow uses three traditions for this claim. The first is based on the work of philosophers who have concluded that wine consumption has an aesthetic dimension (e.g. Coleman, 1965; Fretter, 1971). The second is the sociologist, Georg Simmel, who argued that the form of a meal has an aesthetic structure; its progress is 'beautifully' ordered (Simmel (1910) quoted in Grunow, 1997). The third basis for this assertion uses the arguments of Amerine and Roessler (1976) – oenologists who argued cogently that wine tasting is an aesthetic experience. A refinement of this sociological approach treats wine as a commodity, albeit with an aesthetic purpose, which forms part of a 'lifestyle' for certain consumers (Demossier, 2004). In this case it defines not just the consumer's relationship with others but also shapes self-image and identity (Demossier, 2005). 'The "connoisseur consumer" then, doesn't so much keep up with the Joneses, as keep away from them. "Savvy society" . . . produces connoisseurs at all levels. A bottle of Frascati can be bought for £2.50 from ASDA and served up boastfully with the correct food' (Tomlinson, 1990, p. 27).

'Why do I drink wine?' A consumer-based perspective

What follows is taken from a qualitative research project which examined – amongst other issues – what motivates consumers to drink wine. A number of wine drinkers – including some wine industry professionals – took part in individual interviews or focus groups across Australia, and the resulting data was analysed to examine why people decide to drink wine. The informants for this project covered a range of levels of involvement with wine, from winemakers who drink every day and whose whole life is bound up with the drink, to very occasional drinkers with almost no interest in the product whatsoever.

The informants for the research expressed a number of reasons for drinking wine. These have been broken down into the threefold categorization of experiential, symbolic and utilitarian. The most substantial of the reasons, given by almost all of the informants, seemed to be the enjoyment of the drink. After that the use of wine as a means of socializing, and its role in accompanying food, were perceived to be key important issues. However, it will also be clear that some reasons for drinking wine tended to be more or less important depending on the involvement level of the drinker. Some motivational factors in particular only seemed to apply to high-involvement consumers.

Experiential motivation

Enjoyment

This was the major motivational factor offered for drinking wine; more informants talked about it, and those who did tended to give it more weight, than any other reason, whatever their gender, age or involvement with wine.

Peta: I enjoy wine; for enjoyment, relaxation, pleasure, fun.

Enjoyment comprised a number of related factors, including taste, the effect of alcohol on the body, and the intellectual challenge which wine provides.

Taste: Just as enjoyment is the fundamental reason for drinking wine, so taste is the major (though not the only) element of that enjoyment, as this extract from a focus group suggests:

Interviewer: But why wine rather than water or beer or . . .?

Nell. Taste.

Angela. Tastes better.

For the most highly involved this becomes explicitly an enjoyment of the complexity of flavours available. However, one point is worth noting at this stage; those drinkers who unquestionably made taste the fundamental reason for consuming wine tended to be higher-involvement consumers. Even when consumers with a lower level of involvement determined that taste was important it tended to be more integrated with other reasons for drinking wine, so it became just one amongst a number of reasons for drinking. Florence was one such person:

> Florence: For me it's taste but it's part of the whole experience. Usually for me wine goes with food. I enjoy eating – that's more than an experience of just fuelling the body. I enjoy good food, with good wine, with a complementary situation.

Alcohol: Many informants understood that alcohol has the effect of relaxing you, and felt that this was beneficial.

> Siobhan: I like the fact that it unwinds me at the end of the day. I do enjoy alcohol . . . giving me a certain feeling – just relaxation.

It is worth noting, however, that some would have preferred wine to be without alcohol. The pleasure that they took in its taste was such that they would like to be able to drink more of it, which they were not able to do without the possibility that they would damage their health or endanger lives.

Diversity and intellectual challenge: One informant, asked why she drinks wine, included the following in her reply:

> Danielle: I drink wine because I absolutely adore wine, I adore . . . the differences that you get . . . Every wine's different, every wine's got its own personality so there's always one that's going to stand out more than the others. And I really like appreciating the subtle differences between wines and understanding – evaluating – them I suppose.

The need for difference and the challenge of having to understand wine was less commonly given as a reason for enjoying wine, and again it tended to be the most highly involved consumers who were interested in these possibilities. Sometimes this ability to explore wine was connected with a sense of place, and the ability to travel to different wine regions.

Situation

There were a couple of motivational factors which related to the drinker's social context. Primary amongst these was the desire to use wine as a vehicle for socializing. Additionally, the relationship of wine to food was important for a number of informants.

Social drinking: This was a fundamental reason for drinking wine, for consumers at all levels of involvement:

> Neil: It's affordable and you can derive the pleasure of being sociable with it and it's readily available. It's legal, and it gives a good party atmosphere.

For Neil, in the social context it was the physiological impact of wine which was important – plus the fact that its consumption is licit and inexpensive. Repeatedly friends (rather than, say, business acquaintances) were singled out as the focus for sociable drinking. Additionally wine as a means of binding families – husband and wife or intergenerational relationships – was also considered very important.

Wine and food: Again, the link between food and wine was important to drinkers at all levels of involvement. Thus:

> Kevin: I really enjoy it. I don't drink to get drunk – and love having a glass of red or white with whatever meal is going on at dinner time. That's about it really. It's great on a picnic, or a barbecue, or something like that.

Whilst the wine-food match was a key reason for drinking wine some informants noted that they would drink it on its own. This especially related to certain types of wine:

> Ellie: Some wines aren't [food wines] . . . There are some wines that I wouldn't have with food but I would quite happily sit in a bar and drink.

There is a sense that this separation of food and wine tends to be more important for medium- and low-involvement informants. When high-involvement consumers acknowledged that they may drink wine without food it tended to be almost as a concession – it was an occasional event. It is possible that high-involvement drinkers, being aware of the medical recommendation to drink wine with food to minimize the harmful impact of alcohol, either tend naturally to drink wine with food, or at least are unwilling to admit to consumption in a 'less-healthy' manner.

Relaxation

The third major experiential reason for drinking wine was that it helps one to relax. This reason is often linked explicitly to some of the other reasons already outlined for wine drinking – especially the fact that it aids sociability and also the impact of alcohol on the body:

> Siobhan: I like the fact that it unwinds me at the end of the day. I do enjoy alcohol of a certain percentage giving me a certain feeling, just – you know – relaxation.

The relaxing effect of wine was also mentioned in relationship to food; a meal and wine were perceived by some to be peaceful.

Symbolic motivation

A series of different but related motivations were apparent when considering the symbolic importance of wine consumption. These included its ritualistic role, the way it linked drinkers to their past, how it helps to shape our image, and its significance in establishing status.

The importance of ritual

The use of wine in everyday rituals seemed to have two aspects for informants. The first was the use of wine to mark out the day for drinkers, helping to give a sense of short-term temporal structure, and also signifying the more substantial changes to existence and thus marking rites of passage.

> Rupert: When I finished [work] today I poured myself a glass of wine. I'd finished for the day . . . . I've often sat there cutting my vegetables for dinner, and thought 'oh, there's something wrong here, I haven't got a glass of wine in my hand!'

A glass of wine can symbolize the passage from the public, from work, from what you owe to other people, into the private and personal where you are in control. That marker is crucial for Rupert – and he notices if he misses it when he begins to prepare his evening meal (his time). Ritual such as this can also provide a sense of security for some people:

> Frances: Wine may be a habit for me at meal times particularly the evening meal.
>
> Interviewer: The way you talk about it – warmth, comfort – it's almost as if it's a sense of security?

> Frances: Yes, yes there is possibly that. An element of security. It's difficult. I've never really thought about it in those terms before so – the addiction idea – what it does for me.

In this sense wine drinking is a very personal thing. However, often ritualistic processes act to promote communal cohesion; perhaps with friends or even to strengthen solidarity at work. In the following extract Sue is speaking in a focus group which included a number of informants who all worked in the same organization:

> Sue: For instance, on Friday evening when we sit round and drink at the end of the week, just something sociable, just relax. And when you don't have heaps [of wine] or anything you just enjoy the social gathering.

In this instance the ritually symbolic obviously spills over into experiential consumption, with its focus on sociability.

A historical perspective

When asked why they drink wine a number of informants answered by placing their motivation into a historical context. The following comments – from informants with a range of backgrounds – give some idea of the range of perspectives.

> Oliver: Well I've found it great experience; I was born in Adelaide. I lived 20 years there . . . and I've spent most of the time [since] living in Europe and America, and now in Sydney. I like the social interaction with wine and experiences you can have, and I do enjoy the taste. And I like the experience you have with food so I think it's got a social interaction and enjoyable accompaniment to food and I think you meet a lot of nice people through it too.

> Dan: You'd probably have to say it's tied up being a wine waiter; I've sold liquor for a living.

> Frederick: I think wine for me is so much more than just a beverage. You know it's got 7000 years of history and that's just the most amazing thing. And that all has a role.

Each gives a historical context for his experience, but each of those contexts is subtly different. For Oliver, the historical perspective is broad but personal; it frames the more specific (and more important) social and taste-related reasons for drinking wine. For Dan there was a particular stage in his past which stimulated his interest – when he was working in the hospitality industry. Frederick, who is a wine professional, has a longer-term view; drinking wine helps to link him to a much longer tradition and fix his place, especially as one involved in the wine industry, in the flow of history. For most informants, however, this historical dimension to their wine consumption was focused on one of two processes; the first was the role of family tradition in establishing wine drinking behaviour, and the second on memory as a reason for drinking.

Family tradition: Many informants referred to a family tradition of wine drinking – and when they did, it was often the first reason they proffered for drinking wine. Martha, in the following extract, has just been asked why she drinks wine:

> Martha: The historic tradition in our family, absolutely – I was introduced to wine at an early age, it was put on the table at an early age, and it fascinated me at an early age. So I drink wine because [I have] an ongoing fascination with it and I suppose I might be looking for the ultimate wine – the sort of holy grail of wine.

Martha relates her introduction to wine drinking by her family in South Africa to why she drinks wine now, and to her continuing quest for the perfect wine. There may be a sense that in pursuing it she is trying to fulfil some family-set goal or repeat a sense of belonging which existed in her early life.

Memory: In a reflection of Proust's famous madeleine biscuit (Proust, 1973), one informant, commenting on the reasons for his fascination with wine, took a longer view – fixing what he drinks now in the distant past:

> Tom: I've always had a fascination with flavour, I suppose . . . smells more than anything else . . . I could smell lots of weird things. But as soon as my wife was pregnant I knew from smell . . . . I always remember being whacked as a kid for stopping to smell things. I used to smell everything . . . I think it's a thing we seem to forget a little bit. Smell has a magical link to your youth and places and times and things. It's almost meditative.

This offers a good mirror of the role of wine and recollection: people (his parents), places and events. There is evidence that of all our senses, smell is most closely linked to our emotions (Herz, 1998; 2004); this is possibly because the area in the brain used for processing olfactory stimuli is connected to the amygdalahippocampus, a component of the limbic system which is the part of the brain which manages emotional processes, and the recollection of emotional events (Herz, 1998).

We can develop this general idea of emotional recall by noting the memory of consuming particular wines themselves.

> Frederick: I was in Northern Spain in Basque country . . . overlooking . . . the Bay of Biscay, looking down over fabulous country. All these pergola vines everywhere. Stinking hot day. Had a little bit of a mild hangover because of being out dancing the night before, drinking a bit of whisky. But anyway we were looking at the wine – came into the winery. Mercifully the winemaker didn't take us into the winery and show us his bottling line or anything. He said 'come upstairs.' Had this big oval plate of anchoas – new season anchovies – with parsley and oil and bit of vinegar sprinkled over the top of them. He got his Chacoli de Guetaria out, he poured it in the ceremonial way – this sharp, green, acidic stuff into this glass. And in that moment, in those moments, in that hot, humid, glary climate with this wonderful, tangy sort of anchovy stuff going into your gob and a glass of this wine it was the most perfect wine in the world. And the fact that everyone else was there sharing it and experiencing it made it the most perfect wine and the most perfect situation in the world. It was perfect. Now to plonk that [wine] back in a wine show in Australia you'd probably give it 10 marks out of 20.

Within memory the symbolic importance of a wine may far exceed any intrinsic worth or 'quality' it may attain. This symbolic importance has a certain ambivalent quality. Frederick's job requires him to select quality wines. The event he describes is memorable for the entire experience and is one of his more enjoyable moments in the wine industry. Yet by any 'objective' measure the vinous component of the experience (which was the reason for his involvement) was of limited quality. The event also possessed a ritualistic dimension in the method of pouring the wine. It may be that ritual like this is important in fixing the memory and in framing the event as one worthy of later recollection.

Image

The idea that wine helps to shape our image seemed to have three elements to it in this research. One was focused on how wine fits into an overall lifestyle. Second, was the specific relationship of wine to consumers' image of themselves – whether a precise reflection of who they were, or more of an ideal of who they would like to be. Also important was the role of wine as a marker for establishing status.

Lifestyle: Some drinkers explicitly saw wine as an integral part of their lifestyle, and this was volunteered as a motivating factor by low- as well as high-involvement drinkers. In this way wine is an aspect of an individual's view about the way they want to live, and what is significant in their life. It may not be that wine is important on its own, but as part of a package of activities or interests which together are essential. For at least one informant the consumption of wine was linked, perhaps a little wistfully, with an aspiration for an improved lifestyle.

> Wendy: It's part of what we need to do to socialize . . . When we grew up we always had family dinners and we hear a lot about things now not connecting everyone . . . [families] have dinner at different times. I think it is important to have that time as relaxing. That's the nice thing about France, you have that two hour lunch everyday. I find with the way I live I have constantly to eat things – you have a snack all the time. Whereas if you have a two hour break, where you sit down and have a glass of wine and you have the full lunch that need is not there. Nurturing yourself with a bit of food. Work wise, and for peace of mind, you need to do that. Just stop rather than always [trying to] get to the next stop. Which is what we all do, we're all busy getting to the next stop.

Self-image: The idea that wine is a part of one's lifestyle appeared to be connected to the consumer's self-image. For one informant this was explicitly acknowledged:

> Don: Why do I drink wine? Wine is an alcoholic beverage that, I suppose, stands for a lot. Wine as such has a lot of attributes that make it align with who I am perhaps, who I want to be.

Self-image extends to the specific wine one may select. Belinda (who owned a wine bar) made a point of preferring (comparatively inexpensive) French wine over a reputable and pricey Australian wine.

> Belinda: It depends on what I eat too. I never find cabernet suits what I eat. I very rarely eat a big slice of unadorned steak. I eat duck, I eat chicken, I eat fish, so I tend to have lighter reds . . . I can afford to have a bottle of Moss Wood cabernet if I want but I'd rather have a Cote du Rhone. It's the kind of girl I am.

The explicit rationale for this choice is that she opts for certain types of wine to match certain types of food. Nevertheless, she is also stating that she can make judgments beyond the simplistic cues of price and common reputation – Moss Wood is an expensive Margaret River cabernet sauvignon, Cotes du Rhone a generic and comparatively cheap French red blend. The 'kind of girl that she is' can buck trends and display the confidence to make an unorthodox choice. Belinda is apparently discussing how she views herself, using wine as a means of establishing inner-directed self-image.

Status: There are a number of historical precedents for the use of wine to establish status – a factor discussed further in Chapter 8. One informant, asked about motivation, explicitly talked about 'snob value', then went on:

> Morag: On Sunday there was an absolute classic example. We belong to . . . a wine group, and there is a certain expectation that you will bring a very smart French wine along. And we need to have those very smart French wines in the cellar – because you just don't turn up with a bottle of Peel Estate shiraz, like someone did yesterday – and it was really, really looked down upon.
>
> Interviewer: Of course some people say Peel Estate shiraz is a very good wine.
>
> Morag: Absolutely, it just depends . . . and for some wine groups that we would go to that would be the standard of wine that we would bring. But it just depends upon the expectation. Terrible thing to say but it's true.

Peel Estate is a Western Australian wine producer, making a number of reputable wines, the most highly regarded of which is its shiraz. The suggestion was that even this would not offer sufficient cachet in certain tasting groups, where a wine should be foreign, and probably from a highly reputable origin, in order to be acceptable. Without it, the donor's status within the group is impaired. Morag was aware that this motivation for drinking is flawed, that it detracts from the real – perhaps aesthetic, or more cohesively sociable – reasons for drinking, but she was clear that it is one prompt to consume.

Utilitarian motivation: Lubrication and refreshment

The utilitarian motives for drinking wine appeared much less important than any of the symbolic or experiential reasons but were occasionally mentioned by informants. Nevertheless, some informants referred to the idea, and the following was typical:

> Richard: It's enjoyable, it's refreshing. Well not in the sense that a glass of water is. But as an accompaniment to food, because it's dry and because it's acidic and all those sorts of things. And it refreshes your palate, so that it's very useful as an adjunct to meals in what it does to your mouth.

Richard notes that wine refreshes (although he adds it may not quench thirst), and that it cuts through food (for which the acid in the wine is particularly useful). He also suggests that it stimulates the palate, and maintains a healthy sense of hunger. This use of wine for lubrication and refreshment was referred to by a few informants, but it is important to note that it was mainly high-involvement drinkers who commented on it. It appears likely that lower-involvement consumers naturally use beer or soft drinks as their automatic drink of refreshment, and are inclined to think of wine essentially as an aesthetic accompaniment to a meal, or as the focus of specific social events, rather than as a lubricant. Another, perhaps symbiotic, interpretation is that the high-involvement drinkers have the knowledge to justify their wine consumption in such a functional (physiological) manner – therefore providing themselves a 'legitimate' rationale for their 'vice'.

It's not just a drink . . .

For many drinkers the experiential and symbolic aspects of wine consumption have relevance beyond mere everyday usage; they may have a profound psychological impact. This relevance was expressed not only by high-involvement drinkers, but they did articulate it most fluently.

> Wendy: You're going to ask me to define this too – but I'm not going to be able to – so it's a mystery. Something you can't define. So what is that character that makes that wine so special that everyone enjoys it but no one can actually say exactly what it is? . . . . I suppose that great wine does transport us, it takes us somewhere else . . . Like we did on Friday – open a bottle of 1986 Clos de Mesnil and it was completely transporting. You can sit there and you can say 'it's completely dry, it's got lots of layers of flavour, it's got texture, it's still got varietal definition'. In effect you can definitely pick it as chardonnay. It's got a very fine bead. But the overall effect was that even after one mouthful your day wasn't so bad . . . . And I don't know why that happens . . . . That is

the mystery. I can spend probably 15 minutes describing that flavour of Mesnil – 'it's got this, it's got that', but I can't say why it makes me feel good. I wouldn't know what it was. And I don't think anyone would.

Wendy is a winemaker who has also been a show judge, having finely tuned organoleptic skills to supplement a technical analysis. Yet ultimately the combination of flavours and the structure of the wine do something for her that – with all her knowledge and skill – she cannot explain. Clos de Mesnil is a very expensive single-vineyard Champagne produced by Krug; she can dissect it, and see how it has been produced, she can correct it in the winery, yet the way it 'transports' her remains a mystery. The fact that she chooses an exclusive and expensive wine suggests that such a quasi-spiritual response may not be appropriate for all wines, but at least for some that she drinks it is the case, and it is clearly an experience to be aspired to. This type of response has much in common with the kind of 'profound experience' felt by many who explore aesthetic objects, such as music or paintings (Csikszentmihalyi & Robinson, 1990).

At this level wine consumption can combine almost all of the various factors which prompt consumption. Wendy clearly sees the consumption of the Clos de Mesnil as fitting into her lifestyle, and it is probable that she sees it as helping to shape her image. There is also no doubt that it gave her immense pleasure, both organoleptically and in the sense of the challenge offered by the exploration of its complex taste. It also provided a socially cohesive experience (she talks of 'we . . .') and there may also be a sense of ritual to it; it was drunk at the end of the last day of the working week, a classic time for marking out private time. Yet all of these complex factors together make something that to Wendy is greater than the sum of their parts.

Conclusion

The broad outline of why people consume wine seems to be well understood. Enjoyment is the key factor, a fact well established in previous consideration of the subject (Heath, 2000). Taste seems to be the main element in enjoyment – the paramount aspect for some – which is again well established (Dubow, 1992; Thompson & Vourvachis, 1995). Additionally the physiological impact of alcohol and, for higher involvement drinkers, the diversity, intellectual challenge and opportunities for exploring new wines are also key components of this pleasure, and the latter are perhaps not so well recognized academically. The situation in which wine is drunk is crucial; drinking with friends and family is perhaps the second most important spur to consume, followed closely by the fact that it fits into a meal so readily (Dubow, 1992; Hall & Lockshin, 2000). Most of this reflects previous academic thinking on the subject, although the mental test provided by wine is perhaps not so well recognized.

Although the symbolic use of wine was not so well attested as the experiential, it nevertheless had relevance for many, perhaps most, consumers. It should also be noted that a number of the symbolic elements of consumption stem from the subconscious, and many informants might have been unaware of them. Nevertheless, the ritual relevance of wine was significant for drinkers at all involvement levels, as was the sense, for some, that they were maintaining a family tradition. The former of these is well-understood academically (Douglas, 1987b), the latter not so well. The use of wine to fix memory or as an aid to the recollection of rites of passage is, perhaps, distinctive to wine as a drink, and again not really registered in previous examinations of the role of drink. Wine also seems to be used to help drinkers shape their image, in terms of how they view their lifestyle, their self-image, and the way they may try to obtain status within a wine-drinking community.

Bibliographical note

For the anthropological perspective on alcohol Douglas (1987b) is a fascinating introduction, with some illuminating pieces on wine. This chapter does not focus on the consumer's selection of wine. For those who want to understand that, a good summary of our current knowledge has been prepared by Larry Lockshin and John Hall (Lockshin & Hall, 2003). An investigation of the relationship of involvement to wine consumption is outlined by Charters and Pettigrew (Charters & Pettigrew, 2006).

There is a certain amount of research on the impact consumption situation has on wine drinking, including a couple of papers by John Hall and Larry Lockshin (1999; 2000) and – taking a different slant – Simone Pettigrew (2003). For more information about the relationship of food and wine specifically, see work produced by the author with Simone Pettigrew (Charters & Pettigrew, 2004; Pettigrew & Charters, 2006).

8

The symbolic role of wine: Religion, sex, fertility and status

Having considered what prompts people to drink wine it is necessary to examine in more detail some of the symbolic meaning which drinkers attach to it. Historically there was a close relationship between wine, religious belief and fertility, and of all the symbolic associations related to wine these are the most long-standing. Whilst these associations may be less obvious today in western, Anglophone societies, they still permeate much of European wine culture, and they have an impact on the way wine is portrayed throughout the world. The first part of this chapter will examine how and why that relationship developed, and how it is evident today. The use of wine as a means of establishing status – in modern sociological terms making distinctions – is also long established, and remains highly relevant as a feature of modern wine consumption. The final part of the chapter considers why that relationship developed and how it operates in the modern world.

Historical context

The origins of the religious connection with wine

The first wine was produced by neolithic people who had no understanding of yeast activity and the processes of fermentation which created an intoxicating drink. Early societies will thus have assumed that the transformation of juice to wine was a magical process. (No other product utilized in early societies 'appeared' in this way; bread and foodstuffs, tools and clothes were all manufactured.) Equally magical was the impact that drinking wine had on the body; little other produce could have such an impact; beer may have predated wine, but had a lower alcohol content, and some fungi may have been available in certain cultures but their use was probably limited.

The advantages of wine are that the vine is very productive and easy to tend, with a regular yield – which made it more consistently available than mushrooms. It grows on fairly poor soils on hillsides, and thus did not compete for space with the grains which provided the staple foods. It was also safer and more palatable than other intoxicants. Crucially, it was produced in the area which comprised the cradle of those monotheistic faiths which have shaped the religious belief of Europe. Finally, amongst the first civilizations of Mesopotamia and Egypt its scarcity made it an elite product, unlike beer. It was thus economically controllable and appropriate in terms of status for royal and priestly elites (which were often identical).

It is also evident that wine was one product which, for early societies, signified the distinction between people and animals. It is possible that, as early societies evolved, this distinction which focused on how humanity was superior to the beasts was important to human self-identity.

The story of Enkidu

The story of Enkidu, contained in the Epic of Gilgamesh, highlights the importance of wine as a marker of what it means to be human. The Epic of Gilgamesh is probably the first substantial and complete written story in human history, dating from about 2000 BC and possibly centuries before that (Anon., n.d./1972). The story tells of the rule and travels of a Mesopotamian hero-king, Gilgamesh, who rules in Uruk. Central to the story is his relationship with the wild man, Enkidu. Enkidu lived in the wilderness with wild animals, and ate grass like them – but was seduced (literally) out of savagery by a sacred prostitute from Uruk. However,

> Enkidu had no idea how to eat or drink as humans did and was ignorant of bread and wine. Thus the woman who led him out of the wilderness said to him 'eat bread, it is the staff of life, drink the wine, it is the custom of the land' (Anon., n.d./1972). With this, the tale goes on to say 'Enkidu became a man'; he cleaned himself up, and rubbed himself with oil.
>
> The importance of this is that it was two foodstuffs, wine and bread – plus the third of the Mediterranean trinity, olive oil – which Enkidu uses when he joins civilization. Before he lived with the animals, but animals cannot ferment wine from crushed grapes nor bake bread from milled grain nor press oil – these are processes unavailable to 'dumb' creatures; rather they graze on living plants, or tear at raw meat. For a society which was much closer to nature and to the wildness of the animal kingdom than our own these were key markers – the processes which separated us as 'civilized' people from the savagery of beasts, and which placed us next to the gods in the order of creation. Bread, wine and oil defined what it was to be human.

The 'magical' nature of wine, which could 'inspire' its adherents, can also be seen to be symbolic in a number of other religious ways (Unwin, 1996). Firstly, the vine came to symbolize the concept of death and rebirth. It was one of the few deciduous plants cultivated in any volume in the middle-east and each year after producing fruit it seemed to die in late autumn; there was leaf-fall and dormancy, followed by an apparent rebirth in the following spring. Such seasonal change chimed with burgeoning ideas of the immortality of the soul. At the same time the vine's produce – raisins and wine – lived on and provided sustenance after the plant itself had appeared to die. Thus, in Egypt, Osiris – a god who was killed but then brought back to life – was explicitly referred to as 'the lord of the wine' during a festival which celebrated his role in the annual flood of the Nile, an event which was pivotal to continued agriculture through the country (McGovern, 2003, p. 135).

Another point to note is that – at least when made from red grapes – wine had the colour of blood. Many early religions had myths explaining that wine had originally come as the blood of a divine animal (Fuller, 1996). In religions in which propitiatory sacrifice was significant wine could be seen to have a relationship to blood sacrifice, so that at a very early stage in human history wine became an alternative form of divine offering (McGovern, 2003). The Greeks, for example, would make a libation, where they would pour out wine onto the earth, as a gift to one of their gods, and by extension in some middle-eastern countries wine has come to represent the soul (Saeidi & Unwin, 2004). It is also worth noting that the gods of wine were most powerful where vines were widely grown (Unwin, 1996). In those places wine as a significant product, and an important religious aid, needed to have a powerful god associated with it. It is significant that this symbolic link of red wine to blood has remained until the modern age. Red wine – with the blood-like, perhaps divine, power it can instil – is still often seen as a 'man's drink' and when French soldiers were given a daily ration of wine it was invariably red, as it was more likely to inspire and fortify them (Phillips, 2000).

As a final point about the significance of wine in a religious context one can note the importance of aroma in ritual. It has been suggested that 'an integrative power is also usually attributed to smell, making scent an excellent means of uniting the participants in a ritual . . .. The boundary-crossing nature of smell, in turn, is often made use of to help the participants in a rite of passage' (Classen et al., 1994, p. 123). Thus a distinctive aroma, such as that provided by wine, may by its attractiveness give ritualistic cohesion and by its uniqueness mark out a special event.

The role of fertility

The link between religion and fertility may not be immediately obvious to us but there is a long-standing connection between the two. Whereas in modern western society a harvest failure in one country can be remedied from another, in early agricultural societies fertility was a matter of life and death. Fertility in this context included two factors. The first was the success of the harvest, which was critical in the short term. A poor harvest would at the very least cause major hardship, and could easily lead to a community's extinction. Fertility was also an element in the control of population, especially its growth. This was, in the longer term, essential for one's own longevity (later generations could support the elderly) and also for the community's prosperity generally. Religion, which had a focus on securing the goodwill of the gods and guaranteeing the security of the community and the individual's well-being, was a major mechanism for seeking to ensure fertility both annually in the fields and generationally in the family. It is significant that the Greek myth which records Dionysos' first visit to Greece after he discovered wine tells how he cuckolded his host and then paid him off with a gift of a vine to soothe away his sorrows (Dalby, 2003).

As outlined, wine symbolized fertility and, with its power to reduce inhibitions, could also be seen to promote it (as it still does). It is relevant to note that the first recorded winemaker was a woman (Siduri, in the Epic of Gilgamesh) and in Babylonian society barkeepers were assumed to be women, as the code of Hammurabi – an early summary of the law in Babylon – demonstrates. This probably has its roots in even earlier societies, when hunters tended to be male but gatherers – including those who gathered grapes – tended to be female.

Wine in Greek and Roman religion

The most well-known gods of wine were Dionysos, in Greece, and his Roman equivalent Bacchus. They were significant members of the pantheon of the gods with a substantial mythology surrounding them which both fixed the importance of wine in their respective societies, and also linked it to other key mythological dimensions.

Dionysos

Dionysos was the Greek god of wine. According to myth he was the son of Zeus and Semele, a woman rather than a goddess, but historical evidence suggests that his worship spread from the Black Sea region, probably as the vine itself spread from there. According to one story Dionysos was raised by the Muses – the Greek goddesses of the arts, including poetry and song – a relationship which persists to this day (see Chapter 9). He discovered how to make wine and when he had grown up he journeyed through the world teaching people how to cultivate the vine, and spreading his cult. In this he was accompanied by followers from the woods and fields (satyrs and nymphs), representing the places where vines flourished. Those who refused him were driven mad, but at the same time some variants of his worship were also frenzied and violent, with wild dancing and trance-like states. Quite possibly for 'rational' Greeks he presented an alternative ideal, one side of a duality focusing (in his case) on the emotional and irrational. This may relate to his origin from outside Greece, so that he can be seen to represent an alien, less civilized but perhaps more exciting way of life (Robinson, 1999). He descended into the underworld and returned – symbolizing the idea of rebirth – and his cult developed a later association with the afterlife. He was also credited with prophetic powers – perhaps a reflection of the 'clear-sightedness' which is sometimes perceived to accompany intoxication.

There are some important factors to be noted in the cults of Dionysos and Bacchus. The first is that they were comparatively democratic. They developed in countries were the production and consumption of wine was widespread, and the ritual practices were widely available to free citizens – even to women, who featured prominently amongst the followers of the god and in cultic rites. The gods themselves were often perceived to be the benefactors of humanity, offering them a gift which cheers the downhearted and relieves cares (Robinson, 1999). However, another aspect of the worship of Dionysos and Bacchus is that they were seen to be threatening to good order. *The Bacchae*, a play by the Greek author Euripides, presents a conflict between passion and reason which ends in the women of Thebes tearing apart Pentheus, the king of the city, who has rejected Dionysos but spied on his female followers. This tension between the benefits of wine and the dangers it offers is a constant theme in the relationship of communities with wine until the present, and at times caused the worship of Bacchus in the Roman Empire to be banned.

Wine in the Bible

Wine appears in both the Old and New Testament of the Bible. Again there is a sense of ambivalence about the Jewish attitude to it – something which has continued to pervade Christian thought. Typical are the warnings contained in the book of Proverbs:

> Who has woe? Who has sorrow? Who has strife? Who has complaints?
> Who has needless bruises? Who has bloodshot eyes?
> Those who linger over wine, who go to sample bowls of mixed wine.
> Do not gaze at wine when it is red, when it sparkles in the cup, when it goes down smoothly!
> In the end it bites like a snake and poisons like a viper.
> Your eyes will see strange sights and your mind imagine confusing things.
> You will be like one sleeping on the high seas, lying on top of the rigging.
> 'They hit me,' you will say, 'but I'm not hurt! They beat me, but I don't feel it! When will I wake up so I can find another drink?'
> (Proverbs 23:29–35).

Yet other parts of the Old Testament have a different perspective. The writer of Ecclesiastes, traditionally considered to be the same author as the book of Proverbs, talks about wine making life merry, and advises the reader to 'eat your food with gladness, and drink your wine with a joyful heart' (Ecclesiastes 9:7). Elsewhere the consumption of wine is alluded to approvingly for the enjoyment it provides, and tending the vineyard is an everyday aspect of agriculture. Indeed, wine was so integrated into society that its consumption became a part of the Passover meal, one of the most important annual rituals of the Jewish people, in the later Old Testament period (Thompson, 1986).

Noah and wine

The first time wine is mentioned in the Bible it is said to have been created by Noah. It is recounted that he planted a vineyard and produced wine which made him drunk – with the result that he fell naked in his tent. One son (Ham) saw that he was naked and, laughingly, told his brothers – but they (Shem and Japheth), embarrassed for their father, walked backwards into his tent carrying a cover which they could put over him without seeing him unclothed. When Noah awoke he cursed Ham, saying he would be the slave of his brothers. This curse placed on Ham was considered by some Christians to apply to all the 'Hamitic' (black African) races, and was subsequently used to justify apartheid. Meanwhile, the Bible records, Noah lived for 350 more years – so wine cannot have been too detrimental for his health.

The ambivalent perspective on wine continued into the period of the New Testament. Paul, writing to the Ephesians, urges them to a more spiritual life by saying 'do not get drunk on wine, which leads to debauchery. Instead be filled with the [Holy] Spirit' (Ephesians 5:18), but in another place he urges his friend Timothy to drink wine rather than water for the good health of his stomach. Wine is seen to be good, but drunkenness is unacceptable.

Crucial to the relationship of wine and religion in Christianity is the role of the sacrament. In varying Christian traditions this may be a meal of remembrance or a re-enactment and reprise of the sacrifice of Christ's death. The rite was instituted by Christ on the night before his crucifixion when he passed bread and then wine to the twelve apostles for them to share and urged them to continue to repeat the ceremony to remember him after his death. Wine, as has been noted, can act as a marker for sacrificial blood, and Jesus was explicit about this when he said 'this cup is the new covenant in my blood, which is poured out for you' (Luke 22:20). Given that, according to the Bible, Jesus returned to life two days after his death, the use of wine with its links to death and rebirth was also significant. The celebration of communion was adopted by the early church as a key ritual, although interestingly it took place in the context of a wider meal, shared by the church – the agapé, or love feast. Food had a key symbolic function in bringing together the members of the church as a community and wine had a specific symbolic role within that focus relating to the idea of sacrifice. This marks a key point in the 'socialization' of wine-related rituals; it becomes more than just a mere remembrance, but also part of the social glue which binds a community together.

It has also been suggested that bread and wine together are symbols of transformation. One is baked, the other fermented, changing a raw material into something better in the same way that the soul can be transformed by the sacrifice of Christ (Scruton, 2004). This again echoes the symbolic role of these products noticed in much earlier societies, such as that of Uruk at the time of Gilgamesh.

The role of the church

Christianity was accepted as a religion by the Roman Empire in AD 313 and after the Empire's fall it became the most cohesive institution as western Europe fractured. Wine retained its symbolic importance for the church as one part of the sacrament. As a result it has been suggested that the church was responsible for the continuation of viticulture through the dark ages (Johnson, 1989), although the importance of this has been disputed (Unwin, 1996). However, the church retained its enjoyment of wine as a drink, as well as for its religious significance, and the rule of St Benedict, for instance, prescribed an allowance of 570 mL of wine per day for each monk (Seward, 1979). Religion and fertility remained linked, also, for the church rather than civil authorities retained jurisdiction over matters of marriage, adultery and divorce (these were the responsibility of church courts in England and Wales until 1858) and the prime rite recognizing birth was christening, which took place in church.

As a result of the pervasive social importance of religion until the start of the twentieth century viticulture integrated religion into its processes. Given the vagaries of the weather, God's influence was considered crucial. Even in 1876 in Bordeaux prayers were offered when a humid westerly wind began to threaten the health of the vines and the success of the harvest (Briggs, 1994). In many wine regions the festival of St Vincent on the 22nd January was co-opted to link church and grapegrower – although it is interesting to note that, at least in Champagne, this festival had fallen into abeyance until the end of the nineteenth century when it was resurrected as a sign of the communal solidarity of vignerons who faced the threat of domination by the large Champagne houses (Guy, 2003).

Modern symbolism

In the modern world the link of wine with fertility and religion has weakened. Nevertheless, the relationship still exists, although it may be the former which is more immediately obvious. Sex is regularly used as an adjunct to promoting and selling wine, and Champagne may be explicitly referred to as an agent of seduction even by those responsible for promoting it (Anon., 2005a). Wine also retains its link with the results of sex; we still talk of 'wetting the baby's head', and again Champagne is often thought of as the symbolic drink to celebrate birth.

Celebration of the harvest still functions to link wine, religion and fertility. The following is an extract describing what might have happened a century ago, but it still holds good in many places in southern Europe.

> When the new wine was fermenting quietly in vats or in casks and the air was still heavily redolent with the sweet odours of fresh fruit and the pungency of carbon dioxide gas then he and his family and the rest of the village came together for a celebration combining the awesome solemnity of Christian prayers, of church bells, of chants and hymns, of *Te Deums*, with the unleashed passions of their ancient inheritance, the gorging upon food, the swilling of wine, the ribald songs and the abandon to joyous dancing sweeping up both young and old (Loubere, 1978, p. 240).

However, the explicit relationship between sex, fertility and wine is increasingly under pressure from other directions. Chateau Mouton-Rothschild, in Bordeaux, commissions a different artist each year to design the label for its wine. In 1993 it asked the French painter Balthus to prepare the design, and the wine was released featuring his label, which portrayed a youthful, perhaps pre-pubescent, girl lying naked. This prompted accusations that the chateau was promoting paedophilia and child abuse. The opposition to the label was most vociferous in the United States, and despite their initial protestations that the label was essentially innocent the chateau ultimately released the wine in that market without the offending label, in order to placate critics.

More recently, an advertisement which was part of a generic promotional campaign for wine made in Bordeaux was deemed unacceptable by the French authorities. They invoked the 'Loi Evin', which controls the advertising of alcoholic drinks in the country, because the picture, featuring an attractive female winemaker, was considered 'too sexy' (Randall, 2005). It was replaced by a photograph of the same winemaker but with a 'less sultry' look, and with a glass of wine at a greater distance from her mouth, which made it, so the argument ran, less provocative (Randall, 2005, p. 15). The links between alcohol and sex are increasingly under threat, at least in the public arena, as a direct result of health campaigns which seek to break the connection and thus make wine less attractive.

Wine producers may still make explicit or implicit use of ancient symbolism in what they do. Grant Burge Wines in the Barossa Valley produce a wine called 'The Holy Trinity'; it is made of a blend of three grape varieties, and features a stylized pattern on its label which evokes a stained glass window. There are producers who hold services of 'blessing the vines' before the vintage each year with prayers for a good harvest. It is also possible to see the modern preference for organic wine, especially coupled with the idea of Gaia – a living earth – as a return to the old concept of mother goddess providing for humanity.

The development of wine as a marker of status

It is important to note that the use of any product – including wine – to signify status has two functions. The first is about exclusion; it marks the individual off from those in other social groups whose lifestyle is considered inappropriate; usually, although not invariably, wine is used to differentiate the individual from 'lower' social classes. The second status-related means of using wine is inclusive. In this way it serves to ally the individual to others who share similar interests and perhaps a similar social, economic and educational background; in that sense it acts as a form of self-classification (Groves et al., 2000).

It is also noteworthy that establishing social differentiation can operate in different ways. Vigneron and Johnson (1999), in an exploration of the way that luxury goods (such as Champagne or other expensive wines) are used, apply five categories to consumers of these products. The first group is Veblenian; their focus is on conspicuous consumption, and price is important to them to mark prestige. Next is a group described as snob consumers; they seek products because of their exclusivity, and eschew popular brands. Both of these forms of luxury consumption tend to be exclusive. Bandwagon consumers, on the other hand, seek inclusive status; they want to consume what other socially significant people are using. The next two categories are the hedonist consumers and perfectionists, who are mainly concerned with their own enjoyment, and make their own judgments about wine. It can be posited that these groups also tend to focus on inclusivity and a sense of belonging rather than exclusion. As a general comment it is also worth noting that it is not only the possession of high income but also cultural background (specifically a willingness to accept cultural change) which are jointly the predictors of a desire to own and consume luxury goods (Dubois & Duquesne, 1993).

Wine and status amongst the first civilizations

When wine was first produced supply was limited and it was first made away from the centres of power in the middle-east (Mesopotamia and Egypt). Consequently, although a highly sought product, access to it was reserved to elites. Even when grapes began to be grown in the Nile delta beer remained the everyday alcoholic beverage in Egypt and wine the drink of the country's rulers, used as a prestige drink (McGovern, 2003). The result of this was that, in the early civilizations, wine became a marker for power and privilege – a symbolic function it has retained to the present day in some societies. It also seems evident that not only wine but appropriate, beautifully decorated utensils for the service of wine were important as a marker of differentiation for those who were in the upper classes (McGovern, 2003).

Gradually the consumption of wine became more widespread and, as noted previously, in some countries it became a democratic drink. At this point the mere possession of wine was no longer enough for it to act as a status symbol. Instead it was necessary for comparison to occur; there was a need for 'better' and 'worse' wine so that it could continue to signify the position of the elites. Tutankhamen's tomb contained amphorae marked 'very good quality', but the problem is how do you establish high quality? Formal quality levels were required. The most obvious way for quality to be established was for a wine to have a superior taste but, given the limited numbers of wines available, that was difficult to achieve and to validate, although flavour, and more specifically richness and sweetness, were relevant. However, a more important factor was that quality based solely on taste is not in itself a public representation of what is good wine; it does not proclaim to the world how important a person one is. Instead, as Chapter 5 examined, the creation of differentiation of wines developed, based on origin, vintage or an objective classification (usually based on price, rather than directly on how good it tastes).

Once wine quality has been established, in order for it to continue to act as a marker for status it has to be maintained. If the reputation of a wine is a mere passing fad it has much less symbolic equity than if it continues to be recognized for its quality. At the same time, reputation adds value to a wine, so that economically it was important for those making 'good' wine to preserve the quality of that wine, thus protecting its renown and guaranteeing their income.

In the fifth century BC on the Aegean Island of Thasos the law required that the island's wine must be sold in large jars which were sealed, in order to try to guarantee the authenticity of the wine throughout the Greek world (Unwin, 1996).

The Roman Empire

Empires particularly are organizations predicated on rank and status, and this was especially true of the great Mediterranean empires which functioned economically by exploiting a slave caste. Given that the consumption of wine was widespread the Romans became especially adept at using it to establish status. Four methods were relevant to this process:

1. Classifying wine by its origin. At various times different regions were considered to produce the best wines. Falernian, for instance, produced from vineyards near Naples, was often considered the most prestigious by the Romans (Johnson, 1989) and Pliny offered a list of the best regions, starting with Pucinum, Setian and Caecuban (Pliny the Elder, n.d./1991).
2. Classifying wine by its vintage. If it had the potential to age then 'old' wine (which was defined as being at least one year old (Robinson, 1999)) was generally better. However, most status was established by knowing about, and consuming the wines of, specific vintages. The wine produced in the year that Opimius was senior consul (121 BC) had a general reputation for excellent quality (Unwin, 1996).
3. Classifying by grape variety. According to the Roman author Pliny, for instance, wines made from the Aminean grape were pre-eminent (Pliny the Elder, n.d./1991).
4. Establishing status by the ability to drink. This was a marker based on individuals themselves, rather than stemming from their possession of a particular wine. However, unlike today where such status is based on connoisseurship it tended to be capacity, or the ability to hold one's drink, that impressed the Romans. Pliny refers to Torquatus who could drink without slurring his words or being sick (Pliny the Elder, n.d./1991).

Trimalchio's feast

One of the most famous stories about the attempted use of wine as a marker for one's position in society is Trimalchio's feast. This is part of the Satyricon, a picaresque tale written in the first century AD by Petronius (n.d./1997). Petronius wrote the work as a satire, and Trimalchio is a *parvenu* – a freed slave who has obtained extraordinary wealth, and displays it ostentatiously.

In this episode from the story the narrator and his friends are invited to a banquet by Trimalchio, a meal of great length full of the choicest delicacies. Trimalchio boasts throughout about his achievements. At one point in the meal three sealed jars of wine are produced, with a label which states 'Falernian wine, Opimian vintage; one hundred years old'. Trimalchio comments that he is serving wine which genuinely comes from the vintage of Opimius, which would make it 150 years old at the time! In bombastic fashion he adds that the wine he had served at yesterday's meal was not nearly so good, even though his guests then were much more important people (Petronius, n.d./1997, p. 25). The irony, of course, is that no such wine would still be in existence when Petronius wrote. Trimalchio was rich but stupid, and had been cheated by his wine merchant (Unwin, 1996).

The only variation to these four means of establishing one's position occurred in the second century AD. During this period the cask replaced the amphora as the principle means of storing liquid, and – as noted in Chapter 2 – the means for wine to age so effectively was lost, so that possessing a good vintage became less significant.

The impact of the consumer revolution

Wine continued to be relevant as a status symbol throughout the medieval period, especially so in the developing urban centres of northern Europe and by extension to their overseas settlements such as those in North America (Fuller, 1996). Determining the best wine (primarily based on its origin) remained a key concern, and it was given particular relevance as the feudal system was, like the Roman Empire, a system based on the maintenance of distinctions and the importance of remaining in one's place in society, with status accorded by birth, land ownership and noble titles. Indeed sumptuary laws were regularly passed (though not always effectively enforced) which attempted to determine what clothes, food, drink and other products could reasonably be consumed by each level of society; the intent of this was to prevent those of lower rank from drinking above their station. However, the last French 'price fixing' orders were in 1680 (Briggs, 1994), just as the whole notion of consumption was about to change radically.

The impact of the industrial revolution and the growth of a consumer society in eighteenth century Britain challenged the notion that an individual's right to consume various goods was predetermined. Individual achievement rather than the accident of birth increasingly became accepted as the main criterion for status, and the possession of wealth, rather than nobility, the precondition for consuming luxuries. Consumption widened, but there was an intensification of the need for ever more finely nuanced distinguishing factors allowing the display of one's knowledge of, and ability to purchase, products.

The use of origin as a means of differentiation remained important. However, with the development of a consumer society a number of new and renewed distinguishing factors became important. These are dealt with in some detail, as they are crucial to how wine can facilitate social differentiation in the contemporary world.

- *A return to the importance of 'vintage'*: The ability to use vintage as a means of distinction had been substantially lost with the transition from amphorae to casks. In the seventeenth century, however, the increasing use of glass bottles and the introduction of cork as a stopper changed that. Corks form an excellent air-tight seal and allow the slow development and improvement of the best wines in a reductive environment. Wines which previously would have faded or turned faulty after a year or two could now be kept. This allowed for the comparison of vintages, and the selection of the best purchased, naturally, at a premium.
- *Price and scarcity*: As economic life became increasingly focused on money as a means of exchange, so price became a widespread marker for quality. Scarcity inevitably raised prices, as did the cost of production. Champagne (as a sparkling wine, rather than a still, pale red wine) was developed at the end of the seventeenth century and was a wine made for the consumer revolution. It went through a laborious process of production (second fermentation, riddling and disgorgement) and was a difficult wine to produce; it has been estimated that in some years in the early eighteenth century up to 50 per cent of all bottles were destroyed in the cellars of the region, exploding under the poorly controlled pressure of the second fermentation (Brennan, 1997). Indeed, given the immediately recognizable appearance of such wine in the glass, with its mousse and trails of beads, it can be argued that sparkling wine in its own right became a category of differentiation which enabled the instant visual establishment of social position.
- *Novelty*: A new aspect of social differentiation was the importance of novelty (McKendrick et al., 1982). It was a feature of the consumer revolution that the new – putting the consumer at the forefront of fashion (an 'early adopter', in modern marketing language) – was an

important denotation of sophistication. The development of 'new' wines at the end of the seventeenth century (Unwin, 1996), offered consumers an opportunity to display the currency of their knowledge and their role as a trend-setter. These wines included the new French Clarets which arose when the Médoc was drained, Port, created as a fortified drink at the same time, and a little later Constantia from Cape Town. Novelty and insatiability have become key drivers of modern consumption (Campbell, 1987).

- *The significance of the producer*: Following from the development of new wines was the increasing ability to make distinctions based on the particular producer of the wine. The ability to buy wine from one specific source had always existed but had not been feasible outside the region of production. Samuel Pepys generally bought wines designated as Claret, Malaga and Tent (from Spain) – not the wines of a specific *vigneron*; it was a significant event when he recorded in his diary in April 1663 that he had tried a new wine called Ho Bryan (Haut-Brion). As Port, Champagne and the new Clarets developed, purchasing from a particular shipper, house or chateau became possible for the more wealthy and at the same time a valuable form of intellectual property for the producer (Briggs, 1994). In the case of Claret, particularly, buying a producer's name was purchasing wine from a specific origin, but in practise it also operated as we would see a brand operating in the modern market.
- *The volume of consumption*: In an echo of Pliny's description of Torquatus consumption levels could also, at least in certain social segments, be used to establish status. The appearance of the 'three bottle man' – the person who consumed three bottles of Port during the course of the day – was a feature of this period; some were even renowned as 'six bottle men' (Johnson, 1989). High consumption still offers status in certain segments of society although the wine industry, with its quasi-formal commitment to responsible drinking (see Chapter 12), may, at least ostensibly, argue that it no longer applies to wine, but only to other alcoholic drinks.
- *Classification*: The consumer revolution formed the basis for the development of very formalized classificatory systems, particularly in Bordeaux and Burgundy – as outlined in Chapter 5. The first classification to appear for Bordeaux in a form similar to the current one is recorded in 1786 (Markham, 1998).
- *Imitation*: As the possession of surplus income slowly spread, and with it the facility to spend on non-essentials, so there was a trickle down to lower levels of society who sought, within their very limited

means, to imitate the consumption patterns of those in higher social groupings. This resulted in the spread of wine consumption into non-wine producing areas, and it was during the eighteenth century that wine became the staple alcoholic beverage of Paris. There was, however, a clear distinction between *grands crus* and *vins populaires* in France (Unwin, 1996). Imitation was spawned from a desire for social identification with the rich, but limited economic means ensured that social differentiation was maintained.

An aristocratic wine drinker

A classic example of the use of wine to mark one's social position is fictional. The detective writer, Dorothy Sayers, wrote a short story entitled *The Bibulous Business of a Matter of Taste (Sayers, 1928).*

Her hero, Lord Peter Wimsey, is in France on the trail of two spies who were seeking to gain possession of a formula for a deadly gas, both of whom were masquerading as him. The owner of the formula, a French count, will only pass the information onto the genuine Peter Wimsey, but has no way of determining which of the three visitors he is. In the event the three visitors are required to judge the origin and vintage of the wines served over dinner – a Chablis, a Chevalier-Montrachet, a Rheingau riesling, Clos Vougeot 1911 and a Tokay. Only the true lord can place the wines precisely and show his true credentials.

There are those who would dismiss the possession of such arcane knowledge and skill as a mere adjunct of class, and a form of snobbish superiority. However, for the author it rather exemplified her hero's natural pre-eminence, and complemented his many other talents. Note also the assumption that Lord Peter seems to have absorbed his wine knowledge almost by a process of osmosis. He has not worked to get it, and this symbolizes his aristocratic pedigree; he is born with this knowledge.

Wine and status in the modern world

Wine remains a means of establishing social distinction, and consequently status, in the modern world. It can do this in two key ways. The first is by signalling the price one is able and willing to pay for a bottle, thus conveying signals about wealth. The second is by showing how much one knows about wine and consequently giving messages about one's sophistication. The latter is particularly significant within the community of high-involvement consumers, where rank depends on expertise and association with key opinion formers. This general recognition of the use of wine to establish status is also applied both by sociologists (Bourdieu, 1986) and by anthropologists (Gurr, 1987). Bourdieu (1986) particularly notes the importance of (physical) taste as a means of establishing the distinctions which define taste as an aesthetic concept. The main ways in which wine can facilitate these distinctions are in the wine's style and origin, its classification (both by price and by vintage) and its brand.

The style of a wine is important in making a statement about the drinker. The specific instance of Champagne, with its effervescence, has already been noted. The colour of wine can also be relevant. During the boom in wine consumption in south-east Asia in the late 1990s it was observed that 90 per cent of all wine drunk in Thailand was red. In part this was due to health issues, but it was also suggested by professionals in the country that it was because, in a crowded restaurant, if a patron was drinking red wine others could instantly see it, whereas if it was white wine that was consumed it could easily be mistaken for lemonade or another pale soft drink and observers would not receive the required message. Equally it has long been noted that sweetness in a wine is important to a consumer's image. Dry wines are generally perceived to be more sophisticated to the extent that, irrespective of the level of residual sugar, drinkers will describe a wine which they like as dry and one they dislike as sweet (Lehrer, 1974; Wright et al., 2000).

Brand, as a means of providing security to the consumer, has already been examined in some detail (see Chapter 6). Status may be attached to brand, especially for specific products or in markets in which brand equity is heavily protected, such as Champagne. Champagne generically establishes status when compared to other sparkling wines (Salolainen, 1993), and specific brands of Champagne convey various carefully coded signals of the consumer's expertise and ability (Vignes & Gergaud, 2003) – often irrespective of the drinker's actual ability to distinguish brands on the basis of taste (Lange et al., 2002). It is important, therefore, to note that brand, as a marker of status, may be significant for both high- and low-involvement consumers.

For higher-involvement consumers origin and vintage replace the more general idea of style as key markers of status. The importance of classification and origin as a factor in wine as a product has already been dealt with in Chapter 5 and it was noted that neither guarantee organoleptic quality. Nevertheless, within some wine regions there is no doubt that specific origins convey extra kudos; it is for this reason that the *cru* system developed in Burgundy was based on vineyards. It is well recognized by keen wine drinkers that *grand cru* le

Montrachet is 'superior' to *premier cru* les Pucelles, which in turn is 'better' than AC Puligny Montrachet. Site, reputation and price interact to establish the drinker's knowledge of the product, and their ability to select and access appropriate bottles; each of these together help to set their position amongst the hierarchy of wine lovers.

Drinking a specified vintage is also a crucial element in the process of connoisseurship. As previously observed, there is a subtle distinction between offering your guests 1991 Chateau Latour and the 1990 vintage of the same wine, the former being a mediocre vintage, the latter a great one. Much attention is given by wine journalists (Robert Parker and the *Wine Spectator* being the classic examples) to the evaluation of different vintages from the major wine producing regions, and each year aficionados eagerly await the experts' analysis of weather conditions in the world's premium wine regions so that they can assess how good their future wine drinking may be. The ability to offer a range of vintages in turn depends on effective storage methods – particularly the possession of a suitable and substantial cellar. The usefulness of a range of vintages in allowing for nuances of distinction also means that the ageworthiness of the wine is important. Consequently a wine's ability to age has been raised by some wine critics as one of the key determinants of quality in wine (for instance Broadbent, 1979).

Wine consumption and national self-esteem

The phenomenon of Beaujolais nouveau (the early release of the new vintage of red Beaujolais in November of each year) has waxed and waned each year, with consumption peaking in the early 1990s (Robinson, 1999). Critics, especially, think it too early to drink a barely fermented red wine, particularly one which has often been made from grapes grown in the least appropriate viticultural areas. However, one country in which its consumption has remained popular is Japan. Because it is situated close to the international date line Japan is consistently the first country in the world to be able to drink Beaujolais nouveau on the fifteenth of November. The Japanese enjoy being the first people in the world to get a new product, so Beaujolais nouveau took off because it put them a few hours ahead of the rest of the world. Even people who do not normally drink wine in Japan will partake and talk about the wine, and enjoy being part of a nation which considers it has an elite status.

Conclusion

The symbolic function of wine is significant and long-standing, resulting in part from its nature as a rare but desirable product in early civilizations, as well as the mysterious nature of alcoholic fermentation in pre-scientific societies, its colour relationship to blood, and the way it could symbolize death and rebirth. Together these gave wine a magical dimension and scarcity value, both factors which made them appropriate for the religious caste who tended to form part of the elite.

This symbolism continues to the present and although sophistication is no longer synonymous with religious leadership it can still be conveyed by wine. Wine also retains its religious significance in the modern world and there remains – just – a religious overlay to viticulture for some. More significantly the link of wine to fertility – and by extension to sex – continues to be important for those involved in marketing wine.

Bibliographical note

For a much more detailed discussion of the origin of the symbolism of wine see Unwin (1996), Chapter 3. A good introduction to the Greco-roman mythology is Dalby's (2003) work on Dionysos. For a consideration of the religious significance of wine in Christian societies Fuller's (1996) study on the North American experience is full of detail. A different and interesting approach to the cycle of birth, fertility and death is offered in Patricia Atkinson's (2003) tale of developing a vineyard in Bergerac which is informative and entertaining. The classic sociological work on distinction is Bourdieu (1986) and the use of luxury wines – specifically Champagne – as a marker of status is comprehensively covered by Guy (2003).

9

Wine and the civilized life

Issues around religion, fertility and status are some of the most visible symbolic meanings attached to wine. Less obvious historically, but of equal significance, is the fact that wine is often viewed – albeit unconsciously – as a key part of a civilized life; in modern terminology, it has become a 'lifestyle product'. This chapter will investigate this phenomenon, looking at what it means to be civilized, and then how wine takes on the trappings of civilization – in the pursuit of knowledge, the fact that it is natural, that its consumption is perceived to indicate sophistication and that it may be an art form. The context of wine as a civilized drink is then examined – specifically its relationship to philosophy and the arts, to food and to lifestyle.

Introduction

The idea that wine forms part of a 'civilized life' may seem unexpected in an academic study on the social context of wine. However, it is important for a number of reasons. The first is that one of the major symbolic uses of wine is to communicate messages about the sophistication and culture of an individual or community. This is certainly one way in which it is treated by artists, for wine often appears in paintings, music or literature (as in the Lord Peter Wimsey story in Chapter 8) to convey such a meaning – although, as we shall see, the metaphorical use of wine may be more ambivalent than that. This idea that wine has become a symbol of what it means to be civilized has been encapsulated by one historian of wine:

> Only as man ascended to the higher levels of civilizations did he come to look upon wine as more than a consolation and perceive it as a creation worthy of his advanced culture (Loubere, 1978, p. xvii).

Beyond this, however, the civilizing role of wine has assumed an extra importance in defending the wine industry against anti-alcohol campaigners. In the United States particularly there has been an explicit move to link wine, food and the arts as a marker of an advanced and refined society in the face of what has become termed 'neo-prohibitionism' (see Chapter 13).

It is worth, as a preliminary, being clear about what a civilized life might entail. There are two key definitions of civilization. The first is 'having an advanced state of society – art, science, government and religion' and the second is 'polite' and 'refined' (Delbridge & Bernard, 1998). The two definitions may not necessarily go hand-in-hand. The Aztecs were the most technologically, administratively and artistically advanced culture in northern Central America before the arrival of the Spanish conquistadors. They were not always polite and refined to their captives who were used in regular human sacrifices. For the purposes of this chapter a combination of the two definitions will be used, so that a civilized life is one which is socially, artistically and scientifically advanced, but which is fair, polite and cultured in its dealings with others.

The elements of a civilized drink

In order to explore the concept of wine as a drink of the civilized person it is necessary to understand how wine has taken on that metaphorical role; what factors have ensured that it is seen as the drink of cultured people? Five related phenomena are suggested as catalysts for this transfer of meaning. That wine has an aura of sophistication, that it is a drink of restraint, that it stimulates the pursuit of knowledge, that it is a 'natural' drink, and that it may be considered an art form.

This investigation may, however, be prefaced with a caveat. It can be inferred that in societies where wine is an elite drink it may become denoted as a civilized drink not so much because of anything metaphorical in the product but because of those who drink it. Wine thus is civilized because the elites who drink it consider themselves to be refined and they, by definition, will only drink what is itself refined – rather than because the drink itself symbolically embodies restraint, or artistic creation.

Sophistication

The idea that wine establishes status, and with status comes sophistication, has been examined in detail in the previous chapter. It is worth drawing a distinction between the cultures of democratic wine and elite wine. In the latter, the northern European, Anglophone and – increasingly – east Asian cultures, wine has traditionally been seen to be the drink of the rich and the aristocratic and it has definitely not been a necessity. In non-producing societies wine was exotic and scarcity has value for the more refined part of the population. (In this context one can note the fact that oysters, currently scarce, therefore expensive and a 'refined' taste were in Victorian times so commonly available that they were a foodstuff regularly consumed by the masses (Toussaint-Samat, 1987/1994)).

Part of this sophistication has arisen as wine has been classified and professionalized. There are an increasing number of norms surrounding the tasting, drinking and selection of wine. It has become a complex drink to understand, and those norms can be used for inclusion (those who know their way around them) and exclusion (Demossier, 2004). The more 'advanced' and refined are in the know, and hence more civilized.

The sophistication inferred from the consumption of wine also applies to the style of wine consumed. There is a common belief in the wine industry that consumers move from the less sophisticated off-dry or sweet white wines to more sophisticated reds (Geene et al., 1999), although this trajectory is not invariably born out in research (Muir, 1997), which has noted that consumers may remain with sweeter wines for their entire drinking life.

Finally, one can note that technologically advanced societies have developed more 'advanced' wine. Historically both fortified and sparkling wines have stemmed from technological advance, and the focus in the last few decades on 'fruitier' wines (Demossier, 2004) has arisen from advances in biochemical control over the last half-century, with the ability to manipulate microbiological and chemical activity effectively.

Restraint

The idea that wine is the alcoholic drink of restraint, at least compared to beer and spirits, has a long and widespread tradition. The Greeks considered the careful consumption of wine to be one thing that marked them out from the drunken barbarians around them (Crane, 2003). There is a sense that, despite its potentially deleterious effects, those who drink wine use it with more self-control that those consuming other alcoholic drinks. This view was expressed 200 years ago by many early campaigners for temperance who saw wine as the civilized alternative to spirits, including such noted lovers of wine as the third president of the United States, Thomas Jefferson and the early campaigner against the evils of alcohol, Dr Benjamin Rush (Fuller, 1996). Interestingly, the perspective that wine imparts restraint operates both in southern European countries with high consumption and countries where wine is viewed as an elite drink. In France the term '*les alcools*' (alcoholic drinks) defines spirits and not wine, which confused, in the 1960s, American anthropologists working in France who saw the child given watered wine whilst its mother simultaneously denied that she would ever give alcohol to her children (Anderson, 1968).

This viewpoint, that wine is a drink of restraint, is reflected in advertising. In some countries beer is still promoted, albeit in a humorous manner, by association with the volume that men will drink. Wine tends to be advertised using situations which involve both genders, and in contexts where drinking is more likely to be socially controlled, such as dinner parties.

In principle there may be some truth in this perception that wine is a drink of restraint. The regular pairing of wine with food (see below) and the common context of wine consumption in the public arena of restaurants provides another means of enforcing restraint, and establishing social control over consumption (Demossier, 2004). The fact that wine is consumed for its flavour also means that it tends to be savoured rather than gulped, restricting its intake. To the extent that research has been done on the danger associated with various types of alcohol, bottled wine is perceived to have little or no relationship to alcohol-induced assaults or morbidity related to abuse (Stockwell et al., 1998). However, there is a caveat to this proposition, which is that it applies in specific cultures, particularly those of European origin. Stockwell et al. (1998) make the point that the consumption of cask wine, sold in containers of 4 L or more, does have a significant relationship with assaults and disease which result from alcohol consumption. In many communities of outback Australia with a substantial aboriginal population cask wine is the drug of choice, and is often not consumed with restraint (Stockwell et al., 1998). It can also be noted that in some countries, such as Japan, wine is perceived to be a drink which provides intoxication equally with beer and spirits if the drinker's main aim is merely to get drunk. The idea, therefore, that wine drinkers are more refined because they are more restrained in their consumption is limited to certain social and cultural contexts.

The pursuit of knowledge

Wine, probably more than any other drink, comes in diverse styles, can be made in distinctive ways, and reflects the production approach of many countries and regions. These factors mean that it offers the potential of intellectual challenge, so that the desire to 'explore' wine can be crucial – most notably for high-involvement consumers (Charters & Pettigrew, 2006). This cognitive approach, relying on the gathering of information to aid in the understanding and thus ultimately the enjoyment of a product, can be seen for a number of leisure activities such as sport (Holt, 1995) and artworks (Csikszentmihalyi & Robinson, 1990), and it can be argued that it forms part of a process whereby an interest is given more significant meaning in a consumer's life. Thus, the need to amass and categorize information about a product is a way of developing one's self-image; in essence, of shaping a sense of self (Belk, 1988). Such an intellectual challenge can be an enjoyable process for the drinker.

The amassing of knowledge about wine will be dealt with in greater detail in Chapter 10, but at this stage it is relevant to note the development, over recent decades, of wine clubs, wine literature, wine education courses and even television programmes about wine. Given that wine as an alcoholic drink has a level of ambiguity surrounding it, this process of intellectualizing the product may also give a sense of seriousness to what is otherwise perceived to be an insignificant hedonistic experience.

It can also be pointed out that knowledge establishes distinction (Bourdieu, 1986). We can be 'in the know' about what we drink. Knowledge allows the nuances of the product to be understood, and fine distinctions in evaluation to be applied.

A natural drink

For some consumers wine offers two related symbolic benefits. One is that it is a naturally produced product – that it is, essentially, environmentally friendly. The other is that as agricultural produce, rather than industrially produced like beer, it provides a link to a more bucolic, rural existence; it is a drink which reflects nature, rather than process. Wine, after all, probably began with the spontaneous fermentation of crushed grapes. Beer and spirits both require substantial human intervention in order to produce them and to this extent have always been perceived as manufactured.

The first of these symbolic benefits – the 'green' dimension of wine – can be seen in a number of contexts. It has most successfully been applied in New Zealand's 'clean and green' marketing campaign for its wine. This seems to have been recognized, at least by opinion formers in the food and drinks world.

Plate 1 Contrasting producers: the Araldica co-operative in north-western Italy can bottle 10 000 000 bottles per year.

Plate 2 Garlands winery, in Western Australia, makes 45 000 bottles each vintage.

Plate 3 An advertisement promoting red Burgundy – noting the 'unique' terroir available in the region and stressing that 'true' pinot noir can only come from there. (Photograph by Jeremy Hudson, reproduced by permission of the Bureau Interprofessionel des Vins de Bourgogne.)

Plate 4 The interaction of wine and religion. Above the vines is the hermitage at the top of a hill overlooking Tain l'Hermitage, in the northern Rhone, after which the famous wine region of Hermitage is named. Legend has it that it was constructed by a French knight, weary of the destruction of war. He devoted himself to a life of prayer, and planted syrah wines which he had brought back from the town of Shiraz in modern-day Iran. Unfortunately modern DNA testing has disproved that part of the story.

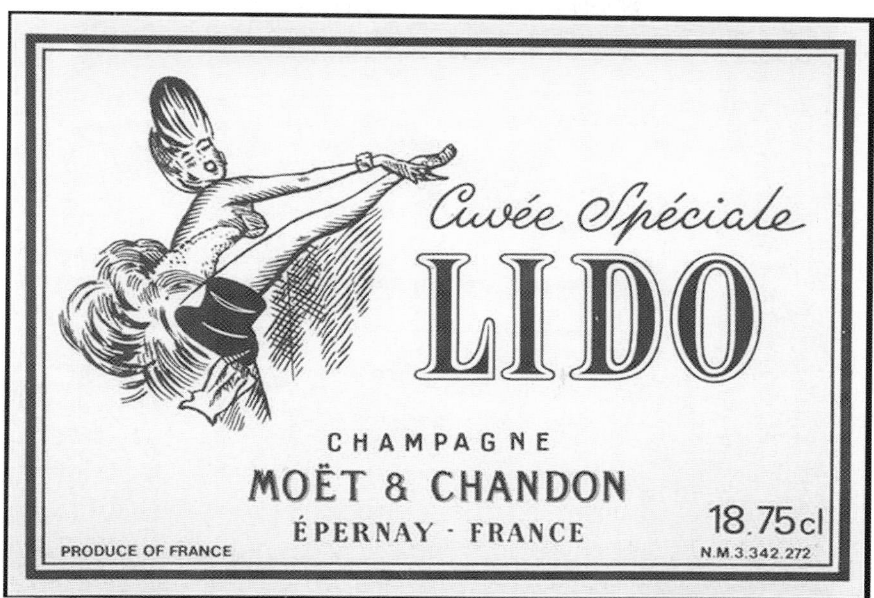

Plate 5 Selling wine by using sex. A label for Moët et Chandon champagne. (Reproduced by permission of Moët et Chandon).

Plate 6 The complex link between wine, status, politics, religion and health. This is the Hospices de Beaune, founded in the fifteenth century by the Nicholas Rolins, Chancellor to the local ruler, the Duke of Burgundy, as a refuge for the sick and elderly of the town, and run by a religious sisterhood. Rolins funded his foundation by donating vineyards, with income from the sale of local wines. Whether he was being altruistic, or demonstrating his (and his patron's power) or securing the future of his soul after death is hard to determine.

Plate 7 The link between wine and health. The sign on the side of a chemist's shop in a small English town.

Plate 8 A vine which grows in the centre of the prison on Robben Island where hundreds of anti-apartheid activists, including Nelson Mandela, were imprisoned. For the fiercely religious Afrikaners the vine would have had religious symbolism. It also represented the alcoholic drinks which their racial group enjoyed. It was thus, perhaps, doubly a symbol of repression for the prisoners.

One review of a New Zealand focused restaurant in London described the food as having the purity of a New Zealand wine and commented that 'the overall impression is that you're eating and drinking from some of the least polluted sources on Earth' (Eyres, 2005, p. 42). Marketing wine as an environmentally sound product is generally seen to have benefits for companies (Pugh & Fletcher, 2002), and an argument has even been made for the continued use of corks rather than plastic or screw-top stoppers on wine bottles because of the adverse environmental impact it would have on Portuguese cork forests (Bruce-Gardyne, 2000). It is significant to note, however, that the impact of the vine is not invariably environmentally acceptable. As one of the six floral kingdoms in the world the Cape Floristic Kingdom is the smallest, covering an area of about 90 000 km^2 around Cape Town (Fairbanks et al., 2004). There is substantial evidence that this unique eco-system is threatened by the expansion of viticulture in the wake of South Africa's burgeoning wine industry (Fairbanks et al., 2004). At the same time Wines of South Africa, the co-ordinating body for the industry there, has launched a marketing campaign in the United Kingdom based on the tag 'variety is our nature' linking wine (and its terroir) explicitly to the Western Cape's diverse flora.

Banrock Station

One wine producer has explicitly linked wine to the natural world by tying its wine production to the environment. Banrock Station wines, launched by BRL Hardy (now part of Constellation Wines) in the mid-1990s, is produced from wines sourced in the Riverland region of South Australia. The area, in the valley of the Murray River, has been subject to growing environmental degradation for much of the past 80 years, due to diversion of the river system and the substantial use of river water for irrigation.

Banrock Station have made both their geographic location in the Murray wetlands, and a commitment to environmental conservation, part of their wine's unique selling proposition (Constellation Wines, 2005). They employ environmental managers and ecologists to look after their property – which is run as a 'Wine and Wetland' centre. Profits from sales have been used to fund projects (Pugh & Fletcher, 2002), and these work to protect endangered Australian species including parrots and frogs, and protecting traditional habitat. The winery's website contains the following:

> The picturesque Banrock Station property includes 3400 acres of bushland and extensive wetlands that are being carefully restored to their natural state.

When the property was first purchased, over a century of rabbit and stock grazing, and timber felling had degraded native vegetation, wildlife habitats and floodplains. Lock's controlling the ebb and flow of the river had interrupted the natural wetting and drying cycles, favouring feral European carp and upsetting the local habitats.

Now, following passionate conservation work by Banrock Station and dedicated conservation groups like Wetland Care Australia, the wetlands and woodlands are carefully being rejuvenated. The re-introduction of natural wetting and drying cycles has spurred life. The replanting of native vegetation has reduced soil erosion, and provided homes for animals to nest. Fish barriers and drying cycles have significantly reduced the number of damaging European carp. Importantly, native water birds are returning to nest at Banrock Station. Native fish, water plants, frogs, insects, birds and reptiles are once again contributing to the diversity of the River Murray.

The success at Banrock Station has encouraged Banrock to make important annual donations to save and restore nature reserves throughout the world. Currently, Banrock Station's wetland sponsorships spans 10 countries throughout the globe.

The countries concerned include Australia, New Zealand, Canada, Denmark, Kenya, the Netherlands, Sweden, the United Kingdom and the USA. All except Kenya are existing or potentially significant markets for Banrock Station wines.

By Christmas 2005 the company had donated Au$3 000 000 to wildlife support, and sent journalists across Australia a bottle of Banrock Station sparkling wine as a sample – a common practice in the wine industry. With it, however, they also added a small sapling of an Australian plant with a request that it be planted within 7 days – much less common, but an indicator to key gatekeepers of the brand owner's dedication to the environment.

Whilst there is no doubting the commitment of the winery to environmental improvement it is paradoxical that many of the immediate problems of the Murray River wetlands, especially salinity, have been caused by land clearance and irrigation, both of which have helped the success of vineyards in the Riverland region. Nevertheless, as part of the company's marketing package it seems that their environmental focus has been successful (Pugh & Fletcher, 2002).

There also seems to be a group of wine drinkers who enjoy wine because of its agricultural roots. Andrew Barr (1995), suggests that 'the fact that wine continues today to reflect the rhythm of the seasons in the countryside makes its appeal especially potent to the increasingly urbanized or suburbanized communities of the Western world' (1995, p. 345). It has been noted in Greece that there is a segment of urban consumers who respond positively to wine which is marketed with a geographic, association, because they perceive it to be more traditional – an authentic drink (Dimara & Skuras, 2003) – and in France, it has been suggested, many urban drinkers see wine as a link to their rural roots (Demossier, 2005).

Wine as an art form

The use of wine symbolically in arts is well-known (see below). However, there are those who would argue not only that wine may figure in the arts but also that it is an artwork itself. These links also give wine a connection to the civilized life, but this assertion is contentious and it is important to note that there are two issues operating here. The first is whether or not wine itself can be considered a work of art, which is relevant to the discussion about what makes a 'civilized drink'. The second issue is whether or not wine can be experienced aesthetically; that is, can it be judged in the way that a picture or a piece of music may be judged.

Is wine an art form? Certainly there are popular wine writers and wine professionals who assume that it is (Amerine & Roessler, 1976; Broadbent, 1979), and winemakers may be described as artistic (Anon., 2003). There is also a philosophical argument that wine is a work of art (Fretter, 1971). The nub of Fretter's (1971) argument is that it can be classed as beautiful, because of the 'aesthetic satisfaction' gained from it as an aesthetic object, which has been shaped by a skilled craftsman. For Fretter these three elements define the work of art, but some philosophers would disagree. Sibley (2001) accepts that smells and tastes can be aesthetically evaluated, but discounts the idea that they have to come from a work of art. Other philosophers would not even accept that aesthetic evaluation can be applied to smells or tastes. There are four key arguments against wine being a work of art:

1 The idea that it satisfies our 'lower' senses (taste and smell) rather than the higher senses of sight and hearing (Scruton, 1979). However, quite why this artificial division exists is uncertain; taste and smell certainly relate to the physically necessary functions of ingesting

food, but then sight and sound are equally necessary for our safety and security.

2 That it cannot engross our full attention, disinterested from any idea of physical benefit; drinking wine is, invariably, linked to other selfish processes (Kant, 1790/1987). This too is arguable; there are many wine drinkers, of all levels of involvement, who would attest to the fact that a specific wine can be all engrossing, and give you an uplifting quasi-mystical experience independently of any utilitarian function it may perform (Charters & Pettigrew, 2005).

3 That enjoying a wine is merely a matter of preference; it cannot be defended by recourse to argument about components of the wine which can 'prove' its quality, unlike, say a piece of music (Shiner, 1996). Again there are those who would argue that dimensions of the wine – components such as balance, intensity, complexity and the interest it generates are definable and can be used objectively in this way (Charters & Pettigrew, 2003b).

4 That wine only offers a single smell or taste, and aesthetic beauty resides in the complex interplay of different components – such as all the lines, various textures, shading and variation of colour in a painting (Beardsley, 1980). However, that is an arguable position to maintain (consider a painting that is entirely one shade of blue, or a piece of music which is a single note). More crucially, good wine – like a good meal – should offer complexity of flavour, with an interaction between a number of varietal fruit characters, acid, alcohol and perhaps tannin and oak (Charters & Pettigrew, 2003b).

A more recent philosophical perspective, influenced perhaps by the tendency of post-modernism to break down disciplinary barriers and shun metatheory, has been to say that the question is irrelevant, for it is impossible and unnecessary to shift the barriers of what is perceived to be 'high art' (Korsmeyer, 1999), so it is ultimately meaningless to ask if wine is an art form when what matters is how drinkers engage with it. Non-philosophical disciplines which consider the nature of art would be less prescriptive than philosophers. Consumer researchers may consider many products, not merely 'high art', as being works of art (Holbrook & Hirschman, 1980). Yet another approach is to see wine not as a work of art, but as a craft; a product which requires skill, though not necessarily artistic expression (Delbridge & Bernard, 1998) – although the distinction between the two is probably false, as crafts become art forms and artistic products require craftsmanship (Becker, 1978).

The philosopher in the vineyard

Whether or not wine is an art form, it has a close relationship to philosophical thought, and is also regularly used in the arts – in each case metaphorically. There are also those who consider that, again irrespective of the nature of wine itself, the drinker's encounter with it may be considered as an aesthetic experience.

Wine and philosophy

Philosophy had its roots in and, at least in metaphysics, retains its link to, theological speculation; the role of wine in religion has already been considered. The Greeks, who initiated philosophical enquiry, saw wine as the civilized drink (Crane, 2003) and used it at their symposium – a formal time of discussion (often philosophical) which followed a meal. Wine, thus, has a long relationship with philosophers, and has regularly been used by them as a metaphor (e.g. Hume, 1757/1998). It has also been used by some philosophers to 'prove' the objectivity of judgments of taste (Gale, 1975; Railton, 1998).

As a philosophical metaphor wine has a number of advantages. It has, however, been used most extensively not in a work of pure philosophy but in a poem – a poem which, nevertheless, expounds a very specific philosophical outlook on life. The Rubaiyat of Omar Khayyam (Fitzgerald, 1989/1859) is based on quatrains composed by a Persian astronomer and mathematician (Omar Khayyam – ostensibly a Muslim – who died in 1132 AD). However, the poetry was not just translated but reinterpreted by the Victorian, Edward FitzGerald, who used it as a contrast with the strict Christian orthodoxy of nineteenth century Britain. In their joint hands wine is used to highlight the pointlessness of traditional religion. Thus wine gives pleasure – perhaps aesthetic pleasure – but unlike works of art it is consumed and only a memory remains; it thus conveys an idea of the transience of life. Conversely, for those who take a more hedonistic approach it can symbolize the need to enjoy the moment. At the same time its apparent frivolity, and its role in mundane social interactions allows it to be used as a contrast with the futile seriousness of dogmatics (Fitzgerald, 1989/1859).

More recently philosophers have turned their attention to wine for other reasons. Carolyn Korsmeyer (1999) has investigated the philosophy of taste (physical, rather than metaphorical) in some detail, looking not merely at wine but more specifically at food. Korsmeyer suggests that food and drink may have aesthetic value, but their importance actually goes beyond that; it is their symbolic role, the way that they function quasi-linguistically which is as important as any philosophical value they may have.

The other area in which philosophers find wine a useful tool is in considering the nature of subjective and objective experience and how we can communicate about something which may seem to be idiosyncratic (Crane, 2003; Smith, 2004). The taste of wine lies not just in its objective chemical properties, but in our subjective response to it. Wine tasting thus offers the possibility of exploring intersubjectivity – the situation where a number of individuals, each with an idiosyncratic physiological response, may share some common understanding of an objective (external) event. We can consider our individual response to the hundreds of components of a wine – albeit using partly metaphorical and thus subjective language – describe to others what we have experienced, and come to some common understanding with them about the nature of the wine we have tasted (Crane, 2003).

Wine and aesthetic consumption

As has been suggested, rather than consider whether or not wine is a work of art (which becomes bogged down in arcane disputes about high art and crafts) it may be better to ask if drinking it shares features with the experience of things like listening to music, viewing art or watching a play. In philosophical terms: can drinking be an aesthetic process, and can wine be evaluated using aesthetic criteria?

The traditional philosophical perspective suggests not just that wine cannot be an artwork, but that enjoying it cannot be an aesthetic experience. This point was made perhaps most famously by the great German philosopher of aesthetics, Kant. Although he enjoyed wine (and knew something about it (Taylor, 1988)) Kant explicitly discounted drink from any aesthetic experience (Kant, 1790/1987). The arguments he raised – that the experience of drinking cannot result in 'disinterested attention' and merely involves judgments of preference rather than objective evaluation – have already been outlined.

This viewpoint is maintained by some contemporary philosophers (Scruton, 1979; Shiner, 1996). Many others, however, are less tied to a traditional 'high-art' idea of what constitutes an aesthetic experience, and explicitly argue that a wine drinker can undergo it. Some maintain that objective judgments of wine can exist (Railton, 1998); others maintain that tastes can be judged independently of one's preference for them (Gale, 1975). Ultimately, wine may give an aesthetic experience just because it is 'worth bothering about' (Sibley, 2001, p. 243).

Consumer researchers tend to a much less restrictive approach to the idea of aesthetic experiences. One can summarize their definition of aesthetic consumption as having four component parts (Charters, forthcoming). First, the experience has a focus on beauty (which is very broadly defined). Second, it is a form of experiential consumption (see Chapter 7), but with a substantial cognitive element which involves thinking and evaluation, as well as the affective sense of pleasure and a substantial sensory dimension. Third, it has a strong symbolic function; when we have an aesthetic experience it speaks both to us and, perhaps, allows us to communicate to those around us. Finally (and unlike the traditional philosophical approach) the experience exists on a continuum from general pleasure to a profound hedonic experience.

The aesthetics of wine: What do consumers think?

When asked if there are similarities in drinking wine and listening to music or looking at a painting, consumers tend to think that there are some similarities. At its most extreme this link has an almost spiritual dimension:

> Simon: Fundamentally you can make the connection between music, literature, art and wine. Without them life wouldn't be worth living. I think that's the fundamental thing. You can certainly drop one or two of them but if you didn't have any expressive qualities in your life then there would be no . . . way of growing as a human being.

Consumers were quite specific about what these experiences had in common. First, they all involve a sense of pleasure. They expressed the idea that pleasure exists on a continuum of intensity, or profoundness. There was also a sense – generally implicit – that this pleasure involved an element of beauty. Occasionally it even became explicit:

> Wendy: [At a concert, art-gallery or wine tasting] you're looking for something that's going to be inspiring and beautiful. Yeah, I guess beauty can be seen in all things. . . . Special bottles of wine, certainly I'd rate in that category [as beautiful].

These processes are all perceived by consumers to involve evaluative responses; judgments are made as part of the response to the product. In order to make these judgments the consumer needs to be very focused on the aesthetic experience and, for the appreciation to be most effective, a level of knowledge and experience aids discernment. At the same time, some consumers noted that similar criteria inform these judgments. Good music, like good wine, needs to be in balance. The experience should be intense and, for the best wine and music it should offer an element of complexity and a sense that the experience is distinctive rather than mundane.

Some consumers also link wine with music or other art forms by noting that both provide the opportunity for intellectual challenge and the exploration of the new (noted above as one factor which imparts to wine a sense of being a civilized drink). Thus, comparing music and wine:

> Gerhard: I think in both cases you need to know what makes it tick. In music you need to know how music evolved, what's behind it. The link between mathematics and music is an obvious one. And once you understand certain things like that you can appreciate music, even if it's not to your liking. Sometimes you find if you realize the amount of work that has gone into growing the wine, that's gone into making the wine, that's gone into storing the wine – you can appreciate it for its quality even if you don't like its style.

In this way knowledge links to challenge and a relish for what is new. For example, even within a small wine region such as Pauillac in Bordeaux, differences between the varying producers and their interpretation of their raw material may be critical to the evaluation and enjoyment of their wines.

Finally, wine and other works of art seem to have a paradox of objectivity. For many consumers personal taste was a key concept linking wine to more traditional artworks:

> Hetty: If I was looking at art or music I think it would come down to my personal taste. Which is the same as wine – so in that way, I think, they are similar.

Thus, for Hetty, the response one makes to a piece of music or a painting is individual and subjective. On the other hand, and in contrast, some consumers considered that there is a common response in the experience of wine and other aesthetic products which unites consumers. Effectively this viewpoint argues that most people sharing the experience tend to concur in how good (or bad) the product is and that aesthetic appreciation has an element of objectivity. One consumer expressed it in this way, when considering art and wine:

> Roger: Often a hallmark of a good work is that it's appealing to everyone regardless of their level of expertise. A painting might be appealing to everyone. They will go 'wow that's really good, obviously someone's talented, they've put a lot into it. There's no way I could do that – it looks really impressive'. Off they go – the punter – and an expert comes along and goes 'wow that is amazing . . . their use of shadow and line and light and all of that sort of thing . . . ' Similarly with wine.

Roger believed that quality in both a picture and a wine is capable of being discerned by anyone, whether amateurs ('punter') or experts – even though the latter may be able to rationalize their reaction with greater facility. This perspective contrasts with the 'personal taste' approach, and exists paradoxically to it.

Consumers thus consider that the appreciation of wine operates – at least in part – in a similar fashion to more conventional artworks. They all involve pleasure, a response which is stimulated by a sense of beauty. They invite evaluation rather than a merely passive reception, and they may involve intellectual challenge, or exploration of the new. Paradoxically, they may be seen to be subject to personal taste, or there may be an element of objectivity or intersubjectivity in the appreciation they evoke (Charters & Pettigrew, 2005).

Wine in the arts

Whatever the debate over the aesthetic nature of wine itself, there is no doubt that it has been represented in the arts at least since *The Epic of Gilgamesh*. It remains most obvious, perhaps, in literature, where its metaphorical or symbolic role can be most articulately exposed, but it can also be found in music, painting and sculpture. Given the breadth of use of wine in literature, most attention will be focused on this art form to allow a detailed exploration of its role. Wine, like many other experiential and aesthetic products, can easily act semiotically. That is, it provides a message without words being spoken, and without the author having to articulate the meaning formally. Thus, in a James Bond film, when the hero buys Champagne to drink with a young woman seduction is implied to the audience without the need for any words to be spoken.

It is important to remember that exactly how wine is treated will depend very much on the perspective of the author. An author rooted in the culture of the Mediterranean, for instance, will pay less attention to status-related issues and more to wine as a medium of conviviality than a writer from northern Europe, such as Dorothy Sayers. Equally, Omar Khayyam writing his verse in a society which ostensibly anathematized wine would, merely by mentioning the drink, be setting his narrator outside the bounds of conventional society.

Finally it can be suggested that – conforming to the generally ambivalent nature of wine – many of these symbolic uses are dichotomous. That means that, depending on context (both of reader and author) wine may symbolize one thing or its opposite.

This can be seen readily in the use of wine as a symbol of status – already exemplified a number of times – including both inclusion and exclusion. A good example of the former is contained in George Orwell's novel 1984, where the hero, Winston Smith, is given wine to try by the bureaucrat who is attempting entrapment; wine is a product entirely beyond Smith's experience. Although in this example Winston Smith the rebel gets to taste wine, it only serves to reinforce the fact that he, and those with whom he mixes daily, are not part of the ruling elite in his country. On the other hand wine may mark inclusion – such as the conviviality that surrounds Falstaff following his consumption of the Spanish wine Sack in Shakespeare's plays. We open a bottle of wine for companionship, which in turn can become boisterous and bawdy.

Wine may be used as a marker for romance and may be an aid to seduction. However, this in itself can be ambiguous. In *Macbeth* there is a well-known scene where a porter expands on the dangers of alcohol; drink, he claims, produces ambivalent results:

> Lechery, sir, it provokes, and unprovokes; it provokes the desire but it takes away the performance. Therefore much drink may be said to be an equivocator with lechery; it makes him and it mars him; it sets him on and it takes him off; it persuades him, and disheartens him; makes him stand to and not stand to (Macbeth act II, scene iii).

In a comic function, wine can be used as a subtle, ironic tool or as a means of inducing slapstick comedy. Chaucer (himself the son of a wine merchant) used it in one of *The Canterbury Tales* – The Merchant's Tale. An old knight who has married a young bride drinks Hippocras (spiced wine) for 'courage' in bed. The message, though not spelt out, is that the knight is too old – and probably in need of an aphrodisiac – but the reader has to infer that from the context and the humour is not immediately obvious.

In a religious context wine may show spiritual ambivalence: it can mark both sacrifice and scepticism. The latter has already been exemplified, the former is reflected in *The Iliad* and *The Odyssey*, written by the Greek poet, Homer, where wine is poured away in a libation, a sacrifice to the gods and a symbol of the sacrificer's piety. One can also contrast such sacred rituals with the profane. In the foxhunting novels of the early nineteenth century writer Robert Smith Surtees a glass of wine features as the essential precursor to the hunt – the stirrup cup. This is a sign that a ritual of social bonding and the maintenance of class status is about to commence – as well as a pointer to the impending spilling of blood.

Wine can signify the relief of worldly cares. The poet, Lord Byron, wrote 'wine cheers the sad, revives the old, inspires the young, makes weariness forget his toil' (Sardanapalus act 1 scene i). This is especially true in the French approach to wine, where it is seen as invigorating rather than debilitating (Barthes, 1957/2000). Yet wine can also create distress, whether temporary in the form of hangovers, or longer term in the reduction of a family to poverty. The consumption of wine may act as a metaphor for the rapid passing of life, as in the *Rubaiyat of Omar Khayyam*. With a fixation on the minutiae of production detail or obsessive collecting it can symbolize selfishness (Meredith, 1995) but paradoxically it can also be used to display great generosity as suggested by the way it is used by Falstaff, in Shakespeare's Henry IV plays.

These examples all feature in literature; similar instances, though without perhaps the nuances which literature allows, can be noted in other art forms. To take one example, wine may be used musically in the sacred (such as the *Good Wine Mass* by the sixteenth century composer Lassus) or the profane, as for instance in the song *Red Red Wine* by Neil Diamond, where it signifies the need for emotional oblivion and, by implication, a rejection of spiritual solace.

Finally, it is worth noting that the arts may have an impact on wine consumption. The recent Oscar-nominated film *Sideways* features a wine tour made by a couple of ex-college friends. During the trip one of them (who is wine-obsessed) forcefully expresses his dislike of merlot, and much prefers pinot noir. Following this – apparently as a result – it seems sales of merlot in the United States slowed whilst pinot noir purchases rose by 57 per cent (Roby, 2005).

Wine and food

There may be a temptation to query why the relationship of food and wine is seen as part of a 'civilized life'. Historically in some cultures, as suggested in the previous chapter, it was the production of wine and the processing of bread which distinguished humanity from animals. There is therefore a long tradition, perhaps now unconscious, which sees these two products as symbolizing the mental, technical and artistic progress of people – the factors which show us to be civilized.

Additionally both wine and food are symbols of conviviality. Conviviality is the result of hospitality, and hospitality implies peaceableness which in turn is predicated on the absence of conflict. It can therefore be suggested that, for those who perceive civilization to rest in part on the minimization of conflict and the non-violent resolution of disputes, good food and good wine may be seen to be helpful.

Additionally, as considered above, there is a perspective which claims that good taste has an aesthetic value, and therefore the appreciation of the complexity and distinctiveness of the two, and the beauty they can offer, may also symbolize the civilized life. Wine is regularly said to be drunk for aesthetic appreciation (Amerine & Roessler, 1976) or enjoyment (Peynaud, 1987). An aspect of that aesthetic experience may be the careful matching of wine with a particular food. This is an aesthetic connection between a pair of products which – literally – offer 'good taste'. It is worth noting, in passing, that beer may not have the same relationship to food (Pettigrew & Charters, 2006).

Introduction

In the past, as suggested in Chapter 3, wine was perceived to be a foodstuff; it has a calorific value, and had some dietary benefits. However, for many modern consumers and popular commentators the true relationship between food and wine goes well beyond the scientific objectivity of calorific intake. There is a generally accepted relationship between the organoleptic pleasure offered by both food and wine (Bode, 1992; Simon, 1996). Louis Pasteur, one of the pioneers of modern oenology, argued that 'a meal without wine is like a day without sunshine' (Exley, 1994). Crucially many popular writers on wine produce publications which explore ideas about pairing food and wine (e.g., Benson & Walton, 2003; Simon, 1996). Thus, for example, a reader is exhorted to drink a chardonnay, preferably with little or no oak (Chablis gets a particular endorsement) with an Indian Korma, to match the creamy-almondy character of the curry sauce (Benson & Walton, 2003, p. 137). Ultimately, the contemporary chef Alain Senderens claims that 'the dish in itself is not enough, the marriage with wine has to occur, and true gastronomy for me lies in research for such harmony' (Spurrier, 2005, p. 96). However, academic investigation into why food and wine good together is sparse, and generally assumes that the relationship exists rather than questions why or how it operates (e.g. Heath, 2000).

Historically, however, this focus on the pairing of the right food and the right wine is of comparatively recent origin – only developing as a major exercise within the last 200 years. Until the middle of the nineteenth century food in Europe was not served in successive courses as now but in just two waves – so on the table there could be fish, game, red meat and sweets at the same time, making the choice of wine problematic. Only with the development of service *à la russe*, which involved starting a meal with soup and ending it with dessert, did the focus on the correct match become important (Briggs, 1994).

The pairing of food and wine is also primarily an issue with the consumption of premium rather than bulk wine. Bulk wine is used as a lubricant with food, or for its alcoholic impact, rather than essentially for any flavour-related aesthetic qualities. In support of the former instance one can cite the general use of a local wine by consumers throughout much of the Mediterranean, irrespective of its colour or style. Historically that drink may have been piquette (Loubere et al., 1985), with little flavour intensity. Even today there are those who will drink merely whatever happens to be locally available. A magazine article on an isolated Italian village (Follain, 2001) describes 'Carmellina', who has lived to be 100, and attributes her longevity to a careful diet. The profile adds that 'she insists on a glass of white wine with every meal' (2001, p. 19). This was the wine that happened to be available in the region. In this kind of society wine is primarily selected not for its aesthetic value, nor to match specific food, but because of the dictates of custom or availability.

One area of research which is relevant to the relationship of food and wine consumption stems out of research into the segmentation of wine consumers, and especially the relevance of the place of consumption in this process. As noted in Chapter 7, the situation in which wine is drunk is important in understanding why people drink, and how they make their consumption decisions (Dubow, 1992). Thus, within an Australian context it has been argued that 'complementing food' is perceived by consumers to be an important occasion to drink wine (Hall & Lockshin, 1999; 2000).

Food and wine: A consumer study

What follows is from a qualitative research study which investigated consumer perceptions of the relationship between food and wine (Charters & Pettigrew, 2004). The study involved consumers (at all levels of involvement with wine) and wine professionals. As a preliminary it is worth noting that none of the informants were asked directly about the relationship of wine with food but merely regarding their feelings about wine. Where the issue was brought up it was by the informants themselves, and consequently the comments that follow are 'top-of-the-mind' perspectives, rather than ideas which were explicitly sought. These perspectives tend to split into three different categories; first the complementarity of food and wine, second the social context of wine and food consumption and third wine as a lubricant. Each will be dealt with in turn.

Complementarity

Most of the informants in the study considered that – after the pleasure afforded by good taste – the major role of wine was to be an accompaniment to food. Thus:

> Dan: I enjoy eating and savouring – eating out. And the wine goes hand-in-hand with that. There's nothing I enjoy more than having a 4 hour dinner. That's one of my big things in life and the wine, you know, it goes hand-in-hand with that.

This approach was common to consumers at all levels of involvement. In this context the complementarity of food and wine seems to operate in two ways. One is the general psychological or emotional effect of pairing food and wine – in the words of one interviewee, the ambience:

> Mary: I guess it's the ambience of it. I really enjoy having wine with a good meal. It's a pleasurable experience in terms of the overall thing – of having a glass of wine with nice food.

Thus food complements wine psychologically; together they may provide enjoyment. It was not mentioned explicitly by Mary but other informants referred to the fact that their consumption in tandem may help one to unwind. Others noted the romantic potential of the two.

However, for some drinkers the link was less obviously about ambient complementarity and more about flavour complementarity – an overtly aesthetic relationship. Often the specific taste of the wine was important. For a number of informants it is taken a step further, with the food planned around the wine:

> Nettie: If I was having what I call a decent bottle of wine . . . then I would plan the meal around the wine and I would sit down and eat it – the meal – and drink the wine simultaneously.

Ultimately there may be a careful marrying of flavours. For Belinda, in the following extract, this complementarity is critical. She runs a winebar, so specific and complementary tastes are essential to her:

> Belinda: I like wine with food and I'm very particular. I don't just drink any wine. If I'm going to eat with friends I find out what they're cooking and . . . I'm very specific. Last night I went to a Chinese and

> I took a viognier. I like food with the wines. If I'm going to eat Asian then dry, austere, so I usually choose a German riesling or gewurtz., or something like that.

Naturally this level of specificity tends to operate at the highest levels of involvement. Nevertheless both forms of food-wine complementarity – the ambient and the flavour – appeared to be equally important for all types of drinker. However, it is likely that the two forms of food-wine complementarity have a varying relative significance depending on the situation; note the comment made by Nettie about planning a meal around a wine 'if I had a decent bottle'. For her that could be a situation where ambient complementarity is of more significance than flavour complementarity – as in the case of an intimate meal as a prelude to seduction. Even for wine industry professionals there were times when the most appropriate wine at a meal was not necessarily the best wine in objective quality terms, if the latter would have been enjoyed less by the company.

The social context of food and wine consumption

In addition to social complementarity the relationship of food to wine had other social features. The two combined often acted in a ritualistic way, marking, during the day, the division between work time and private time. They were also used to set out the boundaries between the working week and the personal time of the weekend, with the quasi-formal 'Friday evening meal' at which wine took a major role.

Thus wine and food jointly may provide psychological pleasure by enabling the preparation and experience of an event which involves both products – although it is also interesting to note that the most significant events, such as millennium celebrations or birthdays, seemed to be marked in the consumer's memory by wine only, rather than a combination of both wine and a meal.

As well as acting in this ritualistic fashion, wine and food together could often represent aspirations for a better life. One Australian informant talked wistfully of living in France, where there is a slower pace of life and a longer lunch hour, so that you can use food and wine to nurture yourself. Pausing, rather than rushing to the next job offered a chance for greater peace of mind.

A number of informants also implied that food and wine in tandem could communicate messages about an individual's level of social sophistication – using the link explicitly to show how 'civilized' they are. Thus it would be a waste to take a 'good' (expensive) wine to a barbecue. On the other hand:

> Waldemar: Having a dinner with white, stunning table cloths and very nice cutlery and very nice tableware really requires something better than cask wine.

One final, and important, point to make about the social context of food and wine consumption is that the match was explicitly seen by many informants to mitigate against alcohol abuse and drunkenness:

> Kevin: I really enjoy it, I don't drink wine to get drunk and love having a glass of red or white with whatever meal is going on at dinner time. Most of my friends are still drinking beer and spirits and other things.

In this sense it was, again, a much more civilized use of an alcoholic drink, overtly contrasted with beer drinking.

Wine as lubrication

Wine was perceived by some informants to have a very corporeal function, acting as a lubricant, helping to wash food down, and stimulating the stomach. Additionally some informants perceived that wine harmonizes physiologically with certain foods (for instance, tannin balancing protein, acid freshening fish):

> Frances: I also think with some foods wine cuts through the food.

At this point the utilitarian or functional reason for wine consumption shades into the aesthetic. Lubrication aids in the appreciation of good taste.

There is also an additional, related, area of lubrication – with the idea that wine can refresh, not so much as water quenches the thirst, but because it cleanses the palate. Nevertheless it is necessary to note that this whole area, lubrication and refreshment, was mentioned by fewer informants than the concept of complementarity. Where it was raised it was generally a concern of higher-involvement consumers, and especially professionals.

Wine and food: A summary

It is necessary to distinguish two ways in which food and wine complement each other. The first is situational complementarity. Aesthetically – in the way flavours marry organoleptically – and socially consumers perceive food and wine to match naturally. This shows a significant experiential and social relevance. The experiential is concentrated on the aesthetic response and sensory enjoyment of products that taste good. Pairing food with a wine which enhances its flavour is perceived to be positive (although absolute precision about the marriage of flavours – 'if I'm going to eat Asian then I choose German riesling' may be too precise for low- and medium-involvement consumers, and they could even find it off-putting). The social element – termed ambient complementarity – comprises both the development of friendship and conviviality and a symbolic element fixed in the messages consumers communicate to themselves and to those with whom they share a meal. Both forms of complementarity – the social and flavour – appeared to be important for drinkers of all levels of involvement (Charters & Pettigrew, 2004). The functional aspect of lubrication which some informants commented on is noted occasionally by academics (e.g. Jackson, 2002). In this sense wine has the significant utilitarian function of easing the consumption of food, stimulating the gastric juices and offering physical refreshment.

Wine and lifestyle

The development of the lifestyle wine

Very few wine drinkers would consider that their imbibing has any relation to the arts or to philosophy. They would be much more inclined to see it as an adjunct to their lifestyle. In the sense that a good 'lifestyle' is predicated on the context of an advanced society, and perhaps even of refinement, then wine as a lifestyle drink can still be seen to reflect a civilized life. Lifestyle has become something of a buzzword, both academically (Featherstone, 1991) and in marketing. A video produced by the promotional body Wines of South Africa claims that chenin blanc, the most widely planted grape variety in the Cape, 'is being reinvented as an exciting lifestyle wine'. The temptation is to ask what a 'non-lifestyle wine' is, and why anyone would choose to drink it, as well as what kind of wine chenin blanc produced before its reinvention.

It can be suggested that there are a number of components to the modern concept of lifestyle. These include individuality and self-expression

(Featherstone, 1991), the development of appropriate and serious leisure interests (Tomlinson, 1990) and the aesthetization of everyday life (Grunow, 1997; Sloan, 2004). As these lifestyle components exemplify the most modern interpretation of wine as a civilized drink it is worth considering each of them in detail.

One aspect that defines the modern 'lifestyle' is an emphasis on the importance of choice (Featherstone, 1991), and consumption as an expression of individuality (Richins, 1994); in a sense this fits into the idea of products allowing people to define who they are (Belk, 1988), and, as has been demonstrated in this and previous chapters, wine is a classic medium to achieve this; informed choice of the apposite wine is the sign of the knowing person (Tomlinson, 1990). Lifestyle is, perhaps, a way of making a busy and mundane existence palatable, and the emphasis is on choice within our own time, rather than within work. In essence, therefore, we consume to define what we would like to be. One element of this is the development of a family orientation; as wine is symbolic of conviviality it fits perfectly into this perspective. Another, linked, dimension is an emphasis on appropriate leisure; the way we spend our private time – our hobbies, pastimes and interests – is crucial in defining who we are. There is a tendency to seek individuality, and the avoidance of what is 'mass produced' (Beardsworth & Keil, 1992). Wine – with its facility to develop knowledge, understanding, collection and exploration – may be one example of this. Wine also has close links to other key leisure activities – food and tourism being the most obvious (Mitchell et al., 2000). At the same time wine is, perhaps, perceived as the most healthful of alcoholic drinks (Smith & Solgaard, 2000), so that its consumption fits into another key lifestyle concern – physical well-being. Wine is, of course, considered to be a key component of the Mediterranean diet which is currently in vogue for its purported health-giving properties. Thus, the back label of an Australian wine, the Mitchelton Triple Blend Red 1993 reads:

> The influence of the Mediterranean has permeated all aspects of lifestyle internationally, in particular its diet which has been hailed by nutritionists as the closest to ideal. And wine has always been its natural accompaniment . . . Grape varieties and wine styles that complement the healthy foods of the Mediterranean evolved over centuries and are gaining increased appreciation (Mitchelton Wines Pty Ltd, 1993).

(In passing it can be suggested that the original Mediterranean diet was somewhat different to its current reinterpretation, with less variety, and less of the gloss provided by modern chefs (Charters, 2002; Santich, 1996)).

The emphasis on lifestyle is primarily a concern of western countries, and its precise outworking may vary from country to country. Given current consumption trends it can be suggested that wine is substantially more important as a lifestyle component in Ireland than France. However, it is also true that there is an element of convergence in the international consumption of alcoholic drinks (Smith & Solgaard, 2000). Convergence is the idea that countries which are the home of natural spirits drinkers (such as Poland or Finland) are increasingly drinking more wine and beer, whilst wine and spirits consumption rises in beer drinking countries (Germany or the Czech Republic), and beer and spirits are consumed more in the traditional wine-producing nations of southern Europe (Smith & Solgaard, 2000).

Whereas traditional aesthetic thought has been limited to high art, one of the effects of so-called post-modernism has been to break down artificial social barriers between high art and other forms of artistic endeavour. Thus advertisements, street signs, graffiti and the design of white goods all become artworks. At the same time the adoption of the aesthetic has become a key feature defining the modern consumer (Featherstone, 1991). Consequently art and design have become key elements of where and how we live. This blurring of the boundaries is apparent with the labels of wine bottles. It became obvious in the decision of Baron Philippe de Rothschild – a noted art lover – to use a different artist each year to design the label of his most prestigious wine, Chateau Mouton-Rothschild – a move copied elsewhere in the world, as at Kenwood Vineyards in Sonoma (Fuller, 1993). Thus the label becomes a work of art. Today labels are designed to convey a 'lifestyle choice'. The artistic label acts as metaphor for the wine; the consumer may be unable to appreciate the aesthetic qualities of the drink, at least until the cork is pulled, but the label signifies what its aesthetic value will ultimately be. Even the bottle itself may become a work of art, to be displayed. At its simplest, this may merely be a bottle used for decoration, such as the wicker covered Chianti flask which is turned into a lamp. At a more complex level it may be the bottle which is itself painted, exemplified aptly by Champagne Taittinger, who have commissioned a number of artists (including André Masson, Roy Lichtenstein and Victor Vasarely) to decorate bottles of their 'collection' series. The bottle, as well as the contents, becomes the art form, so that wine is aesthetic not because of any formal evaluation of its taste, but because presentationally it has visual appeal. At the same time, the aesthetization of everyday life means that aesthetic value becomes increasingly important as a social motivation of activity (Grunow, 1997), and thus the pursuit of wine for the 'beauty' it offers – the propensity it affords for appreciation and cognitive pleasure – attains yet greater validity.

The search for authenticity in wine

As noted above, there is an argument that the 'post-modern' consumer is moving away from what is standard and obviously mass-produced (Beardsworth & Keil, 1992). In wine this has tended to be exemplified in a search for what is authentic, something which is sought by modern consumers (Osborne, 2004), and an entire documentary film in praise of authentic wine has recently been produced (Nossiter, 2004). Thus one modern writer has suggested that classic (i.e. traditional) wines provide authenticity (Michael Schuster, quoted in Anon., 2004a) which is deemed to be a positive factor in their favour. How does authenticity operate in wine? It can be suggested that there are three key ways in which it can be conveyed. One is by creating a story which links a wine to the past, and to tradition. Another is by creating a close relationship with a rural environment, and with the land generally. The third way is by maintaining, at least ostensibly, traditional ways of producing the wine.

Many companies are adept at creating a sense of the history of their product. In some cases, as in the story of Dom Pérignon, the 'history' does not necessarily have to be real but can intertwine with legend. Dom Pérignon is recorded in the mythology of Champagne as the blind monk who invented sparkling wine (McNie, 1999), and his heritage has been taken on by Moët et Chandon, who have bought the remains of the monastery in which he lived, have his statue in the courtyard of their headquarters in Epernay, and have named their expensive prestige cuvée after him. Yet it seems unlikely that he was in fact blind (Bullock et al., 1998) and there is no evidence whatsoever that he actually invented Champagne (Stevenson, 1986); indeed, he may not even have sought to make it. Instead, the myth that he was the father of Champagne was very cleverly cultivated from 1820 onwards (Guy, 2003). First, to help improve the standing of the Catholic church in the post-Napoleonic period then, after 1880 – with even greater vigour – by the merchant community of the region who saw it as an effective marketing device for their wine; associating such a frivolous, transient drink with a great, historic monk attributed mythological qualities to the drink (Guy, 2003). Authenticity has close connections with the idea of tradition and links to 'the past' (Postrel, 2003).

Similarly it has been argued that the 'authentic' past – at least for Bordeaux – is merely an invention, which becomes the authentic as a means of preserving the economic and social power of a wine, and which may underlie the region's claim to wines which are superior (Ulin, 1995).

Images – pictures of eighteenth century chateaux or of the founding fathers of Napa Valley vineyards – are crucial in establishing this idea. The recreation of ancient rituals helps to provide authenticity – in some cases for a region rather than a single producer. The 'rediscovery' of the festival of St Vincent in Champagne at the end of the nineteenth century is a good example of this (Guy, 2003).

The association of wine with a rural place helps. This comprises two elements: the idea that wine reflects a specific site so that by drinking it you can 'partake' of the place (see Chapter 5) and the concept that wine is a natural product, which conveys a 'green' environmental image (Pugh & Fletcher, 2002). The enjoyment of the rural, especially for the vast majority of the population who inhabit an urban environment, is perceived to be very attractive. The use of appellation systems in Greece has been seen specifically to appeal to an urban market segment who seek traditional and authentic wines (Dimara & Skuras, 2003). Additionally it has been suggested that vineyards themselves (which are usually long-established agricultural ventures) offer a sense of constancy and order to life; an idea which – in France at least – may have associations with 'the good life' (Gade, 2004).

The use of traditional methods for wine production offers links both to the sense of history provided by a wine, and to a more artisanal, rural society. There is a sense that consumers want to see wines as crafted – even if in reality they are not (Demossier, 2004). Throughout the world wineries display old basket presses at their cellar door, and pictures of grape pickers in the past, even though they are now using pneumatic presses and harvesting by machine.

Beverland (2005) has analysed the development of brand authenticity for luxury wines. Whilst this is only one niche sector of the wine market, his findings are illuminating. He argues that there are two crucial components to establishing authenticity in high-end wines. The first is to guarantee the quality status of the wine, by using formal and informal classifications, showing a historical tradition of excellence and continuing to work at maintaining the quality of the product with attention to detail, technological advances and continuous improvement. As well as this Beverland maintains that the 'story' has to be sincere; consumers must see the producer as genuine. To do this the use of the history of the company in a mythical capacity, the use of place as a key marker for what the business is doing, and traditional production methods and stylistic consistency are significant. Perhaps most important, however, is the ability to distance the company from any apparent commercial motivation. Thus claims that 'we only aim to make a wine which we like, not which pleases the consumer', downplaying technical developments and avoiding obvious marketing processes, such as aggressive advertising and sponsorship, in favour of a focus on relationships and an image of commercial restraint, help the consumer to see the company as above the grubbiness of actually having to sell the product and interested only in its quality, its reflection of the location and securing its place in history. Beverland's views are echoed by a geographer, Gade (2004) who, in a study of the Cassis region of France, related demarcation explicitly to authenticity, and notes that the impact of an *appellation controlée* was to accentuate quality and develop a series of processes to improve the image of the area. This included emphasizing the historic development of wine production there, making vineyards a key part of the local imagery and developing a cachet for the wines.

The danger for consumers who seek for authenticity is that all they will find is a 'pseudo experience' (Goulding, 2000). It is for this reason that debates about what genuine Champagne is (with the threat of impostors) or whether or not the traditional style of wine made in Bordeaux is changing under the influence of modern winemaking techniques are critical for the consumer's security about the product they are drinking. This is not confined to European countries; disputes about the authenticity of where wine comes from affect the new producing countries also (Fish, 2001; Steiman, 2001).

The future of lifestyle wines

One of the most interesting suggestions about how the modern commitment to lifestyle may be reshaping the way we view products comes from Tomlinson (1990) and this has particular relevance for the future of the wine industry. Tomlinson suggests four trends which are developing:

- Lifestyle as a motivational factor is diminishing the relationship between social class and status. Status may still be important but it is no longer about establishing one's class and much more about affirming one's individuality. One could extrapolate from this, therefore, that traditional wines (for instance Port or Bordeaux) which may be seen to reflect social conformity will become less important, whereas the new fad (perhaps a *garagiste* wine, or the latest micro-producer from Oregon), the knowledge of which separates the drinker from surrounding connoisseurs, will become much more significant.

- Traditional authority will have less sway. This is a related issue to the rise in 'lifestyle'. Labels or classifications will no longer be accepted because they come with the patina of age, or have an established name. There is already some evidence, produced by economists examining the hedonic pricing of Bordeaux wines, that reputation is decreasing as an element of price while reported taste (as mediated by key gatekeepers) is becoming more significant (Cardebat & Figuet, 2004).
- The consumer will take their interests and hobbies more seriously, and will show real discrimination in the application of knowledge and evaluation of their chosen field. One can infer from this that wine education, in its broadest sense, will become more important in the future, as may the influence of gatekeepers who will shape that discrimination.
- For the consumer technical and production factors will become less significant than lifestyle-related issues. This means that the focus will shift from the way that wine is produced (including, perhaps, issues such as terroir) towards the specific experiential needs of the consumer. It has been suggested that this is already happening in a wine tourism context, where consumers are paying less attention to how a winery makes a wine and more to associated recreation such as food, events and the experience of being in the vineyard (Williams, 2001).

If Tomlinson's perspective is shown to be accurate it will have major implications for how wine is marketed in the future. As noted previously, marketers have already begun to segment wine consumers by lifestyle (Bruwer et al., 2001), and that process may develop over the next few years.

Conclusion

One of the key symbolic messages conveyed by wine (especially amongst those who drink premium rather than bulk wine) is the idea that it is a civilized product – and thus that those who drink it are civilized people. Wine is civilized by its nature, being a natural drink, artistic in the way it is made and because it promotes enquiry. It is also civilized due to its association with sophistication and restraint. More than any other drink, perhaps more than any foodstuff, it has been used by philosophers and artists to exemplify concepts, situations and emotions.

The relationship of food and wine is complex but complementary, although it may be understood in varying ways within different cultures and situations. Nevertheless, the links between the two are crucial for most modern consumers. Both food and wine are becoming essential adjuncts to a modern lifestyle and, as individuals increasingly shape their lifestyles – and use lifestyle to shape their self-perception – it may be that issues of status become secondary to issues of image. Lifestyle may be a key focus for making wine in the future but it is important to understand how lifestyle operates and particularly the possible shift from formal classifications and appellations to a more fluid concept of authenticity in wine.

Bibliographical note

Fuller (Fuller, 1996) offers a comprehensive discussion on how wine has – and has not – been considered to be a civilized drink in the diverse context of the United States. As a general introduction to philosophy and food generally (including drink) Korsmeyer's *Making Sense of Taste* (1999) is excellent. On the specifics of aesthetics see Charters and Pettigrew (2005); on the relationship of wine and food see publications by the same authors (Charters & Pettigrew, 2004; Pettigrew & Charters, 2006). A general introduction to wine and lifestyle is given by Demossier (2004; 2005). For a modern and very opinionated but creatively expressed view on authenticity Nossiter's film, *Mondovino*, is well worth watching.

10

The contemporary wine consumer

As wine is moving from being a sophisticated elite drink or everyday bulk beverage to a lifestyle product, so the focus of the modern wine consumer is evolving. Wine is a complex product, and a wider product choice is offered than for most other products. This complexity has led to the increasing importance of external cues which 'help' the consumer make a selection. This part is about how modern wine consumers engage with wine, and covers practices which help them to make decisions, as well as ways in which they can further their enjoyment in wine. In many cases they may make their own choices about wine, but to do this they need to develop an understanding of the product. Thus the chapter will examine some developments in wine consumption which have only recently become important. These are not just enjoyable experiences but also allow the gathering of information, and include wine literature, education and clubs, and the experience of the wine tourist. It also considers the impact on the wine consumer of 'gatekeepers' – the people and organizations who influence consumption – including wine critics and writers, and wine shows. This part of the chapter examines their impact, their consistency in evaluating wine, and dichotomies which develop around them. Finally two other aspects of wine consumption which have developed over the last 60 years are examined. The first is the rise of wine as an investment. Second, and related to this, consideration is given to consumers' use of the secondary (auction) market for wine.

It is important to remember, however, that external cues, which enable the consumer to make a more informed choice, are primarily used by high-involvement drinkers only. Low-involvement consumers are likely to avoid information-seeking activity, and rely on more established marketing devices – extrinsic cues such as brand, price, distributor recommendation or label – to inform their choice (Batt & Dean, 2000; Lockshin & Hall, 2003).

The changing nature of wine consumption

Before considering how the modern wine consumer approaches the drink, it is relevant to examine how wine consumption patterns are changing. The key development has been the growth of consumption in non-traditional markets with a contemporaneous reduction in more traditional, wine-producing, nations. This is exemplified at Figure 10.1.

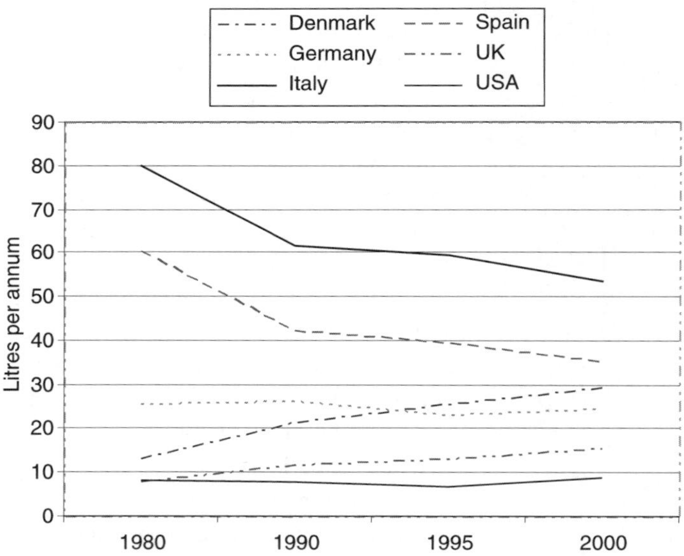

Figure 10.1 Per capita wine consumption in selected markets, 1980–2000.
Sources: International Organisation of Vine and Wine (OIV) and the Wine Institute of California.

The chart shows consumption in two traditional wine-producing countries, Italy and Spain, with a general level of decline over the period. Two adjacent northern European countries, Denmark and Germany, show contrasting patterns. The former shows a rapid increase in consumption, overtaking the latter. In Germany consumption levels remain roughly static over the period. Two Anglophone countries are contrasted. In the United Kingdom there is a marked increase in the population's wine consumption (though not as dramatic as in Denmark). Per capita intake in the United States, on the other hand barely changes over the 20 year period – and in this instance it is like Germany, another country which also produces wine but in which, as with the United States, consumption of beer is much more important than that of wine. Historically wine has come from the periphery of each nation and has been much less significant than in the southern European wine-producing nations.

A number of reasons can be postulated for the rising consumption in some Anglophone and Scandinavian countries. One is the dramatically increased level of overseas travel in the post-war period, particularly to southern Europe, which has changed food consumption behaviour generally (Beardsworth & Keil, 1992), and exposed non-wine drinkers to wine cultures. A second is the increased amount of disposable income available to spend on items which were, hitherto, considered luxuries (Beardsworth & Keil, 1992); this relates to the developing concept of lifestyle, with greater leisure time (Smith & Solgaard, 2000). Third, it may be that there has been a shift from drinking for the sake of drinking (which tended to take place in the bar or pub) towards drinking within the family – the latter more likely to take place in the convivial atmosphere of a meal, and thus to feature wine rather than beer or spirits as the alcohol of choice. Certainly there has been substantial demographic change which has begun to break down traditional social structures and in turn modify what people chose to consume (Beardsworth & Keil, 1992). Within the drinks sector this can be seen in a move away from spirits to lower alcohol drinks, and there is evidence that women are increasingly focusing their drinking behaviour on wine (Smith & Solgaard, 2000). Finally, and most recently, has been the influence of health issues, with the argument that the Mediterranean diet in general and particularly red wine is influential in reducing cardiovascular disease (see Chapter 12).

This changing trend between countries is also mirrored by changing tastes within countries. In 1939 the major supplier of wine to the United Kingdom was Portugal, which had 33 per cent of the market, almost all of it Port. Second was Australia, and third was Spain, with a joint market share of about 40 per cent – again most of it fortified (Faith, 2002). According to records kept by the Wine and Spirit Trade Association by 2004 less than 2.5 per cent of wines released onto the UK market were fortified. Equally, in the United Kingdom over the last 30 years it has been possible to chart a move away from medium-dry wines (principally, but not exclusively, in the form of liebfraumilch) towards drier wines. At the same time, within the traditional wine-producing countries there has been a shift away from the consumption of table wine and towards the consumption of quality wine produced from a specified region (QWPSR). For instance, in the first half of the 1960s the typical French wine drinker consumed 12.6 L of appellation controlée (AC) wine per annum (p.a.) and 114.5 L of table wine. Twenty years later the amount of AC wine had almost doubled and the amount of table wine had declined to 73 L p.a. (Loubere, 1990). By 2002 47 per cent of all French wine was QWPSR (Cholette, 2004).

One final recent change has been the steady increase in wine consumption in east Asian countries. It began from a low base but appears to be rising steadily. Whilst it does not currently figure as a major region for global consumption, given the large population of some of these countries and their growing prosperity consumption in east Asia could become very significant in a few decades. In China, particularly, health issues plus the suggestion that middle-class lifestyles are converging with the lifestyles of those in the west has been suggested as a key driver for this change (Wheatley, 2003).

Wine literature

The development of wine literature

People have been mentioning wine since the first stories were written down (Anon, n.d./1972). However, generally their comments were little more than asides. The first serious attempt to discuss wine was within the context of agricultural texts, particularly Roman authors such as Cato and Columella. The emphasis in these works, however, is not on consumption, nor even particularly on wine styles, but on the effective growing of grapes, with production techniques being considered merely as ancillary to viticultural processes. The only substantial exception to this was Pliny in his *Natural History*, which briefly touched on types of wine, their reputation, and even on consumption practices. Similarly in the medieval period the primary aim of wine books was to focus on grape growing and when they did stray into, for instance, classifying wine regions (as with the French *Maison Rustique*) it tended to be supplementary to that purpose, being particularly aimed at assessing the appropriateness of grape varieties to a specific place (Gabler, 2004). The other main area in which wine writing existed was, from the sixteenth century on, about the role of wine as a medicine.

The shift from treating wine as a solely viticultural activity to one related to production – and even more to cellar management – took place in the wake of the scientific and technological revolution of the seventeenth century. Vintner's texts were published – books such as *The Art and Mystery of Vintners* in England in 1692, and, in 1781, the French *L'art d'Ameliorer et de Conserver les Vins* (Gabler, 2004; Robinson, 1999). These aimed to advise merchants about how to keep their wine and even how to 'improve' them – so that pale red wine, for instance, could be darkened with beetroot juice (Gabler, 2004). The emphasis was still, however, on writing books for those involved in the production of wine, rather than for consumers.

One impact of the consumer revolution was the understanding that consumers required more knowledge about products. At its most basic level this was reflected in the much wider use of advertising, and a greater number of popular journals and magazines (McKendrick et al., 1982). At the same time the rise in the number of people with surplus income and an ability to buy wine resulted naturally in a wider willingness to learn about it.

A number of other social factors can be suggested as influences which meant that there was more need for writing about wine. The technological revolution meant that wine could now be collected and matured; to do that required information so that selection of appropriate wines for keeping could be made. The need for personal differentiation also needed knowledge, so that informed choices about wine preferences could be made. Finally, as consumption took on some more specific aesthetic elements, the need for 'good taste' required education – just as the rich man's visual aesthetic taste needed to be shaped by the grand tour or an equivalent educational process.

As a result, by the beginning of the nineteenth century the first books for wine consumers began to appear, looking at the history and geography of contemporary wines and their styles. These included the grandiloquently titled *Topographie de Tous les Vignobles Connus* by André Jullien (1816), a work which started a trend by attempting to classify wine quality (Gabler, 2004). This was followed by the first works in English to focus on wine *per se* rather than production – Alexander Henderson's *History of Ancient and Modern Wines* in 1824 and in 1833 *A History and Description of Modern Wines* by Cyrus Redding (Gabler, 2004). These books were, however, often polemical, so that Redding was concerned to show up the weaknesses of his predecessors or, as in the case of Baron Joseph Forrester who wrote on Port, to ensure that the wine should not be adulterated in any way – even by fortification.

This style of book, designed as an introduction to wine for the intelligent novice, was later joined by another kind – the book of reminiscences. The first, perhaps, was by Thomas Shaw – a very influential Victorian wine merchant who in 1863 published *Wine, the Vine and the Cellar.* Others followed on, for example the eminent connoisseur George Saintsbury, who wrote *Notes on a Cellar-Book* (1920).

The modern era

From the two streams of literature which developed (for producers and consumers), most modern wine literature has descended. Currently there are guides to the geography of wine (such as Hugh Johnson's *World Atlas of Wine*) and to specific regions, such as the Mitchell Beazley Wine Library series. Production is addressed, as with James Halliday and Hugh Johnson's *The Art and Science of Wine*. Biography and autobiography exist, and there are also works on wine appreciation, such as Michael Broadbent's *Pocket Guide to Wine Tasting*. Thus the key areas of knowledge for the wine aficionado are dealt with: where wine originates, how it is made and how to appreciate it. However, the most common form of guide in the modern world is that which suggests what to buy. Most major wine consuming countries have one or more such books – now updated annually – giving the authors' recommendations on which currently available wines are the best and (not always the same) the best value. A number of these have a specific focus. John Platter produces a guide to the wines of South Africa; in Australia Peter Forrestal writes annually on the country's best wines available for $15 and under.

This form of wine literature is a response to the growing influence of the wine critic, the individual whose tasting ability is respected and who is viewed as a good judge of wine. In this way wine guides also function as a direct response to the fragmentation of the modern wine market. The consumer, faced with a plethora of choice, needs advice about what to buy. This is despite the fact that there is a subjective element to wine tasting, and that in part what a writer tastes and enjoys is specific to his or her physiology, and the timing and environment of tasting (Jackson, 2002).

More recently wine-related magazines have become widely produced and influential. The first in the Anglophone world was *Decanter*, published in the UK, and still considered to be fairly authoritative. *Le Revue des Vins de France*, the *Wine Spectator* and others are also prominent. Although these may publish a range of journalistic pieces on production issues, geography, food and tourism, it is primarily for their drinking recommendations that they are read, particularly comparative tastings which rank a number of wines of a similar type. More recently, and in an attempt to involve younger wine drinkers, magazines which target generation X (those born between the mid-1960s and the end of the 1970s) have been produced. The most successful of these is *Wine X*, in the United States.

Wine education and wine clubs

The rise in the use of wine education and wine clubs fits into the same context as the growth of wine literature. As wine became a substantial consumer product the desire for knowledge spurred individuals not merely to read, but also to sample the product more widely and – as a necessary component of learning about wine – to develop their ability to taste. In order to improve the quality of education and – on occasions – to offer a form of accreditation of trainers, trade associations of educators have been set up in the United States, the United Kingdom and Australia.

Wine education is run in a number of formats. Adult education services offer introductory courses in many countries. Other courses are organized by those with a commercial interest in wine, so that retailers, auctioneers or organizations which represent the wine industry generally may arrange them. Little research has been carried out into their work and effectiveness but, at least in some parts of the world, there is a suggestion that demand for their services is increasing (Ali-Knight & Charters, 2000; Fattorini, 1994). Ultimately high-involvement consumers may attend tastings provided by educational establishments or wine companies or by clubs, in order to expand their tasting skills and improve their knowledge of what is available. It has been suggested that this is one example of the situation where consumers begin to take on aspects of professional activity, for wine tasting is essentially a skill needed by wine buyers and critics. Thus, it has been suggested, 'in this way consumers distance themselves from mere drinkers to become tasters, becoming associated with the glamour and romance of the wine trade' (Fattorini, 1994).

There are a number of ways in which wine clubs can operate. Some of them are consumer-driven. These may merely be mutual-interest organizations designed to promote various tastings and be generally convivial; on occasions they may combine both wine and food. These tend to involve high-involvement consumers, who may spend more than average on wine and be keen collectors and wine tourists (Christiansen, 2004). Other clubs may be created to improve purchasing power. There are cases of groups of consumers negotiating with a retailer to purchase wine in bulk at a reduced rate. This process becomes most developed in the co-operative buying agencies, notably the organizations known as 'The Wine Society' in Australia and the United Kingdom. These bodies are co-operatively owned by their members and buy wines in large quantities, negotiating substantial discounts. Members are free to buy as they wish from the list, which is in each case very comprehensive. Both organizations also organize a number of tastings, and provide wine education as well.

Other wine clubs are distributor driven, with a focus on profit that the mutual ventures do not have. These include mail-order clubs (some specifically attached to non-wine related businesses, such as credit card companies; others the distribution arm of other companies, such as Cellarmaster wines in Australia which is owned by the country's largest wine producer, Fosters). There are perceived benefits to belonging to mail-order clubs. Anecdotally it has been suggested that the ability not to have to enter a shop and display ignorance and uncertainty is attractive to some consumers; mail-order clubs therefore function as a form of risk avoidance. The biggest clubs (such as the Sunday Times Wine Club in the United Kingdom) have a wide range of wines available and issue regular, informative newsletters with their offers. In order to maximize profits such clubs, whilst perhaps offering a few well-known brands for sale, will source some of their wines direct from the producer, or even arrange for a wine to be made to their own specification which the club bottles itself. Margins in such wines are much higher than on the more popular brands.

Wine tourism

Wine tourism is an old activity which is turning into a major adjunct to both the wine and tourism industries. In earlier centuries John Locke and Thomas Jefferson both spent time visiting French vineyards, particularly Bordeaux (Gabler, 1995; Unwin, 2001), and the Germans developed a number of wine routes in the 1920s (Cambourne et al., 2000). However, wine tourism as a widespread consumer phenomenon has only developed over the last 40 years or so and has tended to focus as much on the new producing countries as on Europe. Napa Valley, most Australian wine regions and all in New Zealand are organized to encourage visitors (Cambourne et al., 2000); European wine regions have often been much slower to develop the facilities and culture necessary to facilitate it (Correia et al., 2004).

It is important to remember that wine tourism is not merely an aspect of the wine industry but also of the tourism industry; indeed it could be argued that in some traditional wine-producing regions of Europe, such as Bordeaux, it is more firmly rooted in tourism than in wine. This leads to another distinguishing feature of wine tourism. It is based on a primary industry (grape growing), a secondary industry (winemaking) and a tertiary industry (tourism) (Carlsen, 2004). The former tend to be supply driven, producing a homogeneous, quality-focused product based on technology. The latter is demand-led, with a range of product options and based on the provision of a service. These activities, and the skills required to pursue them successfully, may not necessarily be complementary. They may even tend to pull in opposite directions (Carlsen, 2004).

A definition of wine tourism describes it as follows:

> Visitation to vineyards, wineries, wine festivals and wine shows for which grape wine tasting and/or experiencing the attributes of a grape wine region are the prime motivating factors for visitors (Hall (1996) cited in Hall et al., 2000a, p. 3).

This tends to focus primarily on the experience of the demand side of the process. Other definitions have noted the importance of the service provider and also the links into ideas of lifestyle (Dowling et al., 1999). Crucially the wine tourist can be provided for in a number of ways:

- Events, festivals and vintage celebrations.
- Restaurants and cafes.
- Information centres, education and interpretation.
- Hospitality and accommodation.
- Wine touring and travelling around a region – including wine trails – and winery tours.
- Tasting and cellar door sales.
- Retail outlets – including related 'lifestyle products' such as art and craft galleries and speciality food.
- Architecture and heritage features.

It seems likely that wine tourists tend to be of higher involvement levels than typical wine consumers (Christiansen, 2004). Their motivation is complex, and it is important to remember that a wine tourist probably does not just engage in wine tourism alone but enjoys a wine region alongside other tourism benefits, such as food, heritage or environment (Charters & Ali-Knight, 2002). It has been noted in the United States that wine tourists are likely to be middle aged, with above average incomes and education, and also tend to consume more wine than most drinkers (Dodd, 1997). Other research seems to confirm that profile, although it has been noted that average age, at least, may vary from wine region to wine region and is younger in some parts of the world (Charters & O'Neill, 2000). One motivating factor for the tourist is the desire to learn more about wine (Ali-Knight & Charters, 2000). Another seems to be the idea that visiting wine regions adds benefit to the visitor's overall lifestyle (Mitchell et al., 2000). Counter-intuitively, whilst the quality of wine on offer at a cellar door is important, it is not as important generally as the complete experience – especially the fact that staff are responsive to visitors' needs and that they get a sense of security about the process of tasting (O'Neill & Charters, 2000).

Crucially, two points must be recognized about the motivation of the wine tourist. The first is that it is an experience which is being sought (Mitchell et al., 2000). The experience is a complex interaction of natural setting, wine, food, cultural and historical inputs and above all the people who service the visitor. This can be developed to suggest that the fact that wine tourism acts in a public space is significant; it is a communal act, and thus reinforces the social motivations for wine consumption (Demossier, 2005). A visitor can identify with a specific lifestyle, which involves eating well, appreciating the beauty of nature and enhancing friendships in a convivial setting. Demossier (2005) thus argues that it offers the modern urban consumer a sense of reconnecting with a culture that is alien to them – a culture with a sense of community and of good and healthy living. This echoes the civilizing aspects of authenticity and naturalness offered by wine noted in Chapter 9. The second point that must be understood is that wine tourists are not a single, homogeneous group. It is likely that there are generational differences in expectations of the experience, and of the service offered (Fountain & Charters, 2004); there are certainly gender differences, perhaps focused on different approaches to the idea of shopping and browsing (Charters & O'Neill, 2000), and there are also cultural variations in the wine tourist's perspective (Charters & Ali-Knight, 2002).

The role of gatekeepers

The gatekeepers to wine – those who act as the intermediaries between producer and consumer, and who influence what the consumer will drink – are essentially wine critics; these people may also be wine writers and educators. They may operate in more than one role and can influence wine selection more directly, so that the writer Michael Broadbent M.W. is also an auctioneer and sits on the buying panel for British Airways, thus having an impact on the wines drunk by air passengers, as does another influential writer, Jancis Robinson M.W. Gatekeepers can also act collectively; they may work together on panel tastings for wine magazines, and they may also act as judges in wine shows. Note, however, that the nature of gatekeepers may vary between cultures. Japan, for instance, has few wine writers, but its sommeliers are very highly regarded and extremely influential – even appearing on television to give advice.

Wine critics

As noted previously, individuals have attempted to assess wine for at least two millennia, including the classical authors, Pliny and Strabo who both graded the quality of wines – although there is no evidence that they were accorded exceptional respect for this. A fictional critic, an 'English priest' in a medieval poem, was chosen by Philip Augustus, King of France, to judge the 'battle of the wines', and determine which region produced the best wines of the world (Unwin, 1996). Thomas Jefferson was also renowned for having a fine palate, and used it to advise President Washington on the purchase of wines (Gabler, 1995).

None of these were professionals, however. Amateur critics tended to dominate until the time of André Simon, in the first half of the twentieth century. Simon was French but settled in the United Kingdom, initially as agent for Champagne Pommery. He began by writing a series of articles on the history of Champagne, and discovered that he had a gift for communicating about wine. Over the next 50 years he published widely on wine all around the world (Gabler, 2004). In his wake came commentators such as H. Warner Allen, Edmund Penning-Rowsell, and Hugh Johnson, followed by a subsequent explosion in critics on both sides of the Channel and the Atlantic. Until around the mid-1980s most of these were writers about wine in general who happened also to evaluate and recommend some specific wines. However, over the last couple of decades the focus has been less on education and general information and more on recommendation. This has been the prime focus of magazines like *The Wine Advocate* and many newspaper columns on wine. It has also been a major aspect of other magazines, such as *The Wine Spectator* and *Decanter*.

Robert Parker

Some 'tasters' become so highly respected that they become extremely influential and their ability attains almost mythical reputation for consumers. The classic example of this is Robert Parker. The 'myth' of his entry into the world of wine criticism surrounds the Bordeaux vintage of 1982. At the time it was being evaluated, in 1983, he was a lawyer who had, for a few years, published a small-circulation magazine for aficionados. The story goes that the 1982 vintage was misjudged by most critics who considered it of mediocre quality, whereas Parker recognized its worth and recommended it as such. Later re-evaluations vindicated his position and established his reputation as a judge (Echikson, 2004). In the classic fashion of myths, the story has developed a very dyadic structure, focusing on the clash of good and evil. Parker argues that the traditional 'British' school of wine writing was very flowery and metaphorical and of little use to the consumer and that he was able to revolutionize wine criticism by giving simple descriptions and focusing primarily on whether or not a wine is good or bad (Echikson, 2004). Interestingly, this dyadic perspective is reflected in Parker's own approach to tasting. The French researcher, Frederic Brochet, has analysed the language used by a number of critics, including Parker (Brochet, 2001; Brochet & Dubourdieu, 2001). Brochet's thesis is complex, but broadly he argues that lexically a critic's language reduces to a few categories. Of Parker he notes that essentially his language (for red wines at least) devolves down to just two categories, a good and a bad. Brochet and Dubourdieu (2001) note that new wine enthusiasts tend to see wines as either good or bad, and thus Parker 'evaluates as would a novice, and this could be one reason for the extraordinary success of this writer' (Brochet & Dubourdieu, 2001, p. 193). However, in keeping with the expectations of a myth such a criticism is irrelevant to those who admire Parker, for whom he has taken on a heroic role. After speaking at a seminar in Hong Kong, for instance, he was mobbed by a crowd of devotees who queued to have their photograph taken with him.

As Robert Parker's reputation increased so consumers tended to buy wine according to his recommendation, which in turn has had an influence on wine price (Thode et al., 2002). This gave him great influence, but there are suggestions that there is a 'Parker-style' and fears that he spawns stylistic homogeneity and has become too powerful in influencing markets (Beverland, 2003). He counters this by arguing that he has made wine more flavourful and enjoyable. Another, more subtle, complaint is that by reducing wine to merely good and bad Parker has oversimplified what is a complex aesthetic process, with products which may vary in perceived quality depending on the situation of consumption and the perception of the consumers themselves. Thus the French producer, Bernard Ginestet, made the following comment on him:

> 'Standardized . . . price-conscious. Unsubtle. Square'. Why? 'Americans like certainty . . . If wine contains a truth, it is the absence of certainty. One of the reasons Bob succeeded is that he knows no doubt. Today, there is globalization. Bob is an artisan in the globalization of wine' (Echikson, 2004, p. 222).

Critics can therefore achieve a reputation which allows them vinous power. They may be able to mould markets and influence what the consumer does or does not buy and it is possible that they may also be able to shape how styles of wine change. Many critics begin by being consumers. Some, however, start by being, or later become, producers. Many wine show judges, who are able to influence what is consumed, are winemakers and some winemakers have become renowned writers and commentators on wine. When that also includes making recommendations about wine then inevitably issues of conflict of interest arise, given that they may be evaluating wines which they have been involved with, or for which their competitors are responsible (Allen, 2002).

When critics disagree

Whilst it has objective aspects, there is also a substantial element of subjectivity to wine tasting (Charters & Pettigrew, 2003a). Inevitably, therefore, wine critics do not always agree about wines. A classic example of this occurred with the debate about one particular St-Emilion wine following the first tastings of the 2003 vintage in Bordeaux, and reported in detail on the website of the London-based fine wine merchants Farr Vintners (Anon., 2004a). The wine in question was Chateau Pavie, a long-established producer which had substantially improved its public standing in recent years, partly as a result of stylistic changes which stemmed from its use of the well-known oenological consultant Michel Rolland, and partly from securing a number of positive reviews by Robert Parker.

The English writer, Jancis Robinson M.W., gave the wine a low score and a damning review.

> Pavie 2003 – Completely unappetising overripe aromas. Why? Porty sweet. Oh REALLY! Port is best from the Douro not St Emilion. Ridiculous wine more reminiscent of a late harvest Zinfandel than a red Bordeaux with its unappetising green notes. (I should make it clear that these notes, were written long before I knew what wine it was – and I have witnesses!!) – Jancis Robinson.

This prompted Robert Parker to respond:

> All I can do is write what I truly believe and let the chips fall where they do. I have neither backed off the criticism of some of my favorite estates that faltered in 2003, or hid my enthusiasm for those wines

> I feel are compelling. I suspect most other writers have done the same thing.
>
> I had Pavie four separate times, and, recognizing everyone's taste is different, Pavie does not taste at all (for my palate) as described by Jancis. She has a lamentable and perplexing history of disliking not only all of Perse's wines, but virtually all of the garagiste wines of St-Emilion. The irony is that she seems to be very fond of Le Pin, which some of these wines resemble, and is the inspiration for many of them. That is her opinion, and she will have to answer for it as all of us do that practice this rather whimsical craft. These recent comments (assuming they are accurate) are very much in keeping with her nasty swipes at all the Pavies made by Perse (1998 onward), and mirror the comments of not only reactionaries in Bordeaux, but also segments of the wine trade that are furious with Perse over his pricing shenanigans . . .

This resulted in a vigorous debate between wine writers the world over, reported extensively on the online bulletin board of a magazine *World of Fine Wine*. The American critic, Stephen Tanzer, sided with Robert Parker, as did the eminent French commentator Michel Bettane. Another French critic, Jean Marc Quarin, supported Jancis Robinson, as did a whole host of English experts, including Stephen Spurrier, Clive Coates M.W. and Michael Schuster. There was a sense of American versus British about the argument which, given the timing in the aftermath of the Iraq war, appeared somewhat ironic. More important, however, is the very serious discussion about what Claret should be like. Defenders of 'traditional' Bordeaux wines praise concepts like restraint, structure and elegance. Other critics, led by Robert Parker, look for wines which give fruit, generosity and opulence. The latter tend to have deeper colour and higher alcohol – and specific techniques can be adopted to produce them. This prompts opponents of the style to claim that they are not authentic, that such ripeness is not typical of Bordeaux. In response the 'modernists' counter that, save for exceptional years, much old-style Claret was 'thin, acidic and astringent' and that their 'apologists might mistake the thinness for subtlety' (Echikson, 2004, p. 36).

A slightly different way of seeing this debate is as a collision between the desire for authentic wines (see Chapter 9) and a 'high-quality product'. Proponents of the former subsume quality into an overall goal of authenticity (which includes not just quality but also a relationship to place, traditional methods and a historical context for the wine

(Beverland, 2005)). Those who argue for the latter choose to review wines just as one would a car or toothpaste, assessing its functionality – in this case delivering intense, balanced taste – whilst paying less overt attention to the symbolic meanings bound up in the wine.

In the end consumer preference is a matter for the individual. There is a strong case to argue that good wines can be made both in the traditional and the modern style, although for those who prize *typicité* the former may be more appropriate. However, wine here is being invested with other meaning by the critics; traditionalists wish to uphold ideas of terroir and the importance of historical tradition. The modernists, whilst not necessarily discounting those ideas, see wine as a product like any other (Echikson, 2004), and that its prime aim is to satisfy the consumer rather than represent some mystical idea of place and typicality. This in turn leads back to some of the debates about appellation, terroir and quality outlined in Chapter 5. The average wine consumer, however, will understand little or none of this, and rather just sees two camps arguing about whether or not a wine which costs around £100 per bottle is worth drinking, so is none the wiser about whether or not it is good value.

(All quotations taken from Anon., 2004a.)

Wine show systems and judging

Wine shows are an increasingly important part of the world of wine. They exist in most countries which make wine, and a number which merely consume it. The International Wine Challenge in the United Kingdom, formerly sponsored by *Wine International* magazine, claims to be the biggest such show in the world, whilst most wine regions in France and the new producing countries run shows which judge local wines. Two points need to be remembered, however. First, the very best producers will rarely enter their wines in a competition; they have little to gain if they win, and much potential damage to their wine's reputation may occur if they lose (Robinson, 1999). It is interesting to note that one of Australia's senior show judges, Brian Croser, chose not to enter wines from Petaluma, the label that he managed until 2005, into Australian wine shows partly because he believed that his wines would not win the awards which they deserve, and because he did not market his wines based on medals (Dunphy & Lockshin, 1998). Second, much depends on the quality of the show; in each country there are shows which are considered to be more or less prestigious. That prestige depends on the quality of the judges used, the independence with which they judge, and the organization of the show, which must ensure that wines are tasted entirely blind and in an appropriate judging environment. One show, the International Wine and Spirits Competition, requires chemical analysis of the wines as part of its judging process as well as tasting.

How useful are wine shows to the consumer? Some research suggests that consumers are aware of show medals, and may pay some attention to them (Charters, 2004). Certainly producers consider that consumers respond to them, although it may be that the proliferation of medals is lessening their impact (Dunphy & Lockshin, 1998). Other experimental research, however, suggests that show medals are utilized by consumers less than information on labels about how wine is made, or how it is likely to taste (Shaw et al., 1999).

The Australian show system

The Australian system (possibly the best developed and most cohesive in the world) centres around agricultural society shows. There are a number of shows throughout the country with the six metropolitan wine shows and the National Wine Show in Canberra being the most important. Regional and local wine shows may be limited to wines from that region or state, but that is not invariably the case. Wines are assessed in classes (for instance chardonnay, or lighter bodied-red wines), and may be awarded gold, silver, or bronze medals. Wines are marked discretely – so that conceivably all the wines in a class could win gold, or none could win any medals.

Wines are marked out of 20, but in practice rarely score below about 11. Medals are awarded, so that a wine with points of 18.5 and over wins a gold medal, 17.0–18.4 silver and 15.5–16.9 bronze. Below about 12.5 a wine is likely to be noticeably faulty. Additionally trophies may also be given to the best wine in a class and/or show. These rules are consistent to all shows throughout the country. However, a key aspect of the process is the fact that it is negotiated; whilst judges initially assess the wines on their own they then jointly record their marks and discuss the wines. On occasions they will modify their marks in the light of other judges' opinions.

The Australian show system was originally intended to encourage the exchange of ideas and experience amongst winemakers, to give consumers some idea of the quality of the best wines, and to allow producers a marketing opportunity for their wines. There is substantial anecdotal evidence that it has achieved those goals, and the proponents of the system point to the improvement in the quality of Australian wine and their increasing international success as a sign that shows have been successful (Halliday, 2001). There are, however, increasing concerns about various aspects of wine shows which bear on the validity of their results (Dunphy & Lockshin, 1998; Halliday, 2001; Hooke, 2001). These include a number of organizational and administrative factors:

- There is no hierarchy of shows – wines can be entered indiscriminately and perform variably often throughout the country.
- Judging is dominated by winemakers – who impose their companies' ideas and an ultra-technical perspective on the wines. The result of this is that judging is fixated on faultlessness rather than interest. The wines which win are well made, but not necessarily exciting.
- Classes are too large – often of up to 200 wines. In order for a wine to win it has to stand out in a line-up, particularly on its aroma. Medals consequently tend to be won by 'blockbuster' wines rather than high quality but subtle wines.

There are also some criticisms of the processes of tasting imposed by such a system, and particularly the fact that the speed of tasting required is no way to engage with quality (Jefford, 2002b). However, these criticisms are not universally accepted by those involved in the judging process (Croser, 2001).

Further, as has been noted, professional judgments at shows may not necessarily be accepted by consumers, who will often show surprise at or dislike for wines which win show awards (e.g. King, 2005; Stavro, 2001). Even professionals may have doubts about the usefulness of wine shows as a means of conveying quality judgments to consumers (Dunphy & Lockshin, 1998) and some research suggests that endorsements such as show medals have limited usefulness in influencing consumer choice (Shaw et al., 1999).

Whilst proposals have been made for research into the efficacy of judging (Brien et al., 1987; Cliff & King, 1996), there has been little actual exploration of the process. A number of academic criticisms of the process of judging have been made. These include: the failure of judges to deliver reproducible results; the fact that judges place varying emphasis on different components of the wines; that wine colour will prejudice their judgment; and the inherent malleability of their views when discussing wines (Noble, 1997).

Collecting and investing

At least since the development of cork and bottle in the seventeenth century it has been possible to collect wine and, for the upper classes at least, this became commonplace. The first Earl of Bristol purchased Montilla, Haut-Brion, Margaux, Port, Meursault and Cote Rotie, as well as wines from Tuscany and Chateauneuf-du-Pape at the beginning of the eighteenth century, all in large quantities (Johnson, 1989). Collecting has now become a major aim for very-high-involvement consumers. The wine magazine *Decanter*, for instance, has a regular column entitled 'Collectors' News' giving advice on developing collections of wine. The aims of collectors may be twofold. They may be buying young wine with a view to ageing it so that they can drink it at their peak, and/or they may be collecting it as an investment, with a view to making a profit on it in due course.

Wine as an investment

One of the more recent developments in wine has been its use as an investment tool. In part this reflects the quasi-aesthetic nature of the product; like other arts and crafts (paintings, pottery, books) it offers an element of beauty which is worth possessing. Unlike those other products, however, it has a limited life. There are some bottles which have a substantial value merely for historical interest (for instance, wines which were purportedly once in the possession of Thomas Jefferson, one of which sold for £105 000), because the wine in them is likely to be in very poor condition. Generally, however, wine has an appreciating value whilst the product is considered to be approaching its peak, followed by a perceived slow decline which will be reflected by a decrease in prices. For some prized vintages, such as 1945, 1947 and 1961 in Bordeaux, the period of appreciation may be very long indeed; generally, however, the time-scale for financial return will be more limited (see Figure 10.2). There are others, however, who argue that the auction market is – at least in the first few years after a wine's release, an imprecise guide to how its final quality will be assessed. Ashenfelter et al. (1995) have argued that a close analysis of weather conditions is a much more precise predictor of final price.

How wine prices vary

Figure 10.2 gives an example of how wine prices may fluctuate. The graph gives the auction price for three chateaux in St-Julien, one of the leading communes of Bordeaux, as current in mid-2005, together with the wine's *en primeur* release price for the 2004 vintage on release in 2005. Chateau

Leoville Las Cases is a very highly regarded producer – a 'super-second' growth. Chateau Lagrange is also a classed growth, but without the same very high reputation. Chateau Gloria has a good reputation but was not considered in 1855 as it has only come into existence more recently. Three points need to be made about this. First, the price of Chateau Leoville Las Cases has shown substantial appreciation in the best vintages (1961, 1982, 1990), but its auction price also fluctuates more widely than the other two. Furthermore, as is clear when comparing its 2004 release price against a (moderate) previous vintage such as 1994, it starts at a comparatively high price. Second, from the early 1980s on, when the reputation of Chateau Lagrange began to improve (ownership changed in 1983), its auction price has remained generally higher than the cru bourgeois wine – which is to be expected as a general rule, given that it follows the Bordeaux classificatory system. Third, and most significantly, whilst Leoville Las Cases maintains a reasonable value in the pre-1982 vintages Chateau Lagrange – with the exception of the outstanding 1961 vintage – shows a different trend. Prices begin to rise with the 1982 vintage, and peak with 1990 – an excellent vintage, drinking at its peak in 2005. Thereafter they decline as the quality of the vintage declines. Chateau Gloria, on the other hand, does not show the same curve quite so clearly, but neither does it show the higher prices of Chateau Lagrange at its peak.

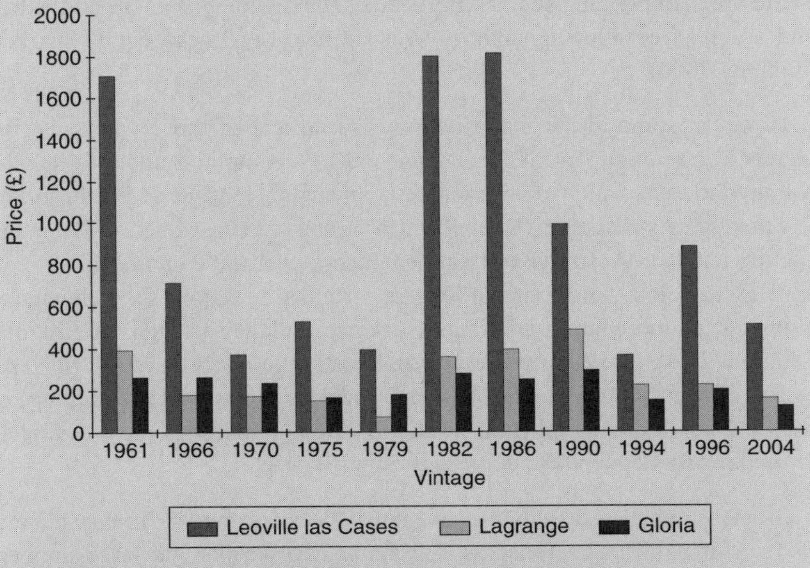

Figure 10.2 Auction prices for three St-Julien chateaux.
Source: *Decanter* Magazine.

In practice the wines which provide good investments are very limited. Regionally only Bordeaux and Port, with Burgundy to a lesser extent (as the wines tend to be less long-lived) have the cachet to appreciate – perhaps a total of thirty labels altogether (Temple, 2004). Some Italian wine regions which make red wines to age, such as Barolo, have certain appeal as do specific Italian wines like Sassicaia. Beyond those some specific wines, such as Caymus Special Selection and Stag's Leap Wine Cellars Cask 23, or Penfold's Grange from Australia regularly gain in value, but even they do not have the same long-standing reputation as classic European wines. Even within the wine regions the number of suitable wines is limited. For instance, only vintage Port (less than 1 per cent of all Port production) has investment potential. However, for those who invest successfully it has been suggested that the return (at least for Bordeaux) has been around 9 per cent p.a. since the 1970s (Temple, 2004).

Given the apprehension faced by many novice wine drinkers, some merchants now offer 'cellar plans' (Stimpfig, 2005a). These require the customer to pay a fixed monthly sum to the merchant, who then buys and stores wines on their behalf, either for subsequent drinking, or as an investment. Additionally, for those who are seeking to use wine primarily as an investment rather than to drink there are a number of wine investment funds which will buy a block of wine, store it and sell to realize a profit in due course. There are also brokers, such as Bordeaux Index, who will quote both a buy and a sell price allowing trading in a similar way to the equity markets (Temple, 2004).

However, some in the wine industry are critical of those who see wine merely as an investment. Jancis Robinson M.W. complains about those who confuse the appreciation of wine with its appreciation in value and of those who buy merely for speculation (Robinson, 1997), and even the owners of Langton's auction house in Australia, noting the concern over the commodification of wine expressed by some wine producers, state that the latter 'see fine wine as ultimately no more than a drinking experience, and they are right' (Caillard & Langton, 2000, p. 9). For those who believe in the importance of wine as a means of signifying conviviality (which involves giving and not gaining) or who feel that it has an uplifting, aesthetic function, to treat wine as a vehicle for making money tends to demean its significance.

Crucially, wine used as an investment may be a way to make money but it is also a symbol of financial success. To claim to have a cellar with large numbers of first growth Clarets, for instance, signifies both that one has great wine knowledge plus wealth and a certain refinement.

The secondary market for wine

The secondary (auction) market for wine developed as wine moved into the aesthetic arena in the eighteenth century; the first company to auction wine was Christies, which instigated sales in the 1760s (Johnson, 1989). From 1966 onwards first Christies and then Sotheby's established wine departments, and wine auctions form regular parts of their business; other auction houses are now involved such as Zachys in the United States, although the law there limits auctions to California, Illinois and New York and the auction market is less developed than that in Europe (Thode et al., 2002). Canada is also now developing an auction market (Gray, 2004) and Australia has had an active one for some time. Internet auctioneers also offer a similar service. The internet has revolutionized auctions generally, as the process can take place over a number of days or weeks and individuals can bid without having to attend physically. The market has, however, expanded mainly in the last few decades (especially after the 1982 vintage in Bordeaux) precisely the same time that wine began to be treated, in part, as an investment medium.

Given the uncertainty offered by the auction market it is clear that consumers make use of external cues to aid their involvement with it. Wine writers are probably used, and there is evidence that the American critic, Robert Parker, has a noticeable influence on the American auction market – an influence which has been quantified precisely (Thode et al., 2002). Thode et al. (2002) have also noted that American buyers pay attention to the European wine auction market, although the same does not happen in reverse.

It can be posited that when wine is auctioned it becomes more than a mere beverage. It has value added to it by the process of the market over its mere worth as an agricultural product. Auctions also give wine a quasi-aesthetic validity – it is treated in the same way as a work of art, or an ancient book. At that point it becomes worth collecting and appreciating. It is no coincidence that there is no secondary market for bulk wine.

Conclusion

The spread of wine consumption in northern European and Anglophone countries, as well as the global shift from bulk to premium wine, means that wine is less than ever merely a drink and is surrounded by activities designed to satisfy the consumer's thirst for knowledge, exploration and challenge as well as the chance to establish status as a connoisseur, and which provide enjoyable experiences which enhance drinking. Most of these activities have their roots in developments which began centuries, even millennia, ago but that have grown at an increasingly rapid pace since the Second World War. Thus literature relating to wine (supplemented now by film, television and radio) education and wine clubs, the opportunity to visit wine regions and specific producers all offer these experiences.

Additionally these opportunities, together with the evaluation of wines by experts, give consumers the chance to extend the range of purchase cues available. However, as with any aesthetic product, the field is not free from conflict and whilst gatekeepers may offer consumers some security their disputes or variability in the assessment of wine may also lead to confusion. Finally, the increasing importance of collecting and investment – both features of general markets for aesthetic goods like artworks – help to add respectability to an interest in wine with a sense that it is a valued and significant product, as well as offering outlets for conspicuous consumption.

Bibliographical note

For those who wish to know more about the literature of wine Gabler (2004) provides a comprehensive analytical compendium of everything which has been written. There is now a substantial body of research on wine tourism, most of it emanating from Australia and New Zealand. This chapter has focused essentially on the perspective of the wine tourist, but the viewpoint of the service provider and the role of wine tourism in developing a modern wine brand have also been investigated by academics. A good overall summary of current knowledge is contained in Carlsen (2004), and the best introduction is the book edited by Hall and his colleagues (Hall et al., 2000b). The influence of wine critics – especially Robert Parker – is much debated and works by Echikson (2004) and McCoy (2005) give an interesting if not entirely impartial assessment. For an alternative perspective on wine and the role of the critic Hugh Johnson's (2005) memoirs are informative. Although a little dated Dunphy and Lockshin (1998) give a detailed assessment of the strengths and weaknesses of the Australian show system.

Part Four: The Social Dimension of Wine

Wine and fraud

The symbolic importance of wine and – critically – its potential value when designated as 'higher quality' means that there is often a great deal of money to be made from it. There is, therefore, even greater profit to be made from fraudulently using cheap wine and then claiming that it is something else with a higher perceived value, or 'improving' it to make it taste different. This chapter will not detail the many wine-related frauds that have occurred but, using a few of them as case studies, will try to unravel the different structures of wine frauds – specifically adulteration, misleading claims, passing off and the modification of wine. It will also consider forms of 'legal deception'.

Introduction and context

It is apparent from what has preceded this chapter that the vicissitudes of growing grapes and producing wine has regularly led to unfair behaviour. It will also be apparent that sharp practice comes in a number of different forms. Sometimes it may be perpetrated by the producer against the consumer, sometimes by a producer against both consumers and other producers, and sometimes by a distributor against the consumer and possibly the producer.

There is also a scale of how the producer or distributor may behave on a moral basis, ranging from the legal through to the illegal (see Figure 11.1), which can be understood as operating on a continuum.

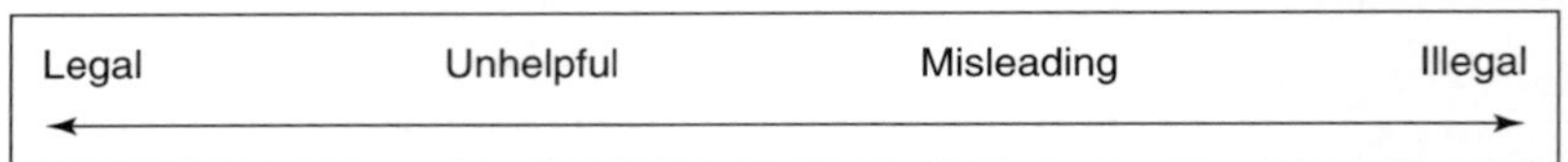

Figure 11.1 A continuum of ethical behaviour.

These can each be illustrated. One form of unhelpful behaviour may be the listing of typical fruit aromas on the back labels of wines. Consumers like this precision (Chaney, 2000a & b), but research has suggested that even highly involved drinkers find it hard to match the actual smell of a wine to the back label descriptors offered (Charters et al., 1999). Thus, to tell a consumer that a wine has peach characters may induce them to buy the wine, yet they may be unable to detect those characters when they drink it. The listing of fruit characters, however, is not designed to deceive the drinker.

As an example of misleading behaviour the allusion, on a wine label, to the use of oak is instructive. As noted in Chapter 6, in many countries it is permissible to add oak chips or staves to give a flavour of oak to a wine whilst all ageing is carried out in stainless steel tanks. This is financially important, for a new French oak *barrique* of 225 L capacity may cost £400–600 – sufficient to add up to £2 to a bottle of wine. Such an additional cost would be unsustainable for a chardonnay designed to sell for around £5. Thus, when a back label refers to 'subtle oak influence' rather than stating that the wine was aged in barrels made from the oak of a specific country for a particular time period, it is likely that some means of flavouring the wine has been used. Most consumers, however, would not understand this, and would merely assume that the wine had spent some time being aged in barrels before bottling. Using oak chips or staves is not necessarily illegal, but certainly misleads most consumers of the wine. (It could, indeed, be argued that these actions are no different from flavouring wine by adding fruit essences, and thus should be banned, or that the label should at least declare that the wine has been 'flavoured by the use of oak products'.)

Illegal behaviour is clear; it is action which breaks the law as part of the production of the wine. Historically lead oxide was frequently added to wine – it helped to inhibit acetification and added sweetness. It was also highly toxic, particularly for children (Robinson, 1999). Naturally its use as an additive is now banned throughout the world.

It is important to note that there is national and cultural variation in all of these potential activities. Chaptalisation – the process of adding sugar to fermenting must to increase the alcohol level of the resulting wine slightly – is legal in northern Europe and New Zealand, but prohibited in Australia, where, given the warm climate, it has not historically been considered necessary (although in some years Tasmanian wines may benefit from it). In Europe the maximum tolerance for the declared alcohol on a bottle of wine is 0.5 per cent. Thus, if a wine has an alcohol level of 13.5 per cent the label is allowed to state any figure between 13.0 and 14.0. On the other hand in Australia the tolerance is 1.5 per cent. Thus the same bottle could give any figure from 12.0 to 15.0 – a substantial variation which is hardly warranted given that modern chemical analysis can deliver very precise data on alcohol levels.

Fraud in the past

Fraudulent practices relating to wine have been a problem that has been recorded since history began. In order to maintain the purity of what was sold the great Babylonian legislator, Hammurabi, stipulated in his legal code in about 1750 BC that tavern owners who were guilty of watering down drink should be drowned. The Greek island of Thasos established a single measuring stone which was used to ensure standard sizes of the Amphorae which were to hold wine; this guaranteed that those purchasing the product would be given a container with a standard volume. Such laws were not isolated, but recur throughout history. From the time when the origin of a wine also added value to the product, protecting the designation of origin against passing off by lesser wines also became important and it has already been noted how the demarcation of the Douro valley and the Chianti region were partly a response to such a problem (see Chapter 5). The impact of demarcation, at least in the Douro, was an improvement in quality, as it also restricted the adulteration of wine by adding substances like elderberry juice to make it darker (Unwin, 1996).

A recipe for Claret

Hallgarten, an authority on wine duplicity (1987), reports the following dating from 1814 which gives details about how to make good Claret:

- 18 L Claret vine leaves;
- 18 kg raw sugar;

- 250 g powdered red tartar;
- 6 handfuls rosemary leaves;
- 6 oranges – peel and juice;
- 4.5 L brandy;
- 83 L water.

It was said to make 81 L of wine in total, after racking and clarification, so quite a bit of liquid must have been lost in the process. The red tartar mentioned may have been a crème of tartar made from red grapes. Such a concocted wine was commonplace in the period before consumer protection legislation and controls on the mislabelling of foodstuffs, and many other examples exist until the end of the nineteenth century. Of interest is the use of leaves and herbs which may have given the resulting drink a distinctly leafy character, akin to a less-ripe wine today. The addition of a yeast source is not recorded (unless some wild yeast were attached to the vine leaves). If not used then the alcohol content of the drink would have been no more than about 2.5 per cent – hardly appropriate for Claret. However, the volume of sugar would probably have raised the alcohol content of the drink by about 12.5 per cent if fermentation was completed – making a final beverage of perhaps 15 per cent alcohol by volume (a.b.v.) – depending on how much alcohol was lost during production and how effective the yeast source was.

The spread of fraudulent practices

Whilst fraudulent activities have been common throughout history the problem accelerated in Europe, especially France, during the nineteenth century as wine became more widely distributed. By 1820 an English writer, Frederick Accum, suggested that wine was more in danger of being adulterated than any other product (Robinson, 1999). There were a number of reasons for this. First, whilst adulteration had always existed it had become much more widespread because scientific developments allowed cheaper, simpler and more varied ways of 'improving' wine (Stanziani, 2004). Second, the imitation of high-quality wine became a major threat during the nineteenth century as the reputation of some regions began to increase dramatically – most notably Port, Bordeaux, Burgundy and Champagne. Thirdly, an impact of phylloxera was that the wine market was fundamentally destabilized and wine supplies were dramatically reduced for a time (Campbell, 2004). Thus, in general, illegal practices developed on two fronts. The first challenged the producers of high-quality wines. The second was over the production of everyday drinking wine. The two types of practice involved rather different methods.

It has been noted that even in 1819 whilst 100 barrels of wine were made from the great Burgundian vineyard of Chambertin, over 3000 barrels were sold (Loubere, 1978). Problems of this nature escalated as the 'golden age' of wine developed. By 1824 fraud was perceived to be sufficient of a threat that the first French statute attempting to protect producers was passed, followed by a series of others over the next century culminating in the development of the appellation controlée (AC) system (Stanziani, 2004). As the century progressed a number of actions were taken by producers to prevent 'passing off' (Duguid, 2003) – the fraudulent claim by one producer that their wine was made by another, or was from another region.

A key impact of phylloxera was to reduce the volume of wine available to French consumers. Consequently a number of alternative 'wines' were developed in an attempt to sustain supplies. Phylloxera led to a rapid reduction in the total area under vine. From 2 643 174 ha in 1869 down to 1 971 000 in 1885 and 1 609 000 in 1900. Meanwhile the average yield fell from 25 hL/ha in 1870–1885 to 15 hL/ha in 1885–1890 (Loubere, 1978, p. 166). As a result producers resorted to adding water to pressed grape skins and re-pressing it to extract a liquid which had some sugar and a little flavour; this was *piquette*, which historically had been considered only good enough to give to vineyard labourers, but now became saleable to consumers. Some producers would re-press up to four times (Loubere, 1978). The insipid nature of this drink meant that it was often bolstered with sugar and colouring agents. There was a backlash from producers who wanted to sell genuine wine which resulted in legislation to counter the fraud, but ultimately it was an upsurge of production in authentic wine in the post-phylloxera period rather than changes to the law which undermined the market for imitation beverages (Loubere, 1978). Even when this problem had passed, however, there were still issues around the modification of wine. Passing *piquette* off as wine was seen to be a deception but even after the Second World War it was remained legal to add Algerian wine to Burgundy in order to bolster it (Brook, 2000c), a practice which generated little adverse comment until the 1970s.

The defence of Champagne

The Champenois, especially, devoted much energy over the century after phylloxera to fighting what was perceived to be the debasement of their wine. The effort was focused on the production of wine marketed as

Champagne which did not come from the Champagne region. Thus when wine was sold in Britain as 'Champagne' made from elsewhere in the world, action was taken (Duguid, 2003), and when Champagne Mercier shipped still wine to Germany for second fermentation action was taken against them by the Champagne Syndicat (Guy, 2003). In these cases it was wine being passed off as Champagne which formed the basis of the fraudulent behaviour. However, another battle was over whether or not grapes from the Aube region could be used to make Champagne. The Aube is in the far south-east of Champagne, growing predominantly pinot noir, and the large houses relied on the area for a steady supply of cheap grapes. To the grape growers around the Marne valley the Aube was not part of the 'true Champagne' being physically closer to Burgundy, and the Aubois were merely seeking to benefit fraudulently from a reputation that was not rightfully theirs (Guy, 2003). For a long time the *vignerons* of Reims and Epernay fought to have Aube producers excluded from the designated region, arguing that they were not part of the traditional Champagne terroir, so that in 1911, when the prototypical appellation law for the region included them, the growers around Epernay and Reims responded with a 'Committee to Defend the Interests of the Ruined Vignerons of the Marne', ultimately rioting to show their displeasure (Guy, 2003). The upshot was that the Aube was relegated to lower status as a 'second zone' (Robinson, 1999). The exclusion of the Aube from the designated region later in the year resulted in demonstrations and tax strikes in the south-east, followed by a 20 000 strong march. There followed almost two decades of dispute, which was only resolved in 1927 with the ultimate inclusion of the Aube in the demarcated area (Robinson, 1999). Today no one disputes its right to produce Champagne, and some of the most notable producers of the region, such as Champagne Drappier, are based there. A shifting perspective means that what was once considered a way of cheating the consumer is now unquestioned as a reasonable practice. It is worth noting that the argument over the Aube was promoted by the growers in the northern part of the region, who were in continual conflict with the large Champagne houses. The idea that the use of Aube fruit was fraudulent was maintained as long as that dispute continued. When both growers and the houses began to see that they had shared interests what had once been 'fraudulent' was no longer considered to be a deception.

Whilst in the nineteenth century it had tended to be individual houses which had sought to protect the Champagne name (which even then had been primarily an activity of the *grandes marques* acting to safeguard their own brands) after the First World War the growers and the houses began to work more closely together. The next stage after the creation of the demarcated area in 1927 was the formation in 1942 of the Comité Interprofessionel du Vin de Champagne (CIVC), with the intention of improving the defence of the generic name of Champagne. From 1956 to 1960 in the United Kingdom they pursued the Spanish 'Champagne' case. The Costa Brava Wine Company was a smaller producer of tank-method sparkling wine in Spain. They marketed their wine in the United Kingdom as 'Perelada Spanish Champagne' (Hallgarten, 1987). The Champagne producers decided to sue the company for passing off their product as something that it patently was not, and won an injunction in 1960 to stop distribution of the wine. That was followed in 1975–1977 by the Babycham case, in which they successfully prevented the producers of that drink calling it a 'Champagne perry' (Barr, 1990). By the 1980s the CIVC's technical section had developed the use of spectrometry as a means of analysing the precise origin of a wine, so that they could pursue anyone guilty of promoting a generic deception. Thereafter the focus has tended to shift back to individual houses defending their brands. In 2001 Veuve Clicquot Ponsardin threatened a Tasmanian producer, Stefano Lubiana, who was bottling a sparkling wine with a label in a colour very similar to the orange of Veuve Clicquot's non-vintage brut wine. The Champagne house argued that the similar colour was sufficient to mislead the consumer and that the colour of their label, 'Clicquot orange', was in itself a trademark (Holland, 2001). The Tasmanians decided to change their label as they felt they did not have the resources to fight a court case over the issue. Finally, the CIVC sponsored an action in France against the company of Yves Saint Laurent which had produced a perfume called 'Champagne', with the Champenois claiming that it was being passed off as a wine (Anon., 2005b).

These most recent developments highlight some of the grey areas around fraud. Most people would probably accept that wine made in Spain should not be allowed to call itself 'Champagne'. It is more arguable whether or not the colour of a label is misleading and could persuade some consumers to buy a Tasmanian wine because they believe it is made by a Champagne house. It is likely that very few consumers, if any, would mistake a perfume for a sparkling wine.

A taxonomy of fraud

The historical context allows us to see that wine deceptions can be committed in three ways. First, wine can be adulterated. This type of fraud in turn can operate in two forms: first, some illegal extraneous substance may be added to the wine to change it; alternatively it may have other wine added to it to modify its taste and structure. The second way in which deception can occur is when misleading claims are made about wine – a form of fraud which often operates in tandem with other means of deceiving the consumer. The third form of deception is cheating customers over price. This may not necessarily be illegal, but plays on customers' ignorance so that they pay more than they should for a wine. In all this it is important to note that what may be illegal in one country is permissible in others.

Adulteration

Any form of adulteration of wine is a deception entirely focused on the consumer. At the very least consumers are entitled to receive what they believe they are buying (in this case a product made to conform to local production laws). Additionally the consumer must have assurance that the wine they buy will not cause them particular harm. In one case in the 1980s Italian wine was adulterated with methyl alcohol (much more toxic than ethyl alcohol, which is the main alcohol component in wine) resulting in the death of at least 23 people. The maximum allowable amount of ethyl alcohol in wine within the European Union (EU) is 0.3 g/L for red wine but one consignment of this wine to France contained 26 g/L.

There have, historically, been regular rumours that winemakers enhance the varietal characteristics of their wine; thus stories abound of French producers of cabernet-based wines who would add a little *crème de cassis* to their fermenting must to accentuate the blackcurranty characteristics of the finished product. Any such addition, however, is easy to identify using modern sophisticated analytical processes. With improvements in flavour technology it is now possible to isolate flavour compounds in wine (Jackson, 2002). As a result it has now become easy to add the precise chemical which creates a specific flavour in a wine. For instance, amongst the key flavour components of sauvignon blanc is a group of compounds known as pyrazines, which contributes a range of aromas to the wine in the spectrum of capsicum, gooseberry and asparagus (Robinson, 1999). The addition of an appropriately selected pyrazine could increase – say – the gooseberry characteristics of the wine (considered attractive – and certainly more generally desirable than cooked asparagus).

Pyrazines in South Africa

In 2003 the highly respected South African wine journalist Michael Fridjhon alleged that various producers were adulterating their wines by adding methoxypyrazines to sauvignon blanc (Matthews, 2003), and that the country's winemakers were therefore not being monitored adequately by government bodies. This allegation occurred just as South African sauvignon blancs were beginning to earn international recognition for their quality and were becoming increasingly popular in export markets. For obvious legal reasons Fridjhon refused to name the culprits, which provoked outrage in some quarters and calls for retraction – but he refused to back down. At the same time an investigation was begun by the South African Wine and Spirit Board which took samples of grape juice to compare against final wines in an effort to locate irregularities (Lechmere, 2004b), an action which resulted in almost 25 per cent of the country's sauvignon blancs being tested. Despite continuing protestations of innocence from many quarters, in late 2004 two winemakers with the large KWV company were dismissed after it was shown that they had added flavouring agents to wines (Lechmere, 2004a). Significantly some of those who object to the addition of methoxypyrazines would accept the use of oak chips or inner staves as a means of giving wine an oak flavour.

Whilst some adulteration is related to enhancing aromatic flavour, other forms seek to modify the structure of the wine. In this case an attempt is made to increase the alcohol content of the wine, or to give it more body, or to vary acid levels. The aroma of the wine may be unchanged but the sensation of the wine in the mouth, particularly its mouth feel, is varied.

The 'anti-freeze' scandal in Austria

One of the natural components of wine, albeit in comparatively limited amounts, is glycerine. Glycerine has a vaguely sweet flavour and adds weight and richness to the texture of wine. It is a natural by-product of fermentation. Clearly its addition could add body to thin wines but, as a form of sugar, it is very easy to detect its addition to wine during analysis. Through the 1970s and after some Austrian merchants wanted to enhance wine which they were blending, adding not the easily detectable glycerine but a related compound, diethylene glycol. This provided similar characteristics to wine as glycerine, making it fuller and sweeter, but it could not be so easily discovered (Hallgarten, 1987). Diethylene glycol is used as a component of anti-freeze – hence the popular title of the scandal. At the levels it was used it was harmless, so its addition hurt no one (and may well have made the wine they drank more enjoyable). Its application was, nevertheless, illegal. In the end the adulteration was only discovered in 1985 because one fraudulent wine producer decided to claim a tax refund on the stocks of the illegal chemical he had purchased (Barr, 1990). Though diethylene glycol was primarily employed by négociants the impact of the scandal on the Austrian wine industry was widespread and all producers suffered as a result. In 1986 exports dropped to 10 per cent of the previous year's total (to four million hL) and stayed low for some time. It also resulted in a rigorous overhaul of the country's wine laws, which in the long run have proved to be to the benefit of Austrian producers, as they are now amongst the strictest in the world.

Misleading claims

The most serious misleading claims made about wine tend to be about origin as, at least in Europe, the idea of quality has been linked closely to where the wine comes from. As observed above one spur for the original appellation legislation was to protect producers in areas with a high reputation. However, as will be seen, that did not entirely eradicate the problem – it merely gave a form of legal redress to those who were cheated. These forms of misleading claims may be generic (a wine claims to be Champagne when it is made from grapes grown elsewhere in the world) or they may be the passing off of one wine as a specific brand, as in a recent case when auction consignments of the Australian wine, Penfold's Grange, were discovered not to be genuine.

It is relevant to note that the making of misleading claims is one area in which attitudes are still changing. Historically, when wine industries developed in new countries they needed to label their wines to give some idea of style. As the concept of using a varietal name is of recent origin, during the nineteenth century in both the United States and Australia when wine was made it was given a European generic wine name to convey a sense of the type of wine it was. Thus 'chablis' was used to denote a crisp, dry wine, and 'white burgundy' to represent a more full bodied style. However, in Australia at least this is changing and following the trade agreement with the European Union (EU) about labelling such generic terms are in the process of being phased out. Thus, what was legal is now becoming illegal, although it must be noted that this may not affect consumer perceptions; it is still normal for a customer in a wine store to ask for a bottle of Champagne when what they seek is a bottle of Australian sparkling wine. However, what is now becoming illegal in Australia remains perfectly legitimate in the USA, where chablis which has no connection with France is still sold without sanction.

The House of Cruse

Historically the strength of the Bordeaux wine trade was based not so much on the chateaux which produced the wine as the négociants who arranged its distribution – as they still do. Many of these négociants were long established Bordeaux traders, collectively known as the *chartronnais* after the part of the city in which their offices tended to concentrate. The *chartronnais* were the elite of the region's wine trade (Faith, 1999).

One of the leading members of the *chartronnais* was the house of Cruse, a family of Danish-German origin which had settled in Bordeaux in the late eighteenth century (Hallgarten, 1987), and were highly regarded, both socially and within the wine trade. In the early 1970s they were involved in a complex fraud which ruined the family. The early years of the 1970s saw a boom in the sales of red Bordeaux; even for the poor 1972 vintage prices accelerated rather than decreased (Faith, 1999). Often producers were selling wine they did not own and could not easily buy, putting their companies under pressure. The négociant firm of Cruse was one such company, and found a solution to the problem; in 1973 they purchased wine from a less well-known Bordeaux merchant with a rather shady past, by the name of Pierre Bert. However, Bert's wine was from the Languedoc, with the papers relating to its origin modified in a complex series of transactions which made it appear to be genuine AC Bordeaux (Faith, 1999). In one fortnight the Cruses were said to have taken delivery of 400 000 L of falsely designated wine. The deception was discovered by the French fraud office, which raided both businesses. Pierre Bert immediately owned up to the crime, but argued that he had done nothing wrong, attacking the whole idea of *appellation controlée* legislation, and suggesting that most AC Bordeaux was of appalling quality (Hallgarten, 1987). Both parties were prosecuted. As Hallgarten (1987, p. 138) records, Bert was cross examined in court:

> 'Had he sometimes mixed white wine with red?' he was asked by the prosecutor. 'Yes it has happened. A little white does no harm to quality when there is too much tannin in the red.'

'But it is not legal,' exploded the prosecutor.

'No, but it is good' asserted Pierre.

Bert later argued that 'there is no fraudulent wine, only fraudulent documents' (Hallgarten, 1987, p. 139). The court was unwilling to accept this and both he and the senior members of the Cruse family were found guilty, although Bert's punishment was more severe than that meted out to the directors of the house of Cruse.

There are, however, some subtexts to the whole affair. When arrested Pierre Bert wanted to know why the matter had not been resolved quietly with the payment of an informal fine, noting that this was how such matters were regularly dealt with (Hallgarten, 1987). Additionally, at the time of the raids on the wine merchants a French presidential election was imminent. One possible contender was Jacques Chaban-Delmas who was the mayor of Bordeaux and a friend of the Cruse family (Faith, 1999). Another likely presidential contender – and the eventual winner of the election – was the Minister for Finance who was active in pursuing the prosecution, Valery Giscard d'Estaing. One claim that circulated was that the négociants had been caught up in a far larger political drama (Barr, 1990).

It is also worth noting that on appeal the sentences imposed were reduced substantially. The suspended prison sentences given to Lionel and Yvan Cruse were quashed, so they were left with a fine of about £2500 each – hardly substantial for such a major fraud. Bert – who had made £360 000 from the deception – had his 1-year prison sentence halved, and his fine reduced to £650 (Hallgarten, 1987). This certainly sent mixed signals about the value of the AC system, and how important it was to defend it.

The fraud was both about misleading labelling and the adulteration of one wine with another. In the end it accelerated the decline of all the elite *chartronnais* merchants and contributed to a major decline in the price of Bordeaux over the rest of the decade – its impact thus went well beyond a mere deception of the consumer.

Price deceptions

There are a number of examples of consumers being persuaded to pay an excessive amount for purportedly high-quality wine. Whilst this has probably occurred throughout history (as the story of Trimalchio's feast recounted in

Chapter 8 illustrates) it is perhaps more prevalent now. The spread of consumption in the modern world, combined with the difficulty consumers have of understanding wine generally and the quality context of specific wines (owing to market fragmentation), as well as increasing publicity about the value of wine as an investment vehicle (e.g. Roberts, 2001; Temple, 2004) all combine to make wine attractive but difficult to buy. Thus, for instance, one unscrupulous trader was recorded as offering a 1996 St Emilion *grand cru classé*, Chateau Troplong-Mondot, for £4200 per case when it could be purchased elsewhere for about a fifteenth of the price (Roberts, 2001). One of the most active opponents of wine merchants who seek to cheat consumers has been the British wine journalist, Jim Budd, who has spent considerable effort trying to expose them, and has a website devoted to such cheats (www.investdrinks.org). Typical of the deceptions he has been instrumental in unmasking was the case of the company Goldman Williams, which traded in Claret, offering stocks to unwary purchasers at grossly inflated prices, whilst misrepresenting that the offer was unexpectedly cheap and the price of the wine likely to rise rapidly in value. In one instance a client purchased Chateau Lafite 1996 for £4600 when they could have bought the same wine elsewhere at the time for £2000. After an active campaign against such deception the company was finally wound up by the Department of Trade and Industry in 2002 'in the public interest'.

Modern deceptions: Variations on a theme

In the United Kingdom selling wine at a substantial premium is not in itself illegal although misrepresenting its value to the consumer would be. Most people would nevertheless consider the sale itself unfair conduct, irrespective of the absence of any misrepresentation. From the foregoing it is clear that fraud still exists in the wine industry. However, less well remarked are instances of borderline deceptive behaviour; this is activity that is probably not illegal – indeed at times it may be explicitly sanctioned by the law – but which nevertheless is not entirely open. Grey areas include wine labelling and production issues, and again requirements may differ from country to country.

Crucially, because the law now takes a very active interest in what is being sold to the consumer, the situation has developed whereby that which is not explicitly prohibited is acceptable, and what is permitted may in fact legally entrench conduct which is not entirely open and honest. Such behaviour either deludes consumers or at the very least does not give them all the relevant information.

Labelling regulations in Australia provide a good example of this grey area. Producers do not have to give any details about the vintage, origin or grape varieties used in a wine. However, if they do then 85 per cent of the wine must come from that vintage and origin and variety. On that basis, if a wine is labelled as a 1998 Coonawarra cabernet then the consumer can expect that at least 85 per cent of it is 1998 Coonawarra cabernet. In practice, however, 15 per cent of it could be 1997 Coonawarra cabernet, another 15 per cent could be 1998 McLaren Vale cabernet, and yet another 15 per cent can be 1998 Coonawarra merlot. In reality, therefore, only 55 per cent of the wine actually has to be precisely as labelled. There is a further argument that even to allow a 15 per cent tolerance on variety, origin and vintage is to allow a legal deception to be perpetrated on the consumer who should be entitled to a guarantee of 100 per cent authenticity. That there is a tolerance at all is designed to allow producers to even out inconsistencies in yield from year to year, and to modify the product in poorer years by using blending material to bolster lesser-quality wine. Against the argument for absolute authenticity the producer could claim that the practice improves the product organoleptically, and is therefore to the consumer's ultimate advantage.

With production issues there are often cultural disagreements about what constitutes reasonable behaviour, as two examples, relating to filtration and blending will exemplify. Most wine is filtered at least once before it is bottled. Filtration removes some impurities in the wine but, more importantly, helps it to be biochemically stable. The alternative to filtration is a long period of settling, usually in wooden barrels, and even then absolute stability may be hard to attain. Some wine critics, however, such as Robert Parker and Kermit Lynch, object to filtration saying that along with impurities it robs a wine of much of its flavour and body. To treat wine in this way could thus be seen to be a deception of the consumer, and indeed a number of wines are now being labelled 'non-filtered' to encourage drinkers concerned about the treatment to buy them. Others, particularly winemakers, argue that filtration does nothing detrimental to the wine, and rather guarantees the consumer a product which will be in a good condition to drink. It is not relevant to analyse the technical side of the debate here (although it is worth noting that critics of filtration tend to be those who focus on expensive, carefully crafted wines where filtration may be less necessary). The issue is whether or not the use, or non-use, of a particular production process may 'cheat' the consumer, and whether the latter is entitled to know how the wine has been handled in the winery. It is also pertinent to ask whether or not the average consumer cares about how the wine they drink was made, any more than they may care precisely how a chicken sold in a supermarket was reared.

Another area of cultural debate concerns blending. In many parts of the world, particularly in new producing countries, interregional blending of wines is common. Thus some Australian wines are sold merely under the geographic designation of 'South East Australia', an area of perhaps some 500 000 km^2 with an extreme range of viticultural environments. To some in Europe this undermines the fundamental element that quality wine should have – a relationship with a particular place – and thus deceives the consumer. For the producers of such a wine, who consider that they are making a consumer product which should show consistency and deliver a reliable flavour (more easily guaranteed by using grapes from a range of areas which are thus less susceptible to idiosyncratic variation from different vintages or other causes) this is a meaningless objection.

Conclusion

It is clear that some wine production and marketing practices are unacceptable. Anything which endangers human life is clearly wrong and deliberately lying about the origin or production processes used in making wine are also objectionable. These practices include adulteration with non-wine related products, modifying it by adding in wine from a different origin, or being deliberately deceptive in the claims made about it, particularly on the label. Beyond that, however, are areas of cultural disagreement, varying legal systems and genuine ethical debate over what should or should not be done to and said about wine.

Bibliographical note

The books by Hallgarten (1987) and Barr (1990) are key introductions to the use of fraud within the wine industry; the former, especially is very anecdotally detailed, the later perhaps a bit more incisive and challenging. Both are now fairly dated. Campbell (2004) and Loubere (1978) are both strong on the fraud which resulted from the phylloxera crisis. Faith's (1999) book on Bordeaux outlines the Cruse case comprehensively.

12 Wine, health and abuse*

Except for about 60 years during the twentieth century, wine taken in moderation has been considered a health-promoting beverage since the time of Hippocrates, the 'father of medicine'. For more than two millennia, wine was also considered a therapeutic agent or medicine. Since the popularity of the 'French Paradox' in the mass media during the early 1990s, there has been a flurry of medical research, including epidemiological, cell culture, animal and human studies. These studies will be considered in the light of the long history of wine as a health-promoting beverage, and an assessment made of the positive and negative impacts of wine on health, including the cardiovascular system, cancer and the antimicrobial properties of wine. The concept of 'moderate' consumption will be considered as will the effect of excessive consumption, particularly the impact of wine on the liver. Finally the social impact of wine abuse will also be explored.

* This chapter is co-authored by Dr Patrick Farrell, M.W.

The historical context

The Hearst Papyrus from ancient Egypt (1550 BC) serves as one of the oldest materials to document wine being used as a therapy. Twelve of two hundred sixty prescriptions specified wine (Lucia, 1963). In the Old Testament, wine was mentioned as a remedy, wound dressing and medicine. The Talmud suggests that wine comforts, refreshes and is nutritious and its health impact is such that if it is absent then medicines are required (Lucia, 1963). A seventh century Greek author described wine as the best remedy for fatigue, distress, pain and sorrow (Lucia, 1963), entities now treated with painkillers, sedatives and Prozac.

Hippocrates and wine

Hippocrates is widely considered to be the father of western medicine. Medical students swear to abide by to the Hippocratic oath upon graduation. An exploration into how Hippocrates and his followers viewed wine and how they used it in treating patients is relevant to the topic of wine and health. Hippocrates lived between 370 and 460 BC. He promoted 'regimen' which referred to what one did on a daily basis to remain strong and healthy. Regimen consisted of food and wine intake, exercise and bathing. Wine was to be consumed in moderation, particularly undiluted wine, as the excessive consumption of wine is debilitating (Cummins, 1976). Unless prescribed for specific ailments, Hippocrates advocated consuming wine diluted with water which served several purposes. As noted in Chapter 3, wine is a sanitizing agent, making the water safer to drink. Dilution with water also promoted moderation. Finally, should consumption to intoxication occur, the additional hydration would tend to mitigate a hangover.

Wine was just one tool available to Hippocrates, his students and their patients. Wine was not used in isolation as a therapeutic agent, but often in combination with other treatments (Smith, 1994). Wine was used as a diuretic, to promote the formation of urine (Adler, 1996). Hippocrates knew that thin, white wines worked best for this purpose, though it was not until the last 150 years that science could ascribe this effect to the action of alcohol and tartaric acid upon the kidneys. Wine was employed as an analgesic and muscle relaxant, in part because of alcohol but also, as science was later to discover, due to the anti-inflammatory effects of wine polyphenols. Hippocrates also prescribed wine as a laxative and as a sedative. Wine was used to cleanse wounds using wine's anti-microbial effect (Adler, 1996), another process only recently understood (Lucia, 1963).

Heavy white wines were considered by Hippocrates to be the most nutritious (Cummins, 1976). It is unclear whether or not these were made in the same manner as red wines, thus having polyphenols. Heartburn was treated with bread and undiluted wine. On the surface this seems paradoxical in that wine's acidity could exacerbate heartburn, though it makes sense in the light of modern evidence demonstrating that wine kills the bacterium responsible for most cases of peptic ulcer disease, *Helicobacter pylori*. White wine was used as an eardrop to treat ear infections (Smith, 1994), again relating to what modern science recognizes as wine's antibacterial effect. Another topical therapy consisted of wine, herbs and honey, boiled and then used to treat skin ulcers (Adler, 1996). Hippocrates' writing and teachings were to live on and influence physicians and medical educators for more than 2000 years.

Other Greek and Roman doctors continued Hippocrates' approach, such as Asclepiades (124–40 BC), and Nicander (190–130 BC) wrote a text entitled *Theriaca*, which was to influence physicians for nearly 2000 years. Theriacs were initially intended as treatments for venomous bites and stings, as well as antidotes to poisons. Nicander's theriac included a host of herbs, including among others: thyme, anise seed, fennel seed and parsley. These were made into lozenges and then soaked in wine (Lucia, 1963). Interestingly, these substances, including wine, are all strong anti-oxidant agents. Celsus (25 BC–37 AD) was a most influential follower of Hippocrates' teachings and wrote a medical text entitled *De Re Medica*, which was used for more than 1500 years. Celsus, too, used wine both alone and in combination with herbs, oils and other treatments (Spencer, 1953). Dioscorides, a Greek surgeon during the reign of Nero, also wrote a medical text, *De Universa Medicina*, which was to remain popular for more than 1500 years. He preferred the Italian wine Falernian over all others as a medical aid. Herbs, flowers, roots and other additives were added to fermenting must (Gunther, 1968), which allowed heat and enzymes from the fermentation, as well as the resultant alcohol, to extract materials from the additives. The fact that alcohol acts as a solvent has been fundamental to its use as a base for medicines through much of history. The use of wine was also developed by Galen (131–201 AD), who was considered the second greatest Greek physician, after Hippocrates, and who used wine as a dressing for wounds.

Some Greek and Roman traditions were included in the New Testament. In Luke, the Good Samaritan binds the wounds of the attack victim, pouring in oil and wine. Paul wrote to his friend Timothy, saying 'stop drinking only water, and use a little wine because of your stomach and your frequent illnesses' (1 Timothy 5:23).

These Greek and Roman usages of wine as a therapeutic agent were continued by the great physicians of the middle ages, with practices spreading especially throughout the Middle-East. These included: Rhazes (860–932 AD), Avicenna (980–1036) and Maimonides (1135–1204) (Lucia, 1963). In Europe, during the middle ages, wine and herbs remained central to treating patients.

Wine continued to be used as therapy during the eighteenth and nineteenth centuries. Following the lead of ancient Greek and Roman physicians, doctors in western Europe promoted the moderate use of wine and advocated specific wines for specific maladies. Graham, a prominent British physician and author, claimed in 1828 that the 'temperate use of wine is conducive to health'. Graham (1828) also wrote that wine roused the powers of the body and mind, accelerated and invigorated the circulation, strengthened the nervous system, and increased the actions and powers of the stomach. In keeping with tradition he felt that wine was especially good for the middle aged and the elderly, describing wine as the 'milk of old age'. Moderation was defined as two glasses per day, after the age of 40, and up to four glasses per day after the age of 50. Dry and light wines, such as those from the Rhine, were used as diuretics and gentle laxatives. Sherry was considered best for the stomach and digestion. Port or Sherry were given to those recovering from acute diseases and taken prior to a meal. For recuperating patients who still had a fever either red Bordeaux or German white wines were prescribed. Graham described red Bordeaux as 'the most wholesome of all vinous liquors' (Graham, 1828).

Writing some 50 years later, Dr Carpenter, a physiologist wary of alcohol abuse, still advocated the use of wine in treating patients with typhus and those with typhoid fever (Carpenter, 1860). Later, Dr Anstie, a fellow of the Royal College of Physicians, wrote extensively about wine in 1877. Like Dr Graham before him, Anstie viewed Bordeaux as being best for health (Anstie, 1877). Moderation, according to Anstie was a half bottle of wine (at around 10 per cent alcohol) for a sedentary adult, and one bottle for an active, vigorous adult, per day. Wine was used to treat children, though sparingly (Anstie, 1877).

With the turn of the twentieth century new medications had become accepted. These included aspirin for pain and fever, barbitals for sedation, and sulphur drugs for infections. Antiseptics, vitamins and improved hygiene came into play as well, diminishing wine's medical usage, though it continued to be stocked in many hospitals to stimulate appetite and improve wellbeing. Even the greatest American physician of his time, Sir William Osler, continued to use wine in the treatment of enteric and pneumonic fevers during the early twentieth Century. Ultimately temperance movements rejected this rich history of wine as a healthful beverage and campaigned for total abstinence (see Chapter 13). Prohibition in the United States was a final death knell to wine as a therapeutic agent, a position accepted by mainstream medical practice, at least until the latter part of the twentieth century.

Wine and health: A scientific assessment

During the twentieth century the fields of epidemiology, microbiology, chemistry, biology, physiology, pathology and medicine flourished. Scientific methods were greatly improved and the sharing of information expanded. Epidemiology has played a central role in determining wine's impact upon both health and disease. Databases can be searched and compared. National per capita wine intakes are compared with the frequency of diseases, such as coronary artery disease (CAD). Population studies have become commonplace. All of this has increased our understanding of the relationship of wine to health.

By late 2005, a computerized medical literature search revealed 4167 published medical journal articles having the term 'wine' in the title or as a major subject heading. Interest in wine's impact upon health has steadily increased since the late 1970s. Forty per cent of these articles had been published during the 5 years preceding this period and 25 per cent had come during 2003–2005. As new research continues to take place at a rapid pace, new information will ultimately clarify some of the observations, deductions and theories described here.

The methodology of epidemiological studies

In retrospective, case–control studies, a group of patients having the same disease are examined with regard to wine intake. These 'cases' are compared with a group of controls, matched for age and other characteristics. Statistical analysis is then performed to determine if there is a statistically significant difference between these two different groups, to discover whether or not a given behaviour, such as moderate red wine drinking, has any effect upon a specific disease.

Prospective studies take a different approach; a population which does not have a given disease is studied over a period of years. Individuals in that population may undergo interviews, physical examinations or tests at the beginning of the study and then at prescribed intervals. Wine consumption at the beginning and throughout the study period can be used to identify groups having shared characteristics, such as non-drinkers and those drinking less than one, one to two, two to four and more than four glasses of red wine per day. These patients are subsequently followed, looking for a specific endpoint such as the development of CAD, or death. Statistical analysis is then performed to determine what effect drinking wine would have upon developing coronary disease. Sophisticated statistical analysis can 'adjust' for potentially confounding variables, such as high blood pressure, high cholesterol, diabetes or a family history of coronary disease. Such studies may then determine the percentage increased or decreased risk that a variable such as wine drinking may have upon the disease being studied. Both common sense and scientific analysis tell us that well planned, larger studies, carried out over longer periods of time, are most valuable. With the confirmation of studies performed by others, evidence then increases to help determine a proven relationship.

Once epidemiological data determine a significant relationship between wine consumption and health, laboratory studies are performed to determine why a specific result may occur and to confirm the epidemiological findings. This is increasingly done with the intention of developing new pharmacologic agents. Studies may be performed on cell cultures in the laboratory. Animals may be studied, especially those that have been selected because they are at particular risk for a given disease. Finally, humans may be studied as well. Individuals may be given wine for variable time periods ranging from a single drink to daily consumption over a period of months. Specific laboratory parameters can be studied, including blood tests such as cholesterol level or anti-oxidant capacity.

Coronary artery disease

The developed world's number one killer is CAD, which is also called coronary heart disease, ischemic heart disease and atherosclerotic coronary vascular disease. In CAD, atherosclerosis takes place in the coronary arteries. This means that a build-up of plaque progressively narrows the arteries, decreasing the supply of nutrients, such as oxygen, carried by blood to the heart muscle. As blood flow to the heart muscle slows patients may develop chest pain or angina pectoris. The heart may begin to function poorly as a pump and begin to fail, causing 'heart failure'. Complete blockage of the artery leads to more pronounced symptoms and may cause actual death of heart muscle. This 'myocardial infarction' is also known as a heart attack. The electrical system of the heart may be affected, causing abnormal rhythms, some of which may lead to sudden death. Up until the beginning of the twentieth century wine was used by various physicians to treat angina pectoris and to stimulate the actions of the heart. Wine, especially acidic white wine, was also used as a diuretic, thus removing fluid from the body, and decreasing the work of the heart as a pump. Pharmacologic diuretics have replaced wine, though diuretics remain a cornerstone in the treatment of heart failure.

In 1819, Dr Samuel Black, an Irish physician, was involved in a number of autopsies in both Ireland and France. Dr Black noted widespread CAD among the Irish, though not among the French. As such, he may have been the first to publish what was much later termed the 'French Paradox'. The French, despite fat intakes similar to, or exceeding, other western nations, have a surprisingly low rate of CAD. Dr Black did not consider red wine as a possible preventative agent, though he did first note the phenomenon (Evans, 1995).

In 1979, St Leger published, in *The Lancet*, the first study purporting to suggest that wine consumption was associated with a lowered risk of CAD (St Leger et al., 1979). St Leger and his colleagues demonstrated that, when national per capita wine consumption was plotted versus the corresponding CAD death rate, there was a strong negative association. In other words, countries such as France, which had higher rates of wine consumption, had far fewer deaths due to CAD. France's per capita CAD death rate was less than one-quarter that of the United States, Australia, New Zealand or Scotland. Such data, though very strongly suggestive that wine was protective against CAD, did not offer absolute proof. For example, national climates conducive to grape growing also are better for fruit and vegetable cultivation and the more widespread availability of produce. The consumption of fruit and vegetables has been subsequently proven to be protective against atherosclerosis and CAD. Such protective fruit and vegetable consumption could be a factor diluting or 'confounding' the results.

A number of good epidemiological studies had previously demonstrated that moderate alcohol consumption was associated with lower risks death from CAD. Following St Leger's (1979) report, several dozen epidemiological studies have been published in the world's medical literature. Most studies have reported a 'U' or 'J' shaped curve when the frequency of heart attacks or coronary deaths is plotted against the frequency of alcohol consumption (Figure 12.1). That is, with light to moderate consumption (up to two or three glasses per day), the risk of developing a heart attack or dying from one decreases by 10–30 per cent, depending upon the study. This would be in keeping with the message of moderation preached by physicians from Hippocrates to Anstie.

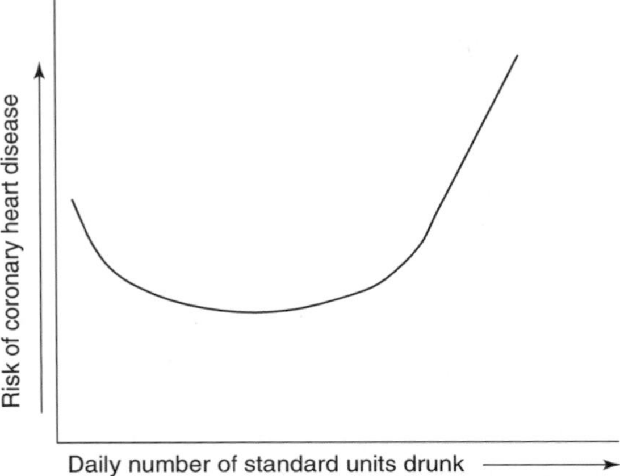

Figure 12.1 The J curve.

St Leger's (1979) report spawned interest in the potential of wine to provide additional protective effects beyond simply its alcohol content. Researchers set up studies to compare wine against beer and spirits with regard to CAD, as well as total mortality and cancer mortality. As with much experimental science the studies do not form a neat picture with a simple answer. The bulk of the evidence supports the hypothesis that wine, particularly red wine, conveys a health benefit with regard to coronary mortality, cancer mortality and total mortality, when compared to those who abstain from alcohol, as well as those who drink either beer or spirits. With regard to total mortality and cancer mortality, the moderate consumption of wine is more protective than the moderate consumption of either beer or spirits. Whereas, in most prospective studies moderate wine demonstrated a survival benefit, beer or spirits showed less survival with increasing consumption (even if moderate), when considering either total mortality or mortality from cancer.

Wine and mortality: The epidemiological studies

A number of studies have demonstrated a 20–40 per cent reduction in CAD risk with the moderate consumption of alcohol (Foppa et al., 2001; Rimm & Ellison, 1995). Sophisticated epidemiological studies, particularly those following large numbers of patients prospectively, have suggested that wine may have an additional benefit over other alcoholic beverages. Some researchers have found consistent results, while others have modified their opinions over time. Klatsky and his associates (Klatsky et al., 1997) initially suggested that alcohol generally decreased CAD, while wine tended to give a minor additional benefit. Subsequently, Klatsky et al. (2003) evaluated data from 128 934 American subjects followed over a 20-year time period. 'J' shaped curves were again demonstrated, though moderate wine consumption showed less mortality risk and less coronary mortality risk relative to either beer or spirits. Klatsky then concluded that those who drank any wine type have a lower risk of mortality than either abstainers or those moderately consuming beer or spirits (Klatsky et al., 2003).

Danish researchers (Gronbaek et al., 1995) reported on more than 14 000 subjects followed for 10 or more years. When considering deaths from either coronary disease or cerebral vascular disease, moderate consumption of either wine or beer was associated with decreased risk, though wine more so. Consuming one to two glasses of beer per day decreased the risk of dying from a heart attack or stroke by 21 per cent, while an equivalent amount of wine decreased the risk by 53 per cent. For three to five glasses per day the decreased death rates were 28 per cent for beer and 56 per cent for wine. Spirits offered either no protection or increased the risk. For other causes of death moderate wine consumption again proved superior to either spirits or beer in decreasing one's risk of mortality. Over the 15-year time period, 1980–1995, coronary death rates decreased 30 per cent in Denmark, while wine consumption increased nearly 16 per cent during the 1975–1992 time period. Though certainly not providing absolute proof, this data is highly suggestive that when consumed moderately, wine provides additional coronary and total mortality survival benefits when compared to abstainers or to the moderate consumption of either beer or spirits. In a subsequent article (Gronbaek et al., 2000), Gronbaek's group reported on another large prospective study. The moderate consumption of wine, up to three glasses per day, showed lower all-cause mortality and cancer mortality relative to abstinence or moderate beer or spirits consumption. Only wine showed fewer cancer deaths with moderate consumption. Interestingly, beer and wine showed equivalent protection against coronary deaths.

The French researcher Renaud has consistently demonstrated that wine decreases both total and coronary mortality. In 1998 he reported that moderate wine consumption decreased cardiovascular mortality by

30 per cent and cancer mortality by 20 per cent (Renaud et al., 1998). Renaud also noted that while France had CAD death rates some 36–39 per cent less than either the United States or United Kingdom, all-cause mortality was only 6–8 per cent lower owing to increased deaths from cancer and violence associated with immoderate alcohol consumption. In 1999, Renaud demonstrated a 33 per cent decrease in total mortality (both coronary and cancer mortality decreased) associated with moderate wine consumption. Moderate beer consumption had less protection against coronary artery deaths (Renaud et al., 1999). In another prospective study, Renaud (Renaud et al., 2004) reported on 36 583 healthy French men followed for 13–21 years. Only moderate wine consumption was associated with a decreased risk of dying during the study period (Renaud et al., 2004).

In 2002 a study evaluated the health and wine habits of more than 4000 university alumni in North Carolina. Wine drinkers were found to have habits that could obtain the cardiac benefits suggested in some studies. As a group, wine drinkers were less likely to smoke cigarettes, and had lower intakes of cholesterol and red and fried meats, whilst having increased intakes of fruits, vegetables and fibre (Barefoot et al., 2002). A cross-sectional Danish study (Tjonneland et al., 1999), found that wine consumers were more apt to consume fruits, vegetables, fish, salad and olive oil, all substances that have been demonstrated to decrease the risk of CAD.

Atherosclerosis and CAD

CAD and atherosclerosis have been studied extensively. CAD takes place over decades and involves a host of processes. The interior lining of the arteries, or endothelium, is damaged by conditions such as: high blood pressure, high cholesterol, oxidized fats, smoking, diabetes, inflammation or infection. This leads to cholesterol and other fats being deposited into the endothelium as fatty streaks. Inflammation inside the blood vessel wall then causes the destruction of normal cells and replacement with scar tissues. Other endothelial tissues proliferate where they should not. Platelets adhere to the growing plaque and the damaged endothelium. These platelets, as well as the damaged endothelium, secrete substances which increase inflammation and clotting, causing smooth muscle in the artery's wall to contract, constricting the blood vessel. Ultimately, the plaque may rupture, causing a blood clot to form over its surface and cutting off blood flow to some heart muscle tissue. Alternatively, the plaque may simply grow large enough to cut off blood flow. The process involves a host of causes including: damage by oxidized fats, inflammation, high cholesterol, thrombosis and constriction of blood vessels, such as arteries.

Oxidative damage and anti-oxidants

That oxygen, something essential for our survival, may cause damage seems paradoxical. Reactive forms of oxygen which are formed during the metabolism of food are the class of chemicals that can cause extensive damage to the body. One may use fire as an analogy. When burning safely in a fireplace or oven, fire provides warmth to the home and heat for cooking. When burning out of control, fire kills and destroys. The same applies for oxidative chemical reactions.

From the time food, particularly fat, arrives in the stomach chemical compounds are oxidized in an attempt to metabolize it into energy and to detoxify harmful chemicals. Some of the compounds formed during oxidation fall into the category of reactive oxygen species which attack normal structures in the body, especially in the bloodstream, causing damage to cell membranes, arteries, organs and DNA. The end result of this may be atherosclerosis, CAD, cerebrovascular disease, dementia and a host of cancers.

Our bodies, particularly our bloodstreams, contain chemical compounds which protect us from oxidative damage. These protective compounds are aptly named 'anti-oxidants'. Some anti-oxidants, taken with a meal, prevent the oxidation of fats in the stomach, thus inhibiting potential damage. The polyphenols found in grape seeds and skins fall into this class of anti-oxidants. These anti-oxidants, when sufficiently absorbed into the blood, serve to raise its anti-oxidant capacity.

Wine may provide both oxidants and anti-oxidants to the body. Alcohol is oxidized during metabolism to form acetaldehyde, a harmful chemical compound responsible for many alcohol-related health problems. On the other hand, anti-oxidants found in the skin and seeds are potent anti-oxidants (including resveratrol, catechins, quercetin, rutin and caffeic acids). These anti-oxidants can prevent the formation of other damaging compounds, such as oxidized low-density lipoprotein (LDL) particles. Anti-oxidants thus represent one potential mechanism by which wine, especially red wine, may decrease the risk of coronary artery and other diseases.

When taken outside a meal red wine will tend towards both oxidation (from its alcohol content) and anti-oxidation (from its polyphenols). Low to moderate intakes tilt the scale in the direction of a net anti-oxidant effect and potential health benefits. Higher intake increases the risk of possible oxidation, as aldehydes overwhelm the anti-oxidant component leading to oxidative harm to the body.

Wine and protection from atherosclerosis

The moderate consumption of alcohol, particularly with a meal, offers protection against atherosclerosis by increasing, over time, the production of proteins which help adapt the body to oxidative stress. Alcohol also decreases the tendency to form thrombosis by accelerating the breakdown of clots. (Note that higher levels of consumption have the opposite effect, that of promoting atherosclerosis, clot formation, constriction of blood vessels, stroke and heart attack). Moderate alcohol consumption also yields a higher level of high-density lipoprotein cholesterol (HDL) which is protective against atherosclerosis and CAD.

Wine, particularly when it contains polyphenols from the skins and seeds, offers other forms of protection. This includes all red wines and those white wines having 18 hours, or more, of skin contact. These polyphenols act as potent anti-oxidants in the stomach, inhibiting the oxidation of fats, thus preventing the formation of LDL particles (Ursini & Sevanian, 2002). White wine without substantial skin contact tends not to offer this protection.

This concept helps to explain the findings by Italian researchers that, independent of amount consumed, those subjects who drank wine only with meals decreased their overall mortality during the prospective study period. In contrast, those who drank wine outside of meals did not have such protection and in fact had increased levels of mortality (Trevisan et al., 2001).

Red wine contains over 200 different polyphenols and related compounds. The amount of these varies with variety, climate and grape maturity. What is important is that the most common polyphenols, such as catechins, quercetin and resveratrol, have varying yet physiologically important functions which are anti-oxidant, anti-microbial, anti-thrombotic, anti-tumour, anti-proliferative and vasodilative. There is also good evidence that these different polyphenols act collectively. The ability of wine polyphenols to inhibit the oxidation of fats in the stomach, thereby preventing the formation of hyper-reactive LDL particles in the bloodstream, seems well established (Ursini & Sevanian, 2002). This would provide a mechanism by which wine polyphenols would have a positive health impact, whether or not they were absorbed well into the bloodstream.

The French paradox

The 'French Paradox' refers to the fact that France has a low rate of CAD and coronary mortality when compared with that of other, developed nations. This is particularly striking, given that the French have significant rates of cigarette smoking and saturated fat intake, both of which are risk factors for CAD. Epidemiologic studies have demonstrated (see above) that one possible explanation for the 'French Paradox' is that the widespread consumption of wine in France is protective against CAD. Subsequent studies have confirmed these findings in France, Denmark and the United States, and laboratory studies have pointed to the polyphenols found in red wine as being responsible, at least in part, for this phenomenon. These findings, and the term 'French Paradox' were popularized during the 1990s by the American television programme *60 Minutes*. Wine sales, particularly of red wines, subsequently rose sharply in the United States and other developed nations.

Wine and blood pressure

Alcohol consumption, even at fairly moderate rates, tends to increase blood pressure. For wine an ambivalence exists. Alcohol increases blood pressure. In contrast, polyphenols cause blood vessel dilatation and a decrease in blood pressure. For high levels of wine consumption alcohol's effect in raising blood pressure tends to overwhelm the protection afforded by the polyphenols. For low to moderate consumption the opposite tends to be the case, with a net lowering of blood pressure. However, there are strong genetic contributions to blood pressure levels as well a host of other factors in its determination. For those drinking alcohol on a daily basis, including wine, who have elevated blood pressure prudence suggests a reduction in consumption. However, some with elevated blood pressure may find that a glass or two of red wine, consumed with a meal, will tend to blunt the rise in blood pressure that follows a meal. In other words there is much individual variation at the low to moderate consumption levels as to how blood pressure is affected by wine, particularly red wine.

Wine as an anti-microbial agent

The use of wine to sanitize water predates Hippocrates. That wine killed pathogenic bacteria was unknown to physicians of the time, though they and lay people recognized that wine added to water made a safer drink that was easier on the stomach and less likely to cause diarrhoea. That wine was used as a medical dressing and a water sanitizer may have given the Roman legions an advantage on and off the battlefield. Modern science has explained how wine kills many of the bacteria that cause human illnesses.

Professor Alois Pick of the Vienna Institute of Hygiene established scientifically wine's ability to kill pathogenic bacteria. Pick (1892) exposed cholera and typhoid bacteria to water and wine mixtures over varying time periods and discovered, that with time, wine killed the pathogenic bacteria (Lucia, 1963; Pick, 1892). Further studies at the Pasteur Institute confirmed this, setting recommendations that white or red wine be added to water 6–12 hours prior to drinking (Lucia, 1963; Sabrazes & Marcandier, 1907). With improved sanitation, hygiene and the availability of other cleansing agents, one would have thought that the use of wine to sanitize water for drinking would have ended in the nineteenth century. However, an American pharmacy student observed during the Second World War that some Italian communities used wine to disinfect their drinking water, escaping the dysentery that befell Allied troops (Lucia, 1963). After the war, he performed a series of experiments demonstrating that wine, when incubated with water killed pathogenic bacteria (Gardner, 1953; Lucia, 1963). This was reconfirmed in 1995, demonstrating that undiluted white or red wine, when incubated with pathogens, killed the 90 per cent of the bacteria after 20–30 minutes (Weisse et al., 1995).

The case of *Helicobacter pylori* confirms this effect. Hippocrates and his followers, over two millennia, had used wine as a digestive agent and to treat maladies of the stomach. As this chapter is being written, Robin Warren and Barry Marshall have been awarded the 2005 Nobel Prize in medicine for discovering that *Helicobacter pylori* was responsible for the vast majority of peptic ulcer disease, and that either antibiotics or bismuth could eradicate the infection and cure the illness. Others have subsequently proven that wine also kills these bacteria and prevents *Helicobacter pylori* infection (Daroch et al., 2001).

The use of wine to cleanse and dress wounds would also be secondary to its ability to kill those bacteria which are likely to cause wound infections and delay healing. The abilities of wine to kill bacteria go beyond alcohol and acidity being inhospitable to many microbes. Studies have demonstrated that wine is far superior to an alcohol solution compiled to mimic wine (Weisse et al., 1995). Some of those anti-microbial capabilities arise from the grape polyphenols, such as resveratrol. There seem also to be other factors such as fatty acids and other substances that are the result of yeast fermentation which create toxins that target bacteria.

Wine and cancer

Strictly speaking, cancer is not a single disease but represents a collection of diseases sharing some medical and biological characteristics. Cancer is the second leading killer after CAD in developed nations, though cancer rates have continued to rise and, in some studies, eclipse that of ischemic heart disease. Wine represents a health benefit for some tumours, while remaining a risk factor for others. As with coronary disease, moderation is a key element as excessive wine and alcohol consumption can lead to increased risk of certain tumours and increase both overall and cancer-specific mortality. Also, as with coronary disease, possible confounding factors may come into play. Though studies have tried to adjust for these in their statistical analyses the reader needs to be aware that in both the United States and Denmark wine drinkers are different, as a group, from abstainers, beer or spirits drinkers, as they are more likely to consume fruits, vegetables, grains, fish and olive oil, while being less likely to consume fatty foods or to smoke (Barefoot et al., 2002; Tjonneland et al., 1999). These behaviours are also associated with lowered rates of overall cancer.

Alcohol consumption, generically, is associated strongly with cancers of the oral cavity, pharynx, oesophagus and larynx. It is also associated, although less strongly, with cancers of the stomach, colon, rectum, breast and ovaries (Bagnardi et al., 2001). Wine-specific studies, by primary tumour site, offer a somewhat different story. An American case–control study (Briggs et al., 2002) found that wine consumption was protective against developing Hodgkin's disease; less than one glass of wine per day resulted in a 20 per cent decreased risk, while one or more glasses per day, netted a 60 per cent decreased risk. If alcohol consumption had begun by age 16, this decrease with one or more glasses of wine per day was 70 per cent. For some other tumours, the message is mixed. White wine, like total alcohol, was associated with an increased risk of basal cell cancer of the skin, while red wine seemed to be protective, at least in women (Fung et al., 2002).

Another Danish study (Pedersen et al., 2003) compared the rates of rectal cancer with the consumption of wine, beer and spirits. Total wine consumption was associated with an increased risk, though not as much as the risk from beer and spirits consumption. Those consuming 14 or more servings of either beer or spirits per week had a 250 per cent increased risk of rectal cancer, while wine consumption at the same level increased risk by 80 per cent. Alcohol consumption, particularly when associated with tobacco use, increases the risk of lung cancer. Wine consumption, though, may be protective. A case–control study from Uruguay (De Stefani et al., 2002), demonstrated a 40 per cent increased risk of adenocarcinoma of the lung by those consuming spirits, relative to non-drinkers. For wine drinkers, however, there was a 60 per cent reduced rate.

Breast cancer rates are on the rise, in part due to obesity and possibly to increasing alcohol consumption by women. Many epidemiologic studies have been performed regarding alcohol and breast cancer, with varied results. Some studies demonstrate that alcohol does not increase the risk of breast cancer among pre-menopausal women (Holmberg et al., 1995; Zhang et al., 1999). Other studies of pre-menopausal women report an intake of more than one drink per day increasing the risk of breast cancer 10–80 per cent (Ellison et al.,

2001; Sneyd et al., 1991). For post-menopausal women the vast majority of studies demonstrate that alcohol of any type, wine included, increases the risk of breast cancer, with one to two drinks per day increasing the risk 10–30 per cent or more (Ellison et al., 2001; Gapstur et al., 1992). On a population basis, this would increase the rate from approximately 4–5 per cent of the population. A family history of breast cancer or of benign breast disease may further increase these alcohol-associated risks (Vachon et al., 2001), as may hormonal replacement therapy during menopause (Horn-Ross et al., 2004).

Wine polyphenols, in dozens of laboratory experiments, inhibit tumour cell growth in cell culture. These polyphenols also posses anti-inflammatory and anti-proliferative properties which may play a role in retarding or inhibiting some cancers. Similarly, dozens of animal studies demonstrate that wine polyphenols are able to delay or inhibit some tumour formation. Whether these results apply to humans will also require further research.

Other health-related issues

The high acidity and low pH of wine, particularly that of white and sparkling wines, tends to de-mineralize and soften enamel (Chikte et al., 2003; Rees et al., 2002). For those consuming wine with a meal, leaving an hour or more prior to brushing one's teeth would seem prudent. Members of the wine trade, particularly those tasting many wines at a sitting, tend to develop problems with de-mineralization, sometimes requiring extensive dental work (Gray et al., 1998; Wiktorsson et al., 1997). The avoidance of tooth brushing, perhaps coupled with the consumption of calcium-rich foods and beverages, may help.

Alcohol is a sedative. Small amounts may act to induce sleep in some while disturbing sleep later in the night for others. Alcohol may stimulate seizure activity and be contraindicated in those with a seizure disorder. On the other hand, red wine decreases the risk of dementia and Alzheimer's disease. A prospective American study found that up to three glasses of wine per day decreased the development of dementia by 45 per cent (Luchsinger et al., 2004), while a French study found that three to four glasses of wine per day decreased the risk of dementia by 81 per cent and Alzheimer's disease by 78 per cent (Letenneur et al., 2004). Bolstering these findings are laboratory studies demonstrating that the anti-oxidant nature of either resveratrol (Savaskan et al., 2003) or grape-skin extract (Russo et al., 2003) protects cells from damage by beta-amyloid, a neurotoxin associated with Alzheimer's disease.

Similarly, moderate red wine consumption may decrease the risk of macular degeneration, one of the leading causes of blindness, another 'wear and tear' disease of ageing, by 20–34 per cent (Obisesan et al., 1998). Another study, suggests that up to two or three glasses of red wine per day may cut the risk of cataract in half (Wysong, 2005).

Wine and appetite

From Hippocrates to Anstie wine was used to stimulate appetite, particularly in those recuperating from disease, those with wasting illness, and the elderly. Does scientific information bear this out? Alcohol stimulates appetite and increases the enjoyment of food. When consumed either before or with a meal an alcoholic beverage will increase the amount of food consumed not only at that meal, but also during the subsequent 24 hours (Buemann et al., 2002; Westerterp-Plantenga & Verwegen, 1999). Dry wines are more stimulatory upon the appetite than beer (Buemann et al., 2002) or sweet wines. In fact, sweet wines, consumed 20–30 minutes prior to a meal, may diminish appetite as a result of sugar content.

Studies done in California during the 1950s (Lucia, 1963) demonstrate that a half glass of dry wine prior to lunch and dinner stimulated the appetites and food intakes of anorexics, leading to some healthy weight gain. Other studies demonstrated that, when allowed by their doctors, patients given wine with their meals not only consumed more hospital food but also viewed the food as more palatable. They were happier with their meals and had an overall improved hospital experience, compared with those used as controls and not offered wine. Studies in nursing homes have demonstrated wine's ability to improve the appetites and food intake of the elderly.

Wine in moderation

This chapter has focused on the potential health benefits of 'moderate' wine consumption. Interestingly, from Hippocrates to the present generation of medical educators an emphasis has been placed upon moderation, as both empirical observations and 'scientific proof' have recognized that excessive consumption of alcohol often leads to disease, addiction, social problems, poor performance and reduced longevity. There is now a large body of research that enables more precise definitions of 'moderation'. Factors to consider include age, sex, disease status and genetic predispositions.

There is general agreement that substantial alcohol consumption is detrimental to children and teens, although those families in which wine is accepted as a part of the dining experience, including those in which children are allowed small amounts to demystify the experience, tend to exhibit lower rates of subsequent alcohol abuse than those in which either abstinence or abuse takes place (Hanson, D.J., 1995). Claims by Anstie and others (Anstie, 1877) that active adults could moderately consume more wine than sedentary ones is an interesting concept which has yet to be tested by science. Middle-aged individuals, who are at increased risks of developing either a heart attack or stroke would seem to be a group into which a definition of moderation could include daily usage. Concerning the elderly, moderation could be limited by functional ability and issues such as a heightened risk of falling.

Gender is important in defining moderation. Males are larger and more efficient, even at the same size as women, in metabolizing alcohol. As such, moderation may certainly be defined as two to four, 125 mL glasses of wine per day. Lower alcohol wines would allow consumption at the higher end, while high-alcohol wines would tend to decrease the definition of moderation. For females, the fact that alcohol increases the risk of breast cancer must be considered. Women thus need to weigh the risk of dying from cardiovascular diseases and the protection offered by wine with the less likely risk of developing and dying from breast cancer, although any increased risk of breast cancer is a serious matter.

It is important to note that one glass of wine per day refers to the day-to-day practice of enjoying a single glass with a meal. This does not refer to an average of one glass per day, all saved up for a single night in the week. Such binging behaviour is associated with increased risk of atherosclerosis, thrombosis, heart attack, stroke, alcoholism and hangover.

Immoderate wine use and abuse

By stressing moderation the converse is that immoderation may be a bad thing. When faced with information suggesting that wine is a health-promoting beverage with therapeutic and preventative properties, one may be seduced into believing that if one glass per day is good, three are better and eight better still. History and current scientific research does not support this. The potential health problems associated with excessive alcohol use can occupy an entire medical text and an in-depth exploration is beyond the scope of this chapter, so a summary only will be provided.

First, alcohol is an addicting substance, with some individuals more prone to addiction on genetic, familial and cultural bases. Alcoholism is a chronic disease which responds to therapy and abstinence but needs to be recognized and treated as a disease. Alcoholics are at markedly increased risks of neuropathy, encephalopathy, pancreatitis, fatty liver, cirrhosis, certain cancers and CAD. Those not addicted to alcohol but who consume immoderately may also be at increased risks of developing these health consequences. There are also the social consequences of intoxication, including marital difficulties, child abuse and poor work performance. One way to pre-empt these difficulties is to follow strictly the moderation guidelines set out earlier, including using wine with meals.

Alcoholism is often used synonymously with alcohol dependence. Alcohol abuse refers to a pattern of use, either daily, weekend or binge, accompanied with a level of drinking sufficient to impair work, school, social or family functioning. There are more individuals who abuse alcohol than are dependent upon it. Nevertheless, alcohol abuse and dependence remain major public health problems worldwide. For those dependent upon alcohol there is usually the phenomenon of tolerance, whereby larger doses of alcohol are required for the desired physical and psychological effect. (One exception is the case of progressive cirrhosis, whereby diminished liver detoxification of alcohol leads to diminished tolerance.) With dependence there are sometimes attempts to cut back that are unsuccessful or short lived. Such dependence should be considered a disease and treated by professionals. Also with dependence comes the possibility of withdrawal, which can be lethal. Withdrawal of alcohol to a dependent individual may result in a spectrum of symptoms ranging from mild anxiety to lethal seizures. Besides anxiety and seizures withdrawal can cause tremors, hallucinations, sweating and an elevated heart rate. Symptoms can rapidly advance from anxiety via mild agitation to profuse sweating, incoherence, hallucinations, seizures and death. As such, alcohol withdrawal must be treated as a life-threatening condition requiring intensive medical therapy. Withdrawal may lead to an attempt to stop drinking voluntarily, though often this is in association with alcohol being cut off abruptly, especially during an illness requiring hospitalization.

Alcoholic liver disease and cirrhosis

Alcohol intake, especially chronic and excessive intake, is a major cause of chronic liver disease. The metabolizing of alcohol to acetaldehyde can yield a pro-oxidative state in the liver with damage to cell membranes and liver cells. These changes result in three general categories of alcoholic liver disease: fatty liver, hepatitis (inflammation of the liver) and cirrhosis (replacement of liver with scar tissue). Alcohol intake may be particularly injurious to the liver in a number of medical conditions including viral hepatitis, iron storage disease and malnutrition. In fact most cases of alcoholic cirrhosis are associated with some degree of malnutrition (Tome & Lucey, 2004), raising the prospect that this may be related to an inadequate intake of anti-oxidants.

One 125 mL glass of wine contains 10–12 g of ethyl alcohol. The daily threshold for the development of alcoholic liver disease is 40 g/day for men and 20 g/day for women (Levitsky, 2004). Thus consuming four or more drinks per day for a man, or two or more for a women, places one at risk for alcoholic liver disease. Daily consumption is not necessary for the development of alcoholic liver disease, as binge drinking, especially most weekends, can lead to similar problems. Nevertheless, most heavy drinkers (those consuming more than 50 g of alcohol per day), do not develop alcoholic liver disease (Levitsky & Mailliard, 2004). Yet some national trends are alarming. In the UK, where alcohol consumption has doubled since 1960, death rates from cirrhosis have increased five- to six-fold since the 1950–1954 time period (Leon & McCambridge, 2006). However, studies in Denmark suggest that when more than half of the alcohol consumed was in the form of wine the increased risk of cirrhosis was cut by more than two-thirds (Becker et al., 2002), possibly because of wine's anti-oxidant effect or perhaps due to better nutritional intake amongst wine drinkers (Tjonneland et al., 1999).

Not all wines are created equal

Although modern viticulture and wine making practices have spread worldwide wines still vary markedly in ripeness, concentration and quality level. Varieties differ with regard to their tannin and pigment contents. These are, in turn, influenced by site, vintage, climate and yield. Varieties also differ in their production of resveratrol. Pinot noir and merlot are varieties apt to develop higher resveratrol levels. Sunlight and fungal pressure also increase resveratrol levels.

The production of healthful polyphenols varies markedly for both white and red wines. Without skin contact white wines have low levels of polyphenols and subsequently low anti-oxidant levels. With increasing skin contact, polyphenol and anti-oxidant levels rise, but so do stability problems. For red wines extraction techniques influence the amount and character of tannins in a finished wine, as do finishing procedures, such as egg white fining. The influence of site, variety, vintage, climate and production techniques upon the 'healthfulness' of a given wine is a slowly developing subject. Upon completion of fermentation and maceration the polyphenol content of red wine is the same as it is for a bottled wine. Interestingly, after several months in bottle, the anti-oxidant level rises (Burns et al., 2001), presumably from alterations in tannin structure, perhaps via polymerization.

Selection of clones in the vineyard for growth and flavour characteristics is an established science. It may also be possible to select clones for anti-oxidant content or the ability to produce resveratrol. Research into the selection of yeast strains for their ability to synthesize resveratrol is ongoing. Ultimately it could be possible to define variety, viticultural and winemaking options that will produce a healthier wine.

Wine and social dysfunction

As has been noted, the abuse of alcohol may result not just in medical but also in social problems. Indeed, until the improvement of diagnostic medicine in the middle of the nineteenth century the medical concerns were less of a focus than social dysfunction (Phillips, 2000) and even afterwards there were doctors who preferred to class alcoholism as a social rather than a medical issue (Nycander, 1998). The roots of this go back a long way. In ancient Assyria at around 650 BC, soldiers were renowned for drinking heavily and often becoming violent. This was probably accepted because the alcohol gave them courage for the battle but records show that the mayor of Assur complained to the king about the soldiers' behaviour and the disruption they were causing (McGovern, 2003).

It has been noted that, whilst alcohol acts to release inhibitions, varying cultural expectations frame the way in which those who are affected by alcohol act. Thus in some cultures excessive consumption of alcohol results in torpor or may have little association with violence (Robinson, 1988). It is possible to go further; it may be that types of alcohol are associated with varying behaviour depending on the subculture which consumes it. Thus the effect of beer drunk at a football match may, between a combination of reduced inhibitions and the excitement of the game, be conducive to aggression and violence. Wine drunk with a meal relaxes, perhaps encouraging volubility, but not inducing hostility. There certainly is evidence in some communities that bottled wine is less associated with social dysfunction, including violence (Stockwell et al., 1998) but that does not mean that wine is never associated with these type of problems. Stockwell et al.'s (1998) research was carried out in Western Australia. They noted that bulk wine was associated with assaults and morbidity, and certainly in some parts of the state wine is the main form of alcohol leading to social trauma, being purchased in bulk form for binge drinking. Thus some communities in Australia have taken action such as limiting the number of sales of cask wine to any purchaser and limiting the hours of sale – controls which have had a notable effect in reducing consumption and, on some occasions at least, a drop in violence and sexual assault (Gray et al., 2000).

Social problems caused by the abuse of wine may affect the abuser's immediate environment such as family and work colleagues; alternatively they may have a much more obvious impact in the wider community. The dangers include criminal activity (from offensive behaviour, via malicious damage to property to violence, sexual assault and child abuse), as well as family disruption and marital disharmony, self-harm, homelessness and work-related issues such as accidents, reduced productivity and absenteeism. One other major concern is death or injury caused by driving under the influence of alcohol.

At its widest, alcohol abuse has an impact on the entire nation. The estimated cost to Australia is over £2 750 000 000 per annum. It is, after tobacco, the second most significant preventable cause of death and hospitalization so that in 1997 there were 3290 alcohol-related deaths and 72 302 hospital episodes. The cost to the UK is said to be £20 000 000 000 per annum (Radcliffe & Piore, 2003). It is not possible, however, to separate wine as a factor in these problems compared with other sources of alcohol.

Nevertheless, whilst cost may be a major concern of administrators, for the general public the more important impact of the abuse of alcohol is its impact on disorder. This is particularly apparent in the UK where, from the end of the 1990s onwards, substantial attention has been paid to anti-social activity and particularly to the role of drinking as a stimulus for such behaviour. The groundswell of public opinion became such that by 2002 the government decided to establish an alcohol misuse study (Hibberd, 2002) particularly aimed at dealing with anti-social behaviour and protecting vulnerable groups.

Whilst there has been a particular focus on the subject of public disorder in the United Kingdom, other European countries are also concerned (Radcliffe & Piore, 2003). However, despite growing concerns about alcohol-fuelled disorder and violence, it is uncertain how far wine is implicated in the problem. In the United Kingdom such disorder is explicitly linked to 'alcopops', also known as pre-mixed drinks (Hibberd, 2002) and, although no research has been carried out into the topic, it is possible that the community as a whole would not generally link wine consumption to disorder. On the other hand it has been suggested that in Spain – which has seen a 31 per cent increase in alcohol consumption amongst young women from 1999 to 2003 – the drink of choice for the young is a mixture of red wine and cola (Radcliffe & Piore, 2003).

There is, however, no doubt that the wine industry seeks to distance itself from anti-social behaviour and, by implication at least, suggests it is beer or alcopops which are the prime cause. In 2002 the noted British wine writer, Andrew Jefford, wrote an article complaining about a violent disturbance on a train which ended in the theft of his laptop (Jefford, 2002c). He pointed out that the event merely confirmed what he already thought of alcopops – that they are 'evil and exploitative' and a form of 'legal drug trade' (Jefford, 2002c, p. 19). He went on to add:

> This product has nothing to do with moderate consumption, with mealtime use, the means of aiding digestion, deepening old friendships or soliciting a restful night (2002, p. 19).

The word wine is nowhere mentioned – but the comparison is nonetheless clearly made between an evil drug which causes violence and a civilized drink, the consumption of which is careful and whose impact is beneficial. Such a perspective reflects what is felt by many in the wine industry around the world – both in distribution and production. Technically, chemically, the drug is the same whether it is in wine or an alcopop. The difference is in its social and symbolic use and, for Jefford, as he went on to explain in the article, in the way that drinks companies promote them. He concludes with an attack on 'drug peddling':

> These drinks are rotten to the core. They exploit the young, the stupid and the gullible. They will blight lives and create the criminals and alcoholics of the future (Jefford, 2002c, p. 19).

Conclusion

Wine had been used as a beverage to promote health, and to treat disease, for thousands of years. With the discovery of antiseptic agents, antibiotics, analgesics, anti-inflammatory medications, diuretics and cardiac medications, wine's role in medicine diminished. Political pressures leading to prohibition and abstinence campaigns further diminished wine's standing as a healthful beverage when consumed moderately. This chapter has explored the rise and fall of wine as a therapeutic agent. The discovery and popularization of the 'French Paradox' has led to a renaissance for wine, particularly red wine, being considered once again to be a health-promoting beverage. Population studies which investigate coronary, total, and cancer mortality along with laboratory evidence support the moderate consumption of red wine as being particularly healthful. Potential mechanisms of action include the possibility that wine polyphenols have anti-microbial, anti-oxidant, anti-thrombotic, anti-proliferative and anti-inflammatory effects, as well as promoting blood vessel dilatation. The concept of moderation has also been shown to have some ambivalence, but to be essential to the healthy use of wine.

Alcohol generally can have a dysfunctional impact on society, although there has been little research into why certain nations or ethnic groups respond in different ways when they have drunk to excess. In many parts of the world wine – in both its bulk and premium form – is seen to be less implicated in abusive activity, perhaps in part because of its links to religion, sophistication, lifestyle and status. However, in the past and today in certain environments wine remains the form of alcoholic drink most associated with abuse.

13

The enemies of wine

The ambivalence with which wine is viewed and its potential for abuse ultimately mean some people are suspicious of it or seek to proscribe it. This chapter will outline the background to these viewpoints, explaining the development of social and religious opposition to wine (and alcohol more broadly) culminating in prohibition in the United States and strict controls in other countries. It will also consider the impact of neo-prohibitionism, particularly in the United States.

Introduction

Given some of the issues which have been discussed in previous chapters it is not hard to see why certain individuals and groups may be opposed to wine. We have noted a marked ambivalence about its use throughout history; it has both positive and negative effects. It may result in illness and addiction (anathema both to many religious organizations and to medical groups, the former because it detracts from the worship and service of the deity, the latter because of its adverse health impact). Those of a conservative social outlook especially may fear the disorder that is considered to come in its wake as well as the reduction in social certainties which follows from the lowered inhibitions induced by alcohol. Those in power may fear the impact of a drug whose effects they cannot easily control or which may give a sense of empowerment to disadvantaged groups. It can also be suggested, however, that along with the well-intentioned there may be some who, for whatever reason, just do not like others to enjoy themselves and see curtailing alcohol consumption as one way of pursuing that end.

In exploring the fear of wine some key contextual factors need to be considered. First, it is important to distinguish wine from alcohol generally. The two may often be grouped together by some of their critics, but there are also times when wine is singled out, perhaps as a 'better' form of alcoholic drink, occasionally as a worse one. Second it is worth noting that those who are opponents of wine may sustain that position for the short term or the long term. War or sudden social unrest may change those who are otherwise sympathetic to the consumption of alcoholic drinks into temporary adversaries. Finally, it is important to remember the substantial cultural differences in attitudes to alcohol generally and wine specifically (Robinson, 1988). Southern European countries have little tradition of opposition to alcohol. Scandinavian countries (except Denmark), North America and the Antipodes – traditionally more focused on the consumption of beer and spirits rather than wine – have been key campaigners in the crusade for prohibition. Interestingly, England has been more lukewarm in its opposition to alcohol consumption, although Wales has had a strong historical commitment to temperance.

The historic origins of opposition to wine

The role of religion

The ambivalence of various religions to the consumption of wine has already been noted. There may be a number of reasons for this. Too great an emphasis on sensory pleasure, including food and drink, may be considered to detract from religious piety or service. Drunkenness specifically may deflect a religious adherent from the path of true religion. Some especially ascetic strands of spirituality also argue that money spent on drink is a wasted resource; rather it could be used either to promote the spread of religion or for charitable purposes. To the extent that religion is a means of social control, or a mechanism for maintaining a particular social order, there may also be a suspicion of wine because its consumption potentially undermines that order. In Rome, in 186 BC, the worship of the god Bacchus was outlawed. This was not because there was any 'spiritual' objection to the cult (this was a society in which myriad forms of religious observance flourished). Rather it was because the rituals of Bacchic observance were performed in secret and involved not only 'free' men but also women and lower socio-economic groups, so that it was considered to present a potential threat to national security (Unwin, 1996); the Roman consul who lead the opposition to the cult went so far as to blame every major crime in the city on the leaders of the cult (Livy, n.d./1983). The Roman historian Livy recorded the transition from religion to 'conspiracy' with a sense of disgust:

> To the religious element . . . were added the delights of wine and feasts. When wine had inflamed their minds, and night and the mingling of males with females had destroyed every sentiment of modesty, all varieties of corruption first began to be practised (Livy, n.d./1983, p. 241).

The crimes were said to include perjury, forgery of wills and evidence, murder and violence. Nevertheless, Roman opposition was not to wine itself but rather to the cult of the god of wine. Proscription of wine on religious grounds was extremely rare in Mediterranean societies until the advent of Islam.

Wine in Islam

The population of Arabia before the time of the prophet Mohammed had consumed wine. Mohammed himself was not originally concerned with wine – it was seen as a sign of Allah's grace to humanity:

> We give you the fruits of the palm and of the vine, from which you derive intoxicants and wholesome food. Surely in this there is a sign for men of understanding; Sura XVI 67 (Mohammed, n.d./1974, p. 308).

In addition the Koran promises believers the use of wine in Paradise, where it will 'flow in rivers' as the drink of the blessed. However, other parts of the Koran are less tolerant:

> They ask you about drinking and gambling. Say: 'There is great harm in both, although they have some benefit for men; but their harm is far greater than their benefit; Sura II 219' (Mohammed, n.d./1974, p. 355).

It has been suggested that parties which included wine drinking meant that followers of Islam ignored ritual prayers. The story is told that the most severe condemnation of wine followed a fight between some of

Mohammed's followers who belonged to different tribal groups which took place during a drinking session. Mohammed asked Allah how this could be avoided and received this response:

> Believers – wine and games of chance, idols and divining arrows, are an abomination devised by Satan. Avoid them so that you may prosper. Satan seeks to stir up enmity and hatred among you by means of wine and gambling, and to keep you from the remembrance of Allah and from your prayers. Will you not abstain from them? Sura V. 90 (Mohammed, n.d./1974, p. 397).

The Islamic interpretation of these contradictory rules suggests that the strongest prohibitions on wine consumption tended to come last – so that Allah was preparing the faithful for a ban which would be unpopular (Ruthven, 1984). A more secular interpretation might also note that the first followers of Mohammed tended to be poor. No grape wine was produced in Arabia, and as the new religion began to expand its rustic adherents would come into contact with the temptations offered by the free-flowing drink of other countries (Hyams, 1987). Thus the strict later prohibition may have been more relevant after the earlier, more tolerant, revelations to the prophet. It is worth noting that wine is excluded by name in the Koran. There were, of course, no spirits at that time and beer was less well known in Arabia.

The consumption of hashish and coffee came to the Islamic world after the time of Mohammed. Although some religious authorities sought to ban them they were unsuccessful – partly because these substances had not been explicitly proscribed by the Koran (Ruthven, 1984), and both are still used, to a greater or lesser extent, in Arab countries. In any event, after the first period of evangelistic Moslem zeal the ban on wine consumption was never absolutely observed. Reading the tales of *The One Thousand and One Nights* makes it clear that the upper classes, at least, were prepared to indulge, and the mystical Sufic strand of Islam explicitly used wine – metaphorically and perhaps in practice – as an element in the mystical path to Allah (Saeidi & Unwin, 2004).

One modern leader of an Islamic country explicitly tried to change the socio-religious opposition to wine consumption. Kemal Ataturk, the modernizing ruler of Turkey from 1920 to 1938, lifted the ban on alcoholic drinks and explicitly encouraged the consumption of wine and the development of a wine industry in his country. Ataturk himself was also said to be fond of the national spirit, raki. Raki is widely drunk in Turkey today and it is possible for Muslims to condone its consumption as it is not wine, and therefore not forbidden to them. Ataturk is reputed to have died from cirrhosis of the liver, hardly a factor likely to incline conservative Muslims to accept the consumption of alcohol.

Despite the opposition of their religion to alcohol, some Muslims are prepared to run off-licences, with a number in the United Kingdom able to square it with their faith (Evans, 2005). One has been quoted as saying that 'if you live in this country then you have got to follow the etiquette. We're not drinking it, and we're not encouraging our fellow Muslims to . . . [but] I can recommend lots of nice wines to customers if I know what they're having with it' (Evans, 2005, p. 36). Such a tolerant approach contrasts with that alleged to be held by the radical British Imam, Abu Hamza, who – it has been claimed – has advocated the murder of those who issue licences for 'wine stores' (Gardham, 2006).

Whilst Islam is often today thought of as a religion of Asia and northern Africa it must be remembered that it has had substantial influence in Spain over seven centuries, and Greece and the Balkans for a longer period. It remains the major religion in Albania and is significant in the former Yugoslavia. Further, although Islam is the most well-known religion which opposes wine consumption in the contemporary world, Sikhs and members of the Bahai faith also proscribe it and some sects of Buddhism, Hinduism and Christianity also ban its consumption.

Alcohol consumption and the rise of temperance

Despite – perhaps in part because of – the opposition of Islam to wine consumption, European societies continued to support the consumption of wine until the start of the nineteenth century. This even included puritan Protestants who, whatever other pleasures they may have criticized, accepted moderate alcohol consumption as a gift of God (Fuller, 1996). It has been suggested that the American temperance movement has its history in the arrival of the Pilgrim Fathers in 1620 (Bruce-Gardyne, 2002) but this is a fallacy. Given that wine was part of the communion service Christian societies could hardly do otherwise than support it. However, from the end of the seventeenth century onwards social changes in northern Europe began to undermine that unanimity of approach, leading first to substantial opposition to the consumption of alcohol and ultimately to prohibition.

The starting point of this process centred on the consumption of spirits – specifically gin – in England. At the end of the seventeenth century in order to reduce the consumption of French brandy and to increase government revenues, the distillation of spirits from cereals was allowed by anyone on payment of a duty of one penny per gallon (Unwin, 1996). By 1694 gin cost less to buy than beer (Barr, 1995). This resulted in an outbreak of gin consumption; from 1688 to 1742 consumption rose from 0.5 million gallons to 19 million gallons per annum (p.a.). This is 10 times the nation's current consumption in a country which then comprised only 5 million people (Barr, 1995). The social impact in London was disastrous. The city was growing – a process which inevitably brought with it social dislocation – and intensive consumption of cheap spirits became the consolation of many of the poorest and most alienated. There was a series of public campaigns against the consumption of gin and a concerted effort to solve the problems it caused. The propaganda against abuse included the well-known series of engravings by the artist Hogarth entitled 'Gin Lane', which graphically portrayed the degradation resulting from widespread public drunkenness. Attempts at reform were hampered by the fact that grain-producing land owners were profiting substantially from the sales of their produce – and these people formed the core of Members of Parliament, thus obstructing any real effort at reform until 1751. Only then was an act passed limiting the sale of gin and increasing the duty on it; that statute, plus a series of poor harvests reducing the amount of grain available for distillation, ensured that the problem subsided (Barr, 1995). Nonetheless the ability to consume to overwhelming excess on a daily basis had, perhaps for the first time, been seen to be available even to the poorest in society. Until this time no European country had seen serious demands for the control of alcohol consumption but suddenly limits to drinking were deemed to be necessary. At the same time the government had also learnt how to tax, and make substantial income from, vice (Barr, 1995).

None of this concern focused on wine, however. Indeed wine was seen to be a drink to contrast with spirits, which had such a devastating impact on individuals. Thomas Jefferson in the United States is famous for his dictum that:

> No nation is drunken where wine is cheap; and none sober, where the dearness of wine substitutes ardent spirits as the common beverage. It is, in truth, the only antidote to the bane of whisky (Johnson, 1989, p. 354).

Jefferson was not alone in this perspective. The 'father' of Australian viticulture, James Busby, first sought to develop vine growing around Sydney as a means of offering a 'civilized' form of alcohol rather than the rum which was pervasive and debilitating throughout the early years of the colony of New South Wales (Faith, 2002).

The temperance movement had its roots in a number of social changes. The rise of the mass-consumption of spirits has been noted. Then, during the eighteenth century came the evangelical revival. This had two results: first, many working people were converted to Methodism, a denomination that came to prohibit its adherents from drinking wine (a ban which continued for Methodist church premises in the United Kingdom until very recently). Evangelicalism also spawned religion with an active social conscience. The prime examples were William Wilberforce who campaigned to end the slave trade and Lord Shaftesbury who worked to limit child labour. Social reformers like this were often also actively concerned at the damage which alcohol abuse caused in their societies. The final spur to temperance came in the 1820s and 1830s, in both England and the United States. In the former a reduction in the price of gin duty in 1825 produced a rapid increase in consumption; a reaction to this liberalized the market for beer and saw a dramatic escalation of sales of that drink – promoting a spiral of abuse (Barr, 1995). Meanwhile in America it was a Protestant religious revival beginning in the 1820s and focused on moral purity which provided the impetus for an active renunciation of the evils of this world (Fuller, 1996).

Four points must be made about the early stages of the temperance movement. First, in both countries the development of temperance movements was in part a response to rapid and destabilizing social change. In Britain this period was at the heart of the industrial revolution and the rapid growth of cities – which were developing appalling slum conditions. One result of this demographic change was a challenge to social order, with a series of events such as the Luddites, the Peterloo Massacre, rural unrest resulting in the burning of hayricks and ultimately the agitation of social reform under the Chartists. Such social unrest was challenging to both social and religious conservatives and dealing with alcohol abuse may have been one way of trying to resolve some of these problems whilst maintaining social order and hierarchies. At the same time other campaigners, seeking an explanation for the extreme deprivation which developed in cities, blamed alcohol dependency – particularly amongst overworked men. Remove the temptation of alcohol, so the argument went, and families will cease to be ground down by poverty. Meanwhile in the United States there was substantial immigration during this period, mainly of Irish Catholics but also (non-English speaking) Germans. These migrants were both poor and of a minority religion, and used to substantial alcohol consumption to alleviate the worst symptoms of their poverty (Fuller, 1996). Their appearance must have threatened both more affluent Protestants concerned about the social stability as well as poorer Protestants who would have felt the economic pressure resulting from such an influx of cheap labour.

Next, it can be suggested that such social dislocation prompted a great deal of personal uncertainty. The social order and one's place in it may have been threatened, which was emotionally challenging for individuals. Temperance, with its focus on self-restraint and personal control may have been one aid in dealing with such psychological challenges. Restraint in the use of alcohol mirrored one's own emotional restraint, and assisted in the sublimation of personal uncertainty in the face of a changing world.

Thirdly, temperance, and even more prohibition, only became viable as the quality of water improved. The campaign for abstinence started in the 1830s but became more substantial and influential as sewage disposal became more efficient and as water was filtered and – increasingly – provided direct to households. This made it safer, and it offered a real alternative to drinks which had some alcohol in them in order to kill bacteria. The pasteurization of milk later in the century added another safe alternative beverage.

Finally, it should be noted that temperance, by definition, is about restraint, not prohibition. Early campaigners sought to limit the consumption of alcohol, not ban it, and like Jefferson and Busby before them one means of doing this was by moving consumers away from the dangers of 'ardent spirits' and onto the refinement and civilizing influence of wine. A proposal at the 1833 National Temperance Convention in Philadelphia to campaign for total abstinence was roundly defeated, in part by those who advocated wine consumption. In part this dispute centred on the fact that wine was considered a 'natural drink', with a spontaneous – and still misunderstood – fermentation, unlike spirits which were industrially produced (Fuller, 1996). As a natural drink it was therefore a gift of God and as such should not be spurned. This view was strengthened by the fact that it was only in the 1820s that scientists confirmed the existence of the substance 'alcohol' in beer, spirits and wine (Phillips, 2000). Until then it had been thought that alcohol itself only existed in distilled spirits, and that fermented drinks had some of the components of alcohol but not the chemical itself.

Nevertheless, the campaign for total abstinence rather than mere restraint continued in both the United States and the United Kingdom. In the former, it had elements both of class and denominational conflict. Temperance (as distinct from abstinence) was the domain of east coast Protestants, especially Episcopalians and Unitarians (Fuller, 1996). These people were suspect to many of the more conservative denominations such as the Baptists and Methodists. The Episcopalians represented an English tradition (and therefore alien), the

Unitarians in rejecting the divinity of Jesus were theologically heretical. Both were part of the upper-class, east coast establishment, and both were perceived to engage in an overly-intellectual faith. If they enjoyed wine (which was after all an expensive drink) then there must be something suspect about wine. A similar division was repeated in the United Kingdom later in the century, with the Liberal party (supported by dissenting Christians and social radicals) tending to oppose alcohol whilst the conservatives (representing the establishment including the established church, and who received substantial financial support from brewers) were against any controls on drinking. Eventually total abstinence became the gospel of temperance crusaders and in 1851 the state of Maine forbade the production or sale of alcoholic drinks within its boundaries (Barr, 1995). The campaign was aided by the conclusion reached by some doctors in 1849 that alcoholism was a medical problem (Phillips, 2000). Meanwhile in the United Kingdom, the term teetotal was coined and teetotal missionaries began to spread out through the country (Barr, 1995). Total abstainers could point to the increasing social dislocation caused by chronic alcohol abuse, particularly amongst the alienated lower classes in the burgeoning cities, although interestingly much of their focus, at least in America, was aimed at the middle class, rather than at serious alcohol abusers in the working class (Fuller, 1996). It was argued that prohibition would benefit a nation economically. It would promote a more stable family life, which would promote the economy, and would allow income to be reinvested profitably – thus spent on essential products which benefited all.

The split between temperance and total abstinence persisted for much of the century, but the latter became more powerful in the aftermath of the American Civil War as successful anti-slavery campaigners turned their attention to another form of 'slavery' – the addiction to alcohol (Fine, 2004). However, one conundrum faced by Christian abstainers was the fact that wine was part of the sacrament, and that according to the Bible Jesus and the early Christians had drunk wine. The first problem was dealt with by replacing wine with grape juice during the sacrament. The second led teetotallers into all kinds of theological contortions trying to prove that Jesus had also only consumed grape juice – a fact which was impossible, given the climate in Palestine and the ignorance of microbiology 2000 years ago which would have ensured the instant fermentation of any grape juice.

Although the teetotallers theoretically sought a complete ban on the sale of alcohol, in both countries in practice they opted for very localized solutions. By 1914, 33 American states were 'dry' (Brook, 1999). 'Local option' was introduced into Scotland in 1913 allowing voters in each local authority area vote every 3 years on whether or not they should be 'dry' – legislation which remained in force until the mid-1970s (Barr, 1995). Similar provisions were used in Wales – and until very recently some Welsh districts were still dry on Sundays. Meanwhile, in Canada and some Scandinavian countries governments established monopoly forms of alcohol distribution in order to guarantee more control on when and how consumers would drink.

A north–south divide

It is relevant to note that, in the European world, there is a split between north and south on the issue of temperance, prohibition and the control of alcohol consumption. Northern Europeans (and their imperial descendants in North America and Australasia) have always been much more likely to advocate control than southern Europeans (and the nations overseas which they once ruled, such as those of South America and Francophone Africa). It is also significant that restrictions tend to get more severe the further north in Europe one goes.

There is no evidence that it was higher alcohol consumption in the northern countries which led to tight controls. However, it has been suggested that consumption is more likely to take the form of binge drinking (Robinson, 1988), often in a quite public fashion, and it may be that this in part had an impact. It is also the case that these countries tend to be Protestant, and the temptation of alcohol abuse was seen to be distracting from the true path of spirituality (and even from the pursuit of worldly economic success which became associated with the Protestant work ethic).

One argument related to this is that over past millennia beer-drinking northern Europeans had less access to higher alcohol drinks such as wine. When they did get high alcohol, in the form of spirits, as something they had long-hoped-for, they had a tendency to drink to excess and thus began to have a genetic disposition to alcoholism (McGovern, 2003). Southern Europeans had more continuous and easy access to wine, and since its discovery have tended to drink more moderately.

The twentieth century and prohibition

The First World War was a critical point in the development of attitudes to wine. Paradoxically, in France, it had the impact of expanding wine consumption. Until 1914 wine had tended to be the drink of the east and south of the country and of Paris. As part of the war effort the producers of Languedoc 'donated' 20 million litres of wine to military hospitals to aid the recovery of the wounded; as a result of this the French government decided to give a daily ration of wine to all serving soldiers – initially 250 mL, and later half a litre (Phillips, 2000). This promoted the spread of daily wine consumption into regions where viticulture was not practised and prompted further expansion of the wine market.

Nevertheless, in most countries wine was seen to be in conflict with the aims of winning the war. In producing countries winemaking diverted energy and resources from munitions and other essential industries. Moreover alcohol abuse was perceived as a threat to efficient and focused working; time spent drinking, or nursing a hangover, was time when armaments were not being made. In the United Kingdom this was the point when rigorous controls on drinking were instituted, particularly the opening hours of public houses, an approach that was adopted in other countries. In Canada, which had had an aggressive campaign for prohibition, all the English-speaking provinces voted to go dry in 1915 and 1916, so that French-speaking (and wine-loving) Quebec was forced to follow suit from 1917 to 1919 as part of a short-term national ban (Phillips, 2000). Nonetheless, it was the aftermath of war, rather than the war itself, which proved the turning point for prohibitionists, when the defeat of the enemy allowed for greater focus on social policy. New Zealand had a referendum on prohibition in 1919 and voted in favour – until the ANZAC soldiers returning from Europe also cast their votes. After years in the trenches they were not going to be denied the pleasures of alcohol, so that prohibition was defeated by a margin of about 1 per cent (George, 1996). Three states in Australia introduced six o'clock closing for bars, which resulted in the form of binge drinking known as the 'six o'clock swill' by workers on their way home each evening (Philips, 1980). Finland also introduced prohibition in 1919 and other Scandinavian countries increased control of the distribution of alcoholic drinks substantially; in 1922 prohibition was defeated in Sweden by 51–49 per cent, but a form of rationing and the abolition of private profit based on alcohol had already been instituted (Nycander, 1998). However, the campaign for total abstinence had its greatest success in the United States.

Prohibition in America

The key to American prohibition lies well before the First World War. Just as was the case in the 1830s and 1840s, the end of the nineteenth and start of the twentieth century had seen a massive influx of migrants – this time from central and southern Europe. These people spoke different languages, ate different food and often worshipped in different ways from the majority population who were northern European Protestants and substantially Anglophone. Some parts of large cities like New York and Chicago became ghetto-like, new and threatening political philosophies such as anarchism and communism became widespread, and economic life whilst vibrant was also uncertain. To a large extent, therefore, prohibition can be seen as the assertion by white Anglo-Saxons of their supremacy in their homeland (Barr, 1995); it was a means of controlling aliens, of putting them in their place, and removing at least one factor which could incite violence and instability. Thus the Volstead Act was passed in 1919, prohibiting the sale of alcohol.

The changes effected by prohibition are well-known. The consumption of alcohol did not stop, it merely went underground, and fortunes were made by smuggling and producing bootleg alcoholic drinks. Demand for the forbidden drug and the profit made from it meant that organized crime became involved, and with that involvement came violence. Government lost revenue on alcohol taxes but, perhaps most important, prohibition did not achieve what its proponents sought; it did not end poverty (Barr, 1995). In the early 1920s, as the American economy recovered from the Great War, it looked as though poverty might be on the wane but from 1929 onwards, with the great depression, it was clear that alcohol consumption was not a substantial cause of impoverishment and social decay, and that macro-economic factors were far more significant. There was little opposition when the Volstead Act was repealed in 1933.

The impact of prohibition on wine in the United States was not as obvious as might be expected. Certainly sales of wine decreased dramatically. Production in 1919 was 208 million litres which had reduced to around 13 million in 1925 (Phillips, 2000). Much more sacramental wine was produced – a product granted an exemption by the Volstead Act (Brook, 1999). Nevertheless, there was actually an increase in the area under vine (Brook, 1999), and probably an increase in wine consumption also (Phillips, 2000). People could make their own wine for home use and grapes, or blocks of dried grapes, were shipped interstate, with the intention that they would be crushed, water and yeast added, and wine made privately; this was how the family of Robert Mondavi first became involved in the wine industry (Robinson, 1999). At the same time financial stress meant that the few wineries which continued paid less attention to the quality of their production equipment (Geraci, 2004).

What prohibition did was not cut wine consumption, but change the kind of wine that people drank. Expensive European wines disappeared – why smuggle them when high-alcohol spirits took up less volume and had far greater demand? Many vineyards were replanted with grapes which were suitable to long-distance transportation to the eastern states (Geraci, 2004). Home made wines tended to be sweet and, as the wine industry resurrected itself after 1933 and the nation rediscovered its taste for legal alcohol, it was these styles which became popular (Brook, 1999). In part this may also have been a result of the burgeoning consumption of sweet cocktails, developed during prohibition to mask the apparent use of alcohol and which began to mould tastes away from drier towards sweeter drinks. Effectively, therefore, prohibition changed the American view of wine. It was no longer primarily an imported, upper-class drink, but rather a cheap, sweet beverage for popular consumption. In 15 years the public taste for, and perception of, wine had been completely reshaped.

The failure of the dream of prohibition in America reduced the influence of temperance movements worldwide. A series of successive social changes accelerated this decline. Integration of migrant populations into host nations – in America before and during the Second World War, in Australia (and to a lesser extent New Zealand) afterwards, reduced social pressure and also meant that wine, which southern European migrants drank, became more socially acceptable. The impact of travel was also significant. Soldiers serving in Europe during the war became accustomed to drinking wine and, from the 1960s onwards, the development of mass tourism to countries like Spain made wine more socially acceptable.

Nevertheless, traces of the temperance movement remain, especially in the United States. This form of 'neo-prohibitionism' sometimes still has a basis in religious belief. Barr (1995) suggested that in the early 1990s 35 per cent of the American population were total abstainers, and half of those cited religious reasons for their behaviour. Allied to these are health campaigners, and those concerned to reduce road accidents (which has only become a serious problem with the growth of car ownership over the last 60 years), as well as those who retain a general fear of the disorder associated with excessive drinking. Health warnings appear on bottles of wine in some countries, and in certain instances, as in the warning about drinking while pregnant on bottles in the United States, providing misinformation by confusing foetal alcohol syndrome (a result of very heavy drinking) with controlled, moderate drinking by expectant mothers (Barr, 1995). A Senate report on underage drinking in 2003 went further, concluding that the problem could only be avoided if there was a total ban on alcohol (Geraci, 2004). The difficulty of selling wine in the United States, with its notorious three tier system whereby in each state there must be separate importers, distributors and retailers of a wine, as well as rules which have prohibited the shipment of wine across state boundaries to mail-order purchasers, is a reflection of a society not at ease with wine. This is shown in the fact that until recently the American controlling body for wine was also responsible for policing firearms and tobacco; one of the controls it imposed was to determine that no wine could be advertised as 'refreshing' (Fine, 2004). According to David Hanson, a sociologist with an interest in the consumption of alcohol, most of these restrictions, many of them varying widely from state-to-state, were imposed essentially to make the consumption of alcohol difficult (Fine, 2004). Even where formal restrictions are not in place, informal controls and the power of lobby groups may impose practical limits, such as influencing the advertising of wine on commercial television stations (Bruce-Gardyne, 2002). Other countries retain similar legal constraints as a hangover from the days of stricter control of drinking. If dining in a restaurant in New South Wales it is illegal to leave one's table with a glass of wine and carry it to diners at another table.

Case study: The development of Finland's retail monopoly

Contemporary economic theory considers monopolies to be regressive, and most modern wine professionals tend to dismiss alcohol distribution monopolies as a device designed to curtail consumption. However, the role of some of these state-owned distributors is changing. Alko, the Finnish drinks monopoly is a good example of this. Its existence is, nevertheless, the legacy of a period of anti-alcohol campaigns and prohibition. Finland's average annual consumption of alcohol is not particularly high (in 2000 it ranked 24th in the world, below most western European countries, Russia and Australia and just a little above the United States). However, this comparative moderation belay an international reputation for binge drinking and in the 1970s its arrest rate for public drunkenness was the highest in Europe (Robinson, 1988). The population's consumption is focused more on spirits than on wine or beer; it has had in the past the highest rates of death from cardiovascular disease in the world (Barr, 1995).

During the First World War Finland banned the distribution of alcoholic drinks except in 'first-class' restaurants, and in 1919 prohibition was introduced (Alko Inc., 2005). Prohibition continued for the same length of time that it existed in the United States, being abolished in 1932, but with the imposition of a state-owned company which was given a monopoly on the production, import and distribution of alcoholic drinks. From 1946 a 'liquor card' was used to record everyone's purchases of alcoholic drinks and a surveillance department set up in the monopoly to monitor individuals' buying behaviour, a practice which continued for 12 years.

Gradually the monopolistic constraints were lifted. From 1959 onwards wine campaigns were launched, initially to shift consumption from spirits towards wine, later to promote the understanding of wine generally. With the accession of Finland to the European Union (EU) in 1994 the monopoly on production, wholesale and importing was lifted, and distributors were allowed to deal direct with on-premises. Yet vestiges of the older social perspectives remain. Alko, the current name for the monopoly, remains under the control of the Ministry of Social Affairs and Health, giving some idea of how public policy makers view it (Alko Inc., 2005).

Despite its heritage the monopoly is generally quite popular in Finland. It stocks a good range of wines (around 1500) with an extra list of 'reserve' wines (which is accessed by less than 1 per cent of all consumers). Any wine can be obtained at any store in the country – and there has been a doubling in the number of stores over the last 30 years. The stores are no longer as atmospherically sterile as they were, and are set out attractively and employ well-trained staff. There is pressure from some distributors to free-up the system, but others actually prefer only having to deal with one retail client.

Even so, there is still a sense in Finland that alcohol is a dangerous drug. In 2004, when the tax on distilled drinks was lowered, consumption of wine immediately dropped and that of spirits rose noticeably; this suggests that amongst some of the population the focus is still primarily on alcohol *per se*, rather than an attachment to wine in particular.

Conclusion

Whilst caution about wine has informed its use almost since it was discovered, the desire for strict controls on it have only appeared comparatively recently – within the last 150 years. Initially they were spurred by religious opposition; later by concern about the social impact of alcohol abuse, although in this case more focused on the consumption of spirits. Only in the last century and a half have health issues *per se* – the concern that the abusers damage themselves physically – come to the fore; it required the precise medical knowledge about the impact of alcohol on the body to focus the concern of campaigners. Even now, however, there remains a tension between those who wish to prevent self-harm, and those who focus on the social and familial implications of abuse.

There has also been – and remains to this day – a sense that wine is different from other alcoholic drinks. It may be in part that its association with religious ritual accounts for this but the fact that wine – more than any other form of alcohol – has been promoted as sophisticated and as a mark of a civilized person gives it this edge, at least in the non-Islamic world. In any event, the experiment of prohibition has been shown to be difficult to make work.

Bibliographical note

For further detail on the impact of wine on classical societies see Unwin (1996). Barr (1995) provides comprehensive coverage of the gin crisis in England in the eighteenth century and of the rise of temperance and Fuller (1996) offers similar coverage of the United States. For the impact of prohibition on American wine Brook's (1999) book on Californian wine is interesting. Although seriously out of date *The Demon Drink* by Jancis Robinson (1988) is useful.

14 The politics of wine

Introduction

The culture of politics

From all that has preceded this chapter it will have become clear that wine's social, economic and symbolic importance gives it a political relevance. However, the way in which governments choose to treat wine, including both its production and consumption, can vary considerably. Two major factors have an impact on the political approach. The first relates to the type of government in a country; democracies, and the rulers who operate in a democracy, will have differing overall aims from those who govern an autocracy. The former may be keen to respond to vocal pressure groups and lobbyists; the latter will be more concerned to suppress civic advocacy, but ensure that the mass of the population are kept quiescent.

The second factor relevant to this chapter is the fact that wine can be perceived to be either a democratic or an elite drink; something for all the masses, or the preserve of a few. It may, in part, be coincidence but it is somewhat paradoxical that – in the western world at least – the most democratic countries have often instigated substantial restrictions on the consumption (and even the production) of wine, whereas in countries subject to more autocratic governments wine has been a more democratic drink and its production and consumption subject to less restriction. On the other hand it has been argued that wine production is something which encourages democracy (Loubere, 1978), although little evidence is adduced in support of this argument, and in many wine-producing countries (Germany until 1945, Portugal under the Salazars and Spain under the monarchy and then Franco) democracy has been hard to find.

The Anglo-Saxon world has always been cautious about wine, having something of a love/hate relationship with it. The 'hate' side of the relationship has allowed alcohol to be used as a political tool. This has been most obvious in campaigns for prohibition but even in countries where prohibition is no longer a serious possibility health concerns can have a major impact. Thus in Australia, which is a major wine-producing nation, domestic tax on wine currently stands at 41 per cent, compared with a normal Goods and Services Tax level of 10 per cent. A major reason given for this is that reducing the tax would send the wrong messages about abuse and the potentially deleterious health impact of wine, even though such a high level of taxation is probably hampering the growth of the domestic market, which in turn could hinder the development of exports. The 'love' side of the relationship has tended to focus on politicians' private enjoyment of alcohol generally, and wine specifically. Winston Churchill was renowned for his fondness of wine, and his enjoyment of Champagne Pol Roger resulted in the house producing a *prestige cuvée* named in his honour. However, this ambiguity has sometimes turned into hypocrisy. Asquith and Lloyd-George both led governments in the UK in the early twentieth century which supported temperance and controls on consumption, but in private they were keen imbibers, resulting in a combination of public abstinence and private indulgence.

Mediterranean countries, on the other hand, have seen wine as a natural part of life and therefore an acceptable element of political culture. Crucially the economic importance of wine in many of these countries has made support for the industry necessary to political success. Thus it is perceived to be reasonable for politicians to take an active interest in the wine industry. When the Médoc classification was established in 1855 four chateaux were designated as first growths. From the mid-1920s Baron Philippe de Rothschild, who was the owner of one of the most prestigious second growths – Chateau Mouton-Rothschild – campaigned vigorously for the promotion of his property to the top level. Having failed to win widespread support for this idea amongst his fellow producers he eventually obtained his goal by having a decree to that effect signed by the French president, Georges Pompidou, in 1973. The idea that the head of state should become formally involved in establishing the status of a specific producer would be alien to the Anglophone world, but in France it was seen to be relevant to national identity. It is also the case that in the Mediterranean world governments will take a more direct role in organizing the wine industry. The establishment of appellation systems is a key example of this.

The political process

It is worth questioning what it is that politicians seek. One can suggest that above all their aim is to maintain power. This may sound like a cynical comment, but is not intended to be. Even the most public-spirited democrats will be convinced that their party's policies are inherently superior to those of their opponents. If that is the case their over-riding goal, quite reasonably and – from their perspective – altruistically, must be their continuance in power, for that is the only way in which they can continue to apply those policies. How do politicians continue in power? In a democracy by winning votes; in a dictatorship or oligarchy by two processes. First, they must maintain stability, which means keeping the populace quiet by giving as many as possible a reasonable way of life. Second, they must ensure security – including both protection against external enemies and the suppression of internal opposition.

All of these political aims require money. Wine is a key means of providing this, either because it is a luxury good in some societies, and therefore will sustain a high level of taxation, or because it is widely consumed and will produce a good return at a low level of taxation. Additionally the widespread consumption of alcohol may help to keep a population quiescent; addiction to alcohol is less likely to produce a social revolutionary, and can dull the impact of alienation in the way that high levels of vodka consumption appeared to in the post-war Soviet Union (although as the history of gin consumption in eighteenth century London shows, in excess this can in turn produce social disruption).

The political process is crucially a process of negotiation. This includes negotiation between people but also negotiation between conflicting demands. The impact of domestic sales tax on wine in Australia has already been noted. Public sentiment (and thus votes) may well make a reduction of the tax popular. Additionally the impact of wine producers within key regional agricultural electorates also makes such a reduction politically attractive. The treasury, on the other hand, which requires the income for other socially useful purposes, needs the tax to remain. Social constraints may have competing demands;

health campaigners and those concerned about the abuse of alcohol (especially in aboriginal communities) see high taxation as a deterrent to the consumption of a debilitating product, whereas social libertarians would argue against a prescriptive or 'nanny' state.

Wine as a political tool

The result of these necessary negotiations is that the relationship of the wine industry to government and the public is one of interaction. They need each other, but there is a tension provided by their competing demands. As a means of teasing out that process of interaction it will be useful to investigate in more detail how politicians use wine.

The aims of the political control of wine

Social control

As has been discussed, wine has an ambivalence. It can cause disorder – and it can also encourage good individual (and thus social) morale. Even without the wholesale social control implied by prohibition, politicians may seek to restrict specific aspects of wine consumption where there is a danger of social order being especially harmed. Thus in 186 BC in Rome it was not wine *per se* which was outlawed, but specifically the Bacchic rituals which were held in secret (and thus away from the gaze of the state apparatus) and which became inflamed by alcohol. The modern equivalent may be the banning of alcohol from football matches, or from town centres. Another area of social control that is worth mentioning is consumer protection; if consumers are cheated or harmed when they buy wine they are likely to react angrily (especially if this realization follows on immediately from their consumption). Consequently ensuring that they are not defrauded may be important for maintaining social order.

However, in contrast to the need to restrict consumption French troops were first awarded their daily wine ration in the First World War in order to improve their morale generally (and perhaps make them less specifically apprehensive about charging towards German machine guns). A side effect of this was that national consumption rose, which in turn benefited producers, especially in the areas where bulk wine was made in the Midi.

Social control is not merely relevant, however, when dealing with the consequences of consumption. Producers in some parts of the world have been vocal dissenters, even radicals, at times. If this seems unusual then it is worth remembering that five people were killed in the south of France in June 1907 during protests against imported and 'manufactured' wines (Campbell, 2004). This is an area where radical vinous protest has continued to the present. During 2001 and 2002 there was a vigorous campaign in the town of Aniane, in Languedoc, against a proposal by the Californian company, Robert Mondavi Wines, to build a new winery. The result of this campaign was to throw out the town's socialist mayor, who was in favour of the scheme, and replace him with a communist (Nossiter, 2004). Subsequently the company voluntarily withdrew their proposal. Later, in 2004, there were protests across southern France owing to declining sales of French wines, including an estimated 8000 marchers in Bordeaux (Anon., 2004b).

Diplomacy and international relations

Historically wine has been used as a tool in shaping the relations between governments – although this in turn may also create conflict between a government and its wine industry (whether distribution or production). A good example of this diplomatic manipulation of wine occurred towards the end of the seventeenth century in England. In 1678 war broke out against France, so that the king, Charles II, banned French wine entirely. In 1685 he died and was replaced by his brother, James II, an overtly Catholic king who sought to promote good relations with the Catholic states in Europe (especially the French king Louis XIV, to whom he was particularly close) and to undermine the Protestant ones. James thus imposed duties on French wine of £14 per tun and on that from Spain of £17 per tun. Conversely on Rhenish wine, which came from the (mainly Protestant) north German states the duty was £19 per tun. In 1688 James was ousted in the 'glorious revolution' and the following year his strictly Protestant successor, William III, changed the duties, so that by 1698 French wine was charged at £47 per tun, Spanish and Portuguese wine £21 per tun and Rhenish at £26 per tun (Briggs, 1994; Unwin, 1996). This combined revenue and diplomacy, for the duties actually rose, but the French were particularly punished for harbouring the exiled James.

There are modern examples of situations where wine is used diplomatically, but these tend to operate specifically to benefit the wine industry itself. The European Union (EU), for instance, operates a tariff-free policy internally, but uses tariff reductions on goods from other countries to gain other benefits for the wine industry. Thus in 1994 the European Union (EU) signed an agreement with Australia for preferential tariff treatment of the latter's wine in exchange for which Australia agreed to phase out the use of generic European wine names such as Burgundy and Champagne as product names. Additionally Australia has agreed formally to delineate regions of origin for its wine (Geographic Indicators), required by the EU which favours the labelling of wine by where it comes from.

Where wine is currently used as a political tool is not so much by governments but by the public at large (albeit on occasions with tacit government support). Thus, in the aftermath of French opposition to the Allied invasion of Iraq in 2003 there were those in the USA who refused to buy French wine in protest against their political stance. Likewise, for much of the 1980s those who sought sanctions against the apartheid regime in South Africa refused to drink South African wine.

Promoting the economy

The fiscal benefits arising from the wine industry have already been mentioned; it is worth noting that excise duty on wine in the UK was worth £1 978 000 000 in 2003 although now that the EU allows the free passage of goods substantial volumes of wine are bought in continental Europe and transported back across the channel without paying duty. The situation in the USA is different, where excise duties are levied by each state and consequently vary. This form of control is indirect – and often compromised as there is potentially a conflict between a government's desire for greater revenue and the social goals. In practice, however, in wine producing countries fiscal returns are often secondary to other benefits to the economy.

Where wine production is a major form of enterprise governmental support for it is often substantial. This may take two forms: the negative protection of a nation or region from external competition and the positive promotion of its wines both domestically and overseas. Thus the earliest attempts at demarcation, especially Chianti in 1716 and the Douro valley in Portugal in 1756 were inspired in part because wine producers from elsewhere (often within the country itself) were passing their products off as coming from those places.

The establishment of co-operatives was clearly a protectionist programme aimed at promoting regional economy, preserving jobs and thus minimizing social unrest. In the Dão region of Portugal 10 co-operatives were established and they were the only organizations allowed to buy grapes, effectively excluding any outsiders and precluding local grapegrowers from becoming dependent on merchants. This may have protected the livelihoods of local smallholders but it also reduced competition, inhibiting technological development, and is generally thought to have had a deleterious effect on the overall quality of wine from what should be a high-quality region (Robinson, 1999).

The vinous oligarchy in the Dão region was ended when Portugal joined the EU, because such a quasi-monopoly breached its competition regulations. However, paradoxically the EU itself promotes non-competitive activities. Whilst it tries rigorously to promote internal freedom of trade with programmes such as the Common Agricultural Policy the EU is non-competitive vis-à-vis the rest of the world.

As another positive exercise, wine tourism initiatives may be taken to support the economy of a region, including help for both those people involved in wine production and others involved in ancillary industries. Thus 11 wine routes have been created in Portugal around its major wine regions like the Douro, Bairrada and Alentejo since 1993. In part this has been stimulated because Portugal has participated with another eight European wine regions in the EU's Dyonísios Inter-regional Cooperation Programme (intended to create economic and cultural exchange across a number of wine regions in the EU, via knowledge transference in the areas of commerce, training and tourism). Additionally a national government regulation (Despacho Normativo no. 669/94) which offers state financial assistance for those in wine tourism has prompted a number of wine regions in Portugal to create wine routes (Correia et al., 2004). Governments in other countries, such as Canada and Australia, have also actively promoted wine tourism by supporting wine industry initiatives and linking them into national tourism promotion.

Trade promotions are a common means of supporting a state's wine industry. Whilst direct export subsidies fly in the face of the current trend towards free trade and reducing the barriers to competition other forms of aid are widely adopted. The Australian government, for instance, supports the Australian Wine Export Council which provides assistance for producers exporting to other countries, and runs promotional offices in New York, London, Tokyo, Frankfurt, The Hague and Toronto. Additionally Austrade, the national body which supports Australian exports can arrange local briefings and contacts for those seeking to export.

Oiling the wheels

Wine may be important in facilitating the political process. The French are unable to have a formal state reception without wine being present – a factor which makes hosting representatives from Muslim nations difficult on occasions (Phillips, 2000). There is a popular perception that all politicians are drunks. Whilst some certainly enjoy their wine – Churchill and Bismarck spring to mind – others, such as George W. Bush, are notoriously abstainers.

One interesting issue, however, is the number of politicians who see wine – or more specifically a vineyard – as a place of retreat. The only surviving written work of the austere Roman senator Cato (renowned for pursuing 'virtue' in the Roman republic concurrently with the aggressive destruction of Carthage) is not about politics or diplomacy but *De Agri Cultura* – 'On the Cultivation of the Land'. This book contains much about the growing of grapes and production of wine, based on his experiences on the family farm. Thomas Jefferson, the third President of the United States, loved wine, and attempted in vain to raise *Vitis vinifera* vines on his property at Monticello. He was defeated, without realizing the cause, by the depredations of phylloxera. Two Italian aristocrats at the forefront of the unification of their country in the mid-nineteenth century were also committed wine producers. Count Camillo di Cavour, the first Prime Minister of the united country had previously been a leading experimental viticulturist in the Barolo region of Piemonte – even employing a French consultant oenologist to help him and other local producers (Garner & Merritt, 1990). One of his political successors, Baron Bettino Ricasoli, is today remembered more because he reformed the production of Chianti, attempting to codify its varietal make-up and production methods (Belfrage, 2001).

It is interesting to speculate on why producing wine may be attractive to politicians. There is no doubt that it was a much safer pursuit than the maelstrom of politics in republican Rome or the Italy of the Risorgimento. It may also be that producing wine, whilst physically active, is more emotionally relaxing than political involvement. There may be other, more unconscious reasons. Possibly there is a sense of peace in nature, where there is a regular flux of natural processes, which contrasts attractively with the uncertainty and unreliability of human actors. Additionally it could be suggested that a failure to change the social and political order, with perhaps a resulting sense of personal failure or inadequacy, makes the natural order – with the predictability of seasonal change and a clear structure to the progress of life – seem attractive. The fact that politicians have been amongst the leaders of those trying to 'reform' wine production suggests that the need to control is significant, and vines may be less prone to resist change than the public.

Methods of political control

As well as examining the reasons for political involvement in the wine industry it is also worthwhile considering how such control is established. The use of revenue raising measures has already been discussed, but they can be justified not merely to raise money, but also for other social ends. Most obviously if higher taxes reduce wine consumption that may be interpreted as a positive outcome for improving health and reducing abuse.

Control of production

The willingness of governments to control the production of wine stems from two goals. The first is that it assists in raising revenue (although this is more generally an issue related to consumption). The second is that governmental support and regulation can act as a means of stimulating national economic growth, and especially development in agricultural regions which may have been suffering with the increasing focus on urban areas over the last century. Government activity in this area can be seen in three ways. The first involves guaranteeing the right of producers in a specific area to legal protection of the name of their product, to preserve its value to them. The second relates to the manipulation of overall production, especially moderate fluctuations in supply. Thirdly, there is activity undertaken by governments to preserve the quality of wine in order to protect the overall return to producers.

The role of governments in trying to protect existing viticulturists has a long history. Vineyard registration occurred in Spain in the sixteenth century, and the later development of demarcation in Tokaji, Chianti and the Douro has already been noted. The more general development of appellation systems explicitly grew out of a desire to protect the value of wine produced in a demarcated region. One of the precursors to the appellation controlée (AC) system in France was the delineation of the Champagne region. By 1900 Champagne was an expensive wine, making a substantial income for those who produced it and a reasonable income for those who grew the Champagne grapes (the two were not necessarily the same). As previously observed, dispute centred on whether or not the large area of the Aube, in the far south-east of Champagne, could be included in the demarcated area. Guy (2003, p. 162) comments that:

> the notion of fraudulent production therefore meant that there were those who threatened the community and, by extension, the nation. The cause in 1911 was thus a patriotic one.

In this case protecting a region of origin – at least when it was as internationally prestigious as Champagne – was about protecting the French people, even if the actual enemy at the time was other French people.

Occasionally governments act to manipulate the production of a country. In around 90 AD the emperor Domitian banned the planting of new wines in Italy and legislated for the destruction of some vineyards in the rest of the empire in response to a glut of wine and a scarcity of grain (Unwin, 1996). More recent times have seen vine-pull schemes in various parts of the world. In the early 1980s there was an overabundance of shiraz in Australia, and formal programmes to uproot it were instituted (Faith, 2002), resulting in the loss of many old-vine vineyards. Paradoxically, with changing trends in consumption shiraz is now the most widely planted grape variety in Australia, and its most successful export (Australian Wine Online, 2004).

The third way in which governments try to influence production is in the control of quality. In 1395 the Duke of Burgundy (at that time a powerful independent state), Philip the Bold, banned the planting of gamay, so that *vignerons* would focus on pinot noir. The argument was that pinot produced better wine – a view which would be generally accepted today, as gamay is unknown on the prestigious slopes of the Cote d'Or. The problem for the peasant grapegrowers was that gamay gave much greater yields and more wine meant a greater return; any 'elitist' view about quality was secondary to the need to eke out a living. Today European legal systems still permit or ban specific grape varieties in various regions, but regulations to enhance quality are increasingly focused on production techniques. Most EU countries have restrictions about the maximum yield that can be used to make 'quality wine produced from a specified region' (QWPSR), and most countries worldwide have controls on – say – the maximum amount of sulphur dioxide that can be added as wine is being made; whilst in part this is for health reasons it is also to avoid the wine becoming unpleasant. In this way guaranteeing the appeal of a specific wine can help to maintain the reputation of the wines of a country in their entirety.

The political desire to promote wine quality may be laudable, but politicians do not always get it right. The dispute about the delineation of the Champagne region shows how balancing conflicting interests may be hard. Other, more blatant forms of partisanship exist. The DOCG system in Italy was established to mark out the highest quality wines. The first awards of DOCG status, to regions like Barolo and Brunello di Montalcino, were non-contentious. However in 1986 DOCG status was given to Albana di Romagna, a wine from a barely known region on the country's east coast with no international reputation – and the maximum yield for the supposed 'quality' wine made in the area was set at a ludicrously high level of 100 hL/ha (Robinson, 1999). That this happened was almost certainly the result of a political deal in national Italian politics to win support from local politicians, but its effect was to demean the whole system and substantially reduce its reputation internationally.

Ideology, as well as processes, may also inhibit production, as the history of Tokaji under the Hungarian communist regime after 1945 suggests. István Szepsy, one of the pioneers of the recent revival in fortune of wines from the region has commented that the government 'was worse than phylloxera or the Turks. It nearly destroyed the basis for producing great wine.'

Hungarian wine: Communism and the control of production

The problems which can occur when governments become too closely involved in the organization of the wine industry are neatly encapsulated by the experience of the eastern European bloc under communism. Political processes varied from country to country, but – with its long reputation for producing sweet wine of great quality – Hungary provides a useful example.

From 1947 the communist regime in Hungary took control of almost all wine processing – although grapegrowing by individuals was allowed on up to half a hectare of land. A single state co-operative, Borkombinat (Friedrich, 2000), and state-owned farms dominated, many of them using Hungarovin, the national wine trust, to market their wines. There was an expectation that production would be achieved by orders coming down from above which is dangerous when snap decisions have to be made during vintage. Investment was haphazard. It has been noted that in neighbouring Czechoslovakia the state wine producer purchased a number of filters from the west. Every wine was filtered to excess – but there was a lack of appropriate barrels for storage and chilling equipment for fermentation (Williams, 1995), and similar situations occurred in Hungary. In Tokaji, in order to capitalize on the wine's reputation, yields were pushed to extremes; the resulting wine would be sugared or even fortified, and aged for up to 10 years in barrel and thus oxidized, to cover the lack of flavour from the over-cropped grapes (Brook, 2000c; Friedrich, 2000). Even before the fall of communism, however, the pressure to be more market focused was growing, with exports to western Europe doubling in the decade following the mid-1970s (Unwin, 1996), and growing competition being encouraged.

With the fall of communism a process of rapid privatization was instigated (Moulton & Botos, 1994). Initially this was popular and for grapegrowing was successful, with 60 per cent of the crop produced privately by 1994; it was less successful with winemaking, with around two-thirds of production facilities still managed by the state at the same time (Moulton & Botos, 1994). Of more significance, however, was the fact that by this stage most producers were effectively insolvent. They had lost major markets in East Germany and the former Soviet Union and failed to sell to the west.

Equally important was the failure of many involved in wine production to adapt to the demands of a competitive environment. Workers, who had had no economic stake in the enterprise and were paid whatever happened, were unwilling to give the time needed to produce better wine. Flying winemakers, brought in from the west to oversee vintage were astonished when staff left at five o'clock on a Friday and refused to return until Monday morning – even though grapes were in urgent need of picking and fermenting must required monitoring.

However, Tokaji has weathered the worst of the transition, in part because its reputation has attracted substantial foreign investment – from Spain, France and England – and in part because dynamic local wine producers like István Szepsy were determined to restore the region to its former glory by producing high-quality wines (Brook, 2000a; Friedrich, 2000). Even so, problems remain. There has been a major dispute about the style that the wine should take, a result of the freedom from the constraints imposed by the communist regime. Some consider that a moderately oxidative wine is historically typical; others vehemently oppose this and pursue pure botrytized fruit character (Friedrich, 2000). Perhaps a more worrying hangover from the days of central control is the requirement for all wines which are labelled as Tokaji to be assessed by a tasting panel – which mainly comprised people left over from the days of communist rule, with palates attuned to the oxidized, fruitless styles of former days. The panel has regularly refused to allow the appellation for most of the new producers (Friedrich, 2000). Finally the regional market for grapes is skewed by the continued existence of a state winery which is obliged to purchase grapes from local growers irrespective of their quality; this gives viticulturists little incentive to improve vineyard practice (Gilby, 2005). This continued state involvement may be because Tokaji is considered to be so significant to the heritage of Hungary (Moulton & Botos, 1994). Nevertheless, despite this the quality and reputation of wines from the region are rising (Brook, 2000c; Smy, 2000). The accession of Hungary to the EU in May 2004 is expected to consolidate the success of sales of Tokaji in the west.

In other parts of the country the improvements have been less marked and harder to achieve. It was suggested in the mid-1990s that the privatization of wine production had been badly handled because it was compromised by aims of political popularity which impeded economic reform (Moulton & Botos, 1994). Total exports declined in value from over 74 million euros in 1999 to barely 57 million euros in 2004 (Gilby, 2005). This can be seen in the performance of another well-known wine region, Eger, which produces Bull's Blood. At the end of communist control its reputation as a fiery, full-bodied red wine had been lost; it tended to be meagre and fruitless (Smy, 2000). Threatened by increased competition from EU membership the region failed to focus on either export or domestic markets and few growers have done much to improve the grapes planted in the vineyard by using more full-bodied varieties (Smy, 2000). There is a need for a new focus on quality but the lack of external investment, lack of any cohesion in its export promotion, failure to improve sales in a now-competitive world and difficulties in adjusting to the marketing needs of a capitalist economy make this hard (Gilby, 2005).

Control of distribution

If governments are to control wine consumption – to ensure social order and to guarantee a flow of revenue – then they need to control how it is distributed. Violence and disputes associated with the consumption of alcohol have been going on almost since the first juice was fermented and smuggling to avoid paying duty is still a major concern of governments.

There are a number of ways in which distribution can be controlled. The licensing of outlets which can sell wine is standard, often with restrictions about how the business can operate – for instance, requiring detailed returns of all wine sold to revenue offices, or prohibiting sales to consumers who are already intoxicated. In countries with a particular history of active temperance movements greater controls may exist. Thus in Ontario, Canada, all wine purchasing is concentrated in the hands of the Liquor Control Board of Ontario, which also manages most of the retail outlets. Sweden and Norway operate an even tighter system, with both purchasing and retail operated by a national monopoly. In an attempt to deter consumers the retail stores were historically made as unwelcoming as possible. Wines are not on display, and are selected from a catalogue (reducing the cues available to customers to make their choice). Shop assistants are dressed in white coats, giving the impression that a purchaser is attending a pharmacist to feed a drug habit, and wines are never available for sampling.

The most comprehensive and confusing system is that operated in the USA (Davis, 2001). As the country is a federal system licensing is determined by the states, and in many cases neo-prohibitionism results in strict controls on distribution. Some states, such as California, have a comparatively free approach to selling wine. Others are much tougher. Many allow a 'local option', so that individual counties may choose to be dry, and have no outlets selling alcohol. Most difficult is the requirement that wine arriving in any state must go through three separate levels of distribution: an importer, a wholesaler and a retailer (Davis, 2001). An overseas producer thus has to appoint an importer in every state in which they wish to sell their product, and then a wholesaler within that state. The result of this is that many companies only concentrate on the few states with a substantial population, in order to focus their export activity. These controls can also apply to domestic American producers. In the wake of fears about children purchasing wine online in the late 1990s a number of states made it illegal to transport wine across their state line unless an 'importer' was involved – effectively wiping out the advantages of mail order sales by producers on the west coast. Other countries would consider this a restraint of trade; in the USA it is integral to the idea of the states' rights.

Political conflict

Wine is an agricultural product with its roots in an age when almost all the population were rural. It may also be a democratic or an elite drink. These factors, grafted onto the changing social and economic environment wrought by the industrial revolution, mean that it can be a stimulus for political conflict. Once it became produced and distributed on a large scale or when, as with Bordeaux or Champagne, it acquired great value, then those with capital sought to control it, and those who produced it determined to protect their livelihood (Guy, 2003; Unwin, 1996). This became most obvious in disputes between grapegrowers – until recently generally peasants – and wine merchants. Brennan (1997) notes how in north-west France the medieval idea of a 'broker', effectively an intermediary who brought together a *vigneron* with wine to sell and an urban merchant, was gradually supplanted in the eighteenth century by the négociant. The négociant would use his economic power to buy, blend and mature large quantities of wine which would then be sold on, at some profit, to retailers or other distributors in major towns. This shifted the balance of power away from the grower towards the merchant. Tension between grower and merchant exists today; Champagne had severe problems over the price charged for grapes sold to the Champagne houses in the early 1990s, as growers sought to increase their own income on the back of rising prices for the finished product (McNie, 1999). Such conflicts may reappear now that EU regulations are prohibiting the CIVC – the Champagne regulatory body – from fixing grape prices in the region; the aim is to ensure a free market for the sale of grapes. Similar conflicts arise regularly in the new producing countries, although disputes there are no longer between growers and merchants, but between growers and large wine companies. In 2001 for instance, the De Bortoli company, based in Griffith, Australia, was involved in major arguments with a number of their growers when they claimed that as a result of a grape surplus prices paid at the winery would have to fall (Ramsay, 2002).

This shift of power from grower to merchant was mirrored – at least in places – in a town versus country conflict. Such a conflict was most obvious around Bordeaux, where economic power was concentrated on the great wine merchants of the Quai des Chartrons. They were responsible for maturing the wine and for selling it on to Paris or the wealthy overseas markets of northern Europe and later the United States. The volumes of wine shipped meant that only companies with access to substantial capital could consolidate and age the product. Until the end of the nineteenth century the Bordeaux merchants, generally family companies, were even more powerful than the great *premier crus* of the Médoc, so that power in the region resided firmly in the city rather than the country. In practice this meant that the merchants indulged in vertical integration, buying some of the chateaux for themselves (Faith, 1999). Only in the last half-century has this balance of power shifted again and even now only the top chateaux of Bordeaux have substantial economic influence. In part this is due to the fact that many of the wine producers have been purchased by large French and international companies – including some, like the insurance giant AXA, who are not based in the drinks industry. These owners have even more economic clout than the merchants had. Additionally the rise of overseas markets, focused on buying wine *en primeur*, has increased the ability of the top chateaux to shape the direction of the market to their own needs.

With the industrialization of modern economies conflicts in the wine industry have paralleled those in society at large; that is, they have become focused more on labour and owner relations. This process accelerated following the devastation wrought by phylloxera and the general agricultural depression at the end of the nineteenth century. It was quite clear that many peasant farmers who lost vineyards during the phylloxera crisis were unable or unwilling to replant their vineyards; surplus viticultural land was thus snapped up at bargain prices by larger organizations, and often the former peasants returned as wage labourers to the same land (Campbell, 2004). This split between labour and capital continues today and is often at its most extreme where there is a racial element. As well as South Africa (see below) the situation in California is instructive. Much of the viticultural labour force there is Hispanic, often of Mexican origin. Low levels of unionization, active attempts by wineries to avoid union contracts, poor worker language skills and the fact that some of them may be illegal immigrants means that pay and conditions are often poor. Some employees may only receive $15 000 per annum (Walker, 2004), a meagre recompense when according to the US Department of Labor average wages in the state were over $41 400 in 2002. This brings the paradox that one of the most obvious luxury products in the world – California is, after all, the home of the cult wine – is produced by labourers who are amongst the most poorly paid in the region.

Finally it is worth considering that general political unrest may have an impact on the wine industry. Following the revolution of 1830 in France (a comparatively tame and bloodless event) wine prices both domestically and overseas were reduced, as demand dropped in response to political uncertainty (Loubere, 1978). More recently the political tension in South Africa both during and after the apartheid regime kept prices of that country's wines artificially low.

South Africa: A case study

South Africa forms a perfect example for the interaction of wine and politics as most of the history of its wine industry is bound up in political decisions, usually made about far more significant and wide-ranging issues than wine, and often determined many thousands of kilometres away from the country itself.

The start of the South African wine industry

The first white settlement in South Africa was made by the Dutch in 1652 at Cape Town. The township was established as a supply station for ships of the Dutch East India Company sailing on to trade in Ceylon (Sri Lanka) and the East Indies. The settlement however was unimportant, and never had the same significance to the Netherlands as their Asian bases. The first vines were planted a year after settlement but the Netherlands has never been a wine-producing nation and it is likely that the wine produced was mediocre at best. One of the first real boosts to the Cape wine industry came from a decision taken in France. In 1685 Louis XIV revoked the Edict of Nantes – the law which had guaranteed the Huguenots (French Protestants) the right to practise their religion in peace. There was an exodus of Protestants from the country escaping anticipated persecution, and some of these arrived in Cape Town. Given the French oenological experience they had greater expertise in wine-making than the Dutch and gave a substantial impetus to the nascent industry. Subsequently wars between Britain and France throughout much of the eighteenth century made Britain a key market for Cape wines, such that British preferences – for fortified and sweet wines – became the dominant style produced. By the 1780s Constantia had become one of the two most prestigious wines in the world (Robinson, 1999).

Politics intruded again when the British occupied the Cape Colony in 1806, later making their control permanent. Britain's prize imperial possession at this stage was India and whilst Cape Town had no intrinsic value for an imperial power it was a key supply station and controlled easy access for ships rounding the Cape of Good Hope; it was thus far too important to be left to the control of a comparatively minor power like the Netherlands. Whilst the Dutch settlers may have resented such an arbitrary seizure of sovereignty, their wine industry benefited substantially from access to the large, rich British market, especially after tariffs were waived in 1813. By the start of the next decade 1 bottle in 10 consumed in Britain came from the Cape (Welsh, 1998), a figure which was boosted after the British government imposed heavy tariffs on French wines in 1825.

The good times did not last for the Boers. In 1834, to their annoyance, the British emancipated all slaves. As a result of this and other grievances many Boers undertook treks, away from the Cape Colony, to found their own states to the north-east. Then, in 1861 Britain signed a commercial treaty with France which almost halved the duty on French wine (Briggs, 1994). The impact of this – which resulted in an influx of cheap French wine from across the Channel – was to ruin the colony's key market almost instantly. To the general decline in agricultural markets over the next 40 years (aggravated in the case of wine by phylloxera) was added the crippling effect of the Anglo-Boer War from 1899–1902, caused by the British determination to take control of the independent states in the north-east. Whilst political decisions had both started and strengthened the wine industry they were also responsible for its long decline.

The South African wine industry in the Afrikaner era

Although the British won the Boer War, a decade later the independent Union of South Africa was established, effectively controlled by the Afrikaners. The new nation began to provide the political support for agriculture generally and the wine industry in particular which had been lost in the previous half-century. The Afrikaners were the agricultural and rural powerhouse of the new nation (the term Boer translates as farmer), and consequently their government felt its priority was to promote wine farmers at the expense of urban merchants (in 1946 Afrikaners controlled 80 per cent of agricultural production but only 6 per cent of manufacturing wealth (Welsh, 1998)). Even before the South African state was established, in 1906, the first co-operative was formed using $125 000 of government support, with the aim of giving farmers greater economic independence. The First World War however again set back the wine industry, so that by 1918 millions of litres of South African wine remained unsold.

The political response was the formation of the KWV. This body was given substantial powers within the industry. It could set minimum prices for grapes (thus preserving wine farmers' income) and at the same time it set grape production quotas to avoid gluts. Whilst it did not sell wine within the country it had a monopoly on exports which, combined with the power to issue or withhold permits to make wine, thus made it exceedingly powerful. Crucially it shifted the balance of power away from merchants and to the farming sector, albeit at the price of granting the co-operative dictatorial powers to control grapegrowing; it acted in a very corporatist way, and against the operation of a free market (Robinson, 1999).

The apartheid era formally began in 1948, although its seeds had been sown before that. For the wine industry the system's political outlook, dominated by a 'laager' mentality (the idea of circling the wagons against all outsiders and becoming both externally aggressive and inward looking) produced insularity. Domination by the KWV continued, as did overproduction, but there was a form of stability in the industry, with the focus on maintaining the production of fortified wines which had been so popular with the British, plus substantial brandy production. From the 1960s onwards there was a growing overseas trade boycott, which merely accentuated the government's own sense that the whole world was against it. As a result it was not just sales that suffered, but production. The industry became cut off from the growing scientific research and technological development which began first in Europe and then grew rapidly in the USA and Australia. For example, many vines were subject to leafroll virus, a disease which severely hampered ripening. The resulting wines taste green, with hard tannin, but the country's political isolation limited the type of critical analysis of the wines which would have exposed those faults, and restricted its access to the means of remedying the problem.

At the same time access to varieties and new clones from overseas was hampered by a stringent quarantine policy (reflective of the country's sense of political and social ostracism). As a result virus-free chardonnay was not available in South Africa until the mid-1980s (Robinson, 1999), long after it had become a boom variety throughout the rest of the world.

An unremarked but longer-term problem was also developing in the apartheid years. The disenfranchized black majority viewed the Afrikaners with especial hatred, seeing them as the particular architects of repression. Wine was produced by farmers, the farmers were Afrikaner, and thus wine was the drink of the oppressor. The black community were beer drinkers (and beer – especially native beer – was after all much cheaper). This antagonism was especially reinforced within the wine industry by particular forms of subjugation, most notoriously the 'dop' system. This was the payment of black workers in whole or in part with wine rather than wages. For an impoverished population this had two effects. It encouraged alcohol dependency which in turn promoted social and economic dependency, and it also hindered workers from building up any capital of their own, or even from supporting a family away from the farm on which they lived and worked. More generally, agricultural workers tended to be offered tied housing with their employment. This meant that they could be paid less, but when their employment ceased they had no home (Ewert & Hamman, 1999). At the same time it was often a condition of a job that a worker's wife would live with him, and be available to work on the farm, particularly at busy times, such as the vintage. There may, however, have been no pay for this (Ewert & Hamman, 1999). It would be wrong to suggest that all – even most – wine farmers were cruel or hard employers. Many could be very generous and supportive – nevertheless, their paternalism operated within an unjust system. As a result it was only to be expected that the black majority would view wine with suspicion. What this means in practice is that in a country of almost 43 000 000, 75 per cent of the population start from an antagonistic perspective to wine – hardly a good proposition for the development of a domestic industry. Additionally, after the alienation of the apartheid years many people, both black and coloured, have alcohol dependency problems – an issue which the industry cannot ignore.

The post-apartheid settlement

In the wake of majority rule the wine industry consequently faces two key economic and political challenges. How is a measure of justice to be brought to the industry, and how are they to break down black prejudice against their product? The former issue takes on an increased measure of urgency due to the requirements of Black Economic Empowerment (BEE). This is a government initiative which aims to start redressing the economic imbalance within the country. As a first stage in the process BEE has set a target of 25 per cent black economic involvement in the industry. As the lack of appropriate land means it is hard to create new wine farms from scratch and give them to the black and coloured populations this target generally has to be met within existing businesses – which naturally unsettles some of the white community. However, BEE does not just have to include ownership, but could also cover training schemes, procurement policies, housing and welfare provision, and a range of other possibilities. All wine farms are going to be 'scored' on their application of BEE, and ultimately those which fail may have their production licence withdrawn. Ultimately, however, the aim of the South African Wine Industry Trust, a government backed project, is that by 2010 a quarter of the industry should be in black ownership. It is worth noting that moves to redress inequitable worker rights began, during the 1990s, at precisely the time when workers' rights were increasingly being constrained throughout the rest of the world. Paradoxically it does appear as though progress has been made in South Africa against this trend (Ewert & Hamman, 1999).

BEE has had some dramatic effects. A few producers, including the long-established and highly reputed Boschendal wine farm, have transferred part or total ownership to the majority population, although in some cases the way this has happened is controversial and not necessarily considered to be as empowering as it could be. Some new black-run wine farms have been set up and the largest producer, the now-privatized KWV, has recently sold 25 per cent of its equity at a discounted price to an investment trust which is run by members of the black community. Additionally some new, black-run enterprises have been established. These have not been without controversy (Williams, 2004b), with complaints that they tend to benefit black elites or are merely another form of paternalism rather than true empowerment, but some initiatives have been successful. The Thandi project, in Elgin – a new cool-climate region – is one of these. Originally it was a settlement for black forestry workers, but a local wine producer, Dr Paul Cluver instigated a wine business with the community, and provided some of the land for vineyards. The project is now jointly owned by the community and the government, and has also involved Vinfruco, one of the country's largest wine producers, particularly to provide support and training for the staff. Thandi has its own vineyards but also buys in grapes, with a focus on sourcing from other communities which formerly were deprived under the apartheid regime. The first winemaker is a former employee of Paul Cluver who has undertaken formal oenological training and is supported by Paul Cluver Estate and Vinfruco, where some of the wines have been made. The community, however, does not only focus on wine and there is a craft shop and a café as part of a wine tourism development. There are other forms of employment on the site, including a community garden which provides fruit for sale at a food store. There is also a crèche for workers.

A parallel development to BEE is the Wine Industry Ethical Trade Association (WIETA). This has been established by a number of producers (including most of the key exporters), and a number of organizations involved in distribution. Interestingly, however, it also includes Trade Unions, some Non-Governmental Organizations involved in alcohol abuse and BEE, and two British retailers (who provide some of the money for the association). By mid-2005 it had 83 members, of which 52 were producers (Simon, 2005). Its goal is to promote ethical processes within the industry. It educates companies and audits and accredits wine organizations for ethical practices. These practices cover issues such as child labour, health and safety and housing as well as discrimination issues. Social auditors have been appointed and trained who are able to scrutinize compliance and those members who do not meet appropriate standards will be assisted to prepare a programme remedying weaknesses. However, WIETA is a membership organization, so its influence currently is only over those who choose to support its aims. It has no coercive powers over non-members and its influence, consequently, relies on the willingness of outsiders to give preference to WIETA members when buying wine. It has also been suggested that ultimately membership will be determined by whether or not a producer can see an immediate financial benefit, rather than purely ethical concerns (Simon, 2005).

The entire history of South Africa's wine industry has stemmed from political decisions. It originated from the politics of exploration, and expanded as a result of wars in Europe. It grew further because of imperial extension, and contracted when the Empire decided to change its relations with Europe, and to fight wars of conquest. Domestic politics shaped its structure and constrained its later growth, and now the new political masters are requiring it to reshape itself. Wine and politics go hand in hand.

Bibliographical note

There is no single or obvious body of research on the relationship of wine and politics. Most of our understanding has to be gleaned from other sources, particularly from historical works (see Chapter 2) or current journalism. For the reader who wishes to follow a number of the ideas in this chapter in a comparatively recent context then, as so often with the production of wine, the Champagne region is especially informative. Two works trace the changes there, the first by Brennan (1997) on the period from the late seventeenth to the late eighteenth century and then Guy (2003), who takes the story up to the start of the twentieth century. For those interested in the impact of war on politics then the Kladstrups' (2001) book on the topic is an interesting introduction.

Part Five: Conclusion

Conclusion

The world of wine is a vast one, encompassing a complete range of people. The aficionado with a cellar of 10 000 bottles worth over a million dollars in Dallas, the teacher in Trier who manages the family's 1 ha vineyard in the Mosel valley at weekends, the Italian aristocrat whose ancestors have been making wine for many centuries and the Portuguese peasant who has been drinking cheap red wine, made by his neighbour, daily for all his life. Critically, it will have become clear through the course of this book that what each person drinks is not merely the result of their choice, but the result of political, economic and social influences and constraints. It may seem like a platitude but the wines that each of us enjoy depend not just on our taste preferences but also on what is technologically acceptable, what is fashionable, what reputation and scarcity allow us to afford and what is politically appropriate. All of these factors in turn are subject to the ebb and flow of historical circumstance.

However, the engagement that each of us have with the product, how winemakers view what they produce and what consumers drink, may have many differences as well as some similarities. Some of the differences in how wine is viewed relate specifically to the approach of those who make it, others are more about the symbolic meaning of wine. It is possible to highlight the differences further, often by focusing on the ambiguities and paradoxes thrown up by wine. As well as examining these paradoxes three other key features of how wine is used will be considered: two are the quasi-religious way in which it may be viewed and its use as a metaphor. Each of these perspectives in turn has an impact on the third feature of wine – the overall social context within which it operates.

A paradoxical drink

The contradictory nature of wine has been noted by at least one outside observer. Osborne (2004, p. 19) comments that wine is 'a bit Jekyll and Hyde'. It can be meditative and meaningful or it can be merely commercial, insignificant and 'soulless'. This sense of ambivalence can be extended into a number of dimensions in which wine operates.

The first element of ambiguity is to note the contrast, made throughout this book, between democratic and elite wines. Democratic wines tend to be consumed both widely and intensively within a community or nation; that is, many people drink wine and they drink very often – perhaps daily. When used in this way wine has less significance as a marker of status (although it is possible to surmise that it may have more relevance symbolically for issues of religion and fertility). Democratic wine may well be seen more as a foodstuff than as an alcoholic drink and it is possible that historically it provided a useful calorie supplement in some places. Elite wines are more common in societies where consumption is less widespread and possibly less intensive. This tends to be in countries, or parts of countries, in which wine grapes cannot easily be grown. In this situation wine drinking is used more as a means of personal and social differentiation and greater emphasis is placed on its aesthetic potential than its everyday function as a beverage.

It may be that this division between democratic and elite is breaking down in the twenty-first century. People in the traditional areas of mass consumption are drinking less but, so it is argued, better quality wine. Areas where wine was formerly an elite product and often associated with higher social class are now consuming more and, rather than providing social cachet, the drink is more about offering lifestyle enhancement. It is of interest to note that in the USA over the last 30 years the lexicon of wine tasting has moved from terms often based on class (such as 'breeding' or 'distinction') to a more neutral, scientific language or to words which have a pastoral aspect, based on fruit or vegetables (Shesgreen, 2003) – or even terms like undergrowth and farmyard. Such a shift may represent a greater emphasis on the significance of rural idyll, or food for the modern lifestyle and less a reflection of status. Nevertheless, what you drink and what you know about wine remains a key means of establishing distinction. At the same time, whilst the democratic and elite distinction may be breaking down and more consumers drinking 'good' wine, they may not necessarily adopt all the attitudes of their predecessors. The complexity of the wine market and the danger of making the wrong choice about wine is tending to increase the number and size of the large-volume branded wines; these may still offer many of the benefits of elite wine drinking (organoleptic enjoyment and aesthetic appeal) but without the plethora of places and producers which had to be remembered by the upper-class drinkers of former ages.

A different dichotomous approach to wine is the conflict between produce and product. The former concept has dominated attitudes to wine for much of history and relates back to the democratic–elite distinction, because it links to the focus on wine as a foodstuff. The idea of produce has also informed many of the mechanisms that have been developed for establishing wine quality, including notions of terroir and the demarcation of origin. The same concept has continuing resonances in an age when urban consumers look for things which will link them to a 'more peaceful' rural existence; this may underpin the success of the marketing campaign for New Zealand wine – 'clean and green' – in some export markets.

Another discrepancy exists between the idea of wine as merely a beverage and the aesthetic dimension of wine. This stems from the democratic/elite dichotomy. When wine is considered to be an aesthetic product it may be treated like other art forms, offering a sense of beauty, wonder or complex sensory enjoyment. Thus it is possible to invest in it and trade it. The winemaker may be considered to take on some of the characteristics of the artist, conjuring from the varying raw material of each year a wine which is both distinctive to his or her artistic tradition yet unique and unrepeatable. The aesthetic imperative in wine means that the pursuit of quality in the production of the drink has, over the last 400 years, become a major goal. Thus, for example, much of the modern development of wine in the leading wine regions of France has been focused on producing better wine. Faced with a growth in cheaper wines from Iberia at the end of the eighteenth century, the French sought differentiation by classification in regions like Bordeaux (Ulin, 1996), a system which became formalized in 1855. Later both the development of appellations (particularly with the use of traditional and authorized grape varieties to exclude the impact of hybrids) and co-operatives which gave less well-off producers access to capital were designed to stimulate further improvements to quality. The creation of the category of top-level table wine in the 1970s, *vin de pays*, took this further. The development of a scientific basis for viticulture and oenology from the nineteenth century academics such as Pasteur and Planchon through to Galet and Peynaud in our time underpinned this process of seeking quality. There is an irony in this today as, with the growing impact of wines from the new producing countries on world markets, the French are driven to defending 'traditional' methods of producing wine and determining wine quality (which once were radical) against criticisms that they produce poor wine and are stultifying the French industry (Jefford, 2002a; Lombard, 2002).

It can also be suggested that wine has both sacred and profane dimensions. Wine has had its gods, and is still used in the expression of religious belief – an issue which is examined in more detail below. However wine has also been disruptive of good order, and may be threatening to piety; the role of Dionysos, who brought frenzy yet punished unbelievers with madness, is an archetype of this. The Christian view on this is especially ambivalent with both the use of wine in communion and active Protestant involvement in prohibition campaigns. However, whilst Christian anti-alcohol activity is now declining (although its influence in the USA should not be underestimated), Islam continues to retain an antagonistic approach and as its adherents become more widespread in some European countries that opposition may create tensions in the future.

Linked to the idea of both the sacred and the profane is the paradox that wine can be seen to be both healthy and unhealthy. Millennia of the use of wine as a means of avoiding bacteria, both as a drink and as a medicine, established the idea of wine's health-giving properties, a perspective which is now reinforced by our understanding of its cardiovascular benefits. Conversely, modern science has exposed the dangers of cirrhosis and alcoholism so that, at least during the twentieth century, the medical establishment shifted from support to scepticism. That scepticism may now be breaking down in part as the potential health benefits of wine are examined by scientists. In the meantime the J curve can be seen as a classic metaphor for many interpretations of wine. Abstinence is suspicious, denoting unnatural behaviour; to drink moderately is healthy and also convivial and stimulating, but as one begins to drink too much that leads not only to medical problems but also to a lack of restraint, disorderly behaviour and disowning social duty. It may also imply that the need for the drug alcohol has supplemented the aesthetic and rational goals for wine consumption – a symptom of the loss of self-control. In this way there may be a social J curve as well as a medical one.

A further dichotomy pits the importance of the business of distributing and selling wine with the mystery of the drink. In part the sense of mystery is a hangover from the days when fermentation and bacterial activity were not understood, and wine was perceived to be magical. Whilst we no longer see wine as magic literally, for some drinkers it retains a form of enchantment in its ability to stimulate conviviality, replicate a sense of place, or even, occasionally, provide a transcendent experience. Such an approach may be adopted by consumers, but is also important for producers who seek to market a particular type of wine by associating it with particular experiences such as relating a wine to a place or experience or suggesting that it may guarantee seduction. Other commentators see such an approach as being designed merely to bamboozle the consumer and sell as quasi-mystical what is no more than another consumer product, albeit one which focuses on delivering good taste rather than a more utilitarian function; this argument maintains that wine is a product like any other, to be produced with care but sold merely for what it is. Connected with this paradox is the debate between those who seek to maintain wine as a traditional beverage (perhaps, in modern parlance, something authentic) against those who consider that product quality should be the end goal irrespective of the history or local context in which the wine is produced. For those who propose the latter, if gamay produces less intense less complex wine than cabernet sauvignon then it should be swept from Beaujolais and replaced, even though cabernet has no local roots and makes an entirely different style of wine. For the traditionalist faulty wine may be defensible if the particular fault – such as high-volatile acidity or spoilage from the yeast *Brettanomyces* – is typical of the wines of a particular region. In many ways this split of business with mystery (and of product with produce) may reflect something about the consumer's motivation to drink. Part is experiential – focusing on good taste – which requires a well made drink. Part is symbolic, responding to what wine says about the drinker. In the latter instance mystery, tradition and uncertainty may be more significant functions for the consumer to focus on.

Finally there is one further dyadic perspective on wine as a product. One view is that it is natural, reflecting the earth or its origin (Fuller, 1996). On the other hand is the idea that it is the result of scientific endeavour and thus something which we control and shape. This dichotomy has clear links both to the product versus produce idea and also the paradox of the authentic versus the traditional. In practice wine from any part of the world is highly manipulated, but most drinkers are unaware of this. Sulphur dioxide has been used as a preservative since the time of the Romans, as has oak which adds flavour. Sugar has been used to manipulate wine's structure for 200 years. A technically advanced producer can now use enzymes to enhance fruitiness, yeast strains to impart greater glycerol, reverse osmosis to extract water and increase alcohol level and micro-oxygenation to add smoothness and texture to the wine. Furthermore, whilst there is a sense that it is the new producing countries which engender such technocratic winemaking, all of these processes and additives are used regularly in France and other European countries. Manipulation in this way almost certainly produces a more organoleptically satisfying product but it conflicts with the clean, natural and environmentally unspoilt view that most drinkers have of wine.

Wine as a quasi-religious experience

The links between wine and religion have already been examined in some depth. It may also be helpful to examine religious experience as a metaphorical means of examining the consumer's experience of wine. One American theologian (Fuller, 1993; 1996) has suggested that, for some, wine consumption is a form of natural religion. This stems from the notion that wine is a natural product. Wine consumption may enhance a sense of community which in turn gives meaning beyond the merely mundane. Wine tasting also has its own creeds, rituals and – for some – mystical experiences (Fuller, 1993).

The sacred dimension of consumption generally has been examined in detail by consumer researchers (Belk et al., 1991), and some of their insights may be particularly applicable to wine. First, Belk et al. (1991) note the importance of place to that which is sacred – particularly for agricultural societies. Place may sacralize the product (wine from a great vineyard) and may also offer a focal point for engagement with the product; the winery as a setting for an experience or the wine festival (Fuller, 1993). Next Belk et al. (1991) suggest that times are significant. This may include both eras (a 'golden age', for instance) and the moments of ritual – such as tastings.

How do objects, such as wine, achieve the status of being sacred? A number of ways have been posited (Belk et al., 1991). Ritual processes, repeatedly used, may help to achieve this. This is a fact which must be considered by the proponents of screwcaps as an alternative closure to a cork and capsule. The latter need to be cut then extracted, with care and perhaps a flourish, using a corkscrew giving a greater sense of occasion and thus of ritual, to the commencement of drinking; this in turn marks wine out as somehow different from, and more significant than, other drinks. Pilgrimage also helps to turn a mere product into something with sacred dimensions; the success of companies offering wine tours and the growing academic interest in wine tourism suggests that this is occurring for wine consumers. Gift-giving and collecting are also important components of sacralization; wine, classically, is considered to be a drink to be shared rather than consumed in solitude, and more than any other form of foodstuff is capable of being collected. Finally, Belk and his co-authors (1991) suggest that products become sacred by inheritance; the old British idea of a grandfather 'laying down' a pipe of Port for his grandson may be an example of how this operates, but more fundamental is the example of the inheritance of land – the vineyard that remains in the family for generations, of which they are less owners than stewards.

Finally it is possible to suggest that the wine world has its own theology and the schisms which accompany dogmatics. The theology surrounds the nature of what wine should be like; thus there are those who maintain that it must show a sense of origin, or be true to its identity, and who will promote wines which fit into that belief. Alternatively, there are those who argue that the purpose of wine is no more than to taste good. Likewise there are those who will – almost as a matter of faith – object to filtration, against those who maintain the process is generally necessary in order to guarantee stability and thus drinkability. Debates about true faith also filter down to the faithful; a tasting for high-involvement consumers may include wines from adjoining vineyards in order to experience the minute differences between them and ensure that these variations accord with similar judgments delivered by experts. Theology thus results in schisms, as the debate over Chateau Pavie exemplifies (see Chapter 10). Theology also needs a priesthood, and both key wine critics and leading winemakers may fulfil this function. Ultimately, death may offer the most influential a form of 'sainthood', a position most obviously filled by a succession of significant *Champenois*, headed by Dom Pérignon.

Wine as a metaphor

Another way of understanding how wine operates culturally and socially is to understand it as a metaphor; that is, to see how it is used to signify something else, perhaps more substantial, that the producer or user wishes to convey. In three ways, perhaps, wine has a metaphorical use. The first, very directly, is in the matter of religious faith – already noted above. From the era when sacrifice required that blood was shed wine, as a deep red-coloured liquid, was capable of representing a sacrifice. The heiress of Chateau Haut-Brion was guillotined in the French revolution. Later there was a move to have her canonized for, it was claimed she had 'spilt for Christ blood more red and more pure than the best of our wines' (Briggs, 1994, p. 155).

The second way in which wine can act metaphorically is to denote civilization. Wine is the drink of the sophisticate, of the connoisseur, of the convivial person. As such it promotes harmony, an appreciation of the finer aspects of life – especially good food and the arts – and its rituals and the sharing it entails encourage polite and respectful behaviour. Tea may have elements of this, coffee less so, and other alcoholic drinks are explicitly not viewed, in some societies, to symbolize such a civilized perspective (Unwin, 1992). By implication the person who does not drink wine (whether President of Iran or of the United States) is somehow seen to be less than civilized. In this respect it is significant that wine has developed as one of the major legal drugs of Europe, the continent which came to impose its cultural and political hegemony on the world from about 1600 until 1940. Wine was the drink of imperial rulers (if not all the foot-soldiers of the empires) and those who would not drink it – whether Indian Muslims, black South Africans or native Algerians – were thus marking themselves out to their overlords as less than civilized.

Thirdly, wine can be seen to symbolize heritage and identity. This has been noted consistently in discussions about Europe, but it equally occurs in other places. Thus in South Africa it is seen to be farm produce, the result of the hard work of the Boers. During the slump of the early twentieth century it was to preserve the identity and economic well-being of these farmers that very corporatist approaches such as the formation of the South African Co-operative Winegrowers Association (KWV) were adopted. During the years of apartheid it was the drinking of wine (and its derivative spirit, brandy) which helped to set apart white from black. Now some South African wines are being deliberately 'recreated' in homage to their symbolic place in a former society. In some situations where wine is under attack, so the nation is considered to be under attack. Phylloxera was seen to threaten the soul of France and today some of the rhetoric which comes from the same country about the danger of industrial wine from the new producing countries threatening authentic French wine which has 2000 years of tradition behind it is similar (Nossiter, 2004; Osborne, 2004). This is a viewpoint which is echoed in some other European wine-producing nations.

The social context of wine

Wine is a social drink; its consumption overwhelmingly takes place with other people and it is generally used as a social lubricant. It has a close relationship to food; it may be seen as a foodstuff or as a social complement to food. Like food it may engender sensory pleasure. Equally, our use of wine generally and choice of specific bottles may say something about us, both to ourselves and to those around us. Ultimately, the chemical make up of wine may mean that our use of it causes social disruption rather than social harmony – both as single events and as repeated patterns of behaviour. This social context gives wine a social impact; just as our relationships with those around us are moderated by legislation so wine, as a catalyst to those relationships, is also controlled politically. In any event, politicians, social policy makers and economists cannot ignore the significance of wine in the world. Whether as a national symbol, a threat to public health, a generator of export earnings, a source of state revenues, or a stimulus to riots, it is a product with which they have to engage.

The complex web of interpretations and paradoxes outlined means that wine has often attained a value beyond the mere cost of processing and packaging the product and, as some of the vinous paradoxes suggest, its production and use spill over into the political sphere. How wine is presented to the consumer and what actually exists in the bottle have been concerns for many millennia. At times, as with Trimalchio (Petronius, n.d./1997), error may have humorous consequences, but for most producers and consumers the integrity of what is drunk is deemed to be crucial. Thus it is argued that accuracy in presenting wine is necessary to protect the consumer. When adulteration leads to illness or death that is undoubtedly the case but, as the consideration of the history of the appellation system shows (Chapter 5), most forms of control on the marketing of wine have been driven by the industry itself. Just as consumers may have little idea of how a wine is actually produced, so they may have little understanding of the constraints around, and latitude allowed, by labelling. Where consumer protection is considered important it has traditionally been in instances where the vested interest of a powerful production group (e.g. Bordeaux producers) is threatened by outsiders, as with the mislabelling of wine from a humble designation with that of a higher appellation. Where all producers benefit equally from less than open behaviour (such as flavouring wine with oak chips) there is little impetus to institute controls. The growing consumer lobby, however, and a contemporaneous emphasis on the safety and purity of production methods and materials, may be changing this, so that increasingly label requirements detailing additives and processing agents are becoming the norm.

Crucially the social nature of wine, like the paradoxes and metaphorical aspects noted previously, is not a static matter. Some aspects – such as alcohol-fuelled violence – have been obvious for millennia. Others, like the problem of drunk-driving, have existed for barely a century. The acceleration of consumption and growth of consumer societies means that consumption behaviour is changing. As more drinkers become interested so wine clubs, tourism and books are of growing importance. Equally the popularity of wines is changing faster. Chateau Haut-Brion has been sought after for 350 years, but some new-wave *garage* wines from Bordeaux rose and then sank during the 1990s. On the other hand it may be that European wines are waning in the long term as wines from new producing countries, often of a different, fruitier style, take their place. It is also possible that, as well as activities and stylistic preferences, consumer attitudes are changing fast. Perhaps traditional wine, wine from place, wine with a sense of heritage, is being replaced by authentic wine. Authentic wine may involve heritage and place as some of the precursors of authenticity but may include other factors such as purity or self-expression (Postrel, 2003), all issues which could be considered secondary by the traditional wine industry. Nevertheless, this final paradox, of a drink which retains meanings and interpretations which stretch back to the dawn of its production, alongside development and change, is part of what makes the production, use and study of wine such a fascinating undertaking.

References

Aaker, D. A. (1996). *Building Strong Brands*. New York: The Free Press.

Adler, M. J. (Ed.). (1996). *Great Books of the Western World Book 9: Hippocrates, Galen*. Chicago: Encyclopedia Britannica Inc.

Ajzen, I., & Fishbein, M. (1980). *Understanding Attitudes and Predicting Social Behavior*. Englewood Cliffs, NJ: Prentice-Hall.

Ali-Knight, J., & Charters, S. (2000). Wine tourism – a thirst for knowledge? *International Journal of Wine Marketing, 12*(3), 70–80.

Alko Inc. (2005). *Information on Alko*. Helsinki: Alko. Retrieved 12th October, 2005, from http://www.alko.fi/frontpage

Allen, M. (2002). Pay per view. *Harpers*, 12th April, 11.

Amerine, M. A., & Roessler, E. B. (1976). *Wines: Their Sensory Evaluation*. New York: W. H. Freeman and Company.

Anderson, B. G. (1968). How French children learn to drink. *Trans-action, 5*, 20–22.

Anderson, K., & Wittwer, G. (2001). U.S. dollar appreciation and the spread of Pierce's disease: effects on world wine markets. *Australian and New Zealand Wine Industry Journal, 16*(2), 70–75.

Anon. (n.d./1972). *The Epic of Gilgamesh* (N. K. Sandars, Trans.). London: Penguin.

Anon. (1998). *The Wines of Champagne*. Epernay: Comité Interprofessionel des Vins de Champagne.

Anon. (2003). *Catalogue of Stock*. Melbourne: Fine Wines of Europe, 18.

Anon. (2004a). *April news*. London: Farr Vintners. Retrieved 13th April, 2004, from http://www.farr-vintners.com/enprimeur/

Anon. (2004b). *Vignerons protest*: Harpers-wine.com. Retrieved 20th January, 2005, from http://www.harpers-wine.com/newsitem.cfm?NewsID=1669&i=1

Anon. (2005a). *Le champagne*. Epernay: Comité Interprofessionel du Vins de Champagne. Retrieved 12th September, 2005, from http://www.champagne.fr/en_vinallegresse.html

Anon. (2005b). *Lookalikes and passing off*: Practical Law Company. Retrieved 25th May, 2005, from http://ld.practicallaw.com/1-100-4964

Anon. (2005c). *Primum familiae vini*. Retrieved 1st February, 2005, from http://www.pfv.org/html/objectives.html

Anon. (2005d). *World wine sales go from strength to strength*: Beverage Daily.com. Retrieved 4th May, 2005, from http://www.beveragedaily.com/news/news.asp?id=11748

Anstie, F. (1877). *Uses of Wine in Health and Disease*. London: Macmillan and Co.

Ashenfelter, O., Ashmore, D., & Lalonde, R. (1995). Bordeaux wine vintage quality and weather. *Chance*, *8*(1), 7–14.

Atkinson, J. (1999). Meaningless brands from meaningful differentiation. *Journal of Wine Research*, *10*(3), 229–234.

Atkinson, P. (2003). *The Ripening Sun*. London: Century.

Australian Wine Online. (2004). Adelaide: Winetitles. Retrieved 11th June, 2004, from http://www.winetitles.com.au/awol/

Bagnardi, V., Blangiardo, M., Vecchia, C. L., & Corrao, G. (2001). Alcohol consumption and the risk of cancer: a meta-analysis. *Alcohol Research and Health*, *25*(4), 263–270.

Barefoot, J. C., Gronbaek, M., Feaganes, J. R., McPherson, R. S., Williams, R. B., & Siegler, I. C. (2002). Alcoholic beverage preference, diet, and health habits in the UNC alumni heart study. *The American Journal of Clinical Nutrition*, *76*(2), 466.

Barr, A. (1990). *Wine Snobbery*. London: Faber and Faber.

Barr, A. (1995). *Drink: An Informal Social History*. London: Bantam.

Barthes, R. (1957/2000). *Mythologies* (A. Lavers, Trans.). Sydney: Vintage.

Bartoshuk, L. (2000). Comparing sensory experiences across individuals: recent psychophysical advances illuminate genetic variation in taste perception. *Chemical Senses*, *25*(4), 447–460.

Basset, G. (2000). *The Wine Experience*. London: Kyle Cathie.

Batt, P. J., & Dean, A. (2000). Factors influencing the consumer's decision. *Australian and New Zealand Wine Industry Journal – Marketing Supplement*, *15*(4), 34–41.

Beardsley, M. C. (1980). *Aesthetics: Problems in the Philosophy of Criticism* (2nd edn.). Indianapolis, IN: Harcourt, Brace and World.

Beardsworth, A., & Keil, T. (1992). Foodways in flux: From gastro-anomy to menu pluralism? *British Food Journal*, *94*(7), 20–27.

Becker, H. S. (1978). Arts and crafts. *American Journal of Sociology, 83*(4), 862–889.

Becker, U., Gronbaek, M., Johansen, D., & Sorensen, T. I. A. (2002). Lower risk for alcohol-induced cirrhosis in wine drinkers. *Hepatology, 35*(4), 868–875.

Belfrage, N. (1999). *Barolo to Valpolicella*. London: Faber and Faber.

Belfrage, N. (2001). *Brunello to Zibbibo*. London: Faber and Faber.

Belk, R. W. (1988). Possessions and the extended self. *Journal of Consumer Research, 15*(September), 139–168.

Belk, R. W., Wallendorf, M., & Sherry, J. F. (1991). The sacred and the profane in consumer behaviour: theodicy on the odyssey. In R. W. Belk (Ed.), *Highways and Buyways: Naturalistic Research from the Consumer Behaviour Odyssey* (pp. 59–101). Provo: Association for Consumer Research.

Benson, J., & Walton, S. (2003). *The Right Food with the Right Wine*. Tadworth: Right Way.

Beverland, M. (2003). Building icon wine brands: exploring the systemic nature of luxury wines. Paper presented at the *3rd Annual Wine Marketing Colloquium*, Adelaide: University of South Australia.

Beverland, M. (2004). Uncovering 'theories-in-use': building luxury wine brands. *European Journal of Marketing, 38*(3/4), 446–466.

Beverland, M. (2005). Crafting brand authenticity: the case of luxury wines. *Journal of Management Studies, 42*(5), 1003–1029.

Beverland, M., & Carswell, P. (2001). An exploratory investigation into consumer behavior in the New Zealand wine market.

Bode, W. K. H. (1992). The marriage of food and wine. *International Journal of Wine Marketing, 4*(2), 15–20.

Botonaki, A., & Tsakiridou, E. (2004). Consumer response evaluation of a Greek quality wine. *Acta Agricola Scandinavia, Section C, Food Economics, 1*, 91–98.

Bourdieu, P. (1986). *Distinction: A Social Critique of the Judgement of Taste* (R. Nice, Trans.). London: Routledge.

Bradley, F. (1995). *International Marketing Strategy*. Hemel Hempstead: Prentice-Hall International (UK) Ltd.

Brennan, T. (1997). *Burgundy to Champagne: The Wine Trade in Early Modern France*. Baltimore, MD: The Johns Hopkins University Press.

Brien, C., May, P., & Mayo, O. (1987). Analysis of judge performance in wine-quality evaluations. *Journal of Food Studies, 52*, 1273–1279.

Briggs, A. (1994). *Haut-Brion*. London: Faber and Faber.

Briggs, N. C., Levine, R. S., Bobo, L. D., Haliburton, W. P., Brann, E. A., & Hennekens, C. H. (2002). Wine drinking and risk of non-hodgkin's lymphoma among men in the United States: a population-based case-control study. *American Journal of Epidemiology, 156*(5), 454–462.

Broadbent, M. (1979). *Pocket Guide to Winetasting* (6th edn.). London: Mitchell Beazley.

Brochet, F. (2001). *Chemical object representation in the field of consciousness*: Academie Amorim. Retrieved 5th February, 2002, from http://www.academie-amorim.com/

Brochet, F., & Dubourdieu, D. (2001). Wine descriptive language supports cognitive specificity of chemical senses. *Brain and Language*, *77*, 187–196.

Brook, S. (1999). *The Wines of California*. London: Faber and Faber.

Brook, S. (2000a). Movers and shakers. In S. Brook (Ed.), *A Century of Wine* (pp. 66–77). London: Mitchell Beazley.

Brook, S. (2000b). Wine in the 21st century. In S. Brook (Ed.), *A Century of Wine* (pp. 182–189). London: Mitchell Beazley.

Brook, S. (2000c). Wine, food, style and pleasure. In S. Brook (Ed.), *A Century of Wine* (pp. 10–23). London: Mitchell Beazley.

Brook, S. (Ed.). (2000d). *A Century of Wine*. London: Mitchell Beazley.

Brook, S. (2003). *The Wines of Germany*. London: Mitchell Beazley.

Brook, S. (2005). High hopes. *Decanter*, *30*(6), 46–49.

Bruce-Gardyne, T. (2000). Stop your wine-ing. *The Ecologist*, *30*(8), 57.

Bruce-Gardyne, T. (2002). Shooting from the lip. *Harpers*, 25th February, 26–29.

Bruwer, J., Li, E., & Reid, M. (2001). Wine-related lifestyle segmentation of the Australian domestic wine market. *Australian and New Zealand Wine Industry Journal*, *16*(2), 104–108.

Bruwer, J., Li, E., & Reid, M. (2002). Segmentation of the Australian wine market using a wine-related lifestyle approach. *Journal of Wine Research*, *13*(3), 217–242.

Buemann, B., Toubro, S., & Astrup, A. (2002). The effect of wine or beer versus a carbonated soft drink, served at a meal, on ad libitum energy intake. *International Journal of Obesity and Related Metabolic Disorders*, *26*(10), 1367–1372.

Bullock, J. D., Wang, J. P., & Bullock, G. H. (1998). Was Dom Pérignon really blind? *Survey of Ophthalmology*, *42*(5), 481–486.

Burns, J., Gardner, P. T., Matthews, D., Duthie, G. G., Lean, M. E., & Crozier, A. (2001). Extraction of phenolics and changes in antioxidant activity of red wines during vinification. *Journal of Agricultural and Food Chemistry*, *49*(12), 5797–5808.

Caillard, A., & Langton, S. (2000). *Langton's Australian Fine Wine: Buying and Investment Guide* (4th edn.). Sydney: Media21 Publishing.

Calabresi, A. T. (1987). Vin Santo and wine in a Tuscan farmhouse. In M. Douglas (Ed.), *Constructive Drinking: Perspectives on Drink from Anthropology* (pp. 122–133). New York: Cambridge University Press.

Cambourne, B., Hall, M., Johnson, G., Macionis, N., Mitchell, R., & Sharples, L. (2000). The maturing wine tourism product: an international overview. In M. Hall, L. Sharples, B. Cambourne & N. Macionis (Eds.), *Wine Tourism around the World: Development, Management and Markets* (pp. 24–66). Oxford: Elsevier Science.

Campbell, C. (1987). *The Romantic Ethic and the Spirit of Modern Consumerism*. Oxford: Blackwell.

Campbell, C. (2004). *Phylloxera: How Wine was Saved for the World.* London: Harper Collins.

Cardebat, J.-M., & Figuet, J.-M. (2004). What explains Bordeaux wine prices. *Applied Economic Letters, 11*, 293–296.

Carlsen, J. (2004). Global wine tourism research. *Journal of Wine Research, 15*(1), 5–14.

Carpenter, W. B. (1860). *On Alcoholic Liquors in Health and Disease.* London: Blanchard and Lea.

Chaney, I. (2000a). A comparative analysis of wine reviews. *British Food Journal, 102*(7), 470–480.

Chaney, I. (2000b). External search effort for wine. *International Journal of Wine Marketing, 12*(2), 5–21.

Charters, S. (2001). The structure of business in the wine industry. *Australian and New Zealand Wine Industry Journal, 16*(1), 97–100.

Charters, S. (2002). The two wines. Paper presented at the *Bacchus to the Future Conference*, Brock University, St. Catherines, Ontario.

Charters, S. (2003). Wine in the modern world. In S. Katz & W. W. Weaver (Eds.), *Encyclopedia of Food and Culture* (Vol. 3, pp. 557–561). New York: Charles Scribner's Sons.

Charters, S. (2004). *Perceptions of Wine Quality.* Unpublished PhD dissertation, Edith Cowan University, Perth, Western Australia.

Charters, S. (2006). Aesthetic products and aesthetic consumption: a review. *Consumption, Markets and Culture.*

Charters, S., & Ali-Knight, J. (2002). Who is the wine tourist? *Tourism Management, 23*, 311–319.

Charters, S., & Loughton, K. (2000). Attitudes to small business in the wine industry. Paper presented at the *45th International Conference on Small Business World Conference*, Brisbane: ICSB.

Charters, S., & O'Neill, M. (2000). Delighting the customer – how good is the cellar door experience? *Australian and New Zealand Wine Industry Journal: International Wine Marketing Supplement*, 11–16.

Charters, S., & Pettigrew, S. (2002). 'Gladdening the heart': a perspective on wine quality. Paper presented at the *Bacchus to the Future Conference*, Brock University Press, St. Catherines, Ontario.

Charters, S., & Pettigrew, S. (2003a). 'I like it but how do I know if it's any good?' Quality and preference in wine consumption. *Journal of Research for Consumers*, *5*.

Charters, S., & Pettigrew, S. (2003b). The intrinsic dimensions of wine quality: an exploratory investigation. Paper presented at the *3rd Annual Wine Marketing Colloquium*, Adelaide: University of South Australia.

Charters, S., & Pettigrew, S. (2004). The relationship of wine and food: an exploration. Paper presented at the *International Wine Tourism Conference*, Margaret River: Vineyard Publications.

Charters, S., & Pettigrew, S. (2005). Is wine consumption an aesthetic experience? *Journal of Wine Research*, *16*(2), 37–52.

Charters, S., & Pettigrew, S. (2006). Product involvement and the evaluation of wine quality. *Qualitative Market Research*, *9*(2), 181–193.

Charters, S., Lockshin, L., & Unwin, T. (1999). Consumer responses to wine bottle back labels. *Journal of Wine Research*, *10*(3), 183–195.

Chikte, U. M., Grobler, S. R., & Kotze, T. J. (2003). *In vitro* human dental enamel erosion by three different wine samples. *South African Dental Journal*, *58*(9), 360–362.

Cholette, S. (2004). A tale of two regions: similarities, differences and trends in the French and Californian wine industries. *International Journal of Wine Marketing*, *16*(2), 23–47.

Christiansen, D. (2004). *Wine Club Members' Enduring Involvement toward Winery Visitation, Wine Drinking and Wine Club Participation.* Unpublished Masters thesis, University of Otago, Dunedin.

Classen, C., Howes, D., & Synott, A. (1994). *Aroma: A Cultural History of Smell*. London: Routledge.

Cliff, M. A., & King, M. C. (1996). A proposed approach for evaluating expert wine judge performance using descriptive statistics. *Journal of Wine Research*, *7*(2), 83–90.

Cobb, P. (2001). Taking port upstream. *Wine and Spirit International* (December), 49.

Coleman, F. J. (1965). Can a smell or a taste or a touch be beautiful? *American Philosophical Quarterly*, *2*(4), 319–324.

Constellation Wines. (2005). *Australia's banrock station: premium wine and environmental conservation*: Constellation Wines. Retrieved 12th September, 2005, from http://www.banrockstation.com/home

Correia, L., Ascenção, M. J. P., & Charters, S. (2004). Wine routes in Portugal: a case study of the Bairrada Wine Route. *Journal of Wine Research*, *15*(3), 15–25.

Crane, T. (2003). A question of taste. *Harpers*, 18th April, 38–40.

Croser, B. (2001). The Australian wine show system. *The Australian Wine Educator* (Spring), 6.

Csikszentmihalyi, M., & Robinson, R. E. (1990). *The Art of Seeing*. Malibu: J. Paul Getty Trust.

Cummins, P. W. (1976). *A critical edition of 'Le regime tresutile et tresproufitable pour conserver et garder la sante du corps humain'*. Chapel Hill: North Carolina Studies in the Romance Languages and Literatures.

Dalby, A. (2003). *Bacchus: A Biography*. London: British Museum Press.

Daroch, F., Hoeneisen, M., Gonzalez, C. L., Kawaguchi, F., Salgado, F., Solar, H., et al. (2001). *In vitro* antibacterial activity of Chilean red wines against Helicobacter pylori. *Microbios*, *104*(408), 79–85.

Davis, J. D. (2001). Wine marketing and its legal environment. In K. Moulton & J. Lapsley (Eds.), *Successful Wine Marketing* (pp. 69–75). Gaithersburg: Aspen Publishers.

De Stefani, E., Correa, P., Deneo-Pellegrini, H., Boffetta, P., Gutierrez, L. P., Ronco, A., et al. (2002). Alcohol intake and risk of adenocarcinoma of the lung. A case-control study in Uruguay. *Lung Cancer*, *38*(1), 9–14.

Delbridge, A., & Bernard, J. R. L. (Eds.). (1998). *The Macquarie Concise Dictionary*. Sydney: The Macquarie Library.

Demossier, M. (2004). Contemporary lifestyles: the case of wine. In D. Sloan (Ed.), *Culinary Taste: Consumer Behaviour in the International Restaurant Sector* (pp. 93–108). Oxford: Elsevier Butterworth-Heinemann.

Demossier, M. (2005). Consuming wine in France: the 'wandering' drinker and the vin-anomie. In T. M. Wilson (Ed.), *Drinking Cultures* (pp. 129–154). Oxford: Berg.

Desseauve, T. (n.d.). *The Book of Wine* (D. Dusinberre, Trans.). Paris: Flammarion.

d'Hauteville, F. (2003). The mediating role of involvement and values on wine consumption frequency in France. Paper presented at the *International Colloquium in Wine Marketing*, Adelaide: University of South Australia.

Dichter, E. (1964). *Handbook of Consumer Motivations*. New York: McGraw-Hill.

Dimara, E., & Skuras, D. (2003). Consumer evaluations of product certification, geographic association and traceability in Greece. *European Journal of Marketing*, *37*(5/6), 690–705.

Dodd, T. H. (1997). Opportunities and pitfalls in a developing wine industry. *International Journal of Wine Marketing*, *7*(1), 5–17.

Dodd, T. H., Pinkelton, B. E., & Gustafson, A. W. (1996). External information sources of product enthusiasts. *Psychology and Marketing*, *13*(3), 291–305.

Douglas, M. (1987a). A distinctive anthropological perspective. In M. Douglas (Ed.), *Constructive Drinking: Perspectives on Drink from Anthropology* (pp. 3–15). New York: Cambridge University Press.

Douglas, M. (Ed.). (1987b). *Constructive Drinking: Perspectives on Drink from Anthropology*. New York: Cambridge University Press.

Dowling, R., Carlsen, J., Getz, D., Charters, S., & Ali-Knight, J. (1999). *The Western Australian Wine Tourism Strategy*. Perth: Edith Cowan University.

du Plessis, I. (2005). *Trade mark protection for distinctive wine bottles*. Cape Town: South African Wine.co.za. Retrieved 12th December, 2005, from http://www.wine.co.za/News/NewsPrint.aspx?NEWSID=7296

Dubois, B., & Duquesne, P. (1993). The market for luxury goods: Income versus culture. *European Journal of Marketing*, *27*(1), 35–44.

Dubow, J. S. (1992). Occasion-based vs. user-based benefit segmentation. *Journal of Advertising Research*, *32*(March/April), 11–18.

Duguid, P. (2003). Developing the brand: the case of alcohol, 1800–1880. *Enterprise and Society*, *4*(3), 405–441.

Dunphy, R., & Lockshin, L. (1998). A contemporary perspective of the Australian wine show system as a marketing tool. *Journal of Wine Research*, *9*(2), 107–129.

Durrell, L. (1969). Landscape and character. In *Spirit of Place: Letters and Essays on Travel* (pp. 156–163). London: Faber and Faber.

Echikson, W. (2004). *Noble Rot: A Bordeaux Wine Revolution*. New York: W. W. Norton and Company Inc.

Edwards, J. (1984). *The Roman Cookery of Apicius*. London: Rider and Company.

Ellison, R. C., Yuqing Zhang, Christine E. McLennan, & Rothman, K. J. (2001). Exploring the relation of alcohol consumption to risk of breast cancer. *American Journal of Epidemiology*, *154*(8), 740–747.

Euromonitor. (2004, 22 July). *The world market for spirits and FABs*: Global Market Information Database. Retrieved 17th August 2005, from http://www.gmid.euromonitor.com/

Evans, A. (1995). Dr. Black's favourite disease. *British Heart Journal*, *74*(6), 696–697.

Evans, R. (2004). Wine lovers influenced by brands, not prices. *Off Licence News*, 1st October.

Evans, R. (2005). An unholy alliance? *Off Licence News*, 14th October, 36.

Ewert, J., & Hamman, J. (1999). Why paternalism survives: globalization, democratization and labour on South African wine farms. *Sociologia Ruralis*, *39*(2), 202–221.

Exley, H. (Ed.). (1994). *Wine Quotations*. Watford: Exley Publications.

Eyres, H. (2005). Prandial pleasure: Kiwi cuisine. *FT Magazine*, 30th April, 42.

Fairbanks, D. H. K., Hughes, C. J., & Turpie, J. K. (2004). Potential impact of viticulture expansion on habitat types in the Cape Floristic Region, South Africa.

Faith, N. (1999). *The Winemasters of Bordeaux*. London: Prion Books.

Faith, N. (2002). *Australia's Liquid Gold*. London: Mitchell Beazley.

Fattorini, J. (1994). Professional consumers: themes in high street wine marketing. *International Journal of Wine Marketing*, *6*(2), 5–11.

Featherstone, M. (1991). *Consumer Culture and Postmodernism*. London: Sage.

Fine, P. (2004). You're barred mate. *Off Licence News*, 26th March, 24.

Fish, T. (2001). *Beringer blass challenges Australia's new Coonawarra appellation*: Wine Spectator. Retrieved 6th November, 2001, from http://www.winespectator.com/Wine/Daily/News/1,1145,1476,00.html

Fishbein, M., & Ajzen, I. (1975). *Belief, Attitude, Intention and Behavior: An Introduction to Theory and Research*. Reading, MA: Addison-Wesley.

Fitzgerald, E. (1989/1859). *The Rubaiyat of Omar Khayyam*. London: Penguin.

Follain, J. (2001). Sample people. *The Weekend Australian Magazine*, 8–9th September.

Foppa, M., Fuchs, F. D., & Duncan, B. B. (2001). Alcohol and atherosclerosis. *Arquivos Brasileiros de Cardiologia*, *76*(2), 165–176.

Forrestal, P. (Ed.). (2000). *The Global Encyclopedia of Wine*. Willoughby: Global Book Publishing.

Fountain, J., & Charters, S. (2004). Younger wine tourists: a study of generational differences in the cellar door experience. Paper presented at the *International Wine Tourism Conference*, Margaret River, Western Australia: Vineyard Publications, Perth.

Fretter, W. B. (1971). Is wine an art object? *Journal of Aesthetics and Art Criticism*, *30*(1), 97–100.

Fridjhon, M. (2004). Three classes of wine? *Circle of Wine Writers Update*, April/May, 27.

Friedrich, J. (2000). Eye on Tokaj. *Wall Street Journal*, 5th October, A 24.

Fuller, R. C. (1993). Religion and ritual in American wine culture. *Journal of American Culture*, *16*(1), 39–45.

Fuller, R. C. (1996). *Religion and Wine: A Cultural History of Wine Drinking in the United States*. Knoxville, TN: University of Tennessee Press.

Fung, T. T., Hunter, D. J., Spiegelman, D., Colditz, G. A., Rimm, E. B., & Willett, W. C. (2002). Intake of alcohol and alcoholic beverages and the risk of basal cell carcinoma of the skin. *Cancer Epidemiology Biomarkers & Prevention*, *11*(10 Pt 1), 1119–1122.

Gabler, J. M. (1995). *Passions: The Wines and Travels of Thomas Jefferson*. Baltimore, MD: Bacchus Press.

Gabler, J. M. (2004). *Words into Wine*. Baltimore, MD: Bacchus Press.

Gade, D. W. (2004). Tradition, territory and terroir in French viniculture: Cassis, France and appellation controlée. *Annals of the Association of American Geographers*, *94*(4), 848–876.

Gale, G. (1975). Are some aesthetic judgments empirically true? *American Philosophical Quarterly*, *12*(4), 341–348.

Gapstur, S. M., Potter, J. D., Sellers, T. A., & Folsom, A. R. (1992). Increased risk of breast cancer with alcohol consumption in postmenopausal women. *American Journal of Epidemiology*, *136*(10), 1221–1231.

Gardham, D. (2006). Hamza had terror manual, court told. *The Weekly Telegraph*, 18–24th January, 10.

Gardner, J. (1953). Anti-bacterial properties of wine. Paper presented at the *American Pharmaceutical Association Conference*, Salt Lake City, UT, USA.

Garner, M., & Merritt, P. (1990). *Barolo: Tar and Roses*. London: Random Century Group.

Gautier, J.-F. (2002). The French soldier's wine during the great war 1914–1918. *International Wine Lawyers Association Bulletin*, *29*, 21–23.

Geene, A., Heijbroek, A., Lagerwerf, A., & Wazir, R. (1999). *The World Wine Business*. Utrecht: Rabobank International.

George, R. (1996). *The Wines of New Zealand*. London: Faber and Faber.

Ger, G., & Belk, R. W. (2005, 28 April–1 May, 2005). Emergence of consumer cultures: a cross-cultural and (art) historical comparison. Paper presented at the *Conference on Historical Analysis & Research in Marketing*, Long Beach, CA, USA.

Geraci, V. W. (2004). Fermenting a twenty-first century California wine industry. *Agricultural History*, *78*(4), 438–465.

Gil, J. M., & Sanchez, M. (1997). Consumer preferences for wine attributes: a conjoint approach. *British Food Journal*, *99*(1), 3–11.

Gilby, C. (2005). Hungary like the wolf. *Harpers*, 2nd September, 18–22.

Gladstones, J. (1992). *Viticulture and Environment*. Adelaide: Winetitles.

Gluckman, R. L. (1990). A consumer approach to branded wines. *European Journal of Marketing*, *24*(4), 27–46.

Goldsmith, R. E., & d'Hauteville, F. (1998). Heavy wine consumption: empirical and theoretical perspectives. *British Food Journal*, *100*(4), 184–190.

Goode, J. (2005). *Boring wine*: Wine Anorak. Retrieved 24th August, 2005, from http://www.wineanorak.com/boring_wine.htm

Goulding, C. (2000). The commodification of the past, postmodern pastiche, and the search for authentic experiences at contemporary heritage attractions. *European Journal of Marketing*, *34*(7), 835–853.

Graham, T. J. (1828). *Sure Methods of Improving Health and Prolonging Life by Regulating the Diet and Regimen*. London: Simpkin and Marshall.

Gray, A., Ferguson, M. M., & Wall, J. G. (1998). Wine tasting and dental erosion. Case report. *Australian Dental Journal*, *43*(1), 32–34.

Gray, D., Saggers, S., Sputore, B., & Bourbon, D. (2000). What works? A review of evaluated alcohol misuse interventions among aboriginal Australians. *Addiction*, *95*(1), 11–22.

Gray, J. (2004). *In vivo* there is cash. *Canadian Business*, *77*(21), 22.

Gronbaek, M., Becker, U., Johansen, D., Gottschau, A., Schnohr, P., Hein, H. O., et al. (2000). Type of alcohol consumed and mortality from all causes, coronary heart disease, and cancer. *Annals of Internal Medicine*, *133*(6), 411–419.

Gronbaek, M., Deis, A., Sorensen, T. I., Becker, U., Schnohr, P., & Jensen, G. (1995). Mortality associated with moderate intakes of wine, beer, or spirits. *British Medical Journal*, *310*(6988), 1165–1169.

Groves, R., Charters, S., & Reynolds, C. (2000). Imbibing, inscribing, integrating and imparting: a typology of wine consumption practices. *Journal of Wine Research*, *11*(3), 209–223.

Grunow, J. (1997). *The Sociology of Taste*. London: Routledge.

Gunther, R. T. (Ed.). (1968). *Dioscorides, 'De materia medica,' The Greek herbal of Dioscordes*. New York: Hafner Publishing Co.

Gurr, L. A. (1987). Maigret's Paris. In M. Douglas (Ed.), *Constructive Drinking: Perspectives on Drink from Anthropology* (pp. 220–236). New York: Cambridge University Press.

Gusfield, J. (1987). Passage to play: rituals of drinking time in American society. In M. Douglas (Ed.), *Constructive Drinking: Perspectives on Drink from Anthropology* (pp. 73–90). New York: Cambridge University Press.

Gutman, J. (1982). A means-end chain model based on consumer categorization processes. *Journal of Marketing*, *46*(Spring), 60–72.

Guy, K. M. (1997). Wine, work and wealth: class relations and modernization in the Champagne wine industry. *Business and Economic History*, *26*(2), 298–303.

Guy, K. M. (2003). *When Champagne Became French: Wine and the Making of a National Identity*. Baltimore, MD: The Johns Hopkins University Press.

Hall, J., & Lockshin, L. (1999). It's not the consumer, it's the occasion. *Australian and New Zealand Wine Industry Journal*, *14*(3), 69–78.

Hall, J., & Lockshin, L. (2000). Using means-end chains for analysing occasions – not buyers. *Australasian Marketing Journal*, *8*(1), 45–54.

Hall, J., & Winchester, M. (2000). Focus on your customer through segmentation. *Australia & New Zealand Wine Industry Journal*, *15*(2), 93–96.

Hall, M., Johnson, G., Cambourne, B., Macionis, N., Mitchell, R., & Sharples, L. (2000a). Wine tourism: an introduction. In M. Hall, L. Sharples, B. Cambourne & N. Macionis (Eds.), *Wine Tourism Around the World: Development, Management and Markets* (pp. 1–23). Oxford: Elsevier Science.

Hall, M., Sharples, L., Cambourne, B., & Macionis, N. (Eds.). (2000b). *Wine Tourism Around the World: Development, Management and Markets*. Oxford: Elsevier Science.

Hallgarten, F. (1987). *Wine Scandal*. London: Sphere.

Halliday, J. (1994). *A History of the Australian Wine Industry 1949–1994*. Adelaide: Winetitles.

Halliday, J. (2001). Australia's wine show system. *The Wine Magazine*, April/May, 95–97.

Halliday, J., & Johnson, H. (1992). *The Art and Science of wine*. London: Mitchell Beazley.

Hancock, J. M. (1999). What makes good wine? Climate versus terroir in determining wine quality. *Science Spectra*, *15*, 74–79.

Hanson, A. (1982). *Burgundy* (1st edn.). London: Faber and Faber.

Hanson, A. (1995). *Burgundy* (2nd edn.). London: Faber and Faber.

Hanson, A. (2000). Burgundy. In S. Brook (Ed.), *A Century of Wine* (pp. 90–97). London: Mitchell Beazley.

Hanson, D. J. (1995). *Preventing Alcohol Abuse: Alcohol, Culture and Control*. Westport, CT: Praeger Publishers.

Heath, D. B. (1995). An introduction to alcohol and culture in international perspective. In D. B. Heath (Ed.), *International Handbook on Alcohol and Culture* (pp. 1–6). Westport, CT: Praeger Publishers.

Heath, D. B. (1999). Drinking and pleasure across cultures. In S. Peele & M. Grant (Eds.), *Alcohol and Pleasure: A Health Perspective* (pp. 61–72). Philadelphia, PA: Taylor and Francis.

Heath, D. B. (2000). *Drinking Occasions: Comparative Perspectives on Alcohol and Culture*. Ann Arbor, MI: Taylor and Francis.

Heijbroek, A. M. A. (2003). *Consequences of globalization in the wine industry*. Bilbao: Great Wine Capitals Global Network. Retrieved 8th August, 2005, from http://www.greatwinecapitals.com/bus-club/Arend%20Heijbroek%20Bilbao%202003.pdf

Herz, R. (1998). An examination of objective and subjective measures of experience associated to odors, music and paintings. *Empirical Studies of the Arts*, *16*(2), 137–152.

Herz, R. (2004). A naturalistic analysis of autobiographical memories triggered by olfactory visual and auditory stimuli. *Chemical Senses*, *29*(3), 217–224.

Hesiod. (n.d./1999). *Theogeny: Works and Days* (M. L. West, Trans.). Oxford: Oxford University Press.

Hibberd, J. (2002). Government announces alcohol misuse study. *Harpers*, 7th August.

Hibberd, J. (2005). House of wildcards. *Harpers*, 28th January, 16–17.

Hirschman, E. C., & Holbrook, M. B. (1982). Hedonic consumption: emerging concepts, methods and propositions. *Journal of Marketing*, *46*(Summer), 92–101.

Holbrook, M. B., & Hirschman, E. C. (1980). Symbolic consumer behavior: an introduction. Paper presented at the *Consumer Esthetics and Symbolic Consumption Conference*, New York: Association for Consumer Research.

Holbrook, M. B., & Hirschman, E. C. (1982). The experiential aspects of consumption: consumer fantasies, feelings and fun. *Journal of Consumer Research*, *9*(September), 132–140.

Holland, J. (2001). *Colour prejudice at Veuve Clicquot!*: ChampagneMagic.com. Retrieved 26th May, 2005, from http://www.champagnemagic.com/newsnov.htm

Holmberg, L., Baron, J. A., Byers, T., Wolk, A., Ohlander, E. M., Zack, M., et al. (1995). Alcohol intake and breast cancer risk: effect of exposure from 15 years of age. *Cancer Epidemiology Biomarkers & Prevention*, *4*(8), 843–847.

Holt, D. B. (1995). How consumers consume: a typology of consumption practices. *Journal of Consumer Research*, *22*(June), 1–16.

Holt, M. P. (1999). Wine, life and death in early modern Burgundy. *Food and Foodways*, *8*(2), 73–98.

Hooke, H. (2001). Australia's wine show system. *The Wine Magazine*, April/May, 92–94.

Hooke, H. (2004). Towering intellect. *Decanter*, *29*(7), 30–35.

Horn-Ross, P. L., Canchola, A. J., West, D. W., Stewart, S. L., Bernstein, L., Deapen, D., et al. (2004). Patterns of alcohol consumption and breast cancer risk in the California teachers study cohort. *Cancer Epidemiology Biomarkers & Prevention*, *13*(3), 405–411.

Hughes, L. (2003). *Constellation-Hardy will be 'the Coca-Cola of winemaking'*: Decanter. Retrieved 17th August, 2005, from http://www.decanter.com/news/46204.html

Hume, D. (1757/1998). *Selected Essays*. Sydney: Oxford University Press.

Hyams, E. (1987). *Dionysus: A Social History of the Wine Vine*. London: Sidgwick & Jackson.

Iland, P., & Gago, P. (2002). *Australian Wine: Styles and Tastes*. Adelaide: Patrick Iland Promotions.

Jackson, D., & Schuster, D. (1994). *The Production of Grapes and Wine in Cool Climates*. Christchurch: Gypsum Press.

Jackson, R. S. (2002). *Wine Tasting: A Professional Handbook*. London: Academic Press.

Jardine, L. (1997). *Worldly Goods*. London: Papermac.

Jefford, A. (2002a). *The New France*. London: Mitchell Beazley.

Jefford, A. (2002b). The quest for autumnal repose. *Decanter*, *28*(1), 16.

Jefford, A. (2002c). Scenes from the real world. *Harpers*, 19th July, 10.

Jefford, A. (2004). Unleashing the dream. *Decanter*, *29*(9), 23.

Jeffs, J. (1992). *Sherry* (4th edn.). London: Faber and Faber.

Johnson, H. (1989). *The Story of Wine*. London: Mitchell Beazley.

Johnson, H. (1996). Struck dumb by appellation controlee. *Decanter*, *22*(4), 22.

Johnson, H. (1997). *Hugh Johnson's wine companion* (4th edn.). London: Mitchell Beazley.

Johnson, H. (2005). *A Life Uncorked*. Berkeley, CA: University of California Press.

Johnson, L. W., Ringham, L., & Jurd, K. (1991). Behavioural segmentation in the Australian wine market using conjoint analysis. *International Journal of Wine Marketing*, *3*(1), 26–31.

Jooste, L. (2005). *25th anniversary media kit*. Cape Town: Klein Constantia. Retrieved 12th December, 2005, from http://www.kleinconstantia.com/m25%/20anniversary/%20draft%20media%20kit

Judica, F., & Perkins, W. S. (1992). A means-end approach to the market for sparkling wines. *International Journal of Wine Marketing*, *4*(1), 10–19.

Kakaviatos, P. (2005). *Garage wines face troubled times*: Decanter. Retrieved 3rd July, 2005, from http://www.decanter.com/news/65453.html

Kant, I. (1790/1987). *Critique of Judgment* (W. S. Pular, Trans.). Indianapolis, IN: Hackett.

King, R. (2005). Drinkers see red at top drop. *West Australian*, 30th April, 3.

Kladstrup, D., & Kladstrup, P. (2001). *Wine and War*. London: Hodder and Stoughton.

Klatsky, A. L., Armstrong, M. A., & Friedman, G. D. (1997). Red wine, white wine, liquor, beer, and risk for coronary artery disease hospitalization. *American Journal of Cardiology*, *80*(4), 416–420.

Klatsky, A. L., Friedman, G. D., Armstrong, M. A., & Kipp, H. (2003). Wine, liquor, beer, and mortality. *American Journal of Epidemiology*, *158*(6), 585–595.

Korsmeyer, C. (1999). *Making Sense of Taste*. Ithaca, NY: Cornell University Press.

Kotler, P., Chandler, P. C., Brown, L., & Adam, S. (1994). *Marketing* (3rd edn.). Sydney: Prentice Hall.

Kupiec, B., & Revell, B. (2001). Measuring consumer quality judgements. *British Food Journal*, *103*(1), 7–22.

Landon, S., & Smith, C. E. (1998). Quality expectations, reputation and price. *Southern Economic Journal*, *64*(3), 628–647.

Lange, C., Martin, C., Chabanet, C., Combris, P., & Issanchou, S. (2002). Impact of the information provided to consumers on their willingness to pay for Champagne: comparison with hedonic scores. *Food Quality and Preference, 13*, 597–608.

Leahy, R. (2003). Champagne: success through diversity and unity. *Vineyard and Winery Management, 29*(2), 70–74.

Lechmere, A. (2004a). *KWV sacks winemakers in additive scandal*: Decanter. Retrieved 6th June, 2005, from http://www.decanter.com/news/60153.html

Lechmere, A. (2004b). *SA wineries to be monitored for additive use*: Decanter. Retrieved 6th June, 2005, from http://www.decanter.com/news/47885.html

Lehrer, A. (1974). Talking about wine. *Language, 51*, 901–923.

Leon, D., & McCambridge, J. (2006). Liver cirrhosis mortality rates in Britain from 1950 to 2002: an analysis of routine data. *The Lancet, 367*(9504), 52–56.

Letenneur, L., Larrieu, S., Helmer, C., Dartigues, J. F., & Barberger-Gateau, P. (2004). Nutritional factors and risk of incident dementia in the PAQUID longitudinal cohort. *The Journal of Nutrition, Health & Aging, 8*(3), 150–154.

Levitsky, J., & Mailliard, M. E. (2004). Diagnosis and therapy of alcoholic liver disease. *Seminars in Liver Disease, 24*(3), 233–247.

Levy, S. J. (1981). Interpreting consumer mythology: a structural approach to consumer behavior. *Journal of Marketing, 45*(Summer), 49–61.

Levy, S. J. (1986). Meanings in advertising stimuli. In J. Olson & K. Sentis (Eds.), *Advertising and consumer psychology* (Vol. 3, pp. 214–226). New York: Praeger.

Liddell, A. (1998). *Madeira*. London: Faber and Faber.

Littlewood, J. (1985). *Milady Vine: The Autobiography of Philippe de Rothschild*. London: Century Hutchinson.

Livy. (n.d./1983). *History of Rome* (Vol. 39). London: William Heinemann.

Lloyd, A. (2002). *Klein Constantia Vin de Constance: An appraisal*: Grape. Retrieved 12th December, 2005, from http://www.grape.org.za/index.html

Lockshin, L. (2002). Brands speak louder than words. *Harpers*, 11th October, 16.

Lockshin, L., & Hall, J. (2003). Consumer purchasing behaviour for wine: what we know and where we are going. Paper presented at the *3rd Annual Wine Marketing Colloquium*, Adelaide: University of South Australia.

Lockshin, L., & Spawton, A. (2001). Using involvement and brand equity to develop a wine tourism strategy. *International Journal of Wine Marketing, 13*(1), 72–87.

Lockshin, L., Rasmussen, M., & Cleary, F. (2000). The nature and roles of a wine brand. *Australian and New Zealand Wine Industry Journal, 15*(4 Marketing Supplement), 17–24.

Loftus, S. (1992). *Puligny Montrachet: Journal of a Village in Burgundy*. London: Random House.

Lombard, J. (2002). A crushing year for the vignerons of Beaujolais. *Australian Financial Review*, 2–3 November, 47–48.

Loubere, L. A. (1978). *The Red and the White: The History of Wine in France and Italy in the Nineteenth Century*. New York: State University of New York Press.

Loubere, L. A. (1990). *The Wine Revolution in France: The Twentieth Century*. Princeton, NJ: Princeton University Press.

Loubere, L. A., Sagnes, J., Frader, L., & Pech, R. (1985). *The Vine Remembers. French Vignerons Recall Their Past*. Albany, NY: State University of New York Press.

Luchsinger, J. A., Tang, M.-X., Siddiqui, M., Shea, S., & Mayeux, R. (2004). Alcohol intake and risk of dementia. *Journal of the American Geriatrics Society*, *52*(4), 540–546.

Lucia, S. P. (1963). *A History of Wine as Therapy*. Philadelphia, PA: J. B. Lippincott.

Mansson, P. H. (1996). Burgundy divided. *Wine Spectator*, 15th November.

Markham, D. (1998). *1855: A History of the Bordeaux Classification*. New York: John Wiley and Sons.

Marlatt, G. A. (1999). Alcohol, the magic elixir? In S. Peele & M. Grant (Eds.), *Alcohol and Pleasure: A Health Perspective* (pp. 233–248). Philadelphia, PA: Taylor and Francis.

Marx, K. (1867/1976). *Capital* (B. Fowkes, Trans.). Harmondsworth: Penguin Books.

Matthews, P. (2002). Clash of the titans. *Harpers*, 17th May, 51–56.

Matthews, P. (2003). *South Africa clamps down on illegal flavouring*: Decanter. Retrieved 6th June, 2005, from http://www.decanter.com/news/47218.html

McCoy, E. (2005). *The Emperor of Wine: The Rise of Robert M. Parker, Jr. and the Reign of American Taste*. New York: Harper Collins.

McGovern, P. E. (2003). *Ancient Wine: The Search for the Origins of Viniculture*. Princeton, NJ: Princeton University Press.

McKendrick, N., Brewer, J., & Plumb, J. H. (1982). *The Birth of a Consumer Society*. London: Europa Publications.

McNie, M. (1999). *Champagne*. London: Faber and Faber.

Mennell, S. (1985). *All Manners of Food*. Oxford: Basil Blackwell.

Meredith, G. (1995). *The Egoist*. Ware: Wordsworth Editions Ltd.

Mitchell, N. (2001). *Ideas with wings: crack open the bubbly*. Retrieved 31st July, 2001, from http://abc.net.au/science/wings/print4htm

Mitchell, R., Hall, M., & McIntosh, A. (2000). Wine tourism and consumer behaviour. In M. Hall, L. Sharples, B. Cambourne, N. Macionis, R. Mitchell & G. Johnson (Eds.), *Wine Tourism Around the World: Development, Management and Markets* (pp. 115–135). Oxford: Elsevier Science.

Mitchell, V.-W., & Greatorex, M. (1989). Risk reduction strategies used in the purchase of wine in the UK. *European Journal of Marketing*, *23*(9), 31–46.

Mitchelton Wines Pty Ltd. (1993). 1993 Mitchelton Triple Blend (back label).

Mohammed. (n.d./1974). *The Koran* (N. J. Dawood, Trans.). Harmondsworth: Penguin Books.

Moran, W. (2001). Terroir – the human factor. *Australian and New Zealand Wine Industry Journal*, *16*(2), 32–51.

Moulton, K., & Botos, P. (1994). Evaluating privatization in Hungary's wine industry: a framework for analysis. *Agribusiness*, *10*(3), 193–205.

Muir, A. (1997). Who decides what we want to drink? The merchant's view. Paper presented at the *Institute of Masters of Wine Symposium*, Perth: Institute of Masters of Wine.

Nahoum-Grappe, V. (1995). France. In D. B. Heath (Ed.), *International Handbook on Alcohol and Culture* (pp. 75–87). Westport, CT: Praeger Publishers.

Ngokwey, N. (1987). Varieties of palm wine among the Lele of the Kasai. In M. Douglas (Ed.), *Constructive Drinking: Perspectives on Drink from Anthropology* (pp. 113–121). New York: Cambridge University Press.

Noble, A. C. (1997). The catch-22 of scoring wine quality. *Slow*, *6*, 14–17.

Norman, R. (1996). *The Great Domaines of Burgundy* (2nd edn.). London: Kyle Cathie.

Nossiter, J. (Writer) (2004). Mondovino [Documentary Film]. US.

Nycander, S. (1998). Ivan Bratt: The man who saved Sweden from prohibition. *Addiction*, *93*(1), 17–25.

Obisesan, T. O., Hirsch, R., Kosoko, O., Carlson, L., & Parrott, M. (1998). Moderate wine consumption is associated with decreased odds of developing age-related macular degeneration in NHANES-1. *Journal of the American Geriatrics Society*, *46*(1), 1–7.

Oliver, J. (2000). A classification of his own. *Australian Gourmet Traveller Wine Magazine*, August, 76f.

O'Neill, M., & Charters, S. (2000). Service quality at the cellar door: implications for Western Australia's developing wine tourism industry. *Managing Service Quality*, *10*(2), 112–122.

Osborne, L. (2004). *The Accidental Connoisseur: An Irreverent Journey Through the Wine World*. New York: North Point Press.

Österreichische Weinmarketing Service GesmbH. (2005). *Facts & figures: viniculture in Austria*. Vienna: Wines of Austria. Retrieved 2nd August, 2005, from http://www.winesfromaustria.com/edaten/fr_facts.html

Parker, R. (1986). *Bordeaux*. London: Dorling Kindersley.

Pedersen, A., Johansen, C., & Gronbaek, M. (2003). Relations between amount and type of alcohol and colon and rectal cancer in a Danish population based cohort study. *Gut*, *52*(6), 861–867.

Peele, S. (1999). Introduction. In S. Peele & M. Grant (Eds.), *Alcohol and Pleasure: A Health Perspective*. Philadelphia, PA: Taylor and Francis.

Peppercorn, D. (1991). *Bordeaux* (2nd edn.). London: Faber and Faber.

Perrin, F., & Lockshin, L. (2001). Australian wine segmentation and distribution of costs. *Australian and New Zealand Wine Industry Journal, 16*(5), 147–150.

Petronius. (n.d./1997). *The Satyricon* (P. G. Walsh, Trans.). Oxford: Oxford University Press.

Pettigrew, S. (2003). Wine consumption contexts. *International Journal of Wine Marketing, 15*(2), 37–45.

Pettigrew, S., & Charters, S. (2006). Consumers' expectations of the pairing of food with alcoholic beverages. *British Food Journal, 108*(3), 169–180.

Pettipher, M. (2005). How image may be changing. *Financial Times*, 19th February, p. 19.

Peynaud, E. (1987). *The Taste of Wine* (M. Schuster, Trans.). San Francisco, CA: The Wine Appreciation Guild.

Philips, W. (1980). Six o'clock swill: The introduction of early closing of hotel bars in Australia. *Historical Studies, 19*, 250–266.

Phillips, R. (2000). *A Short History of Wine*. London: Allen Lane.

Pick, A. (1892). Ueber den einfluss des weingeistes auf die entwicklung der typhus and cholera bacillen. *Zentralbl Bakt, 12*, 293–294.

Pliny the Elder (n.d./1991). *Natural History* (J. F. Healy, Trans.). London: Penguin.

Postrel, V. (2003). *The Substance of Style: How the Rise of Aesthetic Value is Remaking Commerce, Culture and Consciousness*. New York: Harper Collins.

Pritchard, B. (1999). The regulation of grower-processor relations: a case study from the Australian wine industry. *Sociologia Ruralis, 39*(2), 186–201.

Proust, M. (1973). *Swann's Way* (C. K. S. Moncreiff, Trans, Vol. 1). London: Chatto and Windus.

Pugh, M., & Fletcher, R. (2002). Green international wine marketing. *Australasian Marketing Journal, 10*(3), 76–85.

Quester, P. G., & Smart, J. (1996). Product involvement in consumer wine purchases: its demographic determinants and influence on choice attributes. *International Journal of Wine Marketing, 8*(3/4), 37–56.

Quester, P. G., & Smart, J. (1998). The influence of consumption situation and product involvement over consumers' use of product attributes. *The Journal of Consumer Marketing, 15*(3), 220–238.

Radcliffe, L., & Piore, A. (2003). Is Europe drinking too much? *Newsweek*, 3rd November, 37.

Railton, P. (1998). Aesthetic value, moral value and the ambitions of naturalism. In J. Levinson (Ed.), *Aesthetics and Ethics: Essays at the Intersection* (pp. 59–105). Cambridge: Cambridge University Press.

Ramsay, S. (Writer) (2002). The De Bortolis [Television Programme]. In J. Bell (Producer), *Australian Families*. Australia: ABC Television.

Randall, C. (2005). Which poster was too sexy for the French? *Daily Telegraph*, 3rd February, 15.

Ray, J. (2001). Grape Expectations. *The Spectator*, 3rd November, 43.

Ray, J. (2004). *Bloodlines and Grapevines: Great Winemaking Families of the World*. London: Conran Octopus.

Rees, J., Hughes, J., & Innes, C. (2002). An *in vitro* assessment of the erosive potential of some white wines. *The European Journal of Prosthodontics and Restorative Dentistry*, *10*(1), 37–42.

Renaud, S. C., Gueguen, R., Schenker, J., & d'Houtaud, A. (1998). Alcohol and mortality in middle-aged men from eastern France. *Epidemiology*, *9*(2), 184–188.

Renaud, S. C., Gueguen, R., Siest, G., & Salamon, R. (1999). Wine, beer, and mortality in middle-aged men from eastern France. *Archives of Internal Medicine*, *159*(16), 1865–1870.

Renaud, S. C., Gueguen, R., Conard, P., Lanzmann-Petithory, D., Orgogozo, J.-M., & Henry, O. (2004). Moderate wine drinkers have lower hypertension-related mortality: a prospective cohort study in French men. *The American Journal of Clinical Nutrition*, *80*(3), 621–625.

Ribereau-Gayon, P. (2001). *Les vins de France*: Office of the Prime Minister of France. Retrieved 13th December, 2001, from http://www.premier-ministre.gouv.fr/ressources/fichiers/imf/vinfrance.pdf

Richins, M. L. (1994). Valuing things: the public and private meanings of possessions. *Journal of Consumer Research*, *21*(December), 504–521.

Richins, M. L. (1999). Possessions in the expression of self. In M. B. Holbrook (Ed.), *Consumer Value: A Framework for Analysis and Research* (pp. 85–104). New York: Routledge.

Rimm, E. B., & Ellison, R. C. (1995). Alcohol in the Mediterranean diet. *The American Journal of Clinical Nutrition*, *61*(6 Suppl), 1378S–1382S.

Roberts, A. (2001). Wine investment. *Financial Times*, 27th October, 1.

Robertson, G. (1992). *Port*. London: Faber and Faber.

Robinson, J. (1988). *The Demon Drink*. London: Mitchell Beazley.

Robinson, J. (1997). *Confessions of a Wine Lover*. London: Viking.

Robinson, J. (Ed.). (1999). *The Oxford Companion to Wine* (2nd edn.). Oxford: Oxford University Press.

Robinson, J. (2003). *Jancis Robinson's Wine Course*. New York: Abbeville Press.

Roby, N. (2005). After sideways. *Decanter* (California Supplement), 48.

Rokeach, M. (1968). *Beliefs, Attitudes and Values*. San Francisco, CA: Josey-Bass Inc.

Rokeach, M. (1973). *The Nature of Human Values*. New York: The Free Press.

Russo, A., Palumbo, M., Aliano, C., Lempereur, L., Scoto, G., & Renis, M. (2003). Red wine micronutrients as protective agents in Alzheimer-like induced insult. *Life Sciences*, *72*(21), 2369–2379.

Ruthven, M. (1984). *Islam in the World*. London: Penguin.

Sabrazes, J., & Marcandier, A. (1907). Action du vin sur les bacille d'Eberth. *Annales de l'Institut Pasteur*, *21*.

Saeidi, A., & Unwin, T. (2004). Persian wine tradition and symbolism: evidence from the medieval poetry of Hafiz. *Journal of Wine Research*, *15*(2), 97–114.

Salolainen, M. (1993). The marketing of Champagne: The way forward. *International Journal of Wine Marketing*, *5*(4), 15–27.

Sanjuan, A. I., & Albisu, L. M. (2004). Factors affecting the positioning on the value added by the DO certification. *Acta Agricola Scandinavia, Section C, Food Economics*, *1*, 163–175.

Santich, B. (1996). *Looking for Flavour*. Adelaide: Wakefield Press.

Savaskan, E., Olivieri, G., Meier, F., Seifritz, E., Wirz-Justice, A., & Muller-Spahn, F. (2003). Red wine ingredient resveratrol protects from beta-amyloid neurotoxicity. *Gerontology*, *49*(6), 380–383.

Sayers, D. L. (1928). The bibulous business of a matter of taste. In D. L. Sayers (Ed.), *Lord Peter Views the Body*. London: Gollancz.

Scruton, R. (1979). *The Aesthetics of Architecture*. Princeton, NJ: Princeton University Press.

Scruton, R. (2004). Philosophy and the intoxicating properties of wine. Paper presented at the *Philosophy and Wine: from Science to Subjectivity Conference*, London.

Seward, D. (1979). *Monks and Wine*. London: Mitchell Beazley.

Shaw, M., Keeghan, P., & Hall, J. (1999). Consumers judge wine by its label, study shows. *Australian and New Zealand Wine Industry Journal*, *14*(1), 84–87.

Shesgreen, S. (2003). Wet dogs and gushing oranges: winespeak for a new millennium. *The Chronicle of Higher Education*, B15.

Shiner, R. A. (1996). Hume and the causal theory of taste. *The Journal of Aesthetics and Art Criticism*, *54*(3), 237–249.

Sibley, F. (2001). *Approach to Aesthetics: Collected Papers on Philosophical Aesthetics*. Oxford: Oxford University Press.

Simon, J. (1996). *Wine with Food*. London: Mitchell Beazley.

Simon, J. (2005). Good values for money. *Harpers* (South African Supplement), September, 28–31.

Sloan, D. (2004). The postmodern palate: dining out in the individualized era. In D. Sloan (Ed.), *Culinary Taste: Consumer Behaviour in the International Restaurant Sector* (pp. 23–42). Oxford: Elsevier Butterworth-Heinemann.

Smith, B. C. (2004, 10th December). Questions of taste. Paper presented at the *Philosophy and Wine: from Science to Subjectivity Conference*, London, (Unpublished).

Smith, D. E., & Solgaard, H. S. (2000). The dynamics of shifts in European alcoholic drinks consumption. *Journal of International Consumer Marketing*, *12*(3), 85–109.

Smith, W. D. (1994). *Hippocrates* (Vol. 7). Cambridge: Harvard University Press.

Smy, L. (2000). Vineyards fight to rebuild brands. *Financial Times*, 22nd November, 2.

Smyrnios, K., Tanewski, G., & Romano, C. (1998). Development of a measure of the characteristics of family business. *Family Business Review*, *11*(1), 49–59.

Sneyd, M. J., Paul, C., Spears, G. F., & Skegg, D. C. (1991). Alcohol consumption and risk of breast cancer. *International Journal of Cancer*, *48*(6), 812–815.

Solomon, G. E. A. (1990). Psychology of novice and expert wine talk. *American Journal of Psychology*, *103*(4), 495–517.

Spawton, A. (1991). Marketing planning for wine. *European Journal of Marketing*, *25*(3), 1–48.

Spencer, W. G. (1953). *De Medicina, Celus II*. Cambridge: Harvard University Press.

Spurrier, S. (1998). Terroir – myth or reality? *Decanter*, *23*(10), 17.

Spurrier, S. (2005). Sublime dining. *Decanter*, *30*(6), 96.

St Leger, A. S., Cochrane, A. L., & Moore, F. (1979). Factors associated with cardiac mortality in developed countries with particular reference to the consumption of wine. *The Lancet* (8124), 1017–1020.

Stanziani, A. (2004). Wine reputation and quality controls: the origin of the AOCs in 19th century France. *European Journal of Law and Economics*, *18*, 149–167.

Stavro, A. (2001). Judges' top drop stumps amateur taste-testers. *The Australian*, 16th February, 3.

Steiman, H. (2001). *Australian court settles dispute over Coonawarra's boundaries*: Wine Spectator. Retrieved 6th November, 2001, from http://www.winespectator.com/Wine/Daily/News/1,1145,1460,00.html

Stevenson, T. (1986). *Champagne*. London: Sotheby's Publications.

Stevenson, T. (2005). *The New Sotheby's Wine Encyclopedia* (4th edn.). London: Dorling Kindersley.

Stimpfig, J. (2005a). A starter's guide. *Decanter*, *30*(9), 119.

Stimpfig, J. (2005b). The white knuckle ride. *Financial Times: How to Spend it*, February.

Stockwell, T., Masters, L., Philips, M., Daly, A., Gahegan, M., Midford, R., et al. (1998). Consumption of different alcoholic beverages as predictors of local rates of night-time assault and acute alcohol-related morbidity. *Australian and New Zealand Journal of Public Health*, *22*(2), 237–242.

Taylor, C. S. (1988). Prolegomena to an aesthetics of wine. *The Journal of Speculative Philosophy*, *2*(2), 120–139.

Temple, P. (2004). Patience can bring its rewards: alternative investments. *Financial Times*, 4th September, 24.

Thode, S. F., & Maskulka, J. M. (1996). A brand equity strategy for ultra-premium California wine. *International Journal of Wine Marketing*, *8*(3/4), 5–22.

Thode, S. F., & Maskulka, J. M. (1998). Place-based marketing strategies, brand equity and vineyard valuation. *Journal of Product and Brand Management*, *7*(5), 379–399.

Thode, S. F., Taylor, L. W., & Maskulka, J. M. (2002). Information asymmetries in the pricing of fine wines. *International Journal of Wine Marketing*, *14*(1), 5–16.

Thompson, J. A. (1986). *Handbook of Life in Bible Times*. Leicester: Inter-Varsity Press.

Thompson, K. E., & Vourvachis, A. (1995). Social and attitudinal influences on the intention to drink wine. *International Journal of Wine Marketing*, *7*(2), 35–45.

Thompson, K. E., Haziris, N., & Alekos, P. J. (1994). Attitudes and food choice behaviour. *British Food Journal*, *96*(11), 9–13.

Thornton, M. A. (1987). Sekt versus schnapps in an Austrian village. In M. Douglas (Ed.), *Constructive drinking: Perspectives on drink from anthropology* (pp. 102–112). New York: Cambridge University Press.

Tjonneland, A., Gronbaek, M., Stripp, C., & Overvad, K. (1999). Wine intake and diet in a random sample of 48763 Danish men and women. *The American Journal of Clinical Nutrition*, *69*(1), 49–54.

Tome, S., & Lucey, M. R. (2004). Review article: current management of alcoholic liver disease. *Alimentary Pharmacology & Therapeutics*, *19*(7), 707–714.

Tomlinson, A. (1990). Introduction. In A. Tomlinson (Ed.), *Consumption, Identity and Style* (pp. 1–30). London: Routledge.

Toussaint-Samat, M. (1987/1994). *A History of Food* (A. Bell, Trans.). Oxford: Blackwell.

Travers, D. (Ed.). (1999). *Vintage: The Wine Industry Yearbook*. Adelaide: Winetitles.

Trevisan, M., Schisterman, E., Mennotti, A., Farchi, G., & Conti, S. (2001). Drinking pattern and mortality: the Italian risk factor and life expectancy pooling project. *Annals of Epidemiology*, *11*(5), 312–319.

Tustin, M., & Lockshin, L. (2001). Region of origin: does it really count? *Australian and New Zealand Wine Industry Journal*, *16*(5), 139–143.

Ulin, R. C. (1995). Invention and representation as cultural capital. *American Anthropologist, 97*(3), 519–527.

Ulin, R. C. (1996). *Vintages and Traditions: An Ethnohistory of Southwest French Wine*. Washington, DC: The Smithsonian Institute.

Unwin, T. (1992). Images of alcohol: perceptions and the influence of advertising. *Journal of Wine Research, 3*(3), 205–233.

Unwin, T. (1996). *Wine and the Vine: An Historical Geography of Viticulture and the Wine Trade*. London: Routledge.

Unwin, T. (2001). From Montpellier to New England: John Locke on wine. In R. A. Butlin & I. Black (Eds.), *Place, Culture and Identity: Essays in Historical Geography in Honour of Dr. Alan R.H. Baker* (pp. 69–90). Quebec: Laval University Press.

Ursini, F., & Sevanian, A. (2002). Wine polyphenols and optimal nutrition. *Annals of the New York Academy of Sciences, 957*, 200–209.

Vachon, C. M., Cerhan, J. R., Vierkant, R. A., & Sellers, T. A. (2001). Investigation of an interaction of alcohol intake and family history on breast cancer risk in the Minnesota breast cancer family study. *Cancer, 92*(2), 240–248.

Vaudour, E. (2002). The quality of grapes and wine in relation to geography: Notions of terroir at various scales. *Journal of Wine Research, 13*(2), 117–141.

Vigneron, F., & Johnson, L. W. (1999). A review and a conceptual framework of prestige-seeking consumer behavior. *Academy of Marketing Science Review* [*Online*], *2002* (18th January), 1–23.

Vignes, A., & Gergaud, O. (2003). Twilight of the idols in the market of champagne: dissonance or consonance in consumer preferences. *Working Paper: University de Paris II.*

Voss, R. (2005). When wine is not wine. *Harpers*, 2nd September, 14.

Walker, L. (2004). Labour days. *Harpers*, 12th November, 10.

Walker, L. (2005). Standards bearer. *Harpers*, 8th April, 12.

Wallendorf, M., & Belk, R. W. (1989). Assessing trustworthiness in naturalistic consumer research. In E. Hirschman (Ed.), *Interpretive Consumer Research* (pp. 69–83). Association for Consumer Research.

Weisse, M. E., Eberly, B., & Person, D. A. (1995). Wine as a digestive aid: comparative antimicrobial effects of bismuth salicylate and red and white wine. *British Medical Journal, 311*(7021), 1657–1660.

Welsh, F. (1998). *A History of South Africa*. London: Harper Collins.

Westerterp-Plantenga, M. S., & Verwegen, C. R. (1999). The appetizing effect of an aperitif in overweight and normal-weight humans. *The American Journal of Clinical Nutrition, 69*(2), 205–212.

Wheatley, G. B. (2003). *How China made it into top 20 wine consuming countries*: WineBiz. Retrieved 2nd April, 2003, from http://biz.tizwine.com/stories/storyReader$3747

Wiktorsson, A. M., Zimmerman, M., & Angmar-Mańsson, B. (1997). Erosive tooth wear: prevalence and severity in Swedish winetasters. *European Journal of Oral Sciences*, *105*(6), 544–550.

Williams, A. (1995). *Flying Winemakers: The New World of Wine*. Adelaide: Winetitles.

Williams, D. (2004a). Blasons de Bordeaux. *Harpers*, 16th July, 21–23.

Williams, D. (2004b). Power steering. *Harpers* (South Africa Supplement), September, 14–16.

Williams, P. (2001). Positioning wine tourism destinations: an image analysis. *International Journal of Wine Marketing*, *13*(3), 42–58.

Wilson, J. (1998). *Terroir: The Role of Geology, Climate and Culture in the Making of French Wines*. London: Mitchell Beazley.

Wong, N. Y., & Ahuvia, A. C. (1998). Personal taste and family face: luxury consumption in Confucian and western societies. *Psychology and Marketing*, *15*(5), 423–441.

Woodcock, G. (1975). *Anarchism*. Harmondsworth: Penguin Books.

World Trade Organisation (n.d.). *Intellectual property: protection and enforcement*. Lausanne: World Trade Organisation. Retrieved 10th August, 2005, from http://www.wto.org/english/thewto_e/whatis_e/tif_e/agrm7_e.htm

Wright, J. C. (1995). Empty cups and empty jugs: the social role of wine in Minoan and Mycenaean societies. In P. E. McGovern, S. J. Fleming & S. Katz (Eds.), *The Origins and Ancient History of Wine* (pp. 287–309). Amsterdam: Gordon and Breach.

Wright, L. T., Nancarrow, C., & Brace, I. (2000). Researching taste: layers of analysis. *British Food Journal*, *102*(5/6), 429–440.

Wysong, P. (2005). Moderate red wine drinking reduces risk for cataract. *Medscape Medical News*, 5th May.

Younger, W. (1966). *Gods, Men and Wine*. Cleveland, OH: The Wine and Food Society Limited.

Zaichkowsky, J. L. (1985). Measuring the involvement construct. *Journal of Consumer Research*, *12*, 341–352.

Zaichkowsky, J. L. (1988). Involvement and the price cue. *Advances in Consumer Research*, *15*, 323–327.

Zhang, Y., Kreger, B. E., Dorgan, J. F., Splansky, G. L., Cupples, L. A., & Ellison, R. C. (1999). Alcohol consumption and risk of breast cancer: the Framingham study revisited. *American Journal of Epidemiology*, *149*(2), 93–101.

Index